FOOTBALL DEFENSE
OF THE FUTURE:
The 2-Level Model

JOHN M. THOMSON

Queen's University

BILL ARNSPARGER

University of Florida

PRENTICE HALL, Englewood Cliffs, New Jersey 07632

Library of Congress Cataloging-in-Publication Data

Thomson, John M.,
    Football defense of the future : the 2-level model / John M.
  Thomson, Bill Arnsparger.
        p.   cm.
    Includes bibliographies and index.
    ISBN 0-13-324062-2 :
    1. Football--Defense.   2. Football--Coaching.   I. Arnsparger,
  Bill, 1926-   . II. Title.
  GV951.18.T48 1988
  796.332'2--dc19   87-25839
                                                             CIP

Editorial/production supervision and
  interior design: Rob DeGeorge
Cover design: Ben Santora
Manufacturing buyer: Margaret Rizzi
Photography: Arthur Martin

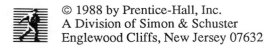 © 1988 by Prentice-Hall, Inc.
A Division of Simon & Schuster
Englewood Cliffs, New Jersey 07632

Printed in the United States of America

10 9 8 7 6 5 4 3 2 1

ISBN 0-13-324062-2 01

Prentice-Hall International (UK) Limited, *London*
Prentice-Hall of Australia Pty. Limited, *Sydney*
Prentice-Hall Canada Inc., *Toronto*
Prentice-Hall Hispanoamericana, S.A., *Mexico*
Prentice-Hall of India Private Limited, *New Delhi*
Prentice-Hall of Japan, Inc., *Tokyo*
Simon & Schuster Asia Pte. Ltd., *Singapore*
Editora Prentice-Hall do Brasil, Ltda., *Rio de Janeiro*

To Bob Gage of the *London Free Press*, the consummate sportswriter....
for thirty years of dedication to high school and college football.

CONTENTS

PREFACE   *viii*

PART ONE: FOOTBALL DEFENSE IN THE EIGHTIES

1 **THE EVOLUTION OF DEFENSIVE FOOTBALL: PAST,
        PRESENT . . . FUTURE**   *1*

Introduction: Football Coaching   *1*
Evolution of the Three Levels of Defense   *3*
    The First Level of Defense   *3*
    The Second Level of Defense   *4*
    The Third Level of Defense   *5*
Offensive Football in the Eighties: Characteristics and Capacities   *8*
Tactical Capacities of the Present Model of Defense   *14*
    The Model's Run Defense   *16*
    The Model's Pass Defense   *18*
Tactical Capabilities of Future Models of Defense   *21*
Notes   *26*
References   *27*

PART TWO: THE 2-LEVEL DEFENSIVE SYSTEM

2 BASIC CONCEPT, PRINCIPLES, AND PERSONNEL   *29*

Introduction: The Unique Problem of Defense *29*
Defensive Principles and Alignments *31*
    The First Level *32*
    The Second Level *33*
    The Deep Safety *35*
Tactical Principles *36*
    The End-Line Concept *37*
    Outnumbering the Offensive Blockers in the Core *38*
    "Automatic" Multiple Alignments *40*
    Defensive Concealment *40*
    Simplicity *42*
    Goal Line-to-Goal Line Continuity *42*
Selection Criteria for Personnel *43*
    First Level Personnel *43*
    Second Level Personnel *44*
    The Deep Safety *45*
Signal System *45*
    Core Structure: First Byte in the Huddle Call *48*
    Stunt Mechanisms: Middle Byte in the Huddle Call *48*
    Pass Coverage: Final Byte in the Huddle Call *49*
Notes *49*
References *49*

3 RUN DEFENSE   *50*

Primary Mechanism of Run Defense: First Level Alignment *50*
    The Positional Alignments for First Level Personnel *52*
    The Eleven First Level Alignments: Personnel Rules *54*
    The First Alignment Call *58*
Primary Mechanism of Run Defense *62*
    1- and 2-Stacks *62*
    Tight End/Slotback Stacks *62*
First and Second Level Stunts *66*
    First Level Stunts *66*
    Second Level Stunts *69*
Secondary Mechanisms of Run Defense *72*
    First Level *72*
    Second Level *73*
    Incorporated Secondary Mechanisms *74*
Notes *81*
References *81*

4 PASS DEFENSE 82

Working Definitions of Pass Defense *84*
    Numbering the Five Mobile Offensive Personnel *84*
    Defining the Offensive Formation According to Areas *88*
    Defining the Defensive Pass Zones *90*
Pass Coverages: Max and Covers *96*
    Max Coverages *96*
    Cover Combinations *100*
    Max/Two-Deep and Cover/Two-Deep *111*
Pass Rush: Core Mechanisms *118*
    5-Man Rush Principle *120*
    Outside Pass Rush Principle *120*
    Overload Principle *120*
    Pass Block Mechanism *121*
Notes *122*
References *122*

5 SHORTYARDAGE AND GOAL LINE ADAPTATIONS 123

Shortyardage Adaptations *124*
Goal Line Adaptations *128*
Notes *131*
References *131*

PART THREE: INSTALLATION OF THE 2-LEVEL DEFENSE: COACHING PROGRESSION

6 RUN DEFENSE: TEACHING PROGRESSION 132

Introduction: Installing a New System *132*
Recommended Teaching Model *135*
Run Defense: First Level *136*
    Nose and Tackles: Fundamentals and Drills *136*
    Ends: Fundamentals and Drills *143*
    Team Drill: First Level (only) *150*
    First Level Stunts: Coordination and Techniques *152*
Run Defense: Second Level *153*
    Interaction of First Level Alignment and Second Level Stack *156*
    Responsibility Sequence: Run Defense *158*
Run Defense: First and Second Levels *175*
Notes *190*
References *190*

7 PASS DEFENSE: TEACHING PROGRESSION 192

Pass Rush *194*
    Nose and Tackles: Fundamentals and Drills *194*

Ends: Fundamentals and Drills *204*
Pass Coverage *210*
    Ends: Fundamentals and Coverage Responsibility *210*
    Second Level: Fundamentals and Coverage Responsibility *217*
    Second Level: Stacked *219*
    Second Level: Not Stacked *227*
    Deep Safety: Fundamentals and Coverage Responsibility *253*
Notes *269*
References *269*

PART FOUR: IMPLEMENTATION OF THE 2-LEVEL DEFENSE: GAME PLAN PREPARATION

8 ANALYSIS OF OFFENSE: BASIC MECHANISMS *272*

Introduction: The Machinery of Offense *272*
Analysis of Offense Prior to the Snap *274*
    Formation Evaluation *275*
    Countering Formation Strength and Tendencies *278*
Analysis of Offense after the Snap *282*
    Analysis of Run Offense *282*
Dynamics of In-Game Analysis *296*
    Alternate Planning *296*
    Sideline Adjustment *297*
    Half Time Adjustment *298*
    Post-Game Analyses *299*
Notes *305*
References *305*

9 ANALYSIS OF OFFENSE: SYSTEMS EVALUATION *307*

Analysis of Run-Oriented Systems of Offense: Option Football *308*
    Four Generations of Option Football *309*
    Defensing the Triple-Option Mechanism *311*
Analysis of Balanced Systems of Offense: Run and Pass *316*
    Components of the Balanced Multiple-Offense *319*
    Defensing the Balanced Multiple System *324*
Analysis of Pass-Oriented Offenses: Three Unique Systems *331*
    The Shotgun *331*
    The Run-and-Shoot *333*
    Quick Passing *338*
Notes *340*
References *341*

GLOSSARY *343*

INDEX *353*

PREFACE

The game of football provides an opportunity of unparallelled challenge in the coaching profession.   Emotion, motivational skills, and personal ego—very human factors—become superimposed upon an impersonal chess board, 120 yards in length by 53 1/3 yards in breadth. Over this huge field both the movement of each player and the flow of the game must be intricately controlled by the coach, first through his circumspect preparations prior to the game, then by his impromptu decisions during the contest. For the past decade and more, the ability of football offenses to score points has been mounting steadily; defensive effectiveness, however, has been eroding increasingly, to the point where it must now seem to many defensive coordinators that they possess only limited means by which to control the destiny of their teams. Even coaches who possess teams of superior athletes can no longer be assured of defensive domination—witness the fate, in the 1984 Orange Bowl, of the University of Nebraska, which had been touted as the *best* college football team of *all time*.

As a defensive coordinator, I have been confronted with this deteriorating situation annually for the past fifteen years. My defenses have consistently been ranked among the top five in Canadian college football, and the members of my present defensive personnel are, if anything, larger, stronger, and possess superior ability compared to the players I coached even five years ago. However, I have increasingly realized, in comparing our game films over successive seasons, that on the field our players were not always in the most advantageous position to make a particular play; and, more critically, that the techniques which were taught and in which we all believed were actually placing them at further disadvantage. For example, the traditional pass coverage techniques (first denying the deep pass routes to a receiver) were allowing passing teams, who now throw in excess of forty passes per game, to complete an unacceptable number of short passes; even more alarmingly, our team pass interception-per-completion ratio fell precipitously throughout the 1970s. The traditional defensive-line techniques for breaking an offensive lineman's charge were being progressively nullified by the increasing use of hands, holding, and forearm extension on the part of the offensive blockers. Our defensive stunts (usually on a passing down) were becoming less effective as the expected gaps between the offensive lineman (i.e., two to four feet) virtually disappeared; in today's football, offensive pass protection now resembles the blocking pattern employed on field-goal attempts. I have coached some outstanding outside linebackers . . . the problem has been that fewer and fewer offenses are employing either tight ends or large slotbacks, the specific offensive personnel against which this particular defensive position evolved. And several other changes and innovations by the offense have rendered our defense progressively more impotent. Our major problem by far, however, resided with our defensive alignments and pass coverages (particularly zone coverages) called in the defensive huddle *before* each down: the static nature of these pre-play decisions (which are only "best guesses" on the part of the defensive coordinator) resulted in a growing number of defensive personnel being out of position at the snap, even though it was obvious *before that play commenced* where the action would take place.

This escalating predicament—and there have been numerous related problems and many short-term solutions—resulted in the gradual development of the present 2-level model of defense. The system itself, and its defensive concepts, evolved from two dichotomous courses of action. Initially, through the 1970s, we instituted a multiple defensive system, the solution with which the majority of coaches reading this text will identify. Ultimately, however, for both theoretical and practical reasons, this course of action had to be curtailed: our multiple system grew in size and complexity, eventually retaining little semblance of continuity; our personnel were required to learn a plethora of techniques and situation reactions; and our signal system became unwieldy. Thus, the second phase in the development of the 2-level defensive model commenced with—for lack of more apropos terminology—a series of experiments. Literally, the "book" governing traditional defensive theory was abandoned, and in its place some rather strange mechanisms and techniques were attempted: in man-to-man pass coverage the short pass routes were denied to the receiver (thus opening up the deep pass routes); in our huddle before each play, defensive alignments were *not* called; progressively, various deepbacks were positioned further and further off the line of scrimmage (eventually it was established that just *one* defender positioned 28 yards deep could be extremely effective within the evolving system); and new defensive concepts and terminology were developed (i.e., levels, core, etc.), and some of the familiar ones, such as linebackers, deepback, etc., were deleted.

The defensive system detailed in this textbook represents the culmination of several years of thinking and innovation, of trial and error and refinement. It presents an alternative concept of football defense which coaches may implement directly or incorporate within their present defensive system for use in specific tactical situations. By coincidence, during the two years in which this text was being written, the success of the Chicago Bears defense employing a 4-6 alignment increased our appreciation of many aspects of the 2-level model itself. On the other hand, the present defensive system is not intended as an ultimate system, and I am sure that one never will exist, as argued in Part I of this text. More probably, this defense represents a *next step* in the dynamic evolution of football, and some of its precepts will not stand for long, given the strategical nature of the game. This text was written from the perspective that this system would provide a beginning for a new mode of defensive thinking. It has been both a privilege and pleasure developing this system over the past decade under the stable influence of a very knowledgeable and forebearing head coach, Professor Doug Hargreaves, and with some very enthusiastic friends, our players and assistant coaches. Finally, in collaborating with Coach Bill Arnsparger in the writing of this text, a very personal acknowledgment is expressed. Prior to his assuming head coaching duties at Louisiana State, Coach Arnsparger's defenses with the Miami Dolphins became legendary. He is the premiere defensive theorist in football today; his vast experience and wisdom have proven invaluable in this coauthorship and are greatly appreciated.

John M. Thomson

ACKNOWLEDGMENTS

The authors are indebted to a number of persons who so generously gave of their talent and efforts, at various times, throughout the two years during which this text was written.

To Anne Thomson, Colleen Zilio, Carol Boyle and Dorothy Daley, all of whom labored over the word processor in typing various sections of the manuscript, we extend our appreciation.

To Arthur Martin, known in inner circles as Canada's greatest sports photographer, who travelled many miles on several occasions to carry out impromptu photo sessions, we pay particular thanks for a job well done.

The assistance of the Graphics Department, Queen's University, in the production of the text's figures is appreciated.

And not least of all, we gratefully acknowledge Jerry Sandusky, defensive coordinator at Penn State, and Gary Jefferies, defensive coordinator at Wilfrid Laurier, who were generous with both their time and their critiques of the manuscript. Coach Sandusky's contributions are doubly appreciated in that his own writings provided valuable information and insight into this intriguing game of defensive football.

John Thomson and Bill Arnsparger

Chapter 1
THE EVOLUTION
OF DEFENSIVE FOOTBALL:
PAST, PRESENT ... FUTURE

INTRODUCTION: FOOTBALL COACHING

The coaching of football must proceed simultaneously on three distinct yet interdependent levels: the teaching of fundamental skills and techniques, the installation of systems to coordinate personnel movement, and then the implementation of the system against a specific opponent (fig. 1). In defensive football these three tiers in figure 1 must be *highly* integrated. For a sophisticated system to function effectively, a solid foundation is provided only by the physical skills and techniques that personnel require to operate the system being thoroughly taught. Next, each player must comprehend the system itself particularly his integral responsibilities and movement patterns within its total structure. Finally, the system must be effectively implemented in the emotional climate of competition against a specific offensive opponent. This highest tier provides the allure and challenge for the coach, but his success is dependent upon his ability to teach and integrate the three tiers in this pyramid.

The major sections in this text deal separately with each of these levels of coaching, in order to assist the defensive coach in both understanding and installing the two-level defense. In part II (chapters 2 to 5) the entire system is detailed; corresponding to the middle tier in figure 1, the total system is developed in stages throughout this section. First, the concepts which form the basis of the system are explained in chapter 2; then the fluid mechanisms within the system for defensing the run and the pass are detailed in chapters 3 and 4 respectively, in chapter 5 the simple adaptations of the 2-level Defense for short yardage and goal line situations are outlined. In part III

1

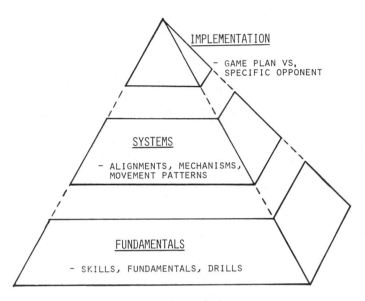

Figure 1 The football coaching pyramid: three tiers at which coaching must proceed simultaneously

(chapters 6 and 7) the individual skills and movement patterns required by this system are detailed for each player position. This corresponds to the lower tier, the essential base of the coaching pyramid, and in chapters 6 and 7 the progression for both teaching the requisite fundamentals and installing the entire system in sequential phases is presented. In the final section of this text, part IV (chapters 8 and 9), suggestions for implementing this defensive system into the game situation are outlined. The top tier of the coaching pyramid must be constantly modified from week to week, throughout the season. The system must be adapted to combat the offensive potential of the upcoming opponent, and the defensive coach cannot effectively implement his game plan without a thorough understanding of offensive systems and theory. In chapter 8 the methodology for dissecting and categorizing offensive strengths and potentials is explained. The final chapter integrates the theory and specific mechanisms in the 2-level Defense that may be used in countering various offenses, for each week the appropriate elements within the system must first be highlighted by the defensive game plan, then thoroughly practiced on the field.

From several perspectives, many elements within the comprehensive system presented in this text contravene contemporary "defensive orthodoxy." More conservative coaches may be highly skeptical of this system—its concepts, specific personnel requirements, and the mechanisms built into the system. Others may argue that the 3-level defense presently employed maintains its viability. Alternate viewpoints are discussed in this chapter which traces the evolution of defensive football as a reaction to the pervading offensive trends of each era. The mounting defensive problems—de facto and potential—are analyzed here in light of the dynamics of offensive football in the eighties. In essence, this chapter argues for a radical change in defensive thinking; in point of fact, there have been few conceptual changes in the basic precepts governing football defense for the past thirty years.

Few of the texts which deal with technical aspects of football trace its evolutionary strategies. Yet this perspective is necessary in order to appreciate both *how* the game has evolved and, more importantly, *why*; for the past hundred years of football have most definitely influenced the game as it is played today. This chapter examines the logical (and brilliant) changes that have taken place in the game from the standpoint that they were defensive reactions to successive innovations by the offense. The point to appreciate, however, is that although offensive evolution has greatly accelerated since the 1950s, in 1987 the defense still utilizes many of the basic concepts developed to combat the offense of the '50s. Although mechanistic improvements have been made over the past thirty years both in techniques and, more recently, in substitution of personnel according to tactical situations on the field, the concepts which govern defensive football have remained relatively static, particularly in comparison to the dynamics of the offensive arsenal. This chapter argues for changes in defensive thinking and explains why specific changes must be made.

EVOLUTION OF THE THREE LEVELS OF DEFENSE

The First Level of Defense

The origins of American football began in 1874 when the Canadian university McGill, in Montreal, played Harvard. There were fifteen players per team, the field was 140 yards by 70 yards, and the Canadians had perfected the use of the lateral (not forward) pass. Harvard liked the Canadians' playing style and adopted aspects of their rules and strategy. Then, early in the 1880s, through the efforts of Walter Camp at Yale, further rule changes were implemented, and the strategical elements of the game of football as we know it today became entrenched (1).

1. Each team was limited to eleven players on the field.
2. Positions were established: seven men "up front," with four "back"; these positions had their origin in the English game of rugby.
3. The size of the playing field was reduced to 110 yards by 53 1/3 yards, its present width. (In the twentieth century the length of the field was standardized at 100 yards, with ten-yard end zones and goalposts located at the end lines.)
4. A brilliant innovation was instituted—a system of downs: if the offense gained five yards within three downs, they achieved another first down.

Strategically, with these rule changes, maintaining possession by advancing the football became the major focus for the offense: the responsibility of stopping this advance fell to the defense. Suddenly, on this smaller field, each yard gained or lost became important, so the concept of massing the twenty two players at one point on the field quickly developed. The seven linemen opposing each other across a line of scrimmage established the concepts of line-play—that each offensive lineman must struggle against his opposite number, that each defender was primarily responsible for a limited area along the line of scrimmage. Melèe and fisticuffs, however, were the only components of line technique in that era, thus, the aggressive physical nature of the game became firmly entrenched. In addition, the practice by the four defensive "backs" positioned just off the line of scrimmage of *marking* their opposite number on the offense established the beginnings of the man-to-man concept on defense. Finally, the arbitrary ratio of seven line personnel and four backs as legislated for the offense in the late 1800s *continues* to dictate the structure of defense even in the late 1900s: in the Pro 4–3 and its prototype the 6–1 Defense, and 3–4 Defense originally the Oklahoma 5–2, seven defenders still are positioned along the line of scrimmage with four deepbacks off the line.

The Second Level of Defense

By the turn of the century these new strategies of the game had led to violent physical contact and, combined with grossly inadequate equipment (little padding, no helmets), resulted in an unacceptable number of traumatic injuries. In the 1905 season alone, eighteen deaths and 149 serious injuries were recorded, even though only a handful of players were competing at the time (2). In that same year a threatened edict by President Theodore Roosevelt which would have abolished football, precipitated the second major transformation in the concepts and conduct of the game. Between 1905 and 1912 a series of rule-changes were instituted, making the game more wide open and dynamic. The offense was permitted four downs, with a first down being achieved if ten yards were gained. The game was reduced in time to sixty minutes, segmented into fifteen-minute quarters, with a mandatory rest period at half time. Rules governing blocking and tackling modified the brutality of the game, and the wearing of rudimentary equipment for protection became obligatory. The points allotted for a touchdown were increased to six, giving further impetus to the offensive focus of the game. A pass *forward* was legalized, but with the following restrictions: the passer had to throw the ball from (at least) five yards behind his line of scrimmage to a receiver downfield over the line of scrimmage, but not deeper than twenty yards (3). Thereafter forward passing underwent successive modifications, but it was not until 1933 that the forward pass as we understand it today was fully installed in the professional game, and not until 1945 in college football. The screen pass was not legalized until the 1950s, while the shape and size of the football is still being modified to improve its aerodynamic qualities.

As a result, the period from 1905 to the start of World War I saw the development of the dynamic forces which still characterize the conduct of football. Several important concepts became entrenched as well and even today remain part of the psyche of the game. On the offense, the majority of forward passes are *still* thrown from a depth of five to seven yards behind the line of scrimmage, released by the passer in (approximately) 2 1/2 seconds after the snap, and caught twelve to eighteen yards downfield by the receiver. Defensively, in reaction to the complementary threat of the run *and* pass, two lasting concepts evolved. The backs are *still* placed off the line of scrimmage at a depth of six to eight yards in order to cover their receiver, the technique forecast by Camp in 1908 (4). Initially, when the positioning of specific backs was deepened, parts of the defensive line were left exposed without any immediate backup personnel. Thus, the idea developed that all seven of the defensive linemen need not be aligned *on* the line of scrimmage, and from the 1920s through the '50s a multitude of defensive alignments were deployed: basically, the center and one of the guards (rarely a tackle or end) shifted back and forth, from being on the line of scrimmage in a four-point stance to a stand-up line-backing position (5).

The Third Level of Defense

By the 1980s, only three of these *down* linemen remain on the defensive line in the popular 3-4 Defense: two ends and one nose tackle. So the question must be asked: what offensive leverage forced the evolution of defensive theory to the point where eight of the eleven defenders must now be either deepbacks or linebackers? The answer is found in the next major transformation of defensive theory, which occurred in about 1950.

From the technical writings on defense it is not clear how the concept of zone pass defense evolved, but the concept of permitting the receivers to run *to* the defenders and the technique of defending specific areas of the field eventually proved brilliant and effective. Most probably the prototype of today's complex zones had its origins in the techniques of double coverage (two defenders on one pass receiver) and combination coverage (two defenders on two receivers; if, however, the receivers' pass routes crossed, the two defenders *switched* their man assignments). Zone concepts are discussed in defensive system texts written in the 1930s (6) and 1940s (7, 8, 9). By today's standard, however, their theory is quite naive. Even as late as 1957, Jones and Wilkinson, the foremost defensive coaches of their era who pioneered the brilliant 5-2 Defense at the University of Oklahoma, wrote in their text *Modern Defensive Football*:

> The weakness of the 'zone' defense, however, is . . . if defensive [backs] are dropping quickly to cover the deep outside and deep middle zones, and if other men are rushing the passer, there are not enough defensive players remaining to cover all of the hook and all of the flat pass areas . . . . (10)

On offense, from the 1920s into the 1950s, some rather astonishing pass receiving records which still stand today were established against the man-to-man system of pass defense, and in 1940 the modern-day spread T formation (11) emerged (fig. 2). These two factors combined to precipitate the next evolutionary step in defensive football. Today, coaches are realizing that their defensive strategy is in jeopardy . . . and it is; similarly, by the late forties it was clear that against the spread T formation, defending the split pass receivers man-to-man was suicidal. Former pro quarterback Norm VanBrocklin (first with the Rams, then with the Eagles) is one of the few writers to document , from recollection, the emergence of the modern zone. He describes how, in

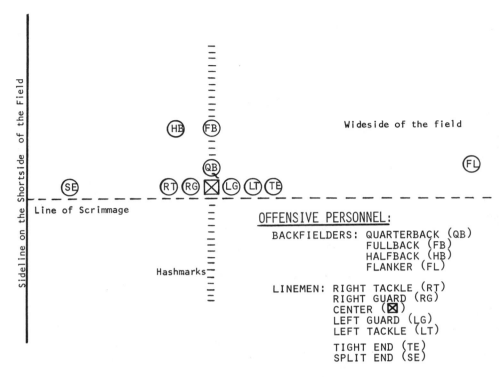

Figure 2 The spread T Formation: the split end (SE) moved out to one side-line. One halfback — now called a flanker (FL) — moved across the field to the other sideline, with the remainder of the T Formation intact.

1950, the New York Giants initiated the conversion of the 6-1 Defense into the modern-day Pro 4-3 Defense: " . . . Coach [Steve] Owens dropped the two outside [ends] of the six-man line off into the flats, thereby enabling the halfbacks [now the cornerbacks] to play loose and cover deep." (12). Later in his text, VanBrocklin documents the true emergence of the third level of defense: " . . . the first time I saw it,[1] was when the Los Angeles Rams played the Detroit Lions in 1951, but I have heard that it was used earlier." (13) The underneath zone coverage functioned, in 1951, much as it does today (fig. 3): rotation of the deepbacks covering deep zones and the strong flat zone; counter-rotation of the linebackers covering the hooks and weak-side flat zone; the stand-up technique by the two outside players on the defensive line converting them from static defensive ends to mobile outside linebackers; the emergence of the inside linebacker as the dominant force against *both* the run and the pass.

Since the 1950s, sophisticated systems of defense have been developed. Successive innovations in defensive construction and technique, combined with the imposing physical stature now required at specific positions, have steadily improved defensive performance. In 1945 at the University of Michigan was born two-platoon football (14) which has led in the eighties to the emergence of highly skilled defensive specialists–

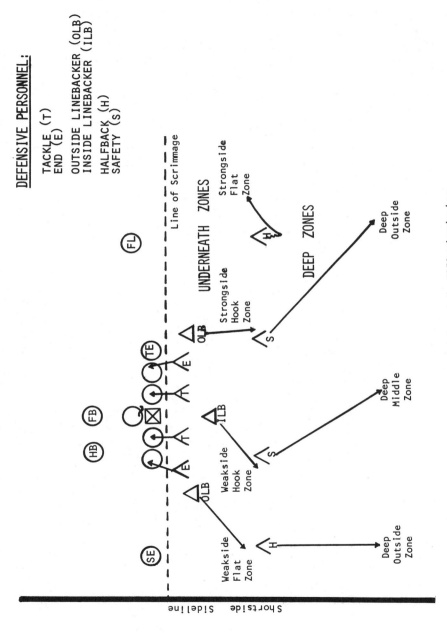

Figure 3 The emergence of the present-day zone pass defense in the 1950s: denying long passes to the offense by means of deep zone coverage; flooding the underneath zones and picking up receivers as they enter these zones; the emergence of the linebacker as the dominant force against *both* the pass and run, the third level of defense.

huge linemen and linebackers, and deepbacks possessing extraordinary speed and athletic ability. From the technical writings on defensive football, it seems that every conceivable combination of personnel alignment, zone and man-to-man pass coverage, and stunting mechanism has been invented (see ref. 15 for an example of the diversity in today's multiple defensive systems). Yet the basic concept of defense remains today as it evolved through the 1950s: the third level of defense still providing the crucial connecting link between the first two levels, and thereby, requiring zone coverage as the basic mechanism of pass defense. What has changed since the fifties is the strategic arsenal of the offense; quite literally, the offensive chess game has continued unchallenged.

OFFENSIVE FOOTBALL IN THE EIGHTIES:
CHARACTERISTICS AND CAPACITIES

The rule changes instituted in 1905-1912 were purposefully designed to open up the game of football and have succeeded far beyond the perceptions of even Walter Camp (16). Throughout this phase of the game's development the offense has always been the instigator of change, and the defense, of necessity, has assumed the reactionary role. Throughout, the instrument for change has been the judicious application of the principles of leverage: spreading the defensive manpower across the width and depth of the field, exploiting vulnerabilities in the defense's systems, and manipulating specific defensive personnel by taking advantage of their stature, technique, or movement pattern. Periodically the defense has been forced into untenable strategical situations, and as a result, for limited periods of time several offensive systems have experienced remarkable success, independent of coaching, personnel, or locale (table 1).

Exploitation of the defense by a specific offensive system has only been curtailed by defensive adjustments to the pressures imposed (or by rule change(s), although for the most part the rules of the game have benefited the offense). Throughout, as the defense successfully countered one offensive system, new, manipulative principles of leverage were evolved. And so the cycle has continued. In the 1980s, however, it appears that a crisis has been reached. The offensive arsenal has been evolving at a very rapid rate over the past twenty years, and the defense's capacity for further strategical adjustments within its existing conceptual framework has now been eclipsed. One less lineman versus one more linebacker or deepback, an additional alignment or defensive stunt, a new zone rotation or inversion, formulating another multiple defense (the current trend) . . . in the long run such expediencies will not solve the strategical dilemma posed by the offense.

Modern offensive football began in the 1940's with the consolidation of three diverse offensive concepts into one cohesive system (17); the leverage which each can apply against the defense is being fully exploited in the 1980's (fig. 4).

1.   The *Spread Formation* initially stretched the defense horizontally across the width of the football field; with the subsequent refinements in forward passing, the eleven defenders have been stretched vertically as well to their end zone.

TABLE 1. *The Evolution of Football Offense: 1920s-1980s.*

1920s	Development of the forward pass.
1930s	Single-wing offense: power running, limited passing.
1940s	The T formation revolution.
1950s	Spread T offense: dropback passing.
	Wing T offense: power running.
	play action passing.
	Split T offense: belly series option.
1960-75	I formation offenses: emergence of the tailback.
	sprintout passing.
	Wishbone T & veer offenses: Triple Option Series.
	Pro-style offenses: Multiple-flanker formations.
	Sophistication of the passing game.
1980s	An explosion of offensive innovations.

Figure 4 The mechanisms of offensive leverage built into the T formation: for periods of time, from 1940 through the 1980s, specific combinations of these mechanisms, defined as an "offensive system," placed the defense in untenable predicaments.

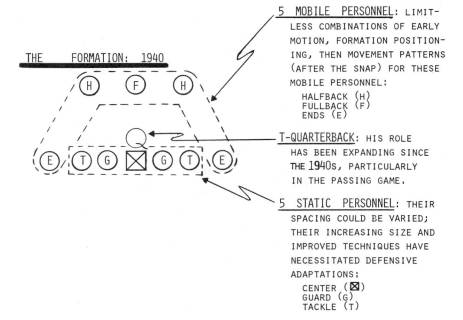

THE   FORMATION: 1940

5 MOBILE PERSONNEL: LIMIT-
LESS COMBINATIONS OF EARLY
MOTION, FORMATION POSITION-
ING, THEN MOVEMENT PATTERNS
(AFTER THE SNAP) FOR THESE
MOBILE PERSONNEL:
HALFBACK (H)
FULLBACK (F)
ENDS (E)

T-QUARTERBACK: HIS ROLE
HAS BEEN EXPANDING SINCE
THE 1940s, PARTICULARLY
IN THE PASSING GAME.

5 STATIC PERSONNEL: THEIR
SPACING COULD BE VARIED;
THEIR INCREASING SIZE AND
IMPROVED TECHNIQUES HAVE
NECESSITATED DEFENSIVE
ADAPTATIONS:
CENTER (⊠)
GUARD (G)
TACKLE (T)

2. *Early-Motion* by the eligible pass receivers prior to the snap, and a multiplicity of offensive formations, forced mobility upon the defense; in the 1980s the need for much greater defensive mobility, more than any other single factor, has placed the defense in serious jeopardy.

3. The installation of the quarterback receiving the snap directly from under the center established the *T-formation* and launched the modern era. (The strategical implications of the T formation are discussed elsewhere—see ref. 18.)

Cooperatively, these innovations have eventually revolutionized offensive football. In the 1940s and '50s, the T-quarterback emerged as the central focus of the offense, and his role has been expanding ever since. Over the past four decades new techniques have constantly been developed, as required by each new offensive system. Until the mid-seventies the offensive revolution followed two distinguishable trends: more conservative, run-oriented offenses were highlighted in college football, and the wide-open passing game in professional football. While these two offensive philosophies have always shared common characteristics, in the 1980s they have become almost indistinguishable from the standpoint of system and strategies; it is apparent that offensive coaches have converged on a universal approach for tactically dominating the defense (19). Present-day offenses have been characterized as conglomerates—in actuality, multiple offenses, as summarized by Rogers and Smith:

One other development is significant in [this] evolutionary story . . . The weaponry approach today accounts for more offenses than does any one of the integrated approaches, such as the Pro-T or the Wishbone-T . . . . Coaches find offensive success in . . . the best plays which have been used in the T . . . . an isolation, an option, a trap, a bootleg pass, a quarterback sweep, a scissors, et cetera—with all of them assembled into one offense. (20)

In strategic terms, what capacities does such an offense possess to manipulate the defense so effectively in the 1980s, and what does this portend for the defense?

The *multiple offenses* of the 1980s have incorporated the best and most successful plays from past eras, both running and passing. From the defensive perspective, defensive systems must now be flexible enough to defense power and speed running, option football, and dropback, sprintout, and quick passing; in addition, special tactical offenses have been developed for short-yardage and goal-line situations, in third-down and long-yardage, and so on. These multiple offenses are now executed from *multiple formations*, and there seems an almost limitless combination of formations and early-motion which an offense can assume. Therefore, in the 1980s defensive systems are forced to build in dynamic mechanisms which can effectively handle this vast offensive diversification; in turn, this has provided a pivotal focus for the offensive leverage, since, by its very structuring, the three-level concept of defense is innately static. As a result, many of the adjustments which it is *forced* to make can place the defense at a distinct disadvantage tactically. Defenders are now burdened with problems of offensive recognition, which can cause confusion or disrupt their mental concentration;

many of the defense's adjustments before the snap allow the offense (particularly the quarterback and receivers) to read their pass coverage; impossible adjustments for the defense to make, or adjustment errors, result in structural weaknesses, such as an undefended running lane or an open pass receiver.

By the 1980s the strategy that characterized offensive line play also was being used to manipulate the defense. Prior to the establishment of the spread T formation, the offensive formation always included two ends, principally blockers, who created the seventh and eighth (outside) gaps in the offensive line (fig. 5). By the 1950s one of

Figure 5 The strategical lever of the tight end (TE) and slotback (SB): the defense must always be prepared to defend eight offensive line-gaps; this necessitates outside linebackers under present defensive concepts.

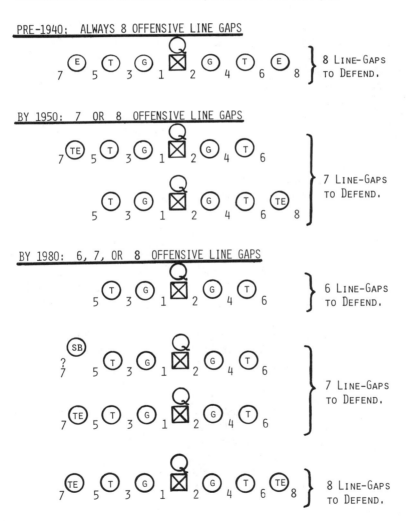

these ends (called a split end) had been spread out while the remaining tight end could be flip-flopped to either side of the offense. This strategy provides an excellent example of offensive manipulation: the tight end was both large in stature—and thus a viable blocking threat—fast and sure-handed, posing a deep pass threat. To counter his presence, the defense in the 1950s was forced to replace its static defensive ends with more mobile outside linebackers. Soon after, the offensive slotback evolved, smaller than the tight end but very mobile, and by the late 1970s slotbacks and even tight ends routinely went in early-motion, thereby eliminating line-gaps 7 and 8 altogether. In the mid-1980s, however, the *two* outside linebackers remain in the defensive construction, a personnel luxury the defense can ill afford yet *must* retain, for in any given situation the offense can insert two tight ends into its formation.

The tactics of the interior offensive line (i.e., the center, guards and tackles) have also undergone significant changes. Progressively, with the evolution of the T quarterback and the passing game, the need to protect the quarterback reached a critical point. Therefore, the distance between these offensive linemen (i.e., gaps 1-4, see fig. 5) was closed, from sizable gaps two to four feet in the older T formations to less than twelve inches in the passing offenses of today. In addition, the rules of the game have been modified in the 1980s to permit these blockers greater use of their hands in order to grapple with the onrushing defenders; this modification in blocking technique must eventually alter the course and concepts of the game of football. These changes have placed the defense's pass rush, the crucial element of pass defense in the 1980s, at a distinct disadvantage: first, the defensive (team) stunts for pressuring the quarterback require rushing lanes between the offensive linemen; second, the defense's superior pass rush techniques have now been effectively neutralized.

Finally, the latest offensive dimension being perfected in the 1980s has been termed *quick* passing (21), a modification of the brilliant principles of the run-and-shoot offense (22) but without the sprintout action of the quarterback. By 1960, the skills and tactics of the offensive passing game had been precisely honed. Quarterbacks had perfected two throwing actions: the dropback pass, which threatened the defense downfield, and the sprintout pass which pressured the defensive flanks. The offensive receivers were executing sophisticated pass patterns with amazing skill, timing, and intelligence. A variety of screen passes (and draw plays) had been incorporated into the offensive arsenal as well. On defense through the sixties and early seventies, offensive domination via the pass was constrained by a succession of complex zone innovations, notably the Two-Deep Zone (fig. 6) pioneered by Coach Arnsparger, then with the Miami Dolphins. Firmly entrenched, therefore, within both the offensive and defensive systems were the *conventions* which defined the passing game: the football thrown after 2 1/2 seconds following the snap (screen passes and trick plays being excepted), with the defensive techniques and movements predicated on this timing factor and on the patterned actions of the quarterback and receivers. Quick passing not only adds a new dimension to the offensive passing game, it *negates these established conventions* (23). The strategy behind this type of pass is simplicity itself: to move the football quickly to the perimeters of the offense allowing a fast flanker to run with the ball, unfettered by the interior defenders. Thus, quick passes must be thrown in less than 1 1/2 seconds, the

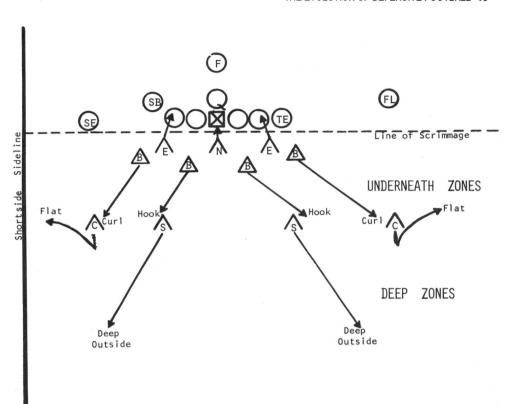

Figure 6 The Two-Deep Zone: developed in the 1960s, it permitted up to six defensive personnel to flood the underneath zones.

pass routes are very shallow, yet at the snap the pass defenders cannot discern if a quick or dropback pass will be thrown; as a result, they are forced to utilize the established man-to-man and zone techniques, and both are proving inappropriate against this type of passing. Execution of the quick pass poses few problems for the offense, compared to those it presents to the defense (fig. 7). Usually employing multiple motion, four or all five of the receivers are spread along the line of scrimmage before the snap, which permits both the quarterback and these receivers to read the defensive pass coverage (the problem of *defensive concealment* is analyzed further in the next section). In comparison to dropback pass protection for the quarterback, pass blocking is much less of a problem for the offensive line, because the elapsed time that the quarterback holds the ball is so short; alternately, this time factor renders the defensive pass rush almost obsolete. Most importantly, this new offensive leverage has created a dilemma for defensive personnel: to defend effectively against the quick pass, *more than* four deepbacks are required (see discussion, p. 23), thus, one (or more) linebacking

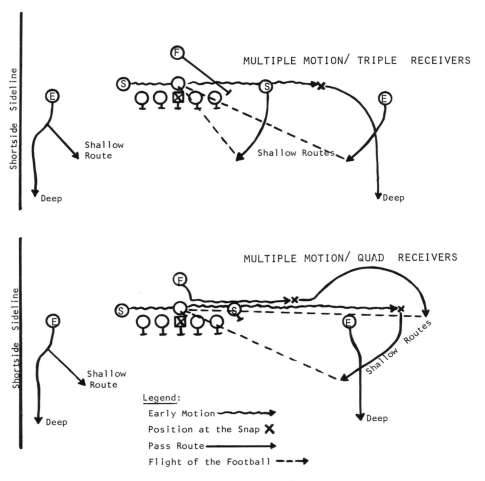

Figure 7 The simple yet effective quick pass routes run by the spread receivers: in zone pass coverage, the defenders are caught between these shallow receivers; in man-to-man coverage, they must defend against the deep pass first.

position(s) must eventually be occupied by non-linebackers. Even at the present time, in long-yardage situations extra deepbacks must temporarily be inserted into the defensive alignment.

TACTICAL CAPACITIES OF THE PRESENT MODEL OF DEFENSE

Since the 1940s the tactical capabilities of the offense have been rapidly expanding, and over the past decade this expansion has become a virtual explosion. Exactly the opposite trend has occurred in defense. In 1957, the most up-to-date football text of that era detailed no fewer than ten defensive models (30). In the 1980s the number of viable defenses has been reduced to basically two (fig. 8), Both contain similar alignment variations for shifting to strength or to the weak side, and identical pass coverage adjustments within their systems: the Pro 4-3-4 (i.e., four down linemen, three linebackers, four deepbacks) and Okie 3-4-4 defenses. In figure 9, the tactical capabilities of these models are summarized, and while differences exist between these

Figure 8 The evolution of one dominant model of defense in the 1950s and its Pro 4-3 and Okie 3-4 Alignments: the *only* advantageous personnel alignments for the three-level model.

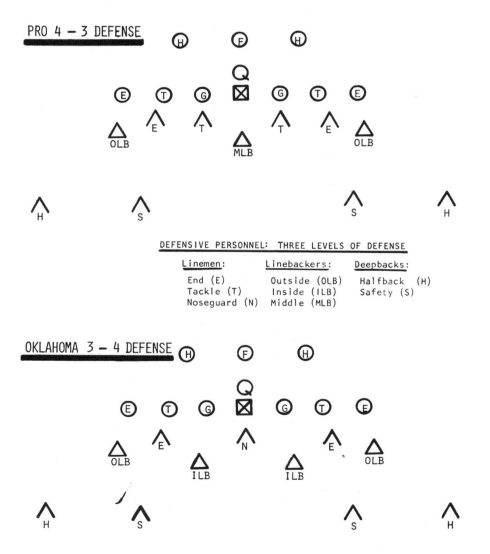

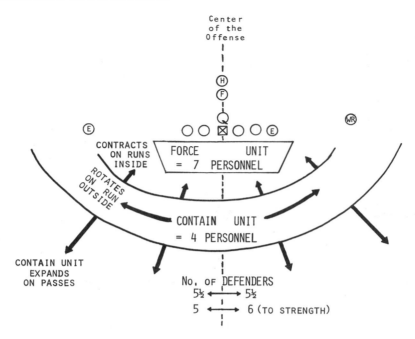

Figure 9 The present models of defense: limitations.
Three Levels of Defense: Line and linebackers = Force unit. Deepbacks = contain unit.
Force Unit: 7 personnel; each player defending one offensive line-gap.
Contain Unit: 4 personnel; defending against the pass by "expanding," against the run by "contracting" or "rotating."
Spatial Deployment: Optimal structural strength requires 5 1/2 personnel to each side of th offensive center; thus, limited mobility in model.
Pass Defense Limitations: Pass rush by the defensive line; employing additional personnel can weaken the defensive structure.
In man-to-man coverage, the *third* receiver to one side of the offense reads this coverage.
In zone pass coverage, this model can only defend against three pass receivers to one side of the offense; up to one-third of the defensive personnel defending deep zones.

two alignments (i.e., at three interior positions in the force unit–see below), for purposes of this critique they have been amalgamated into a single working model (25).

The Model's Run Defense

To defend against offensive running plays, this model grouped the defensive personnel into two subunits: the *Force Unit*, composed of the seven linemen and linebackers, and the *Contain Unit* comprising four deepbacks. The Force Unit's role was to attack the ball directly, and to accomplish this each player was assigned one offensive line-gap to defend. In the eighties the Force Unit can still effectively perform its role of attack, but the mobility of linebacking personnel is still restricted by the model itself. These personnel may not move far from their assigned offensive line-gap (i.e., their primary run responsibility) until the football, post-snap, has moved away from their area.

For this model to operate effectively against the run, the Contain Unit had to limit the movement of the ball, laterally or forward, by containing it within the immediate area of the field where it was put into play (fig. 9). As early as the 1970s, fewer deepbacks were positioned to perform this coordinated function *as it was originally designed*, because at the snap the four deepbacks had been strung out across the width of the field by the offensive formation—and, in the 1980s by *multiple* early motion as well—then run downfield by the offensive flankers. Progressively, therefore, the outside linebackers (originally the defensive ends of the Force Unit) have had to assume the primary responsibility for containment in the majority of defensive alignments while, at the same time, they have been burdened with other crucial responsibilities as well:

- at the snap to prevent the tight end /or a slotback from releasing inside;
- underneath zone coverage responsibility;
- providing primary support against running plays off-tackle;
- gradually assuming primary containment against outside running plays.

Against the run this defensive model has proven most structurally sound when the eleven personnel are positioned, relative to the center of the offense, five personnel to one side and five to the other (i.e., one defender in the Force Unit is viably positioned to defend to *both* sides of the offensive formation: the noseguard in the Okie 3-4, the middle linebacker in Pro 4-3). Seldom, however, does the offensive formation dictate such a balanced distribution of defensive personnel; and the limited flexibility within this model has become most apparent when specific defensive systems have attempted to *permanently* position a 6th defender to the strong side of the offensive formation (thus five personnel away-from-strength), the so-called monster defenses tried in the past (26, 27). These defensive mechanisms were very quickly taken advantage of by the offense: by running from the I-formation and the triple option, and also by passing to an isolated split end (away from strength).

Finally, defensive football in the eighties must be characterized by aggressiveness, because of the preemptive need to pressure the quarterback. The pass has now become the premiere offensive weapon, and on any or every down some offenses will pass. Translated into defensive tactics, aggressiveness means *initiating* the action as opposed to *reading*, then *reacting*, after the snap. But initiating positive action poses a dichotomy for this defensive model. In the 1950s it was structured as a reactionary model, used principally to react to the movement and blocking patterns initiated by the offense, and this concept *still* remains an integral characteristic of the model. Quite often a cornerback, for example, is isolated on a wide flanker without help, and dares not be overly aggressive. If Force Unit personnel are to play aggressively, on one hand their action can only be initiated *through* their assigned offensive line-gap or against a running play a structural weakness will immediately be created: on the other, if they have not gambled prudently, the Force Unit may be weakened in any case—a blitzing inside linebacker may take himself out of his critical pursuit role on sweeps, or a slanting lineman may be sprinting in the wrong direction, away from the play.

The Model's Pass Defense

Since the inception of the forward pass, two elements have been essential in defending against it: pass coverage of the five eligible receivers, and a pass rush at the quarterback.   However, until the 1960's, pass defense was essentially reactionary: receivers were covered man-to-man as they raced downfield, and pass rush was defined as a *secondary* Force Unit responsibility in the defensive systems prior to the '60s (30). Since then, the quarterbacks and receivers have elevated the pass-and-catch almost to an art-form, and the passing game has taken over as the primary offensive weapon. As a result, over the past twenty years numerous techniques and mechanisms have been incorporated *ad hoc* into this defensive model to combat the ever-increasing effectiveness of the offensive passing game. Some of these mechanisms have remained within the model, while others have failed, or became obsolete. For purposes of this discussion, these have been categorized into three general mechanisms of pass rush and three types of coverage (table 2).   By the 1980s, it was apparent that a minimal pass rush (*i.e.*, line rush only) in combination with saturation zone coverage by linebacker and deepback personnel provided the least consistent *but safest* strategy to thwart a potent pass offense. Most critically, the minimal rush, even with superior defensive line personnel, did not exert enough pressure on the quarterback, and the improved offensive blocking techniques, smaller line-gaps, taller quarterbacks, and recent rule changes have only exacerbated this situation. In addition, zone coverage was designed primarily to combat traditional dropback passing, and fewer of these were being thrown; it now appears that even eight defenders spread over the football field in zone coverage possess a finite capacity to defend against today's multiple pass offenses.

By the 1980s effective pass defense had been resolved to pressuring the quarterback but this required more personnel than just three or four defensive linemen. In turn, a number of combination coverages (29) have evolved where man-to-man and zone principles are employed together, permitting tighter coverage when the offensive formation (and not the field) is zoned and providing even greater variety in pass coverage. Pressuring the quarterback with additional personnel, however, exposed other vulnerabilities in this defensive model that cannot be rectified. First, blitzing additional personnel to pressure the quarterback requires aggressive action by linebackers, and occasionally by a deepback, which renders the defense more vulnerable against the run. Second, the greater the number of defenders involved in pass rush, the more man-to-man pass coverage *must* be employed, for there simply are not enough defensive personnel remaining for saturation zone coverage. Third, offensive sophistication and its ability to read the various pass coverages employed by this model *before the play* has also heightened the hazards inherent in blitzing (fig. 10); check-off passes and quick passing have negated the traditional man-to-man coverage

Table 2. To defend against the pass three basic mechanisms of 'coverage' and 'rush' have been developed in conjunction with the three-level model of defense.

PASS RUSH	P A S S C O V E R A G E S		
	ZONE THE FIELD (2-/3-/4-DEEP)	MAN-TO-MAN (REGULAR, BUMP-&-RUN)	COMBINATIONS - ZONING THE FORMATION - DOUBLE COVERAGE(S) - DEEP ZONE /MAN-TO-MAN UNDERNEATH
LINE RUSH (DEFENSIVE LINEMEN ONLY, WITH LIMITED SLANTING, TWISTING, ETC.)	'SATURATION' COVERAGE	LIMITED USE	USED PROGRESSIVELY MORE: - PROVIDES TIGHTER COVERAGE - GREATER VARIATION IN COVERAGE
LIMITED BLITZ (LIMEMEN WITH ONE LINEBACKER /OR A DEEPBACK)	LIMITED USE	WIDELY USED	USED SPARRINGLY, AS A CHANGE-UP
OVERLOAD BLITZ (BLITZES DESIGNED TO RUSH MORE DEFENDERS THAN AVAILABLE OFFENSIVE BLOCKERS)	NOT POSSIBLE	WIDELY USED	(INSUFFICIENT DEFENSIVE PERSONNEL TO PROVIDE BOTH COMBINATION COVERAGES AND MAXIMAL BLITZ AT THE SAME TIME)

technique (where a receiver's deep routes are eliminated *first*), thus bump-and-run man coverage must frequently be employed in conjunction with all-out blitzes.

Since the establishment of the third level of defense in the 1950s, its vulnerabilities against both the run and the pass have been progressively exposed through methodical experimentation and probing by the offense. Over the past thirty five years, at the end of each era (*i.e.*, when unique offensive innovations were finally countered by the defense's reactions) the three-level model slipped without coaches realizing it, deeper into a classic catch-22 dilemma: in countering its most immediate vulnerability, others were exposed. In the mid 1980s, there remains only a thread of continuity in most defensive systems, since so many mechanisms and adjustments have had to be incorporated to handle the offensive diversity. Defensive systems have become large and unwieldy, and even superior defensive personnel (a rare luxury in any case) cannot guarantee a short-term solution to the problems as they once could. Pre-game preparation has been reduced to a game-by-game predicament, a firefight, a

A. MAN-TO-MAN PASS COVERAGE

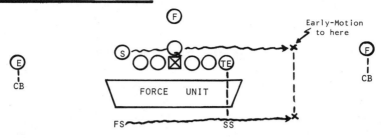

B. ZONE PASS COVERAGE

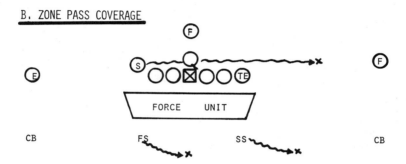

Figure 10 Reading the defensive pass coverage:

A. The free safety (FS) carries the slotback (S) across the offensive formation; cornerbacks (CB) tight on wide receivers = man-to-man coverage.

B. The free- and strong-safety (SS) rotate to the offensive strength side = zone pass coverage.

rehearsal of those mechanisms which the coach believes will accomplish the job against a specific opponent rather than the practicing of a coordinated, systematized attack. And during games, too often a defensive coordinator is reduced to prudent guessing. However the most difficult argument for coaches to believe and accept, is yet the one at the very heart of the problem: this dilemma is *unresolvable* because of the limitations imposed by the three-level concept of defense. For thirty five years, the three-level concept has been ingrained as the definitive model for defensive football. Unfortunately, as the first 100 years have proven, there are few *absolutes* in the game of football—certainly not the systems of offense and defense, nor the playing positions and techniques, nor the rules of the game . . . not even the shape and size of the ball itself. The quintessence of the game is dynamic; what appear to be *universal* at the present time are the more important elements in the game's history, merely taking a little longer to complete their evolutionary contributions.

TACTICAL CAPABILITIES OF FUTURE MODELS
OF DEFENSE

If defensive coaches continue to adapt and readjust the three-level concept of defense, this predicament can only escalate in the foreseeable future. The present trends in offensive football should continue with even greater dispatch, including: increased offensive mobility, even more play diversification for the defense to handle, and a greater number of specialists continually inserted into the offense (particularly in passing situations). From a tactical perspective the most immediate threats would appear to be larger, more mobile quarterbacks who are excellent runners as well as passers, and an ever-increasing use of multiple early-motion and multiple formations. As these offensive trends progress there is also ample precedent to predict that complementary rule changes must follow: from 1905 into the 1950s the successive rule changes which legalized forward passing *in stages* were, in several instances, instituted to alleviate the referees' difficult discretionary calls, and this same rationale has been responsible for several of the rule changes governing offensive blocking. Hence, *unlimited* early-motion must eventually be legalized, in any direction (back of the line of scrimmage), at any time, and by any one of the five eligible receivers; in the future, even the offensive ends may not be stationary for one full second before the snap.2 Whatever the future holds, one thing remains certain: offensive systems, personnel, and techniques will continue to probe the vulnerabilities of the present defensive model.

Therefore, to speculate on the magnitude of the defensive capability in the future, it is necessary to establish a list of priorities, distinguishable elements within the defensive philosophy which must characterize its play. First and foremost, the basic assumption of the three-level concept of defense—that defensive personnel can only *react* to offensive actions and initiatives—must rapidly change. More and more, the primary characteristic of defense must be *attack-oriented*; on every play, coordinated pressures must be initiated against the offense which simultaneously eliminate the major offensive options (fig. 11). For example, if a running play has been called by the offense, at the snap the offensive line-gaps would be jammed by charging defensive linemen, backed up by secondary personnel, and contained from the outsides by crashing ends; if a pass play had been called, however, the quarterback would have to release the ball quickly, regardless of the type of pass action, because of these rushing personnel, while the secondary defensive personnel played each eligible pass receiver aggressively. Thus, the only reacting by defensive personnel would be their decisions as to which specific run or pass would ensue (fig. 11, lower portion), and the offense would have to declare this quickly because of these systematic defensive pressures. Realistically, however, there are several problems with this ideal model of attack. It would require a majority of the defensive personnel to execute all these assignments simultaneously. Thus, in the future, up to one-third of the defensive personnel (at present the deepbacks) could not be regularly assigned coverage of the deep zones.

Prior to the snap, defensive *mobility* would appear to be another prerequisite of defense in the future. But this would have to be achieved without compromising either

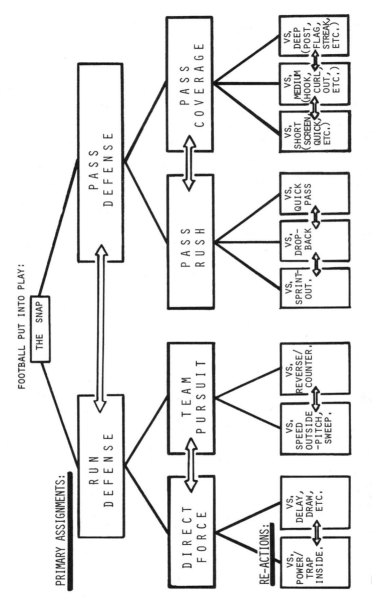

Figure 11 Model for a balanced defensive attack: specified personnel assigned to eliminate the major offensive run and pass options; as the offensive play developed, only then would defensive personnel re-act, adjusting their specific attack assignment accordingly.

the defensive structure or its ability to attack once the play began. In figure 12 this mobility requirement is determined: a maximum of three mobile defenders would be required, and each must have complete flexibility to shift quickly (before the snap) to either side of the offensive formation to counter any early-motion by the mobile offensive personnel. To allow these defensive personnel *unlimited mobility*, however, they could not be assigned specific offensive line-gaps to defend (as linebackers, for example, are presently assigned); thus again in such a model, attaining optimal defensive mobility would require a majority of the available defensive personnel. Absolute *concealment* of the defensive intentions (*i.e.,* before the snap) would appear to be another critical element, for a mobile, attacking defense would be placed at a distinct

Figure 12 The defensive mobility requirements: prior to the snap, the inherent mobility of the defense must permit three personnel *unlimited* mobility without jeopardizing the structural integrity of the defense or its ability to attack (after the snap).

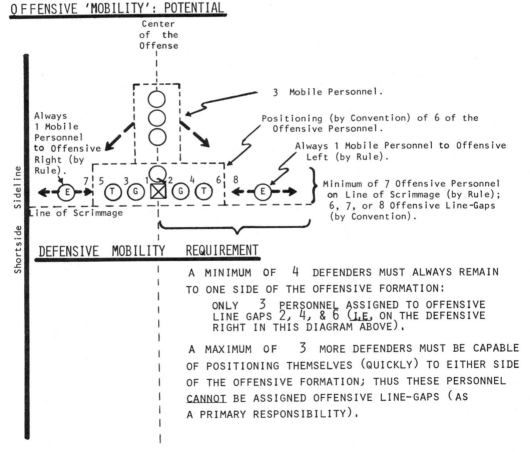

OFFENSIVE 'MOBILITY': POTENTIAL

Center
of the
Offense

3 Mobile Personnel.

Positioning (by Convention) of 6 of the
Offensive Personnel.

Always
1 Mobile
Personnel
to Offensive
Right (by
Rule).

Always 1 Mobile Personnel to Offensive
Left (by Rule).

Minimum of 7 Offensive Personnel
on Line of Scrimmage (by Rule);
6, 7, or 8 Offensive Line-Gaps
(by Convention).

7 5 3 1 2 4 6 8

Line of Scrimmage

Sideline

Shortside

DEFENSIVE MOBILITY REQUIREMENT

A MINIMUM OF 4 DEFENDERS MUST ALWAYS REMAIN
TO ONE SIDE OF THE OFFENSIVE FORMATION:
  ONLY 3 PERSONNEL ASSIGNED TO OFFENSIVE
  LINE GAPS 2, 4, & 6 (I.E, ON THE DEFENSIVE
  RIGHT IN THIS DIAGRAM ABOVE).

A MAXIMUM OF 3 MORE DEFENDERS MUST BE CAPABLE
OF POSITIONING THEMSELVES (QUICKLY) TO EITHER SIDE
OF THE OFFENSIVE FORMATION; THUS THESE PERSONNEL
CANNOT BE ASSIGNED OFFENSIVE LINE-GAPS (AS
A PRIMARY RESPONSIBILITY).

disadvantage if an offense were able to predetermine any defensive actions (fig. 10). However, this may prove to be one of the simpler elements to install in any future defensive system: prior to every play and independent of the actual defensive mechanisms or pass coverages, the defense would simply employ *constant* principles of movement and alignment. Given the (almost) unlimited number of offensive formations and early-motion, these most probably should involve man-to-man movement principles to achieve pre-snap adjustments. Therefore, the offense would obtain an *identical* read from this defensive movement prior to every play, thus, their read would be meaningless.

Several other elements should also be built into the defense in the future. Simplicity and continuity remain two important defensive characteristics, but at the present time are given only lipservice by coaches because defensive systems have become so unwieldy. *Simplicity* minimizes both the complexity and the number of decisions which an individual defender must make in any given situation; in defensive football decisions must be kept to a minimum, and must never be so complex that the player's ability to carry out his responsibilities effectively and aggressively is compromised. *Continuity* in a defensive system involves its universal application. Defenses freely employ unique concepts, strategies, alignments, and even personnel for different tactical situations, according to the down-and-distance situation, using middle-of-the-field versus goal-line defenses, to defend against a specific offensive system (such as the triple option), and so on. The importance of continuity in defensive football is that one system can be universally applied against a wide range of offensive situations and opponents, with significant effectiveness in every instance. Finally, at the heart of any defensive system lie its signals, the terminology employed to direct the defensive personnel. More and more it is becoming apparent that defensive signals must be visually cued: with the greater offensive mobility spreading the defensive personnel across the field before the snap, attempts to maintain verbal communication on defense are becoming futile. In practical terms, the defensive huddle call—predetermining alignment, stunts, pass coverage, etc.—has become the least effective mode of communicating defensive signals.

In designing a viable defensive model for the 1980s therefore, many tactical questions must be considered, and obviously major changes and compromises will have to be made in the present concepts of defense. Surprisingly, at the present time there is already one *very effective* defensive model which encompasses many of these prerequisite conditions and tactical capabilities: the 6-5 Goal Line Defense, successfully performed and popularized by the late Coach Bryant at Alabama (29). In figure 13, the football has been positioned on the defense's own ten-yard line, the location on the field where this goal-line model gains maximum effectiveness. In the 6-5 Defense, all eleven defenders are massed near the line of scrimmage, while the end line (at the back of the end zone) imposes a twenty-yard maximum on any pass that can be completed over the line of scrimmage. Each of the defensive linemen is assigned an offensive line-gap as his primary responsibility, and each of the five defensive personnel backing up the linemen is assigned to one of the mobile offensive personnel, with both run and pass responsibility (fig. 13:A). With minimal verbal communication, this model

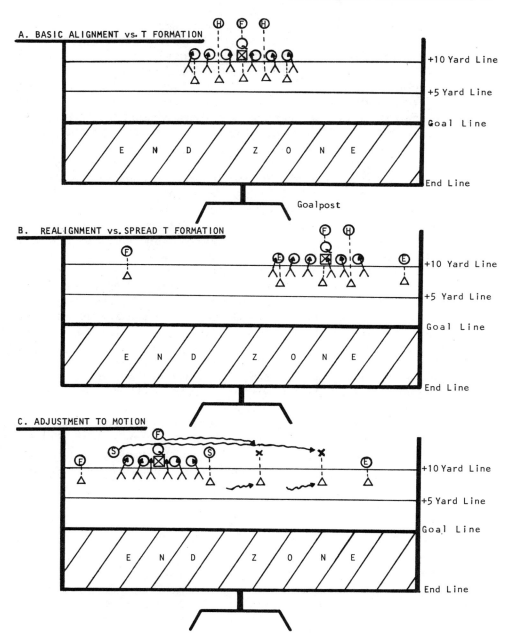

Figure 13 The 6-5 goal line defense and its dynamic adjustments to: A) the threat of power running; B) power running *and* spread passing; and C) spread passing from multiple early motion (before the snap).

already incorporates the mobility that permits these defensive personnel to adjust to every combination of offensive formation, to unlimited early-motion by the offense, while maintaining both the structural and tactical integrity of this defense (figs. 13: B and C). Against the run, this model also provides the *best* defensive attack against any incursion into its interior or flanks while ensuring immediate and maximum pursuit response.   Against the pass, the defensive linemen put *immediate* pressure on the quarterback, and from *all* directions; at the same time, the five backup personnel can provide aggressive and tight coverage against the receivers—but not necessarily man-to-man pass coverage (30)—because the end line (at the back of the end zone) is only twenty yards away. As offensive coaches have realized since the 1960s, this specific combination of defensive pressures against both the run and pass has always made this two-level model extremely difficult to move against. However, the 6–5 Goal Line Defense only possesses these tactical capabilities because the position of the football (*i.e.,* within the defense's ten-yard line) greatly reduces the playing area of the field (to 53 1/3 yards wide by 20 yards deep). Obviously, nearer the middle of the field or in the offense's end, the extreme advantages of this attack model of defense are outweighed by its vulnerability to the deep pass. On the other hand, if mechanisms could be incorporated which in effect compressed the immediate defensive area to approximately this size *regardless* of the location of the football on the field, many of the tactical mechanisms and pressures of this effective model could be reinstituted.   This is precisely what occurred, for example, in both the 1984 and 1986 Super Bowls. In 1984 the defensive game plan of the Los Angeles Raiders relied upon (to quote Head Coach Tom Flores) "attack football" (31) and (according to Defensive Coordinator Charlie Sumner) "bump-and-run pass defense . . . to shut off the short [passes] . . . . and the swirling winds [throughout Tampa Bay Stadium] would take care of anything deep" (*i.e.,* any passes thrown over twenty to twenty-five yards deep) (32).   As a result throughout the game the Raiders were able to mass all eleven defenders within five yards of the line of scrimmage in a two-level 5-6 alignment. In the 1986 Super Bowl the Chicago Bears utilized their vaunted 4-6 defense, massing ten defenders along the line of scrimmage, assigning the eleventh (the free safety) to assist on deep passes.

Notes

1. Of greatest significance in this quote, is the fact that at the time of writing, some fifteen years after the event, VanBrocklin was the premiere NFL quarterback with over a decade of experience against zones and rotational coverages; yet, in recollection, his reference to "it" reveals the true impact which this 1951 event had on him.

2. For example, these rules govern early-motion in the Canadian college and professional football leagues, but not, however, in the United States.

References

1. ROBERT L. DODD, *Bobby Dodd on Football* (Englewood Cliffs, N.J.: Prentice-Hall, Inc., 1954), pp. 3-4.

2. "College Football: Babes in Wonderland." *Time,* October 28, 1966, pp. 54-61.

3. ALLISON DANZIG, *Oh, How They Played the Game* (New York: MacMillan, 1971), pp. 187-188.

4. NORM VANBROCKLIN, *Passing, Punting, Quarterbacking* (New York: Ronald Press Co., 1961), p. 4.

5. JOHN F. BATEMAN and PAUL V. GOVERNALLI, *Football Fundamentals: Basic Strategy and Teaching Methods* (New York: McGraw-Hill Book Co., Inc., 1957), pp. 246-282.

6. B. W. BERNIE BIERMAN, *Winning Football* (New York: McGraw-Hill Book Co., Inc., 1937), pp. 73-75.

7. V-FIVE ASSOCIATION OF AMERICA, *The Naval Aviation Physical Training Manuals: Football* (Annapolis, Md. U.S. Naval Institute, 1943), pp. 171-172.

8. DANA X. BIBLE, *Championship Football* (New York: Prentice-Hall, Inc., 1947), pp. 148-152.

9. H. O. FRITZ CRISLER, *Modern Football: Fundamentals and Strategy* (New York: McGraw-Hill Book Co., Inc., 1949), pp. 164-166.

10. GOMER JONES and CHARLES BUD WILKINSON, *Modern Defensive Football* (Englewood Cliffs, N.J.: Prentice-Hall, Inc., 1957), p. 217.

11. DANZIG, *Oh, How They Played the Game*, pp. 396-403.

12. VANBROCKLIN, *Passing, Punting, Quarterbacking*, p. 29.

13. Ibid, p. 33.

14. CRISLER, *Modern Football: Fundamentals and Strategy*, pp. 6-8.

15. S. E. SULLINS, *Complete Book of Multiple Defenses in Football* (West Nyack, N.Y.: Parker Publ. Co., Inc., 1978).

16. DANZIG, *Oh, How They Played the Game*, pp. 10-11.

17. Ibid, pp. 396-399.

18. MURRAY OLDERMAN, *The Pro Quarterback* (Englewood Cliffs, N.J.: Prentice-Hall, Inc., 1966), pp. 11-21.

19. JOHN ROBINSON, "Similarities between College and Professional Football" (paper presented by the head coach of the Los Angeles Rams at the University of Michigan, eighteenth Annual Football Clinic, Ann Arbor, Michigan, April, 1984).

20. PEPPER ROGERS and HOMER SMITH, *Installing Football's Wishbone-T Attack* (West Nyack, N.Y.: Parker Publ. Co., Inc., 1973), p. 9.

21. WALT HARRIS, "Tennessee's quick game package," *Scholastic Coach*, 54:28-31, 77, 1984.

22. GLENN ELLISON, *Run-and-Shoot Football: Offense of the Future.* (West Nyack, N.Y.: Parker Publ. Co., Inc., 1965).

23. HAL LOCKHART, "A simple one-step, drop-back, short passing game," *Scholastic Coach*, 53:28-30, 106, 1983.

24. BATEMAN and GOVERNALLI, *Football Fundamentals: Basic Strategy and Teaching Methods*, pp. 246-284.

25. JONES and WILKINSON, *Modern Defensive Football*, pp. 52-88.

26. DALE FOSTER, *The Slanting Monster Defense in Football* (West Nyack, N.Y.: Parker Publ. Co., Inc., 1970).

27. JACK OLCOTT, "Monster Pass Defense," *Football Coach's Guide to Successful Pass Defense* (West Nyack, N.Y.: Parker Publ. Co., Inc., 1970), Chap. 8: pp. 107-116.

28. BATEMAN and GOVERNALLI, *Football Fundamentals: Basic Strategy and Teaching Methods*, pp. 64-69.

29. MICHAEL JANOFSKY, "Cornered," *New York Times Magazine*, September 29, 1985, pp. 52-53, 74-75.

30. PAUL BRYANT, *Building a Championship Football Team* (Englewood Cliffs, N.J.: Prentice-Hall, Inc., 1960), pp. 48-51.

31. PAUL BRYANT, "Alabama's 6-5 Goal Line Defense," *The Best in Football From Scholastic Coach* (New York: Scholastic Coach Athletic Services, 1970), pp. 20-23.

32. TOM CALLAHAN, "Perspective on a Screen Pass," *Time*, February 6, 1984, p. 59.

33. PAUL ZIMMERMAN, "A Runaway for the Raiders," *Sports Illustrated*, January 30, 1984, pp. 16-17.

Chapter 2
BASIC CONCEPT, PRINCIPLES, AND PERSONNEL

INTRODUCTION: THE UNIQUE PROBLEM OF DEFENSE

A football system is a complex integration of coaching intellect, precise movement patterns, and specific physical skills (fig. 14). Whether designed for offense or defense, a system originates in the mind of a coach when he conceptualizes a unique sequencing of *tactical principles* for applying pressure and leverage against the opponent. Next, appropriate *mechanisms* must be devised and integrated into the system: discrete movement patterns for personnel to execute from specified *positional alignments*. In order to coordinate concept with mechanism, an esoteric vocabulary must also be developed, the *signals* of the system. Finally, at the root of any system are the specific football *skills* and *techniques* that each player must learn for his position, the physical elements that impart the system's advantages to each personnel position. As the first century of football has demonstrated, the possible permutations for manipulating the eleven personnel on the field, even within the structured rules of the game, appear almost limitless.

Implementing a defensive system, however, poses a unique set of problems. All of the successful *offensive* coaches, both past and present, have known precisely what concept(s) they were implementing, and the end result each had determined to achieve: a Vince Lombardi or a Woody Hayes was determined to run the football, directing a power-oriented system at the heart of the defense; a new generation of coaches is bent, with equal determination, on passing the football, implementing complex and sophisticated systems of offense. By comparison, the aims and objectives of a *defensive* system

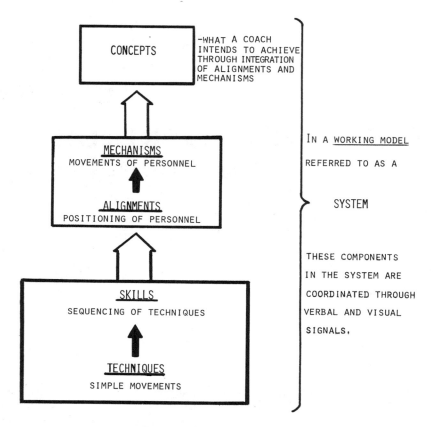

Figure 14 Elements in a football system.

can never be as succinctly defined: defensive systems are forced to embody more universal characteristics, to build in diversified mechanisms. Additionally, offensive coaches have always been afforded the luxury of experimentation; on defense, errors committed at the technical level (usually) cost six points; at the systems level, however, miscalculations are potentially disastrous. As a result of these circumstances, over the past one hundred years there have been few prominent defensive systems, as the major transitions in defense have required years of refinement before gaining popular acceptance. Consequently, proven defensive systems have never been discarded carelessly, but the eventual passing of each has marked the demise of one football era and the beginning of the next. In essence, this cycle goes to the heart of the defensive quandary. A mediocre performance by an offense need only result in a lower-scoring game, and victory *versus* defeat seldom hangs in the balance; but even a substandard performance by a defense forebodes defeat.

In defensive football, therefore, the *system* must always provide the main focus for the coach. There is a clichè in football that systems should always be suited to the player personnel. Categorically, this philosophy has *limited relevance for the defense*. It is a product of the offensive experience, in which coaches do have many choices when suiting a specific offensive system to their available personnel; by comparison, in defensive football today there is a dwindling number of systems from which to choose. Due to the injury factor in football, or to a substandard performance by a superior defense, or to inadequate game preparation, at least once *every season* the offense's arsenal will prove superior to the defenses capabilities (and this usually occurs in the most crucial games). Therefore team defeat is imminent in such circumstances unless the defensive system, and the coaching of a superior system, can compensate for this disparity.

From several perspectives the 2-level Defense detailed in this text represents a complete break with the defensive concepts of the past. Vince Lombardi was often quoted as saying "that football is blocking and tackling," and while this remains the essence of the game, the coaching of football has evolved into an exciting science built upon these more simplistic precepts. From this chapter, when a basic understanding of the 2-level model has been assimilated, the reader should begin to appreciate the aggressiveness and preemptive attack that this concept of defense allows. The specific defensive mechanisms for accomplishing these objectives against the run and the pass are discussed in detail in chapters 3 and 4, respectively, with goal line adaptations briefly outlined in chapter 5. In order to best describe the internal operations of the system, throughout this chapter and chapter 3 the defense's *base* alignment is employed (i.e., five defensive personnel operating in the First Level and five in the Second Level). In chapters 4 and 5, several additional alignments and personnel substitutions are introduced, but the reader should note that these variations require no change either in the working model as formulated or its systems of operation.

DEFENSIVE PRINCIPLES AND ALIGNMENTS

The *First Level* (i.e., the actual name given to this defensive subunit) includes five defenders playing on the line of scrimmage, and corresponds quite closely to the present defensive line. The *Second Level* is also comprised of five defenders who play up to five to seven yards off the line of scrimmage but are neither linebackers nor deepbacks as these conventional subunits of defense are presently understood. A degree of flexibility is built into the attack of the First Level; *absolute* mobility is the keystone of the Second Level. On each play personnel in the First Level are assigned *specific offensive line-gaps* to defend, according to the huddle call. In contrast, each second-level player *mirrors* (i.e., another new "systems" term) one of the eligible pass receivers: by this mechanism the five second-level personnel are free, within the limitations of the system, to quickly adjust their location *across* the football field, according to the positioning of the flankers, ends, and backfielders in the offensive formation. The eleventh defender, the *Deep Safety*, is positioned at a depth of twenty eight yards from the line of scrimmage, inside the field's hashmarks, at the approximate midpoint of the offensive formation. The tactical capacities of this new position allow the 2-level defense to function more aggressively than is presently possible with the three-level model: ten of the eleven defenders, the first and second levels, can execute their responsibilities aggressively because of the deep safety's *range of movements*. Finally, the coach implementing the 2-level system should appreciate that specific physical characteristics are required at several key positions in this defense; these important implications are discussed at length at the conclusion of this chapter.

The First Level

In the system's nomenclature the offensive linemen, tackle-to-tackle, are defined as *static* personnel because they are always positioned in the offensive core and must (by the rules of the game) remain motionless once they have assumed their pre-snap positions (fig. 15). The *core* is defined by an elliptical area on the football field, extending to five yards outside each of the offensive tackles and circumscribed by (imaginary) boundaries five yards deep on either side of the line of scrimmage; the point from where the football is snapped provides the epicenter of the core. The established names for defensive line positions have been retained: the *Nose* and *Tackles* always set in the conventional three-point stance; however, the *Ends* may assume either

Figure 15 The static offensive personnel and the defensive first level positioned in the core.

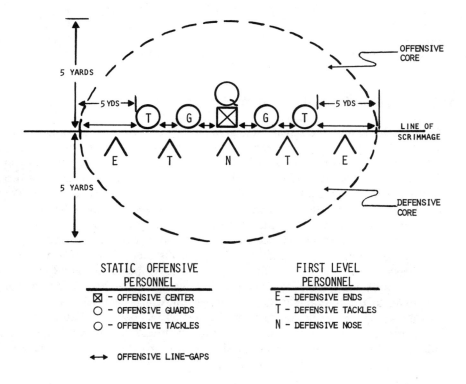

STATIC OFFENSIVE
PERSONNEL

⊠ – OFFENSIVE CENTER
○ – OFFENSIVE GUARDS
○ – OFFENSIVE TACKLES

↔ OFFENSIVE LINE–GAPS

FIRST LEVEL
PERSONNEL

E – DEFENSIVE ENDS
T – DEFENSIVE TACKLES
N – DEFENSIVE NOSE

the down or a standing, two-point stance. There are two major differences between the First Level and conventional defensive line-play.

1. Regardless of the offense's formation, *only* six offensive line-gaps are defined: two center-guard gaps, two guard-tackle gaps, and two off-tackle gaps (fig. 15). The First Level is responsible for defending these areas, and individual gap responsibilities vary according to the system's attack format on any given down.

2. Therefore, the ends are not linebackers; rather, the First Level is an integrated, five-man subunit and functions as such, carrying out its coordinated assault through assigned line-gaps.

Generally, the ends attack from the extremities of the core in order to restrict the movement of the football laterally (and this movement pattern and technique is termed *crash*); the nose and tackles attack specific internal line-gaps in order to limit the penetration of the football across the line of scrimmage. And of course, on a forward pass play the First Level would carry this attack pattern to the quarterback, continuing its coordinated assault from all directions.

The Second Level

According to the nomenclature developed for the 2-level defense, the *eligible* pass receivers are defined as *mobile* because of their (almost) unlimited positional alignments in the offensive formation, and Second Level defenders *mirror* these five personnel; that is, wherever the offensive flankers, ends, or Backfielders align, inside or outside of the core or even in early motion (prior to the snap), as each looks downfield at the defense he sees his "mirror image," a second-Level defender across the line of scrimmage and up to seven yards deep off the line of scrimmage (fig. 16). *Lou* and *Rose* are always the two outermost defenders in the Second Level; Lou always mirrors the mobile personnel positioned furthest to the left side of the defense, while Rose mirrors the widest personnel furthest out on the *right* side. *Strong* aligns to the strength side of the offensive formation, *Bandit* aligns away from the strength side, and *Gael* is always positioned in the middle *between* Strong and Bandit, mirroring his mobile offensive personnel. In this ordered sequence across the football field, their final positioning is always dictated by the alignment of the five mobile offensive personnel across the line of scrimmage from them. In mirroring an offensive backfielder in the core, however, these personnel do *not* become linebackers in the conventional sense: they do *not* assume primary responsibility for an offensive line-gap against the run, as linebackers must in the 43 and 34 defensive models. In addition, inside the core Second Level defenders align immediately behind the First Level and up to five yards off the line of scrimmage; outside of the core, Second Level defenders may align eye-to-eye with these (potential) pass receivers *or* up to seven yards off the line of scrimmage. The Second Level always attacks in a very structured, predetermined manner, according to the defensive pass coverage called.

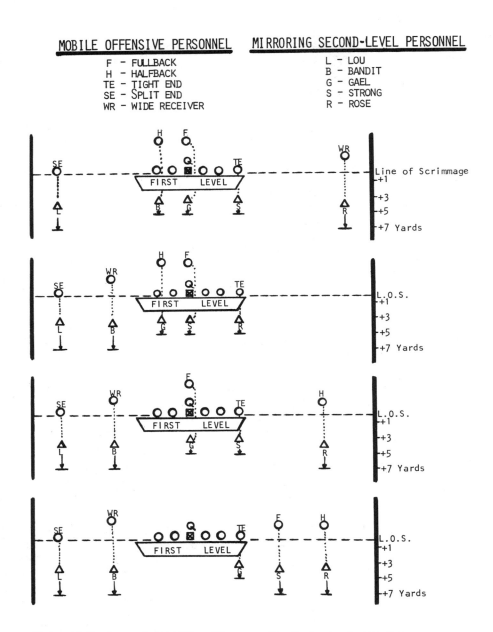

Figure 16 Realignment capabilities of the second level: mirroring (....) the five mobile offensive personnel, eligible pass receivers, up to 7 yards off the line of scrimmage, inside amd outside the core.

The Deep Safety

In figure 17, the movement patterns for the *Deep Safety* are diagrammed. His role in the 2-level defense is to enforce an *end line* across the football field at a depth of eighteen-plus yards from the line of scrimmage, duplicating, in effect, the end zone's end line (as explained at the conclusion of part I—see fig. 13). The establishment of an end

Figure 17 The end-line concept: the deep safety (DS), aligned 28 yards from the line of scrimmage, intersects the football at a depth of +18 yards (or deeper if a longer pass is thrown), in effect establishing an end line across the field at that depth.

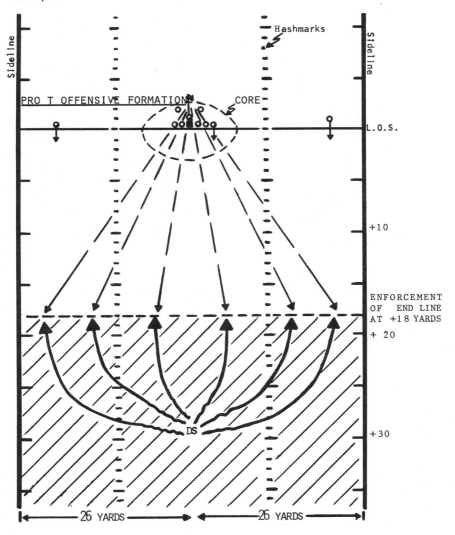

line at eighteen-plus yards from the line of scrimmage is *independent* of the location of the football vertically, up and down the field, and remains in effect until the football has penetrated deep into the defensive end of the field (i.e., until the field's end line becomes operable). Four interacting mechanisms (detailed in the following section) make the establishment of such an end line across the football field a viable concept within the 2-level defensive system. In fact, the end line becomes a devastating reality using this system, and forward passes attempted deeper than fifteen yards downfield are only thrown into the sidelines; the offense's reason for this decision is extremely judicious: fear—of injury and of pass interception.

1. The deep safety is always moving forward and thus is sprinting at almost *twice* the speed of a defensive back backpedalling, with little need to stop or change direction.

2. He is, therefore, able to effectively cover *twice the area* of the field (i.e., twice that which the conventional deep back can cover) within the same time frame, and arrive at the moment of impact with much greater momentum, usually hitting an overextended pass receiver who is looking back in the direction of the quarterback.

The longest sprint for the deep safety can be calculated at just over thirty yards (fig. 17). In most instances, however, this distance is reduced by the second level defenders' attempting to steer the offensive pass receivers in predetermined directions. In the development of the 2-level Defense several other depth combinations for the prealignment of the deep safety, then enforcement of the end line concept, proved effective. Through extensive experimentation in both scrimmages and game situations, however, the combination of twenty-eight yards depth alignment for the safety, between the hashmarks, and the establishment of the end line at eighteen-plus yards from the line of scrimmage, proved optimal. That is, this combination proved very effective in eliminating medium-depth passes thrown to from fifteen to eighteen yards without encroaching upon the overall *safety factor* of the defense.[1]

TACTICAL PRINCIPLES

The integral role of the deep safety within this defensive system cannot be over-emphasized. At first glance coaches may conclude that they would be playing with only ten defenders should they implement this defense . . . *yet this is precisely the point:* this defense is designed to utilize ten of the eleven defensive personnel *directly* and *effectively* on every play. It is a two-level concept with the First Level countering the offensive running threats on every play, including rushing the quarterback on passing plays. The Second Level is assigned to the potential ball carriers or pass receivers, whichever type of offensive play results, and both zone and man-to-man coverages are interchanged with regularity according to the tactical situation confronting the defense. Many defensive personnel are required to execute these responsibilities *simultaneously*:

- • certainly seven personnel cannot accomplish it (i.e., the number of defenders originally allocated to the Force Unit in the three-level model);
- • nor can the personnel be fragmented into small defensive subunits (i.e., three to four defenders per unit).

Therefore, this model of defense is only made possible by the deep safety: a commitment of one defender who, by prealigning twenty-eight yards deep, can virtually eliminate the long pass (and run) as well as exerting considerable influence against an offense's middle-depth passing game. Two or three defenders are *not* required to secure this deep area because the football can only cross the end line at one location; thus one defender integrated within the appropriate system can secure this entire area.

The End-Line Concept

Prior to any down, many offensive options are available to the versatile arsenals of today. Traditionally, the philosophy governing defensive play has been to react to whichever option the offense has selected, and the increasing importance of the defensive game plan has incorporated an element of "highest probability" into this philosophy. In the 1980's, however, it is evident that all of the offensive options cannot be effectively countered by this approach, principally because the defensive subunits in the three-level model are fragmented to such a degree. The 2-level Defense offers an alternate concept: the first premise of this system is to *limit* the offensive options on any given play through the imposition of two mechanisms. First, the end line constricts the area of the field in which the offense may effectively operate, thereby reducing some of its options. Second, the time frame in which the offense is permitted to operate is reduced through defensive pressures; again, specific offensive options must lose their viability because of the premeditated attack directed at the football. In this Defense these two complementary factors must operate in close concert; combined, they are the main tactical advantages of the system, but their coordination presents the major problem in implementation.

Primarily, the concept of the end line is a tactical mechanism for reducing an offense's passing options. Four interacting factors enable the deep safety to establish, de facto, an end line across the football field.

1. There is only one certain means of preventing a pass completion: to attack its source, force the quarterback to throw within a shortened time frame and under maximal defensive pressure. In this 2-level system this is accomplished through coordination of the First Level's pass rush with blitzing by Second Level defenders mirroring in the core.

2. Additionally, independent of the pass coverage (man, zone, or combination), precious time elapses while pass receivers are delayed on their way downfield by the mirroring Second Level defenders. Combined with the pressure exerted on the quarterback, receivers are seldom able to run pass routes over twenty yards downfield.

3. The third factor in the establishment of the end line requires pass defenders, particularly in man-to-man coverage, to get *underneath* their receivers *between* the quarterback and receiver, in order to deny medium-depth passes. Thus, if the pass is thrown on a flat trajectory, there is little margin for error in the quarterback's accuracy.

4. When these three factors are effectively implemented by the first and second levels, the concept of an end line across the field at eighteen-plus yards becomes a reality, because the football can only cross the end line *at one point* (whether in the air or on the ground), and the deep safety has the tactical capability to intersect it. The final factor then becomes his method of enforcing the end line, and physical intimidation must play an integral role in the concept at this point. If a medium-depth pass cannot be thrown by the quarterback on a flat trajectory with velocity but must be arc'd, the time that the deep safety has to reach the intersection point is increased, and his momentum will be maximized, yet the receiver has placed himself in the most extreme position of vulnerability—arms outstretched, trunk completely exposed, head and eyes turned back towards the quarterback, unable to protect himself physically by any means.

In this regard, an important coaching point for the deep safety involves his timing in getting to the point of the intersection: the safety is only at fault when he arrives late; if he arrives prior to the football, he disregards this and completes the hit as his preestablished timing schedule dictates. This can result in pass interference calls against the deep safety and is one of the liabilities of the Defense; but, the physical element in the safety's enforcement of the end line must remain unrestricted (see chapter 7, final section).

Outnumbering the Offensive Blockers in the Core

A problem of the first magnitude has recently arisen by which the defense seems nonplussed within the limitations of the three-level defensive model. Offensive blockers are being permitted much greater use of their hands, arm extension, and actual holding of the defender. In many leagues throughout North America, although the written rules governing offensive blocking may not have been modified, in practice the referees' interpretations of these rules permit the blocker to grasp a defender's clothing, equipment, or body parts, provided this occurs along the frontal plane of the (defender's) body (that is, the blocker cannot encircle an arm or leg). Except for very blatant holding, the rules governing offensive blocking have become excessively lenient, to the detriment of the defense, and this trend probably will accelerate as offensive systems and techniques continue to evolve. Therefore, any time the number of offensive blockers is equal to the number of defenders at the point of attack each defender can be tied up quite effectively by an offensive player's literally grabbing hold of him. The mobility built into this 2-level Defense provides a tactical solution to this problem. In the core, the defenders *always* outnumber the available blockers at the offense's point of attack; thus, *all* of the defensive tacklers cannot be neutralized, even by offensive holding. The defensive principle for securing this numerical superiority is diagrammed in figure 18; pictorially, the principle is shown in reference 2, in film sequences illustrating U.C.L.A.'s defensive strategy against Ohio State in the 1979 Rose Bowl (2). On every down the offense is free to select the formation it requires;

Figure 18 It is built into the core structure that the defensive core personnel always outnumber the offensive blockers at the point of attack.

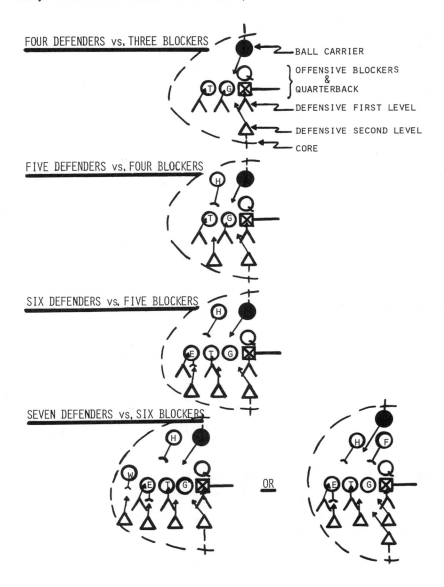

but any formational change is achieved through *relocating its mobile personnel*. This 2-level system mirrors the movements of these mobile personnel, in effect always augmenting the defense's structure in the core at the points where the offense has chosen to locate these personnel for additional blocking. On running plays, one of the mobile offensive personnel must carry the football; this player is therefore not available for blocking, and thus the number of defenders will always outnumber the offensive blockers in the core. It should be noted that there is one important exception to this tactical principle: when the quarterback becomes the ball carrier on option plays or sprintout passes. In these situations, however, the number of defenders will *equal* the available offensive blockers, as this system can *never* be caught at a numerical disadvantage in the core; this safeguard has been built in.

"Automatic" Multiple Alignments

Two additional mechanisms are build into the 2-level Defense which further strengthen its core structure: *multiple* core alignments and *stacks*. Eleven discrete alignments for the First Level are possible within this system (see chapter 3); these are either called in the huddle or checked-off at the line of scrimmage. On the other hand, as Second Level defenders move through the core mirroring the offensive backfielders and end(s), they stack behind these First Level personnel according to a simple system of rules (see chapter 3), and this never needs to be called. Combining First Level alignment and Second Level stacking the number of core structures that are possible exceeds fifty discrete combinations; in addition, the stacked positioning always assumed by the Second Level presents a constant tactical problem for the offense's blocking system.

Defensive Concealment

It has become more and more difficult for the defense to conceal its strategy prior to the snap. Offenses now stretch the defense horizontally across the field, employ multiple formations, and execute various early-motion patterns, all to read how the defense adjusts. The present 2-level concept requires that a majority of the defensive personnel always align in a uniform fashion prior to *every* play, whether in short− or long−yardage situations. Thus the offense always obtains an *identical read* from this defense prior to every play, in effect exhibiting a *meaningless* read, relative to the defensive strategy for that play. This principle is illustrated in figure 19 and can be applied in every defensive situation throughout this text. Note that the deep safety always aligns between the field's hashmarks, at the midpoint of the offensive formation, twenty-eight yards deep; the Second Level mirroring the five mobile personnel in the offense are always spread across the field, according to the positioning of these offensive personnel. The only subunit in this 2-level Defense whose alignments might allow the offense to read something of significance is the First Level, but these five defenders are constantly shifting and realigning along the line of scrimmage, both from play to play and while the quarterback is calling the offensive signals prior to each play (see chapter 3).

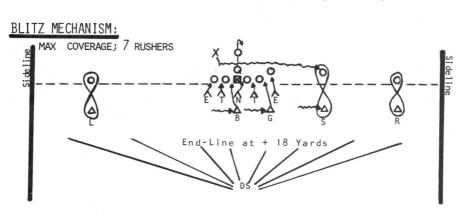

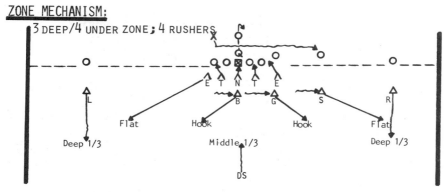

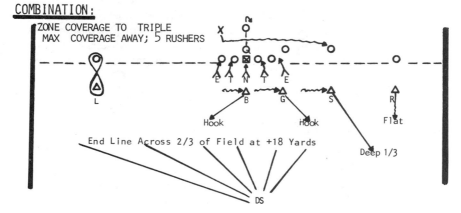

Figure 19 Example of absolute concealment: the offense has selected a pass play from a triple slotback formation, with the halfback in early motion; independent of the defensive mechanism (*i.e.*, blitz, zone, or combination), the defense's alignment at the snap is identical.

Simplicity

Today, football does not remain the simple game many traditionalists recollect. Over the last four decades the conceptual and mechanistic elements in the game have greatly escalated, and the days of playing football without learning even a minimal amount of its theoretical and technical bases are long past. Successful performance within an offensive or defensive system now requires years of coaching exposure and playing experience. In the three-level model of defense, all three levels have evolved into highly sophisticated subunits, and the linebacker and deepback units in particular now require a high degree of mental processing within the compressed time frame of one football play. With all of the alterations and nuances that have been incorporated into the three-level model, the chances of making an incorrect decision have increased as well. This has shattered the principle of simplicity. It would be naive to claim that the present system solves this major defensive dilemma, and any return to simple, basic defensive football would be both impossible and of benefit only to today's sophisticated offenses. Rather, the 2-level model incorporates within its system two additional principles which relegate the importance of the principle of simplicity.

1. Security. As this defense becomes fully operational, personnel gain great confidence in the security of having one defender aligned deep and always in position to make the play; defensive errors are reduced to fifteen-or twenty-yard mistakes, or occasionally to twenty-five-yard losses, but *never* result in the long touchdown score that demoralizes a defense. In turn, this increased safety factor results in more calculated aggressiveness and greater risk-taking on the part of the First and Second Levels.
2. Consistency. From the players' perspective, many of the advantages in the model can be translated directly to gain personal advantage. For example: mirroring ensures that the Second Level can *never* be misaligned; much of the system's dynamic mechanisms are cured *visually*, including zone coverages (see chapter 4); and assignments and techniques for personnel are very repetitive (i.e., attack a specific line-gap in the First Level, mirror a running back or receiver in the Second Level).

Goal Line-to-Goal Line Continuity

Maximizing learning, making economic use of practice time, perfecting performance... for football coaches these are bellwethers. As the complexity of football increases, however, coaches are being forced to economize with their practice time more and more, for significant time and resources are required to perfect the defenses utilized in a growing number of special tactical situations: for example in short yardage, in long yardage (3), in goal line (4), against specific offenses (i.e., triple-option (5), shotgun, etc.). If for no other reasons, coaches must examine the practicality of the present 2-level Defense: this system possesses much greater goal line-to-goal line continuity, thus only tactical changes—not major model alterations—need be implemented in order to optimize its effectiveness against *every* offensive situation or threat. How can one defensive system possess such a wide range of tactical applications? Simply stated, the 2-level model is based upon more universal principles than the 3-level model.

1. In any combative situation, there is greater strength in numbers; thus, the larger personnel subunits of the 2-level model exert greater pressure and leverage upon an offense.
2. In the 1980s, the doctrine of deliberate and premeditated attack has superseded the older 3-level theories of action-reaction.
3. Purposely delimiting both the *time factor* and *field area* in which an offense may operate incorporates more effective principles for pressuring and controlling that offense.
4. And finally, Second Level mirroring provides a simple yet universal mechanism for always matching the defense's strength against the offense's.

SELECTION CRITERIA FOR PERSONNEL

A disadvantage of implementing the 2-level model of defense is its requirement of personnel who possess *specific* physical characteristics. On the other hand, personnel selection has always been of prime concern to coaches in implementing *any* system of defense or offense, so perhaps the personnel problems inherent in this system will prove no greater than those previously faced. On the positive side of this issue, the superiority of the 2-level system can compensate for inferior athletes[2] in much the same way as zone defense in the 1950s initially assisted the man-to-man pass defender in that era. Certainly the problem of securing appropriate personnel is surmountable. There are, however, important physical characteristics which specific personnel must possess, particularly at the end positions in the First Level and the interior of the Second Level (Strong, Gael, and Bandit positions). In this section some of these specific concerns are addressed.

First Level Personnel

While there is usually a minimum body weight for defensive linemen, which varies of course with the league and caliber of competition, the need for players with a larger body mass should *never* supersede the need for quickness and agility in the First Level. In other words, quicker but lighter (compared to heavier and slower) personnel should always be inserted into the First Level; several factors within the system dictate this important agility-versus-size trade-off. This defense is based foremost upon a fluid, movement-oriented concept. If, however, one of its integral subunits is composed of more ponderous personnel, this *first principle* of defense is reduced by a corresponding amount: the greater the mobility and quickness of the First Level defenders, the more effective becomes their swarming. In addition, these personnel must be constantly moving and shifting their alignments prior to the snap (as the quarterback completes his pre-play checkoff), then slanting or twisting in one of three directions at the snap. The era of the larger, less mobile lineman, defending a small area of real estate (for example, the Okie tackle), has long past. There is, however, one important exception to this criterion: the ends *must* possess size in both body mass and height, as well as speed and quickness. Physically, the ends must be very superior athletes, and for this reason they are more difficult personnel to develop. The implications of the recent offensive trends are quite clear, however.

1. Pass Rush: The new offensive blocking techniques and smaller line-gaps have stymied any consistent *internal* pass rush by the defense; thus, the ends crashing unimpeded from the extremities of the core now must provide the defense's primary pass rush. With this greater distance to sprint (in order to reach the quarterback), speed must be an important prerequisite and superior agility a distinct advantage for the ends. In addition to the offensive blocking trends, "quick" passing has dictated that new stunts be devised in order to maximize defensive pressure in *all* passing situations; thus, superior height (relative to the quarterback's stature) is another physical characteristic which the ends must possess in order to reduce the quarterback's field of vision in these evolving concepts of pass rush (see discussion, final section of chapter 4).

2. Run Defense: The other component of an end's unit responsibility is the defensing of the run. For this critical role, both end's require substantial body mass, greater than required for either the nose or tackle positions in the First Level. On any play, the offense can run at an end, yet, by chance, his adjacent defensive tackle and nose may be slanting *away* from that end. Thus, he would find himself quite isolated in that situation, with his only immediate assistance coming from Second Level personnel; without superior size (relative to the offensive blockers), the defense is placed in serious jeopardy.

Second Level Personnel

Employing the 2-level Defense at any level of football, *speed* is the primary physical prerequisite for all personnel in the Second Level, because every competitive league or conference has at least one very superior pass receiver, and most boast several receivers of outstanding ability. In addition, the offense has become particularly adept at isolating various pass defenders, and the mirroring mechanism renders this defense particularly vulnerable to such manipulation. Defensive speed is the *only* assurance against a precarious mismatch—receiver dominating defender—occurring play after play.

On the outsides of the Second Level, at the Lou and Rose positions, there is no substitute for speed, and only a *slight* reduction in sprinting speed can be afforded in favor of a very superior athlete, possessing great agility and quickness. The other physical characteristics (height, body mass, etc.) of the Lou and Rose personnel are not critically important, but one *personality* trait should predominate in these players: a highly competitive spirit—even to the point of braggadocio. In Freudian terms, these personality types must willingly put their egos on the line in front of thousands of spectators, and never embarrass themselves.

In the Second Level, physical stature is a primary consideration for personnel only at the three internal positions. Body mass is crucial, and height will prove advantageous as well. These players are continually moving into the core, where they encounter the largest offensive linemen, yet outside the core they must defend against speedy receivers. As with the defensive ends in the First Level, availability of players with these specific physical qualifications is limited. Ideally, a large linebacker possessing the speed and instincts of a deepback is required at the Strong, Gael, and Bandit positions. When selecting potential players for these positions, never sacrifice speed for larger size. Speed is too important a prerequisite in the Second Level, and the greater number of players in this subunit compensates for having physically lighter personnel. Alternately, individual players may be substituted according to the tactical situation on the field: for example, in running situations larger linebacker types may be inserted, particularly at the Gael and Bandit positions; in longer yardage, faster, deepback types may be substituted, and so on.

The Deep Safety

Even though much of the present 2-level system is dependent upon his performance, the deep safety can be, paradoxically, its most average athlete; and this should provide coaches with an even greater appreciation of the tactical capabilities of this position. Above-average speed is required; sprinter's speed being a distinct luxury. Height is not a critical requisite, but a certain "ranginess"—like that of a basketball forward—can be an advantage. In addition, intelligence, timing, and football sense are all distinct assets in this position. But there is one critical prerequisite for the deep safety, and every football team has at least one deepback of above-average ability who possesses it: he must relish the physical contact of tackling. Safety personnel are best selected during drills and live-contact situations in practice; they will be noticeable but unspectacular deepbacks who always go out of their way for *solid contact* . . . then get back onto their feet smiling.

SIGNAL SYSTEM

Not by coincidence, the term used by both learning theorists and computer analysts to define a basic information unit is a *byte*. And while the brain is capable of storing almost infinite bytes, the rapidity of the human computer in processing information has very finite limitations (6). Superimpose the emotional climate of a football game, as confusion reigns inside a crowded stadium, onto the few seconds available prior to each down for the communication of information—from the sideline to field, and amongst defenders in their huddle—and every information byte in the defensive signals must be succinct, yet must maximize cognition. Compounding this problem is the fact that in defensive football *no more than three* information bytes should be communicated by one set of signals; the reasons for this are twofold:

1.   The defensive huddle call often has limited relevance to the offensive situation on the field by the time the football is actually put into play.
2.   On defense, when signals are missed, or mental errors made due to information overload, dire consequences (i.e., the six-point error) can result.

By comparison, an offensive signal system can impart many bytes and more regimented information, since the offense initiates and dictates the action. If their communications break down, the consequences are usually minor—a small loss of yardage, an incomplete pass, a down squandered. The authors have encountered defensive signal systems which defy the laws of information processing, given the impending circumstances that the defense faces *on every play*.

On defense, there are two practical modes for communicating signals: verbal and visual. *Verbal signals* should be confined exclusively to the defensive huddle call, although this is almost impossible to achieve due to the dynamic character of the game today. Certainly a defensive signal system should not rely upon any *new* information being communicated verbally after the huddle, as the quarterback's checkoff at the line of scrimmage complements the offensive huddle call. Rather, any verbal signals at the line of scrimmage should only *verify* the initial information imparted in the defensive huddle, and even this should be minimal because of the spread of the defensive personnel across the field, the noise of the crowd, and the total concentration that each defender must devote to his immediate duties as the play unfolds. After their huddle breaks, the only certain means of disseminating additional information to defensive personnel is through visual cues, *and these are provided exclusively by the offense* (rather than by one defender waving frantically to a teammate). Several examples of this means of communication within the present system have already been explained:

*   mirroring is a totally visual set of signals with 100% reliability.
*   the deep safety's intersection of the football at the end line is also totally visual, determined by specific offensive cues and keys.
*   in chapter 4 it is explained how the precise coverage for each pass defender may not be determined until immediately prior to the snap, how Second Level stunts are visually cued, and so on.

In fact, following the huddle call, the only mechanisms that are not visual signals are used to verify the First Level's alignment at the line of scrimmage. A schematic of this signal system is diagrammed in figure 20, and the total number of signals required to operate the defense are enumerated in table 3. The information communicated from

I. ESTABLISHMENT OF DEFENSIVE MECHANISMS

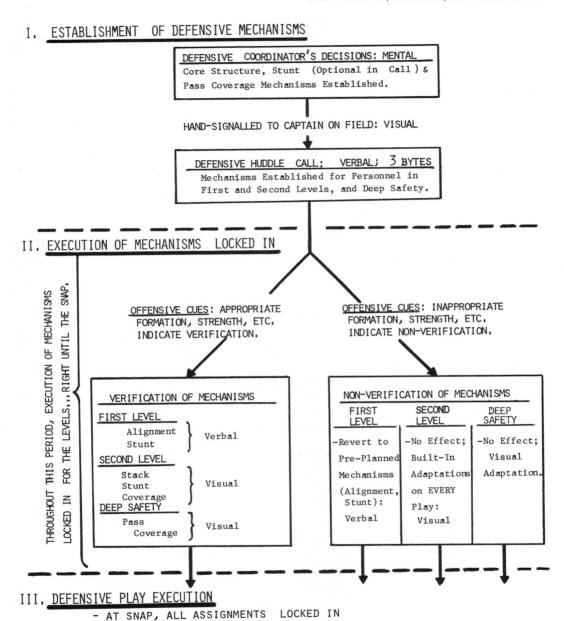

Figure 20 Schematic of the defensive signal system: flowchart of information bytes from coaching decisions to execution of play.

Table 3 Signal system for 2-level defense: summary.

CORE STRUCTURE		STUNT MECHANISM		PASS COVERAGE[***]	
FIRST LEVEL ALIGNMENTS	SECOND LEVEL[*] STACKS	BY THE FIRST LEVEL	BY THE SECOND LEVEL[**]	BASIC COVERAGES	VARIATIONS
1 ⎫ SHIFT 2 -TOWARD STRENGTH 3 -AWAY FROM 4 STRENGTH 5 ⎭	1 - STACK 2 - STACK AREA C STACK	SLANT (NOSE & TACKLE) TWIST (NOSE & TACKLE; TACKLE & END)	DOG CUSHION SWITCH	MAX COVER	⎰ MAX/TIGHT- CUSHION ⎱ MAX/DOUBLE ⎰ COVER-A ⎱ COVER-B COVER-C ⎭ ⟩TWO-DEEP
	* Stacks are not called in the defensive huddle.		** Max (Basic) must be the cover-age with Second Level stunts.	*** Max is the term used to call man-to-man pass coverage; Cover includes zone and combination pass coverages; Two-Deep means two safeties in the defense (via substitution).	

the defensive coordinator on the sideline to the huddle is minimal. The visual information processed after the huddle call (i.e., as the play proceeds, but before the snap) verifies or modifies the defensive mechanisms called, and this means of signals communication complements the urgent need for defensive mobility. Each information byte in the huddle call is succinct and meaningful (the terminology has a descriptive quality), and up to three bytes initiate the specific defensive mechanisms for the upcoming play: its core structure, stunt, and pass coverage. Compared to many defensive systems at the present time (see references 7-9), the total number of signals listed in table 3 are relatively few.

Core Structure: First Byte in the Huddle Call

The defensive structure in the core results from the interaction of two factors: the First Level's *alignment* and the Second's *stacks*. (Note, these two terms, *alignment* and *stack*, are used throughout the text to differentiate between the Levels.) Alignments are designated by a number and a directional call (table 3, left-hand column). Stacks, however, are so simple to form that they are never called: at the line of scrimmage stacks are formed almost incidentally as a result of the internal mechanics of the system, principally mirroring.

Stunt Mechanisms: Middle Byte in the Huddle Call

Only five stunts are incorporated into the system, with each being designated by a specific *descriptive* term. Two stunting mechanisms—*slant* and *twist*—are performed by

First Level personnel (only); the three remaining stunts—the *dog*, the *cushion*, and the switch—involve the Second Level (table 3, middle portion). The execution of all stunts are defined and controlled by rules. If one of these stunts is not called, the (verbal) huddle call has only two information bytes; on the other hand, if a Second Level stunt is called, max pass coverage is employed *automatically*, and therefore the third byte in the huddle call need not be made.

Pass Coverage: Final Byte in the Huddle Call

In the interest of simplicity, only two *basic* pass coverages are defined in this system: *max* and *cover* (table 3, right-hand columns). *Max* is the term employed to call man-to-man coverage, while *cover* primarily employs zone principles. But, all coverages involve elements of both man-to-man *and* zone principles with the specific combinations being *visually cued* according to the (final) positioning of the mobile offensive personnel on any given play.

Notes

1. While a free safety prealigned at twelve to eighteen yards' depth can provide support against shorter passes over the middle, the defense's vulnerability to deep passes (and long runs) greatly increases; on the other hand, without the immediate threat created by the end line at eighteen-plus yards' depth it becomes increasingly difficult for the Second Level to effectively eliminate medium-depth passes.

2. That is, "inferior" compared to the general caliber of offensive personnel in a league off conference.

References

1. NORM VANBROCKLIN, *Passing, Punting, Quarterbacking* (New York: Ronald Press Co., 1961), pp. 27-35.

2. JED HUGHES, "U.C.L.A.'s 'Woody defense'," *Athletic Journal*, 50(2):21-23, 100, 1980.

3. CHARLIE GOEHL, "The nickel defense," *Athletic Coach*, 64(6):16-25, 1984.

4. S. E. SULLINS, *Complete Book of Multiple Defenses in Football* (West Nyack, N.Y.: Parker Publ. Co., Inc., 1978), pp. 143-147.

5. PETE DYER, *Coaching The Wishbone-T Triple Option Attack* (West Nyack, N.Y. : Parker Publ. Co., Inc., 1973), pp. 108-122.

6. MARGARET D. ROBB, *The Dynamics Of Motor-Skill Acquisition* (Englewood Cliffs, N.J.: Prentice-Hall, Inc., 1972), pp. 38-59.

7. GENE ELLENSON, *Coaching Linebackers and the Perimeter Defense* (West Nyack, N.Y.: Parker Publ. Co., Inc., 1972), pp. 232-251.

8. SULLINS, *Complete Book of Multiple Defenses in Football*, chapters 2-9.

9. BOB TROPPMANN, *Football's New Master Defense Guide* (West Nyack, N.Y.: Parker Publ. Co., Inc., 1983), pp. 159-196.

Chapter 3
RUN DEFENSE

The era of the *static* structure in defensive football is almost terminated, and even at this point in time few defenses remain in a stationary three-level alignment. By the late seventies offensive systems had become very proficient in dissecting these static structures, even against superior defensive personnel. But the quandary confronting the defense has been the development of viable alternatives. Through the eighties, coaches have basically adopted a dual approach in attempting to solve this dilemma. First, multiple defensive systems have been devised, employing variations of the 43 and 34 structures, with the multiple combination that a coach selects before each play being highly situation-oriented, according to the down and distance and an offense's tendencies. Second, a progressively greater substitution of specific defensive personnel has taken place, either to complement a particular multiple combination or to physically match the offensive personnel on the field. The 2-level defensive model offers a third alternative. In this chapter are detailed, first, the primary mechanisms of run defense inside the core—the eleven alignments that the First Level may assume, and the stacking by the Second Level. Following this, the five core stunts in the system are explained, as well as several novel *secondary* mechanisms that are critical to maintaining the integrity of the core against the run.

PRIMARY MECHANISM OF RUN DEFENSE: FIRST LEVEL ALIGNMENT

Recently, a debate (1) has arisen concerning the techniques of defensive line-play (fig. 21, top portion): should the pre-snap alignment of a defensive lineman opposite an offensive guard, tackle or tight end, be *head-on* (face-to-face across the line of

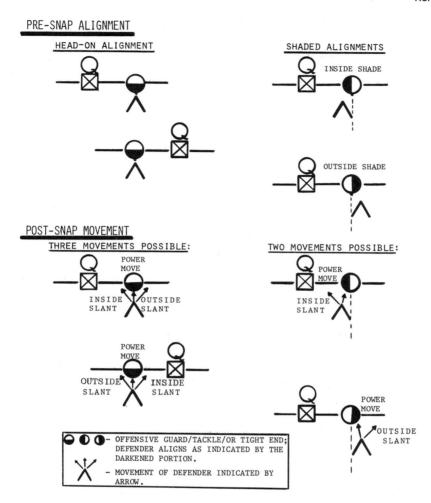

Figure 21 Alignment of personnel in the First Level, head on or shaded, and their movement against the offensive lineman opposing them: power move to control blocker, or slant to penetrate an offensive line-gap.

scrimmage) or *shaded* (positioned on either the offensive lineman's inside or outside shoulder)? To ensure structural stability, most three-level models of defense have required a shaded alignment; this gave the defender an advantage in controlling his assigned offensive line-gap by physically aligning to that side against the offensive blocker. However the core structure of defense is changing radically, defensive line-play has become movement-oriented, and a shaded alignment is more static in nature because the defender can perform only two basic movements from this alignment. By comparison, from a head-on alignment three directional movement patterns are possible (fig. 21, lower portion). Also, the new offensive blocking techniques, permitting the use of hands, have further limited the viability of shaded alignments: when the defender attempts to work to the other side of the blocker, to assist on a tackle or pursue the play, the blocker (although somewhat illegally) grabs and locks onto the defender. In the First Level, therefore, the nose and tackles assume head-on alignments, and this accomplishes three defensive objectives.

1. Greater movement potential: on whichever offensive lineman they align, these defenders have 3 possible movement directions.
2. Greater blocking problems: when these defenders have the option to move in three directions, this creates increased uncertainty for the offensive lineman blocking them.
3. Simplicity: when required to shift their alignment quickly prior to the snap, realigning head-on eliminates one additional cognitive factor (i.e., in shaded alignments the defender must always be concerned that he has aligned with the correct shade).

On the other hand, the ends in the First Level always "crash" to the inside, into the heart of the offensive core from their perimeter alignments on the line of scrimmage; for this reason, these personnel always assume a shaded, *outside* alignment against opposing offensive linemen.

The Positional Alignments for First Level Personnel

In figure 22 the positional alignments and primary offensive gap responsibilities for personnel in the First Level are diagrammed. All positional alignments are designated by name to facilitate communication, but these names are not included in the system's verbal signals.

1. Positional Alignment for the Nose: Odd or Even In an *Odd* alignment, the nose aligns head-on with the offensive center in a three point stance and is primarily responsible for both center-guard gaps. If, however, he is slanting or twisting (see First Level stunts in the following section), the nose then will assume primary responsibility for the gap through which he is moving (only one of the center-guard gaps). When the nose aligns head-on with one of the offensive guards in an *even* alignment, his primary responsibility is *only* the center-guard gap to that side; again, a slant or twist stunt can alter this primary gap responsibility.

2. Positional Alignment for the Tackle: Open or Closed In *open* alignment, the defensive tackle aligns head-on with the offensive tackle in a three-point stance and is primarily responsible for the guard-tackle gap to his side of center. In *closed alignment*, he aligns head-on with the offensive guard; if the nose is positioned in odd, the tackle is still primarily responsible for this guard-tackle gap. On the other hand, in closed alignment, when the nose is aligned in even (that is, head-on with the *other* offensive guard), the defensive tackle becomes primarily responsible for both the center-guard and guard-

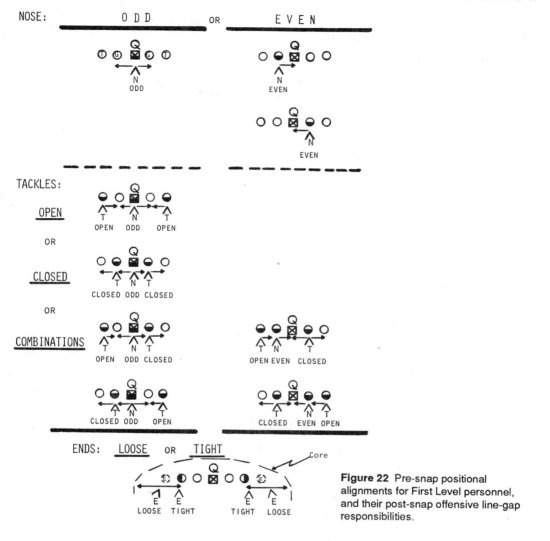

Figure 22 Pre-snap positional alignments for First Level personnel, and their post-snap offensive line-gap responsibilities.

tackle gaps to his side of the offensive center (fig. 22, middle portion on the right). Again, for either of the defensive tackles, a slant or twist stunt can change these offensive line-gap responsibilities.

3. Positional Alignment for the End: Loose or Tight In *loose* alignment, the defensive end aligns three to five yards outside of the offensive tackle, at the perimeter of the defensive core on the line of scrimmage; this alignment greatly improves his crash angle. If a tight end or slotback is positioned across from him, the end aligns shaded-outside on this offensive player to maintain his outside leverage to turn a sweep or quick pitch inside. In *tight* alignment, the defensive end aligns shaded-outside on the offensive tackle; it is, however, more difficult for an end to crash from this alignment. In both loose and tight alignments, the end's primary responsibility is the off-tackle area, stretching from the offensive tackle out to the core's perimeter (fig. 22, lower portion). On a twist stunt with his adjacent defensive tackle, the end's assigned gap is interchanged with the tackle's. In *either* positional alignment the defensive end can assume a two-point (standing) or three-point stance; as a general rule, however, when a defensive end aligns tight and an offensive tight end or slotback is positioned immediately outside of him, the defensive end should utilize his three-point technique (see chapter 6).

The Eleven First Level Alignments: Personnel Rules

Combining these positional alignments for the nose, both defensive tackles, and their adjacent ends, only eleven discrete combinations have been incorporated into the system (fig. 23). In figure 23, note that each alignment is identified by specific nomenclature: always a numerical digit using the numbers one through five, with the directional indicator *link* (L indicating left) or *rip* (R indicating right), included after the four single-digit alignments 2, 3, 4, and 5. These are the system's verbal signals[1] (table 3). These signals are organized sequentially so that *universal* alignment rules can be defined for each First Level position; that is, *simple rules have been established for each position* which determine the correct positioning for that player according to the alignment called. The critical advantage of this method for calling First Level alignments is that individual personnel need *never* be concerned with the Level's composite alignment on the line of scrimmage; rather, each player need only apply his rule in order to quickly determine his correct positioning within any alignment (table 4).

1. Universal Rules for the Nose The positional alignment for the nose is either odd or even, therefore, when the nose hears an *odd-numbered* alignment called he knows to align odd, head-on against the offensive center. Since his positional alignment is predetermined, the nose simply ignores any directional indicator that is included with odd-numbered calls. (Additionally, to increase the pre-snap movement and shifting by the First Level, with *any* odd-numbered alignment call the nose initially may align even, then quickly shift into his odd alignment just prior to the snap). Conversely, if the nose hears any *even-numbered* alignment called, he knows to align even, head-on against one of the offensive guards, and in this instance the directional indicator *always* specifies which guard, the one to his left if the directional call is "link" or to his right if "rip" is called (see diagrams in table 4). (And again, to enhance the general pre-snap movement by the First Level, with even-numbered calls the nose initially may align odd then quickly shift into his correct even alignment.) Whatever shifting patterns are programmed for the nose by the game plan, the critical factor to appreciate is that the nose is *never* concerned with the First Level's actual alignment on the line of scrimmage. Rather, in the defensive huddle *he need only listen whether an odd- or even-numbered alignment is called, then apply his rule.*

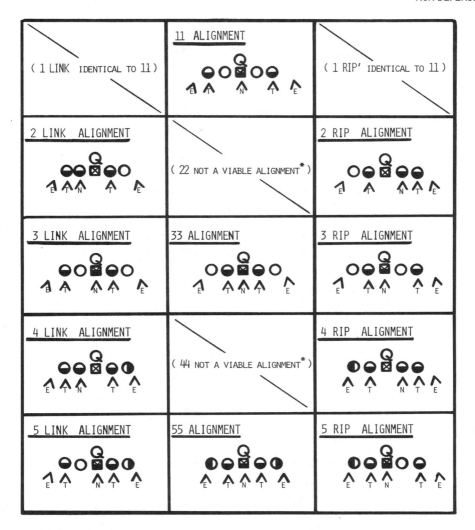

Figure 23 The eleven discrete alignments for the First Level: the *double-digit* alignments (11, 33, or 55) are identical to both sides of the offense; corresponding link/and rip alignments (2, 3, 4, 5) are mirror images of each other. (*Nose and one tackle would align on same offensive guard).

    2. Universal Rules for the Tackles The two alignment rules for the defensive tackles are equally as simple and as universal: in the huddle the tackles only listen for whether a double-digit or a single-digit alignment is called. The positional alignment for these personnel is either open or closed, and when a *double-digit* alignment is called, their positioning is *predetermined*: in the 11-alignment both tackles align open,

TABLE 4, FIRST-LEVEL ALIGNMENTS: 'UNIVERSAL' RULES FOR PERSONNEL

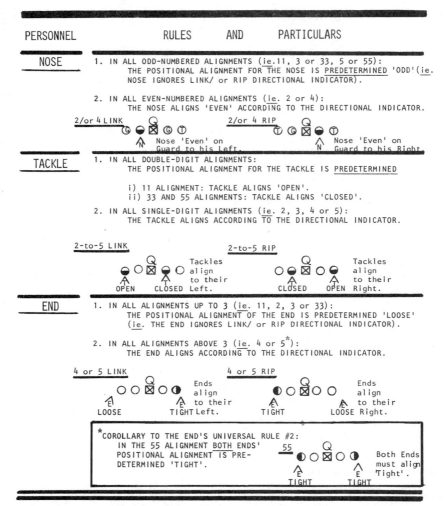

PERSONNEL	RULES AND PARTICULARS
NOSE	1. IN ALL ODD-NUMBERED ALIGNMENTS (ie.11, 3 or 33, 5 or 55): THE POSITIONAL ALIGNMENT FOR THE NOSE IS PREDETERMINED 'ODD'(ie. NOSE IGNORES LINK/ or RIP DIRECTIONAL INDICATOR). 2. IN ALL EVEN-NUMBERED ALIGNMENTS (ie. 2 or 4): THE NOSE ALIGNS 'EVEN' ACCORDING TO THE DIRECTIONAL INDICATOR.

2/or 4 LINK — Nose 'Even' on Guard to his Left.

2/or 4 RIP — Nose 'Even' on Guard to his Right.

| TACKLE | 1. IN ALL DOUBLE-DIGIT ALIGNMENTS: THE POSITIONAL ALIGNMENT FOR THE TACKLE IS PREDETERMINED i) 11 ALIGNMENT: TACKLE ALIGNS 'OPEN'. ii) 33 AND 55 ALIGNMENTS: TACKLE ALIGNS 'CLOSED'. 2. IN ALL SINGLE-DIGIT ALIGNMENTS (ie. 2, 3, 4 or 5): THE TACKLE ALIGNS ACCORDING TO THE DIRECTIONAL INDICATOR. |

2-to-5 LINK — OPEN CLOSED — Tackles align to their Left.

2-to-5 RIP — CLOSED OPEN — Tackles align to their Right.

| END | 1. IN ALL ALIGNMENTS UP TO 3 (ie. 11, 2, 3 or 33): THE POSITIONAL ALIGNMENT OF THE END IS PREDETERMINED 'LOOSE' (ie. THE END IGNORES LINK/ or RIP DIRECTIONAL INDICATOR). 2. IN ALL ALIGNMENTS ABOVE 3 (ie. 4 or 5[*]): THE END ALIGNS ACCORDING TO THE DIRECTIONAL INDICATOR. |

4 or 5 LINK — LOOSE TIGHT — Ends align to their Left.

4 or 5 RIP — TIGHT LOOSE — Ends align to their Right.

> [*]COROLLARY TO THE END'S UNIVERSAL RULE #2:
> IN THE 55 ALIGNMENT BOTH ENDS'
> POSITIONAL ALIGNMENT IS PRE-
> DETERMINED 'TIGHT'.
> 55 — TIGHT TIGHT — Both Ends must align 'Tight'.

and in 33- and 55-alignments both must align closed. On the other hand, when the tackles hear a *single-digit* alignment called, it is the directional indicator (not the alignment number per se) which specifies their positional alignments (table 4). If link is called (after *any* single-digit alignment), each tackle assumes the positional alignment to his left; therefore, the left defensive tackle aligns open while the right tackle must align closed. Exactly opposite, when rip is called both tackles assume their right-hand positional alignments, with the left tackle aligning closed and the right tackle open. In *all* instances, it should, again, be appreciated that the tackles need not be concerned with the First Level's final alignment on the line of scrimmage; rather, in the defensive huddle *they need only listen whether a double- or single-digit alignment is called*, then apply their appropriate rule.

During a game, the universality of these two rules also permits the defensive tackles to initiate a great deal of pre-snap movement in the First Level, particularly in concert with the shifting of the nose and the ends. And their pre-snap shifting may be accomplished quickly and precisely by several means, for example:

1. When the alignment called is a single-digit number, if *both* tackles initially align open or closed, just prior to the snap *one must shift*.
2. When the single-digit alignment called includes the directional indicator link, if *both* tackles initially align rip just prior to the snap *both must shift*, and vice versa.
3. When the alignment called is a double-digit number (and thus, the final positional alignments for both tackles are predetermined), if one defensive tackle independently or both tackles in unison initially align at their alternate position, shifting just prior to the snap will again be necessary.

And so on; the entire shifting of the First Level *before the snap* can be precisely orchestrated by the defensive coordinator and form an important (or minor) aspect of the defensive game plan to combat a specific opponent's blocking scheme (see part IV).

3. Universal Rules for the Ends The two alignment rules for the defensive ends have been made extremely simple because their role in the defense is so vitally important. In the huddle they only listen for whether the alignment call includes any digit(s) *up to* 3-link, 3-rip, or 33, or for whether the call is *greater* (than 3). The positional alignment for the defensive ends is either loose or tight, and *in all alignments numbered up to (and including) 3/33, both* ends always align loose; seldom, however, should these players attempt to move from tight into loose just prior to the snap (only the nose and tackles are able to shift in this manner without jeopardizing the structure of the defensive core). The only positional shift that either end can execute with impunity just prior to the snap is the shift to tight, and this will occur only *when the alignment call is numbered above 3*. Again, the directional indicator (and *not* the digits 4 or 5) specifies each end's final alignment (see diagrams in table 4): if "link" is called, each end assumes the positional alignment to his left, thus the left defensive end aligns loose while the right end must align tight; when "rip" is called, both ends assume their right-hand positional alignments, with the left end aligning tight and the right end loose. An important corollary to the latter rule involves the 55-alignment (which does *not* require any directional indicator because it is a double-digit number). When 55 is called in the defensive huddle both ends must assume their tight alignment, shifting just prior to the snap. Finally, again it should be appreciated how simple and universal these two rules are for the defensive ends. These personnel never need to be concerned with the First Level's actual alignment, yet either alignment rule can be executed swiftly and with absolute surety.

The First-Level Alignment Call

In the defensive huddle the initial information byte of the call always designates the alignment of the First Level for the upcoming play (see table 3), and during most games almost one-half of the alignment calls can be verbalized *in their entirety* in the defensive huddle.

1. The double-digit alignments (*i.e.*, 11, 33, 55) do *not* require a directional indicator and the positioning of all First Level personnel is *predetermined* by these calls (fig 23).
2. For single-digit alignments (*i.e.*, 2 through 5) when the location of the football, in relation to the shortside or wideside of the field, will *predetermine* the directional indicator, "link" or "rip" will be included in the huddle call.

In both these tactical situations, therefore, when the defense breaks its huddle each First Level player will know his complete play assignment: his positional alignment at the snap determined according to rule, with his pre-snap movement (if any) precisely orchestrated according to the defensive game plan. On the other hand, as many as 50 percent of the First Level alignments, and often more, cannot be completed in the defensive huddle because the correct directional indicator is unknown at that point in time (that is only the single-digit number can be verbalized).

3. Following single-digit alignment numbers, when *the formational and personnel strengths of the offense will dictate the directional indicator,* "link" or "rip" cannot be specified in the huddle call.

In other words, given this tactical situation, it is impossible to finalize the directional indication *while still in the defensive huddle.* For example, in all 2- and 4-alignments the nose will align even, but on which offensive guard—link or rip—in order to solidify the defensive core during the upcoming play? In all single-digit alignments one defensive tackle must align closed, the other open, but which combination will guarantee the structural integrity of the core? In 4- and 5-alignments, which end must shift into tight just prior to the snap and which one will remain loose? The "link" or "rip" indicator, therefore, must be verbalized (and very loudly in a noisy stadium) *at the line of scrimmage,* according to the strength and personnel alignment of the offense. This unique method of completing the single-digit alignment calls provides another integrated mechanism for quickly shifting the entire First Level *in unison* just prior to the snap with this system.

Therefore, when the directional indicator will be modulated according to the offensive formation, in the defensive huddle an alternative directive must be included that will instruct which call, "link" or "rip", must be made at the line of scrimmage. Very simply, this alignment directive is either *Toward* or *Away.*

1. *Toward* directs that at the line of scrimmage "link" or "rip" must be called *in the direction* of a specific offensive cue.

2. *Away* indicates the opposite direction, that is, away from the cue.2

In the huddle one of these directives, "Toward" or "Away", is addressed *only to the ends,* and to no other defensive personnel. In their two-point stance on the line of scrimmage, before the play both ends have a clear view of the offense for several seconds (before shifting into their three-point stance if required by the alignment called); therefore, at the line of scrimmage it is the ends who locate the defined offensive cue, then *yell* the appropriate "link" or "rip" call, shifting the First Level into its final alignment. Examples of this call sequence are presented in figures 24 and 25, where the tight end (E) has been designated as the offensive cue defining "form-

Figure 24 Examples of the First Level alignment sequence when "away" is included after a single-digit alignment number in the huddle call (note the offensive formations are identical in fig. 24 and 25): the link or rip call made away from the offensive tight end's side; then final alignment of the first level according to rule on the line of scrimmage.

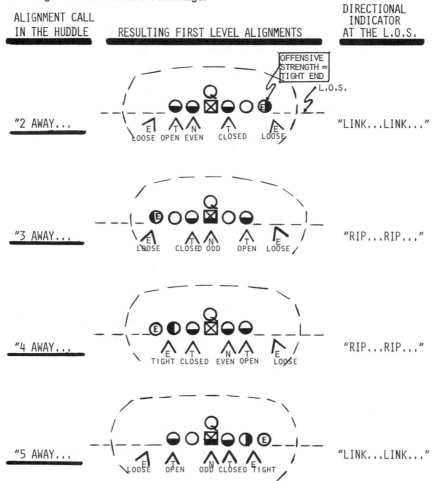

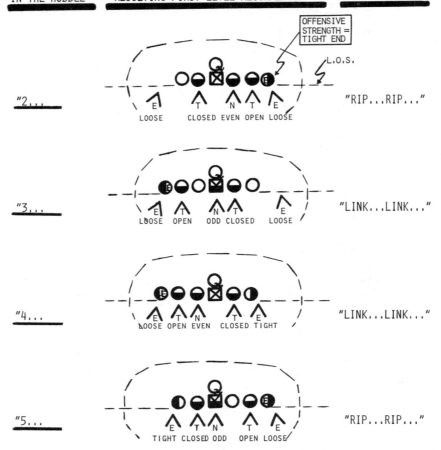

Figure 25 Examples of the First Level alignment sequence: the alignment number call in the defensive huddle; link or rip call towards the offensive cue (to the tight end's side); final alignment of the First Level according to rule on the line of scrimmage.

ational strength." Therefore, if the First Level is to assume its final alignment on the line of scrimmage *away from* the tight end, in the huddle call "Away" is verbalized following the single-digit alignment number; then the appropriate link or rip call can be made at the line of scrimmage according to this directive (fig. 24, examples "2 away . . . " through "5 away . . . "). In actual game situations, however, the preponderance of final alignments are executed *toward* the defined offensive cue, that is, toward the offensive strengthside, or toward a specific offensive personnel. In the huddle call, therefore, the directive Toward is *never actually verbalized* in order to economize on the number of information bytes which must be communicated; rather, if "Away" is *not* specifically verbalized, *"toward" is always understood* (fig. 25, examples "2 . . . " through "5 . . .").

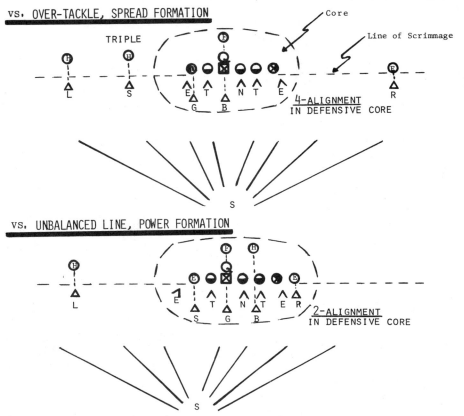

Figure 26 Adjustments of First Level vs. over-tackle (⊗) formations: 2- or 4-Alignments. (note: the Second Level mirroring also brings additional defenders into the core vs. the over-tackle run threat.)

In summary, it must be understood that only two additional information bytes can exert any influence over the First Level's signals called in the huddle: either "link" or "rip". Also appreciate the tactical importance of this call. The defensive ends merely locate the defined cue at the line of scrimmage (such as an offensive tight end, and even this can be changed at any point during a football game), then call the First Level alignment *away from* or *towards* this cue. In addition, each First Level player has only two alignment positions, and in every alignment call his choice is determined unequivocally *by rule*. Appreciate that the only complexity in the First Level's alignment is shouldered completely by the defensive coordinator in his mental manipulations of the system, and not by individual players on the field. Yet, in combination with the Second Level the multiplicity of discrete core structures built in to the system exceeds fifty: many are fabricated incidentally as a function of the system's internal operations, all are structurally viable, and personnel can never be outnumbered at the offense's point of attack. Additionally, First Level alignments are adaptable to *all* offensive formations, whether in shortyardage, on the goal line, or even against surprise formations such as an unbalanced (offensive) line (2) or the tackle-over formation that is becoming increasingly popular (fig. 26).

PRIMARY MECHANISM OF RUN DEFENSE: SECOND LEVEL STACKS

When referring to the positioning of the Second Level within the core structure, the term *stack* is used to differentiate this mechanism from First Level *alignments*. Second Level stacks need *not* be called in the defensive huddle, since the mechanism is so simple for personnel to execute. Also, the number of Second Level defenders who will form stacks is never certain, being dictated by the offensive formation. Basically, stacks position the Second Level within the structure of the core where they are most likely to find a First Level teammate to stack behind, but the Second Level is *never* responsible for an offensive line-gap. Inside the core, as well, these defenders need not stack directly across from the backfielder they are mirroring, and may align *up to five yards deep* off the line of scrimmage.

1- and 2-Stacks

When there is only one Second Level defender in the core (and, thus, only one offensive running back), the 1-stack is preferred, with the Second Level personnel positioned over the offensive center (fig. 27). Thus, in 11-, 3-, and 5-alignments this defender would be stacked behind the nose; in the 2- and 4-alignments, however, there would not be a First Level player directly in front of him. When two running backs are present in the offense, *two* 2-stacks are the most advantageous, positioning the mirroring defenders over both offensive tackles, each stacked behind a First Level tackle (aligned open) or an end (aligned tight). Very seldom in a 2-stack are these Second Level personnel exposed to any immediate blocking threat from the offense, yet to each side of the defense both defenders are established in commanding tactical positions. Each threatens an attack in three directions: firing through the guard-tackle gap into the heart of the offensive core and providing immediate support for the First Level against running plays into the center of the defense; firing through the off-tackle area against outside running plays; and given their speed, the pass threat against these Second-Level defenders (usually) is considered *minimal*, particularly the defender mirroring the offensive fullback.

Tight End/Slotback Stacks

In the defensive core, up to two additional Second Level defenders also may be present, mirroring the tight end to one side and a slotback (or a second tight end) to the other, whatever formation the offense has chosen on a given play (fig. 28). The stacked defender mirroring a tight end or slotback must be concerned primarily with the pass threat, but also can provide *run support* when this offensive player blocks. With an adjacent Second Level player aligned over the offensive tackle in a 2-stack, however, if this defender remains directly over his mirrored tight end or slotback, he may obstruct his teammate (in the 2-stack) on outside running plays to their side or when the

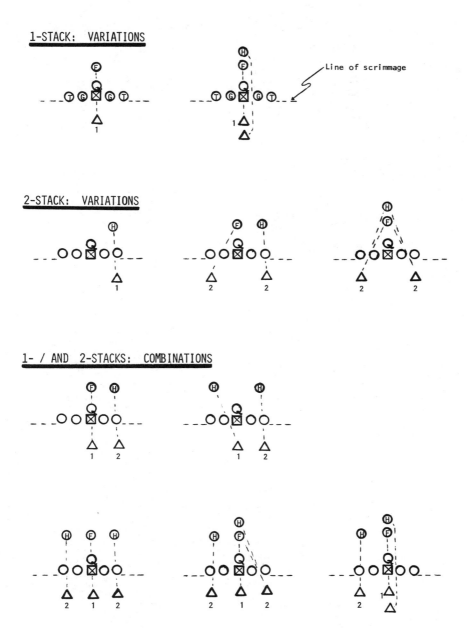

Figure 27 1- and 2-Stacks for the Second Level (△): when mirroring an offensive backfielder in the core personnel position over the offensive center, termed 1-Stack, or over an offensive tackle, termed 2-Stack.

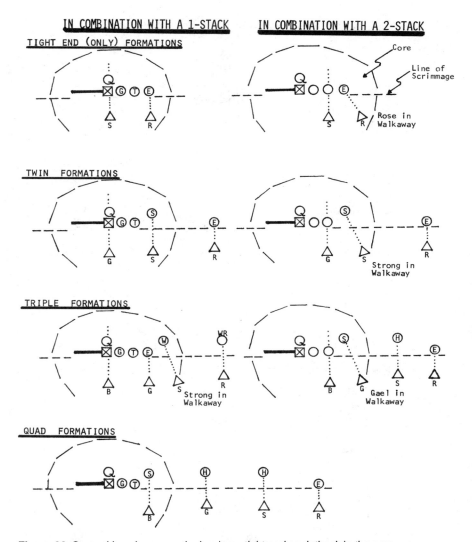

Figure 28 Second Level personnel mirroring a tight end or slotback in the core, in combination with 1- and 2- Stack variations.

offensive halfback moves outside on a pass route (fig. 29, upper diagrams). To alleviate this predicament, three adjustments are possible.

1. The defender can simply align wider than his mirrored tight end or slotback in *Walkaway* (fig. 28).

2. The switch stunt can be executed by the two Second Level personnel (see next section); this stunt sends *both* the First Level end and this Second Level defender crashing from the outside of the core.

DEFENSIVE END ALIGNED LOOSE   STACK TECHNIQUE

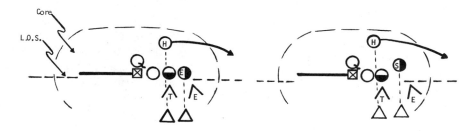

DEFENSIVE END ALIGNED TIGHT   JAM TECHNIQUE

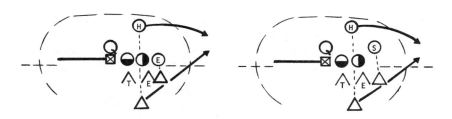

Figure 29 Adjustments of the second level mirror technique against a tight end
(E) or slotback (S): when defensive end aligns loose (upper portion), or tight
(lower portion).

3. If a tight end or slotback is present in the offensive formation, the mirroring
   Second Level defender *automatically* steps up onto the line of scrimmage
   whenever the First Level end aligns tight (fig. 29, lower diagrams). This
   technique, termed *jam*, incorporates important advantages: the Second Level
   personnel in the 2-stack can once again move to his outside unobstructed while
   being *completely hidden* from the offensive guard, tackle, *and* tight end. The
   disadvantages of this adjustment are the blocking-angle which the tight end
   has been afforded against the First Level end, and the mismatch created if the
   tight end is physically larger than the jamming Second Level defender.

In summary, from figures 27-29, one can appreciate the extreme simplicity in
forming these stacks. Essentially, in the core Second Level defenders have three positional choices, over the center (1-stack), or one of the offensive tackles (2-stack), or
mirroring the tight end or a slotback. They encounter little difficulty in identifying
these locations as they move through the core, and both mirroring and stack technique
are simple, quickly becoming second nature for these defenders. The ordered
relationship of the Second Level is maintained at all times—Gael in the center between

Strong and Bandit, with Lou and Rose always to the outsides; therefore when one of these players assumes his stack in the core, the adjacent defender selects the corresponding (and adjacent) stack location. Yet, in assuming any of these positions the Second Level knows that at least minimum stability in the core is secured. Lastly, appreciate that the Second Level operates *independently*, that the First Level's alignment and mechanism(s) are of little practical concern to them. They only rely upon First Level personnel for the creation of stacks (and this latter factor can be totally controlled, when required, by the defensive coordinator's manipulation of the system).

FIRST AND SECOND LEVEL STUNTS

The middle portion of the defensive huddle call designates the *stunt mechanism(s)* to be performed by core personnel at the snap; however, the system includes only five mechanisms: two stunts for the First Level and three for the Second, with each being designated by name in the huddle (table 3). The primary reason for so few mechanisms lies in the essential nature of the 2-level defensive model itself: First Level personnel are always shifting, then penetrating specific offensive line-gaps; and when the Second Level player mirroring the running back carries his attack over the line of scrimmage this often appears to be a stunt rather than the natural, swarming type of play which *must characterize* this defense. On the other hand, specific tactical stunt mechanisms are necessary in order for the defensive coordinator to finely control the aggressive characteristics of this defense.

First Level Stunts

Slant. The slant mechanism involves only two First Level personnel: the nose and one of the defensive tackles. Determination of which tackle will slant with the nose and the direction of their slant is incorporated into the mechanism itself.

1. Slant from 11-, 3-, and 5-alignments must always be *to the offensive strengthside*; thus the defensive tackle away from offensive strength must slant into the nose's defensive area on the line of scrimmage, as the nose slants to strength (see examples, fig. 30; again the offensive *strengthside* has been designated by the location of the tight end in this figure).
2. Slant from 2- and 4-alignments always involves the nose and the defensive tackle, aligned closed; its direction must always slant the nose (aligned even) *towards the offensive center,* thus the defensive tackle slants in a parallel direction (i.e., away from the offensive center; see examples, fig. 30).

Because it occurs after the snap the slant is viewed essentially as a mechanism for *absolutely concealing* the actual First Level alignment. Examine the diagrams in figure 30: if the defensive coordinator actually wishes a 2- or 4-alignment *to strength* but does not want the offense to read his intention, he calls the corresponding 11-, 3-, or 5-Align-

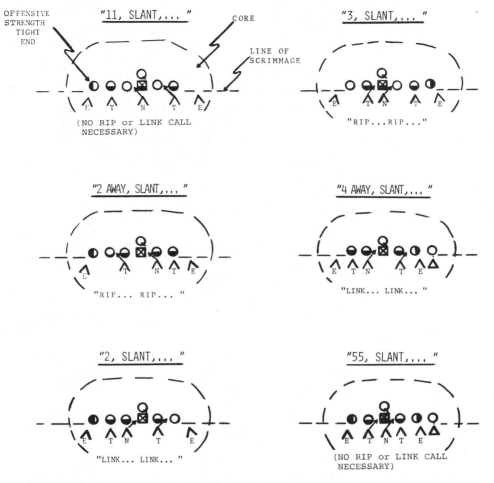

Figure 30 Examples of the slant mechanism: the huddle call, the first level alignment according to the rip or link call at the line-of-scrimmage, and the execution of the nose and tackle slant.

ment and adds "slant" to his call. Conversely, if an 11-, 3-, or 5-alignment is required, the defensive coordinator calls the corresponding 2- or 4-alignment, then adds "slant" to this call. In addition to concealment of the First Level's true alignment, the slant mechanism initiates preemptive movement and attack without necessitating any changes in personnel gap responsibilities (fig. 22).

Twist: T.N.T.; T.E.T. On the other hand, the twist is a mechanism for *interchanging* defensive line-gap responsibilities between (two) adjacent First Level personnel. A defensive tackle is *always* involved in this mechanism, with the nose in a tackle-nose twist (T.N.T.), and with his end in a tackle-end twist (T.E.T.). Again, the prerequisite conditions for either twist to be executed are built into the system; in addition, the two personnel completing the twist assume each other's gap responsibility, as defined in figure 22.

1. A twist can *only* be executed by two First Level personnel when they are *immediately adjacent* to each other. Specifically: in T.E.T., the tackle and end can only be open and loose (respectively); but T.N.T. can be executed, by the nose and one tackle, from either odd-closed or even-open positional alignments. Thus, through manipulation of the First Level alignment, the defensive coordinator is able to finely control the execution of this mechanism by placing the two First Level defenders immediately adjacent to each other (fig. 31).

Figure 31 Examples of the twist mechanisms: huddle call, the first level alignment according to the rip or link call at the line of scrimmage, and the execution of the twist(s).

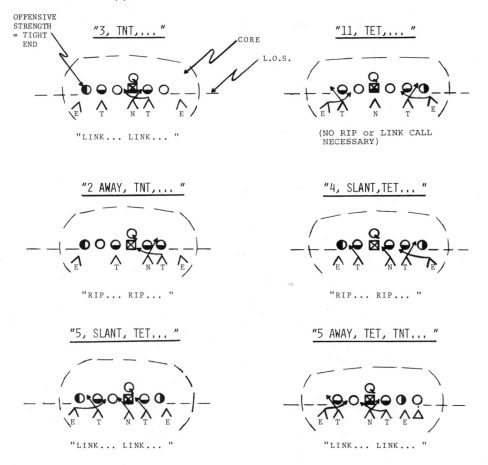

2. The rule, in executing any twist, always requires that the *inside* First Level personnel immediately *slant out* at the snap away from the offensive center, *in front of* the adjacent defender to his immediate outside, who will then *cross behind* him, moving inside towards the offensive center (see examples, fig. 31).

The twist is essentially a mechanism by which two defenders exchange line-gap responsibilities and is not primarily a pass rush mechanism, as coaches currently employ this technique (3). Twisting retards a slow-footed rusher even more; outstanding pass rushers don't really require its mechanistic assistance, and on a sloppy field (where championship games are played, in November) poor footing renders the twist a liability. On the other hand, the twist mechanism initiates preemptive movement by First Level personnel at the snap; it is also the critical (and only) mechanism which enables the nose from an even alignment to slant outside through a guard-tackle gap, and a defensive tackle (aligned open) to slant outside through his off-tackle gap (fig. 31).

Second Level Stunts

Dog. While the First Level executes a specific stunt, the defensive coordinator may wish to include a complementary stunt involving the Second Level (and this is another advantage of operating two independent subunits on defense). In the three-level model of defense, coordination of its stunting, linebackers with line, assigns each of these personnel to specific rushing lanes. In the 2-level model, however, such a high degree of integration is neither attempted nor possible, as Second Level personnel can be off mirroring at some other locale when needed. Six offensive line-gaps are defined by the system yet *only five* First Level players are available to defend them; further, when slanting, twisting, or pass rushing, the nose or one of the tackles can no longer viably defend two gaps (fig. 22) as these personnel can only attack and penetrate one of their gaps in these tactical maneuvers. Quite literally, therefore, an offensive line-gap is waiting for the Second Level personnel to fire through; with the 2-level model this is the practical implication of a complementary Second Level stunt—filling *every* offensive line-gap with rushing defenders. And the Second Level personnel involved encounter little problem in finding this line-gap: by cutting off the backside of the nose in the odd-numbered alignments or a defensive tackle in 2- and 4-alignments, this gap opens up in the center-tackle area to the side of the offensive center *away from the nose.* Where the actual term "dog" and its derivatives—"red dog," "all dog," etc.—actually originated, the authors have been unable to learn; the term itself is succinct, but unmistakable in the defensive huddle, and universally understood. Dog calls require only Second Level personnel *who are mirroring an offensive backfielder* to fire through an interior offensive line-gap *at their discretion.* This last phrase, the discretionary elements incorporated within the dog stunt, cannot be overemphasized: no Second Level player is ever locked into a futile blitz. If he judges that a fire would be inappropriate, little is lost defensively, for already almost 50 percent of the defensive personnel (i.e., the First Level) are rushing. There are three discretionary elements for the Second Level defender to consider quickly, for the offensive backfielder he is mirroring can execute one of three actions at the snap (fig. 32, top portion): A) set up to block; B) sprint laterally towards the perimeter of the offensive core (i.e., to block the defensive end or to go downfield); or C) dive straight ahead, full-speed, at the defensive core. On the first two actions, the Second Level defender is free to fire, and his backfielder now becomes the pass responsibility of a defensive end (see chapter 4). However, on the third action this defender must *continue mirroring* until he is certain this running back is not in possession of the football, or is not sneaking through the line of scrimmage to go downfield for a pass.

Figure 32 Second level stunts: dog, cushion, switch. Note that only in cushion is any restriction placed on the First Level (*i.e.* the defensive end must align loose).

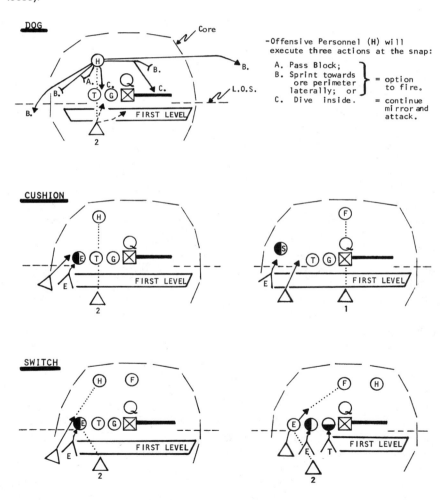

Cushion. The Second Level *cushion* and *switch* stunts provide mechanisms for crashing an extra defender from the outside perimeters of the core against expected sweeps, quick pitch, the triple-option, a quarterback sprintout, etc. But, a Second Level defender cannot be involved in a cushion or a switch unless he is mirroring a tight end or slotback. In cushion the defensive end, at the snap, attacks and max's this receiver (if the offense's play is a pass—see chapter 4), while the Second Level defender crashes (fig. 32, middle portion). In cushion the Second Level defender is relieved of all pass coverage responsibilities and may therefore crash with abandon; on the other hand, this is one of the few instances where this defensive system curbs the end's aggressiveness. And the system places an additional restriction on the end's positional alignment: pre-snap, the end must align loose in his two-point (standup) stance.

Switch. This stunt incorporates a mechanism for crashing *two* defenders, the end and a Second Level player, from the outside perimeter of the core (fig. 32, lower portion). This stunt is particularly effective to the side of the offensive tight end, while often proving more difficult to execute against more mobile slotbacks. While the preceding advice is strongly suggested, the following is a prerequisite condition for proceeding. When "switch" is called in the defensive huddle, its verification at the line of scrimmage is dependent upon the *adjacent Second Level defender in the core being positioned in a 2-stack* (fig. 32); more simply, switch is verified *visually* if there are *two* offensive backfielders. The switching mechanism involves an interchange in max pass assignments between these two Second Level defenders:

1. The player in 2-stack max's the tight end on any passes, as this defender is (almost) aligned over the tight end before the snap in the 2-stack, thereby concealing the switch mechanism (fig. 32, lower diagrams).
2. At the same time, the Second Level defender who is mirroring the offensive tight end at the snap crashes in unison with the defensive end; for this reason, switch provides an effective mechanism to employ against outside running offenses or sprintout quarterbacks.

In summary, each Second Level stunt is *visually verified* before the snap: in dog, to participate the defender must be mirroring an offensive backfielder; in both cushion and switch there must be a tight end or slotback in the offensive formation *in the first instance.* If a stunt mechanism is not visually verified, the built-in system controls of the defense actually are dictating that another stunt or the basic First Level rush would be more appropriate against that formation and the circumstances presented by the offense.[3] Thus, the defensive coordinator can manipulate the system to gain the advantage(s) he seeks, yet never be locked into inappropriate mechanisms at the line of scrimmage. In operating this phase of the defense, however, the defensive coordinator need only remember two cautions: 1) that slant and T.N.T. *cannot* be called simultaneously as First Level stunts; and 2) in cushion that the defensive end must *outflank* the offensive formation to his side (i.e., be aligned loose).

SECONDARY MECHANISMS OF RUN DEFENSE

In the older texts, highly structured primary and secondary responsibilities were always defined for individual players within the defensive systems. In the vernacular of football, secondary responsibility are the actions and tasks defined within a specific system that defenders must perform *in rapid succession* following completion of their primary functions (4): Force Unit pursuit, Contain Unit rotation, gang-tackling, and so on. Team defense is essentially the integration of secondary functions, and defensive teamwork traditionally has depended upon both the sequencing, and the successful execution of these responsibilities. To this point, chapter 3 has dealt with the primary responsibilities for personnel within the 2-level system of defense: this final section focuses upon specific *secondary* mechanisms built into the present system. Into both the First and Second Levels unique mechanisms of defense have been incorporated and their success and shortcomings are discussed. In addition, this defensive concept has permitted the development of four unique mechanisms in which the First and Second Levels must work in unison: these are detailed at the conclusion of the chapter.

First Level

Trailer. Traditionally, every defensive system has assigned one defender whose secondary role has been to trail the football back of the line of scrimmage; that is, at the snap, when the offense masses its blockers against one side of the defense (establishing that area as the frontside), one defender has been assigned to guard against reverse and misdirection plays. The obvious personnel for this role are the defensive ends, but this previously minor secondary mechanism has taken on major proportions due to the tailback search play that the offense has recently developed (5). No specific hole is opened for the ball carrier—usually the tailback running from an I formation—rather, this back searches for any opening as his blockers engage defenders along the line of scrimmage. Far too often this play gains positive yardage when the tailback cuts back (toward the backside of the defense); in this system, however, the backside end can exert considerable leverage by executing his trailer responsibility *aggressively*. Crashing, the ends quickly penetrate into the offensive core. When the movements of the offense establish a backside role for one of the ends, he *continues to crash*. Once inside the offensive core, by flattening out his crash angle and moving more parallel to the line of scrimmage this defensive end can effectively remove the entire backside as a viable area for the tailback to search, even as far frontside as the guard-tackle area if the end is particularly agile and determined. This greatly reduces the tailback's search area, in effect isolating him on the frontside for the defensive pursuit to overwhelm. On the other hand, like any system that would employ such a secondary backside mechanism to gain an advantage frontside, this defense is vulnerable to deeper reverses when the ends crash this vigorously.

Tear Line of Scrimmage. Before a play, First Level and stunting Second Level personnel are gearing up to attack. At the snap, however, if the offensive blockers fire out across the line of scrimmage at the defense, this is a *run key* (chapter 6), and these personnel must immediately "throttle down"; and even for the highly intelligent, superior athlete this consistently proves a difficult transition to make instantaneously. Older systems of defense seldom experienced this dichotomy because pass rush was always defined as a *secondary* responsibility, not primary (6), and therefore their defensive linemen could play along the line of scrimmage, executing the traditional fundamentals. In contemporary defenses, however, this is not possible, and so the critical mechanism of team pursuit is weakened. In the present system, *tear* is the secondary mechanism invoked in order to maximize First Level pursuit without impinging upon their primary function. First Level personnel are instructed to go behind an offensive blocker if necessary, to spin out, circle, or power through, only *move laterally*, parallel to the line of scrimmage, as quickly as possible in the direction of the football. They should not continue to gain depth into the offensive backfield area; this is solely the territory of the trailer end. This secondary mechanism has not solved the problem of First Level pursuit, but, combined with the head-on alignment and techniques used by the nose and defensive tackles it at least gives these personnel a viable chance for pursuit in both directions along the line of scrimmage.

Second Level

Aggressive play by the Second Level also can weaken team pursuit against the run, the exception being the Second Level defender in max coverage who mirrors the offensive ball carrier: his pursuit is immediate and foolproof. For other Second Level defenders, however, especially those moving downfield with eligible pass receivers, the question is, *when do these personnel commence team-pursuit*? Leaving an eligible receiver is the decision with which these personnel are ultimately faced? In the three-level defensive models, this dilemma is partially solved by greater reliance upon cognitive processes, offensive key reading (pass vs. run keys), and through the use of zone pass defense. But, all defenses must employ man-to-man coverage—especially in the 1980s—and the defenders manning the eligible pass receivers in the three-level model can easily be taken out of pursuit if their assigned receiver runs a deep pass route. Using the present system, the solution to this problem has been quite successful to date: Second Level defenders may leave an offensive receiver moving downfield to initiate run pursuit immediately at any time without fault . . . . even before the snap, if they gamble with a degree of certainty. This no-fault assurance is ironclad within the system; however, personnel should never take it as license for failure to execute primary responsibilities to the fullest. This mechanism simply relieves Second Level personnel of that momentary hesitation which provides talented running backs with all the time they require to break clear of pursuit. Obviously, this simple commandment from deep within the 2-level model requires considerable explanation, and is part of a secondary mechanism that requires coordination with the deep safety and the First Level (see final section of chapter). The point of emphasis here is that unique mechanisms have been developed for the Second Level which enhance its secondary response capabilities. These are very simple mechanisms that are easily implemented by the defensive personnel yet have universal application.

Incorporated Secondary Mechanisms

Stratified secondary responsibilities for all personnel, correctly sequenced then well executed, are the backbone of defensive teamwork. However, perfecting secondary mechanisms is the most difficult and painstaking element of defensive coaching, requiring hours of practice. More than physical skills are required. Cognition and experience exert considerable influence in their execution. More than one defensive subunit is involved, and there are crucial elements of coordination that must be rehearsed. Secondary mechanisms are executed during the free-flow period of each play, and thus, specific situations are unpredictable to some degree, with each one being slightly different from the last. In addition, a critical timing factor is involved in their implementation: *overpursuit* frontside actually means that the defensive personnel have travelled too far too quickly, *overrotation* backside that deepbacks advanced frontside too soon, and so on. A crucial reason to orchestrate the defense's secondary mechanisms against the run is the *unknowing* factor: during every play most defenders proceed rapidly through primary to secondary responsibilities yet some players may not have recognized the offensive running play, and always one or two will still not have located the football.[4] At the same time, because the referee's whistle has not sounded, these players realize that a primary assignment probably has been blown, and thus immediate action must be taken. Unless specific courses of action have been well programmed, however, defensive solidarity can erode rapidly when key personnel execute inappropriate secondary actions. This section focuses on four unique mechanisms incorporated into the present 2-level defensive model: the power of stacks; overshift mechanisms; defending the sixth offensive line-gap; and containment and pursuit against the run. Each mechanism serves a specific secondary function, and the nature of the mechanism initiates the appropriate actions for the personnel involved.

The Power of Stacks .   The stacking mechanism of the 2-level Defense was described in connection with the core structure, a Second Level defender aligned directly behind a First Level teammate. Some of the structural advantages gained from this technique are self-evident:

1. The immediate area of the offensive line is double-covered by the two stacked personnel.
2. The stacked Second Level defender is hidden from any head-on blocking threat; any block by the offense   must be made at an angle, with the blocker travelling several feet to reach him.
3. The stacked defender is far more mobile than if (for example) he were an Okie inside linebacker aligned over an offensive guard, with a specific of-fensive line-gap to defend.

The more subtle advantage of stacking in the defensive core is not the stability that is provided by a single stack, but rather the intermeshing strength imparted by a *series of stacks*. This important structural principle is illustrated in figure 33.

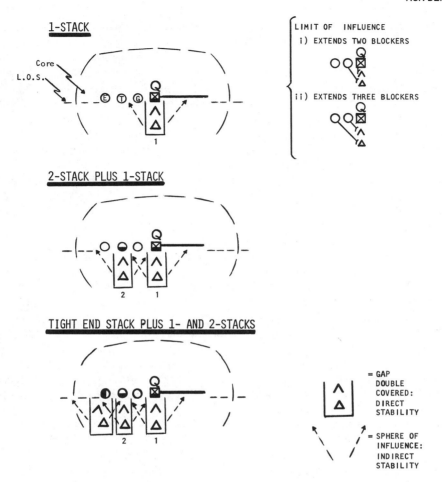

Figure 33 The power of stacks: a series of stacks adds intermeshing strength and stability to the defensive core.

Basically, the core is structured as a *series of stacks*. A single stack accomplishes two important objectives: first, the area of the stack is secured from immediate penetration by the offense; second, depending upon the playing abilities of its personnel the stack can exert a *sphere of influence* to both its left and its right, and this sphere extends as far along the line of scrimmage as the number of consecutive offensive linemen that are required to block the stack effectively (fig. 33 top portion). As a series of stacks are created along the line of scrimmage (fig. 33, lower diagrams) not only are immediate areas secured where the stacks align, but their spheres of influence *intermesh*. Thus this mechanism improves the inherent structural stability of the core as well as creating a much greater blocking problem for the offense; and the constant multiple alignment and shifting immediately prior to the snap escalate this latter factor.

This inherent structure of the stack is employed as a crucial secondary mechanism to defense the seventh and eighth offensive line-gaps (fig. 5) should the offense choose to create them by aligning a tight end (or slotback) next to an offensive tackle. Only six offensive line-gaps are defined in the present system and assigned to the First Level. Without the power inherent in a series of stacks, this arbitrary definition could not have been possible. If the defensive end aligns loose on a tight end, and the Second Level defender (mirroring the tight end) stacks, additional structural elements are incorporated within the larger core structure: the immediate off-end area is secured, while the stack mechanism permits the Second Level personnel to be smaller in stature (than an outside linebacker, for example, performing the same structural function). The stack is never structured in isolation but unites with the *series of stacks* which form the core of the 2-level Defense; its sphere of influence can mesh with a 2-stack immediately adjacent, even with a 1-stack further inside, and both a 1- and 2-stack to its side of the offensive center provides the greatest stability for that off-end area (fig. 33, lower portion).

    Overshift Mechanism.   In chapter 2 it was explained how this defensive model always outnumbers the potential offensive blockers at the point of attack; Second Level mirroring was the defensive mechanism responsible for achieving this numerical superiority in the core (fig. 18). When the opposing team possesses *superior* offensive personnel, (larger or more talented athletes), even this advantage may not prove sufficient. Therefore, two overshift mechanisms have been built into the present system which: 1) gain a numerical superiority of two defenders to one side of the offensive center; 2) *without losing* the effect of the core's numerical advantage of one defender to the other side of the center. While this may seem highly suspect, these secondary mechanisms actually take advantage of the tactical superiority of the nose technique coupled with the inherent blocking limitations of the offensive center position. Explained in tactical terms, when an offense runs to *either* side of center, this action immediately positions its offensive center *on the backside*, thereby reducing his potential blocking effectiveness; conversely, the nose technique is designed to always place this defender frontside, thereby *increasing* his potential tactical capacity. As proof of this principle it may be noted that since the 1950s it has been well established, initially within the Okie 5-2 defensive model (7) then in the 3-4 Defense (8), that the nose can tactically defend both center guard gaps. Unless all nose personnel have been super-men, this could not have been possible without an inherent tactical advantage.

1.   To the Overshifted Side. The mechanisms that accomplish this overshift principle are the 2- and 4-alignments and the slant stunt (fig. 34). Prior to the snap, the 2- and 4-alignments position the nose in even. This gains the defensive core an immediate numerical advantage of two personnel *to that side*. Against an expected running play to that side, the added personnel strength this mechanism provides is obvious. Also, when a First-Level defender is substituted for an additional pass defender (see chapter 4), the overshift mechanism provides the defensive coordinator with a means by which to hedge his bet. He has an enhanced pass coverage capability while still main-

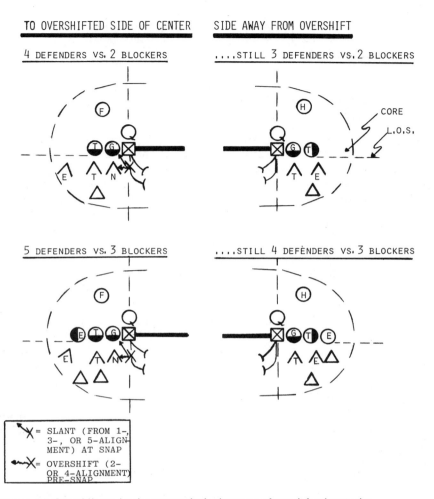

TO OVERSHIFTED SIDE OF CENTER   SIDE AWAY FROM OVERSHIFT

4 DEFENDERS VS. 2 BLOCKERS   ....STILL 3 DEFENDERS VS. 2 BLOCKERS

5 DEFENDERS VS. 3 BLOCKERS   ....STILL 4 DEFENDERS VS. 3 BLOCKERS

X = SLANT (FROM 1-,
    3-, OR 5-ALIGN-
    MENT) AT SNAP
X = OVERSHIFT (2-
    OR 4-ALIGNMENT)
    PRE-SNAP

Figure 34 Overshift mechanism: numerical advantage of two defenders to the overshifted side of center; maintenance of the mirror advantage to side away from the overshift.

taining a numerical superiority in the core. The major disadvantage of the even-digit alignments is their vulnerability to a fullback quick-trap play; this play is run over-center, and thus the offensive center's blocking potential is maximized (9). On the other hand, the slant is a mechanism for concealing the overshift while still gaining its tactical advantage for the defense. An overshift achieved by this means must be executed from the odd-digit alignments. The disadvantage of the slant mechanism involves the loss of the tactical advantages of the nose (i.e., his alignment and technique) if he is slanting in the incorrect direction, away from the play side.

2. Away from the Overshifted Side. To this side of the offensive center, another tactical advantage of the 2-level defense should be noted. The system is structured so that the core can commit the nose to one side of the offensive center, yet maintain its numerical superiority to the other side in most situations (fig. 34). What suffers, of course, is the structural strength of the core: with one fewer First Level personnel to this side, the potential stacks that can be formed is also reduced by one.

Defensing the Sixth Offensive Line-Gap. One problem encountered in developing the present 2-level model from the 6-5 goal line model was the number of First Level defenders that were available: five had to be the absolute maximum of First Level personnel, yet at the minimum, there must always be *six* offensive line-gaps to defend. In the defensive literature dating back to the early 1920s, the authors were unable to find a precedent for simply *leaving one offensive line-gap unassigned*; every structured line-linebacker unit always has included some mechanism for defending all the offensive line-gaps, including one defender being assigned two gaps, stacking mechanisms specifically designed to defend a two- to three- gap area, and several other combinations.   After a season of experimentation, the essence of this problem crystallized. First and foremost, the gap for which the First Level did not have a defender (hereafter, referred to as the *sixth gap* regardless of its exact offensive location) could never be one of the off-tackle areas through which the ends crash. That was entirely too risky; ergo, the sixth gap must always be located BETWEEN the offensive tackles. However, always assigning the nose the two center guard gaps reduced his aggressiveness considerably, while making the defense itself highly predictable. Assigning the Second Level the task of finding the sixth gap in the heat of battle, plus their mirroring responsibility, plus the job of personally defending themselves, all proved futile. In given situations, the closest Second Level personnel was positioned nowhere near the location of the sixth gap; even worse, this solution established a mutual dependency between the First and Second Levels, negating one of the first principles in the model.

Thereafter, it was accepted philosophically that the sixth gap could remain *unassigned*, and thus the solution to the problem resided in developing viable mechanisms for defending the sixth gap at various times and by various means. To achieve this, three general principles were followed. First, one First Level player could be assigned the sixth gap (and thus be assigned two offensive line-gaps), with the understanding that this assignment must be rotated between the nose and both tackles. Second, the actual location of the sixth offensive line-gap had to be *constantly moved* between the four interior gaps in the offensive line. And the third option was, very simply, to leave the sixth gap unassigned on occasion. Once accepted, these principles ultimately led to the development of many of the primary and secondary mechanisms in the present 2-level model.

1. Traditional Assignment of the Sixth Gap: all odd-numbered alignments assign the nose to the sixth gap (i.e., both center-guard gaps); the 2- and 4- alignments assign the two gaps to a defensive tackle (fig. 22).

2. Power of the Stacks: the series of stacks also provide immediate support at the sixth gap; this secondary mechanism is dependent, however, upon stacks being created nearby.

3. Mirroring: when the offense attacks the sixth gap, this *primary* mechanism provides immediate assistance at the sixth gap from the Second Level defender mirroring the ball carrier.

4. Leaving the sixth Gap Undefended: the First Level stunt mechanisms (slant and twist) generally leave the sixth gap undefended; once the defender assigned the two-gap responsibility commences his attack post-snap, he must select one gap to penetrate, or the stunt itself will prove ineffectual.[5]

5. Second Level Stunting: to coordinate a dog stunt by the huddle call proves futile and any attempt to do this at the line of scrimmage requires additional verbal signals; thus, the sixth gap provides a *waiting* rushing lane for Second Level defenders and is easily located by them (based on the actions of the nose), while the offense *cannot* know ahead of time the sixth gap's actual location.

Containment and Pursuit. Foremost, the mechanisms of run defense must include containment of the ball carrier physically surrounding and trapping him in a highly coordinated fashion. The talented running back is seldom just tackled; first the defense must *grind him to a halt*, deny him openings through which to run, obstruct and delay him. When containment is accomplished the pursuit, additional defenders from other areas of the field, can overtake and overwhelm the ball carrier by force of numbers. This concept of run defense was one of the strengths originally built into the three-level model of defense (10): the line, then linebackers, then deepbacks, three successive waves of tacklers.[6] In this 2-level Defense specific mechanisms have been incorporated which provide primary containment, immediate support personnel, and two pursuit waves, shallow and deep. To illustrate this, an offensive quick pitch play is diagrammed in figure 35, but, the general mechanisms described are applicable against both inside and outside running plays.

PRIMARY CONTAINMENT. The frontside end's crashing must accomplish one of three objectives: 1) secure the tackle on the ball carrier (the most preferred); 2) turn the running back immediately inside *back into pursuit* (the next best alternative); or 3) his crash angle must force the ball carrier *to deepen*, making the running back circle around him (the least preferred).

SECONDARY CONTAINMENT. To the frontside this is provided by any Second Level defenders outside the core leaving his mirrored wide receiver *immediately* when the football leaves the quarterback's hands; these defenders sprint toward the inside, adjusting their movement to provide *back-up* containment. *On the backside* the crashing trailer end traps the ball carrier to the frontside, as explained earlier.

SUPPORT PERSONNEL. This is provided by the Second Level defenders located in the core on the frontside, particularly the ball carrier's mirror. Immediate pursuit also is provided by the First Level tackle and nose on the frontside "tearing" along the line of scrimmage. Deep pursuit is initiated by the deep safety moving up, and backside by any Second Level defender leaving his mirrored offensive receiver (again *on key*, by the quarterback pitching or handing off the football) gaining depth immediately. As the safety moves up and backside personnel rotate deep, they must *visually* locate any eligible pass receivers continuing to run downfield (examine fig. 35).

Figure 35 Mechanisms of defensive containment and pursuit: primary (I) containment by frontside defensive end; secondary (II) containment by frontside Second Level outside core, and by the backside defensive end; immediate support by Second Level in core to the frontside and immediate pursuit by the First Level, deep pursuit provided by the deep safety and backside Second Level personnel rotating deep.

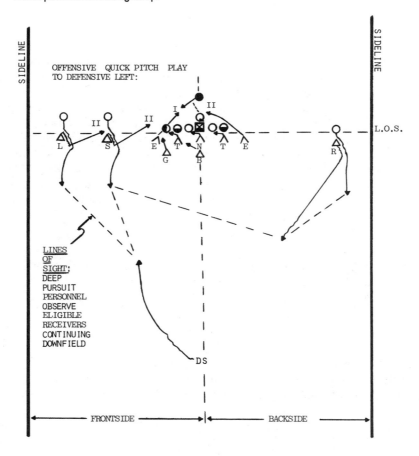

Finally, the halfback option-pass would seem to be open for the offense to throw, yet nothing could accommodate this defense more. At most, the halfback pass will net the offense fifteen yards because of the deep safety's presence, and the ball carrier's actions of stopping, gripping the football, cocking his arm, and *throwing under pressure* provides all the time and keys that the safety requires for an interception. (And most talented running backs cannot throw well, which is why they became runners and not sprintout quarterbacks.)

Notes

1. The directional terms *left* and *right* are employed for many general purposes in defensive football. Thus, unique nomenclature must be defined to cue specific defensive mechanisms; in this system link and rip apply *only* to First Level alignments.

2. There are numerous offensive "cues," defined according to specific systems of offense and/or the opponent's personnel strengths; several of these are analyzed at length in part IV. For the remainder of part II, however, the defined cue will be exclusively the offensive tight end, the most commonly employed cue for defining formation *strength.*

3. These safeguards also are built into many of the pass coverages.

4. By contrast, most pass plays are quickly diagnosed by defensive personnel, and it is assumed that the quarterback retained the football.

5. The identical choice must be made by the First Level in pass rush; the nose or tackle assigned the two line-gaps must select one en route to the quarterback.

6. As a historical aside, the older football texts (11, 12) actually refer to the linebacker unit as "the Secondary," while the deepback unit was called "the Tertiary"; it is significant to note that today it is the deepback unit that is called "the Secondary" implying that any *third tier of defense* has all but vanished from the three-level model.

References

1. MILAN VOOLETICH, "Linebacker Fundamentals: Drills and Techniques." (Paper presented by the Assistant Football Coach, University of Michigan, at the University of Guelph, March, 1984).

2. DAVID M. NELSON, *Football Principles and Play* (New York: The Ronald Press Co., 1962), pp. 317-321.

3. S. E. SULLINS, *Complete Book of Multiple Defenses in Football*, (West Nyack, N. Y.: Parker Publ. Co., Inc., 1978), pp. 171-172.

4. GOMER JONES and CHARLES BUD WILKINSON, *Modern Defensive Football* (Englewood Cliffs, N.J.: Prentice-Hall, Inc., 1957), pp. 12-22.

5. DAVID W. BRYAN, "Techniques and Drills for a 'run-to-daylight' Offense," *Illustrated Football Drills from the Coaching Clinic* (West Nyack, N.Y.: Parker Publ. Co., Inc., 1975), pp. 15-20.

6. JOHN F. BATEMAN and PAUL V. GOVER- NALLI, *Football Fundamentals: Basic Strategy and Teaching Methods* (New York: McGraw-Hill Book Co., Inc., 1957), pp. 246-282.

7. JONES and WILKINSON, *Modern Defensive Football*, pp. 107-113.

8. ROBERT TROPPMAN, *Football's New Master Defense Guide* (West Nyack, N.Y.: Parker Publ. Co., Inc., 1983), pp. 24-27.

9. NELSON, *Football Principles and Play*, p. 243.

10. JONES and WILKINSON, *Modern Defensive Football*, pp. 52-58.

11. DANA X. BIBLE, *Championship Football: A Guide for Player, Coach and Fan* (New York: Prentice-Hall, Inc., 1947), pp. 134, 138.

12. J. F. EDWARDS, *Canadian Football* (Toronto: The Copp Clark Co., Ltd., 1947), pp. 129-138.

Chapter 4
PASS DEFENSE

Employing the 2-level model run and pass defense can be unified under a singular philosophy of defense: on every down, a coordinated assault is directed *at* the football. This strategy has proven consistently reliable against the run (1). Against the pass, this philosophy provides both a high degree of compatibility with run defense and the only *certain* means of pass defense: even the bravest quarterbacks experience difficulty in throwing the football with poise and consistency under constant defensive harassment. This is the first principle of the 2-level Defense, especially its pass defense, for only immediate attack can provide the critical mechanism for shortening the time frame in which an offense is permitted to operate: whatever pass the offense has selected, the football must be launched quickly; only in this way can the end line be patrolled effectively by the deep safety. Therefore, rather than attempting to conceal the First Level's five-man rush, possible blitzing by Second Level personnel in the core, or the Second Level's mirroring mechanism, the theory of this defense is to permit the offense to read *only this* before every play, which is a complete reversal of present defensive philosophy. Several important advantages accrue from this strategy, however.

- In the three-level model of defense, so many complex mechanisms and nuances are executed in order to conceal its pass defense. Mirroring is so much simpler!

- At the present time so much of the offense's manipulation is directed at pre-reading the pass defense. Employing this defensive strategy, the offense's read becomes meaningless, being *identical* prior to every play (fig. 19).

- With Lou and Rose usually showing tight max coverage before the snap the quick-out pass, with its minimal gain and dire consequences if intercepted, becomes too great a risk.

- Finally, by employing this strategy the surprise element of zone pass coverage is complete. Pre-reading the defensive coverage before each play has become so much a part of the offensive strategy that mirroring pre-snap automatically presumes man-to-man pass coverage post-snap, but against the 2-level Defense this validation can *never* be assumed.

In this system, max coverage incorporates an important new strategy into the defensive pass repertoire, while there is essentially no change in the execution of zone coverage. In zone, the medium and deep zones are defended, pass receptions in front of these defenders are acceptable, with any yardage gained kept to a minimum (2). On the other hand, in max the Second Level's jamming of the offensive receivers effectively eliminates their short pass routes (less than ten yards) while the deep safety, in conjunction with the First Level's pass rush, neutralizes the threat of their deep pass routes (deeper than eighteen to twenty yards). Therefore, against max coverage medium depth passes thrown twelve to fifteen yards downfield become the viable alternative. These two contrasting pass coverages, zone and max, when blended tactically during a game, introduce an important new dimension into the defensive chess game. Against max coverage, under pressure, the quarterback must arc the football over the Second Level defenders and in front of the deep safety sprinting towards the end line, leaving little room for error. Prior to the snap, however (and quite often after the snap), the quarterback and primary receiver(s) may not be certain of the pass coverage, and arcing a medium depth pass into zone coverage is precarious, while attempting short passes against aggressive max coverage will prove discouraging at the very least.

There are several other fundamental advantages to the 2-level system of pass defense. In the First Level both ends constantly crash, and this action imposes specific restrictions on an offense's passing game. First of all, unless a quick pass is being thrown, the offense is forced to retain eligible pass receivers in its core for blocking purposes: in turn, with fewer receivers in the pass pattern, zone coverage proves particularly effective. Additionally, the crashing ends discourage both sprintout passes and the more mobile quarterbacks from running out of their protective pocket on dropback passes. In the Second Level's pass responsibilities, the 2-level Defense includes one major "systems" advantage over the three-level model: in zone coverage, against an isolated wide receiver, *one* defender in max (with end line coverage on top) may be all that is required in specific situations, thereby enabling other defensive personnel to saturate more vulnerable pass zones or to pass rush. Finally, there are important personal considerations coaches should examine: not only is this pass defense more compatible with its run defense, coaches will find that their defensive personnel actually appreciate playing this system much more. Consider the job of the First Level ends compared with present outside linebacker play: their tactical responsibilities, particularly in pass coverage, are greatly reduced, and the ends play more aggressively, continually crashing, harassing quarterbacks . . . and this they enjoy! Mirroring gains both a numerical superiority for the 2-level Defense in the core *and* positions Second Level personnel in stacks; therefore, the pressure on these personnel to defend *both* the pass and the run is reduced, compared to the pivotal role that inside linebackers must play in the three-level defensive model. Consider the frustration of the cornerback: a competitive young man who, accepting the challenge of football and relishing its physical contact, finds himself constantly isolated on a wide receiver, defending a deep outside zone—yet an error, one mistake in judgment, can cause his team defeat. For Lou and Rose, this situation is reversed; they may initiate contact with their wide receivers on almost any play, bumping and running, aggressively steering, even occasionally cutblocking their receiver as he releases off the line of scrimmage. When inevitable errors are made, however, the deep safety's presence provides the safeguard.

WORKING DEFINITIONS OF PASS DEFENSE

A critical variable for every system of pass defense is the *final* location, at the snap, of the five eligible pass receivers. As emphasized in chapter 1, an almost limitless number of offensive formations are possible, and during the present decade the tendency to employ less conventional formations has escalated (3, 4). Therefore, within the pass defense system three categories of working definitions have been established in order to delimit these for the defensive personnel, while also ensuring that this system of pass defense can operate *visually* against all offensive formations:

1. Numbering the five mobile offensive personnel;
2. Defining the offensive formation according to specific areas *on the offensive side* of the line of scrimmage;
3. Defining specific zones *on the defensive side* of the line of scrimmage.

Numbering the Five Mobile Offensive Personnel

Prior to the snap, Second Level mirroring is predetermined *by rule* according to a simple numerical scheme that is independent of the offense's specific formation on that play. Conceptually, by this numbering scheme the five mobile personnel are perceived as being *spread across the football field*, either on the line of scrimmage or just back of the line. In power formations these offensive personnel are bunched in much closer proximity to one another while in spread formations they are dispersed, literally, from sideline to sideline (fig. 36). But, irrespective of their spacing in a specific offensive formation, the five mobile personnel are always numbered sequentially: the two *widest* receivers (to either side) of the formation are designated as No. 1, the next mobile personnel positioned *inside* each of these receivers are both designated No. 2. while the fifth mobile personnel (always positioned, sequentially, *in the middle*) is designated as No. 3. This foolproof numbering scheme is illustrated in figure 36, and the only problem that Second Level defenders may encounter occurs when two (or more) mobile

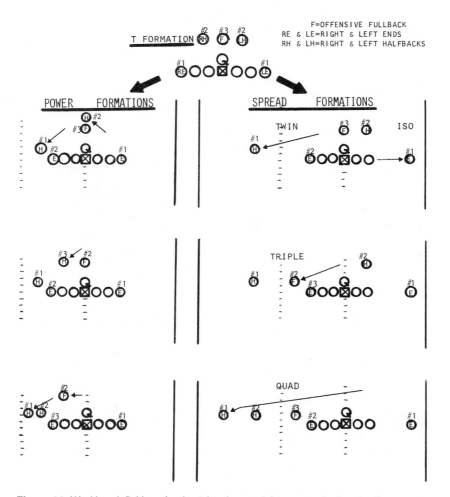

Figure 36 Working definitions for the 2-level pass defense: numbering the five mobile pass receivers relative to their final positioning across the football field (note also the descriptive terminology which describes specific receiver sets to each side of the offense).

offensive personnel are stacked one directly behind the other at the snap. As shown in figure 37, however, specific rules for these personnel govern each situation.

The Second Level defenders always mirror the five mobile personnel by rule: Lou and Rose mirror the No. 1 receivers to each side of the offensive formation, Gael mirrors No. 3, while Strong and Bandit always mirror the No. 2 personnel (with Strong initially positioning himself either to the strength side of the offense, or the wideside of the field). Whenever an offense chooses to interchange the relative position of its mobile personnel through formational variations or by early-motion, the numbering

OFFENSIVE BACKFIELDERS IN AN I FORMATION

WIDE RECEIVERS IN A (STATIONARY) STACK

WIDE RECEIVERS IN EARLY-MOTION TO A STACK

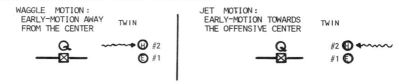

Figure 37 Numbering the mobile offensive personnel when two (or more) of these eligible receivers are positioned *directly behind* each other at the snap: note in the offensive backfield the assignment of the lesser number(s) to the deeper backfielder(s) in the I formation (top portion); and outside the backfield area the assignment of the *higher* number(s) to the deeper wide receiver(s) in the stack (middle & lower portions).

scheme is *never* altered; this working principle, illustrated in figure 38, is crucially important to the total operation of this defense for two reasons:

1. For zone and combination coverages to operate, the relative positioning of the Second Level personnel—Lou and Rose on the outsides, Gael in the middle between Strong and Bandit—may *not* be altered.

2. Solidarity against the run would be substantially diminished if Second Level defenders had to race across the football field before the snap mirroring *individual* offensive players; this situation can become chaotic against multiple early-motion patterns (see fig. 38, for example).

Finally, this numbering scheme provides an important assistance in the dynamic operation of the Second Level: in employing this system every offensive formation can be immediately identified by means of a simple computation. This principle is

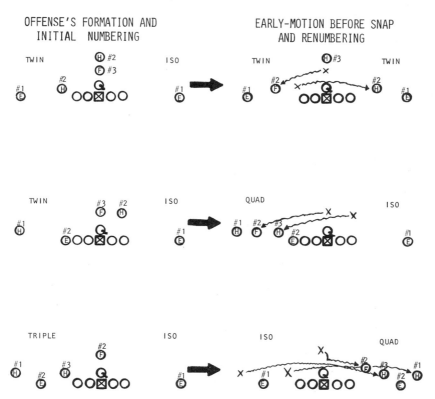

Figure 38 The effect of offensive early-motion on numbering of the five mobile personnel; note that the numbering sequence remains constant, always 1,2,3,2,1 relative to their positioning across the football field at the snap.

illustrated by the following: if only two fingers of one hand are extended in full view, an observer can rapidly compute that three fingers remain hidden *from view*; or if four fingers are held up, then only one cannot be seen; and so on. The application of this simple principle in identifying and calling offensive formations is illustrated in figure 39. In example A (fig. 39, upper portion), because Strong (S) always mirrors No. 2 (an offensive slotback in this particular formation) and can visually count two additional mobile personnel in the offensive backfield, he quickly determines that only one receiver threatens the other side (the right side) of the defense.   If this slotback subsequently jet-actions across the offensive formation, by immediately yelling "Twin . . . Twin . . ." Strong alerts Bandit (initially positioned in the core, mirroring the fullback) *who must mirror No. 2 in ANY Twin formation to his side*; and forewarned by Strong's call, Bandit can be waiting for the slotback as he emerges against the right side of the defense.   Therefore, the offensive formation, and particularly *any major alteration due to early-motion*, is identified for the Second Level from the *other side* of the defense, not by defenders *to the side* of the formational change who may be too

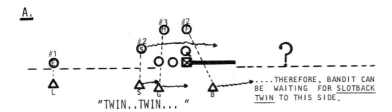

....THEREFORE, BANDIT CAN
BE WAITING FOR SLOTBACK
TWIN TO THIS SIDE.

"TWIN..TWIN... "

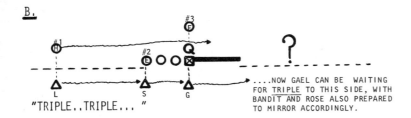

....NOW GAEL CAN BE WAITING
FOR TRIPLE TO THIS SIDE, WITH
BANDIT AND ROSE ALSO PREPARED
TO MIRROR ACCORDINGLY.

"TRIPLE..TRIPLE... "

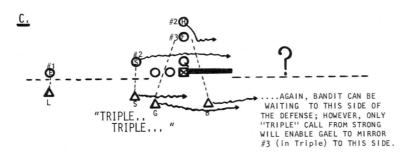

....AGAIN, BANDIT CAN BE
WAITING TO THIS SIDE OF
THE DEFENSE; HOWEVER, ONLY
"TRIPLE" CALL FROM STRONG
WILL ENABLE GAEL TO MIRROR
#3 (in Triple) TO THIS SIDE.

"TRIPLE..
TRIPLE... "

Figure 39 Identification of offensive formations: by counting the number of mobile offensive personnel that are visible (to one side of the offense and in the backfield) the Second Level can quickly identify the formation as well as *anticipate* any formational adjustments(s) to one side of the defense via calls from the *other side* (of the defense).

preoccupied adjusting to and mirroring the incoming offensive personnel. By contrast, note further, in example A, that once the offensive slotback jet-actions, Strong has little else to do but verbally identify the (new) formation for the Second Level as he steps to his right assuming a 2-Stack (to mirror the offensive halfback, now his No. 2). When *multiple* early-motion is employed by an offense (fig. 39, example C), the ability of every Second Level defender to immediately identify the offensive formation in this manner reduces any complex offensive maneuver to a routine adjustment for these personnel. In example C, Strong observes both the slotback (his initial No. 2 mirror), then the offensive tailback (his subsequent No. 2), jet-action against the right-side of the defense; his immediate "Triple . . . Triple . . . " call notifies both Bandit and Gael to move to the right side of the defense (that is, always the side *away from* where the formational call is made) and prepare to mirror No. 2 and No. 3 (respectively) in the forthcoming triple.

Defining the Offensive Formation According to Areas

Dating as far back as 1940, by convention, the prevailing *offensive* terminology has always been employed *by the defense* to define both the formations and the systems of offense (5, 6). While this tradition may *appear* reasonable, for most defensive systems this singular vocabulary has served little purpose other than to facilitate communications, and in the 1980s the offensive vocabulary has become very extensive. The present defense employs a much simpler system for defining the offense. The football field *on the offensive side* of the line of scrimmage is mentally sectioned by imaginary boundaries into discrete areas, in much the same way as the field *on the defensive side* of the line of scrimmage was subdivided by zones in the 1950s. At the line of scrimmage, prior to every play the positioning of the five mobile offensive personnel is always defined according to these areas; thus, many of the systems decisions that defenders must make during that play can be dictated according to their *visual definition* of the offense's formation. In figure 40, the location and physical dimensions of the *seven* areas defined in the present system are described:

Figure 40 Working definitions for the 2-level defense: areas A, B, C, and the backfield *on the offensive side* of the line of scrimmage; before every play the offensive formation is defined according to these areas, *not* by the conventional *offensive* terminology (triple, I formation, etc. are descriptive vocabulary for communication purposes only).

A. FOOTBALL POSITIONED BETWEEN THE HASHMARKS

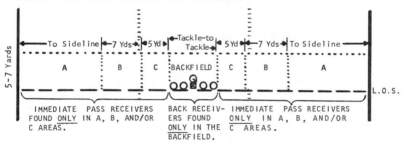

B. FOOTBALL SCRIMMAGED FROM THE LEFT HASHMARKS

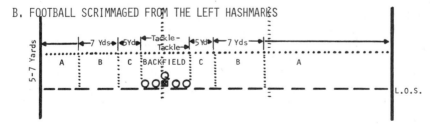

C. FOOTBALL SCRIMMAGED FROM THE RIGHT HASHMARKS

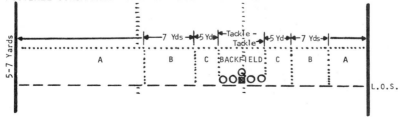

- The *backfield* is defined as the area immediately behind the offensive linemen in the core, extending both to the left and to the right of the center as far as the outside leg of each tackle.
- Two *C areas* are defined, one to each side of the offensive formation; the C areas are also located inside the core and extend from the offensive tackles to the perimeter of the core, a distance of approximately five yards.
- Two *B areas* and two *A areas* are defined outside the core; each B area is immediately adjacent to C on either side of the offensive formation, and A continues from the boundary of B out to each sideline. Area A begins approximately twelve yards outside of the offensive tackle, thereby extending each B area approximately seven yards outside of C.

These seven areas stretch as deep as the mobile personnel positioned in a particular area: for example, a split end by rule must be positioned on the line of scrimmage, while a tailback will be seven yards off the line. In figure 41, the more conventional offensive formations are defined according to area and numbering; further, when one of these eligible pass receivers is positioned in area C, B, or A he is referred to as an *immediate* receiver. And the only restriction placed upon any formational definition involves areas C and A: while *more than one* mobile player may be defined as being located in the backfield or in either B area, *only one* area C and A immediate receiver may be defined (fig. 41 and 42). In figure 42, less conventional formations are also defined; note particularly that this method of defining the offense is applicable to every formation and, more importantly, that both categories are foolproof and uncomplicated.

Defining the Defensive Pass Zones

It was during the 1940s that the football field *on the defensive side* of the line of scrimmage initially was subdivided into (imaginary) sectors called zones (7, 8). Zones were located where the offensive receivers of that era were most likely to run their pass routes: the underneath zones were expansive areas stretching approximately eight to ten yards deep from the line of scrimmage and up to one-half the width of the field; most usually, four deep zones extended from the rear boundaries of the underneath zones (9). By the late sixties, up to six underneath zones had been defined (fig. 6); in turn, this trend necessitated a progressive redefinition of the deep zones—from four to three and then to two sectors. And by the eighties much greater emphasis had been placed on zoning the offensive formation (10) rather than saturating the entire field with up to eight defenders. Particular facets of this evolutionary process have influenced the zone mechanisms of the 2-level Defense. Essentially, its zones are conceptualized as *targets*, areas on the football field at which each defender initially aims during his drop-off but whose final location is finely adjusted according to the offensive formation prior to the snap and the individual pass routes in that area of the field. The intersection of specific landmarks on the field defines each *target* (fig. 43).

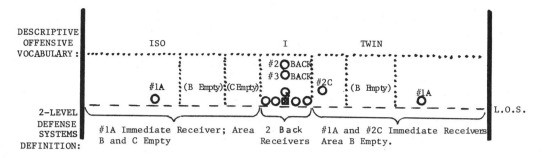

DESCRIPTIVE
OFFENSIVE
VOCABULARY :

ISO   I   TWIN

2-LEVEL
DEFENSE
SYSTEMS
DEFINITION:

L.O.S.

#1A Immediate Receiver; Area 2 Back   #1A and #2C Immediate Receivers
B and C Empty   Receivers Area B Empty.

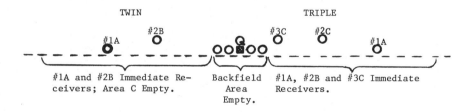

ISO   ACE   TRIPLE

#1A Immediate Receiver; Area 1 Back   #1A, #2B and #3C Immediate
B and C Empty.   Receiver. Receivers.

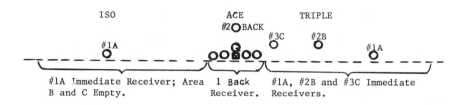

TWIN   TRIPLE

#1A and #2B Immediate Re-   Backfield #1A, #2B and #3C Immediate
ceivers; Area C Empty.   Area   Receivers.
                                Empty.

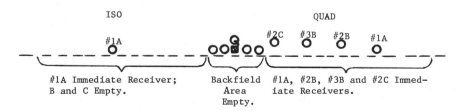

ISO   QUAD

#1A Immediate Receiver;   Backfield #1A, #2B, #3B and #2C Immed-
B and C Empty.   Area   iate Receivers.
                                  Empty.

Figure 41 Examples of offensive formations defined according to the positioning of the five mobile personnel *by offensive areas*: by definition, only *one* of
these personnel may be positioned in an A or C area, while *one or more* B and
backfield area personnel may be defined; also mobile personnel positioned in
an A, B, or C Area are termed *immediate receiver(s)*.

TWO (OR MORE) RECEIVERS POSITIONED IN CLOSE PROXIMITY

STACKED RECEIVERS

AN IMMEDIATE RECEIVER IN EARLY-MOTION AT THE SNAP

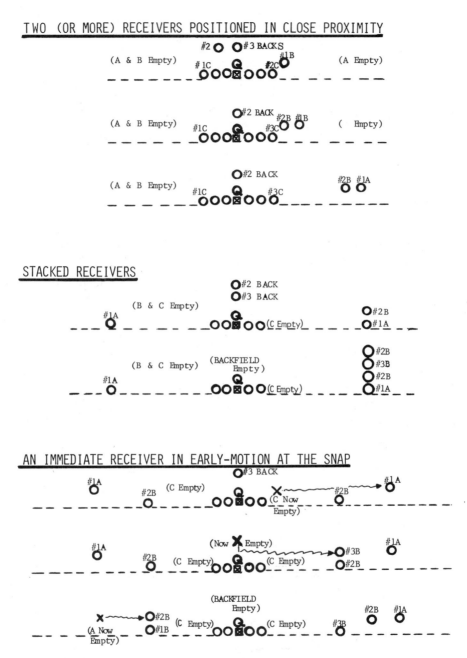

Figure 42 Defining less conventional offensive formations: only *one* A and one C area receiver, may be defined *by rule;* therefore, any additional immediate receiver(s) in an offensive formation must be defined as B area receiver(s).

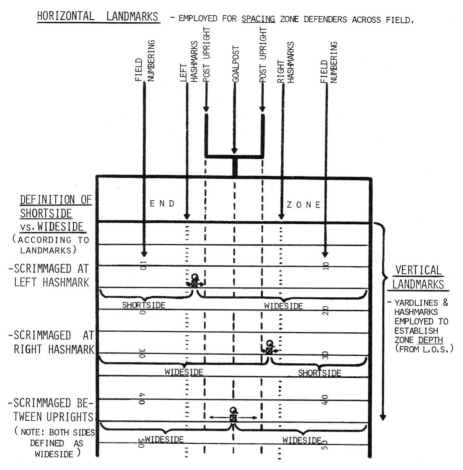

Figure 43 The horizontal and vertical landmarks for defining the football field; establishment of wideside vs. shortside of field according to the horizontal landmarks.

VERTICAL LANDMARKS: the yardstripes marked across the field at five-yard intervals and the hashmarks between that mark one-yard distances. These vertical markings indicate the approximate *depth* from the line of scrimmage to which each zone defender initially must sprint (fig. 43, right hand side).

HORIZONTAL LANDMARKS: five discrete markings are employed as horizontal coordinates for *spreading* the zone defenders equidistant across the width of the field (fig. 43, top), the numberings on the yardstripes, the hashmarks labelled the entire length of the field, and the (imaginary) line down the middle of the field, between the goalposts.

In addition, before every play the point of scrimmage between the hashmarks defines both the *wideside* of the field and the *shortside* (fig. 43, left-hand margin). If the football will be scrimmaged by the offense within three yards of either hashmark, then to the far sideline is defined as the wideside of the field, to the near sideline the shortside. If, however, the football will be scrimmaged *between* the goalposts, *by definition* both sides of the field are defined as wideside (fig. 43, lower portion). Therefore, the precise coordinates of each underneath zone are defined according to the point of scrimmage, wideside or shortside.

Figure 44 Definition of underneath hook and flat zones according to the field's landmarks; defender's target in each zone (▨) is determined by the wideside vs. shortside definition. (*shortside square is only defined to the side of the offensive formation *away from* a triple or quad and covered exclusively by a First Level end).

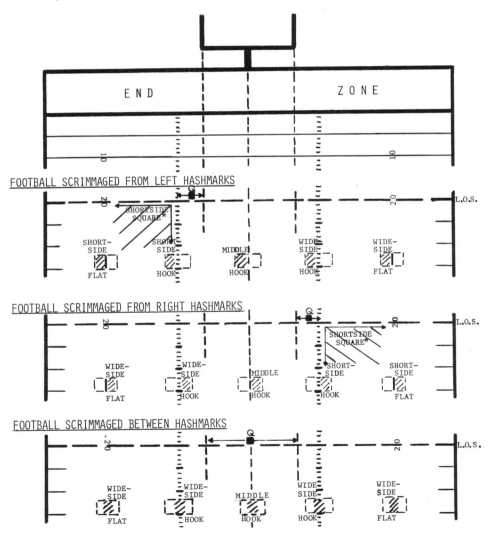

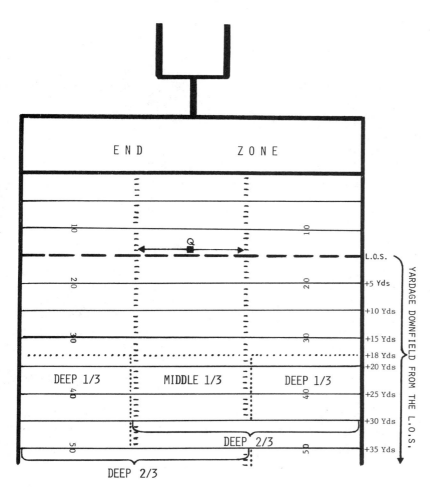

Figure 45 Definition of deep zones according to the field's landmarks: deep zones begin at +18 yards (from the line of scrimmage), extend as deep as the deepest pass receiver in zone, and are *never* altered (wideside vs. shortside influences only the underneath zones).

Defining the Underneath Zones. In figure 44, the *underneath* zones are identified according to specific landmarks. Vertical coordinates are set at approximately twelve to fifteen yards depth from the line of scrimmage, with the precise depth being adjusted according to the defensive game plan. Therefore, the two outside zones at the numbers are called *flats*, while the three interior zones are all identified as *hooks*, specifically the shortside-, middle-, and wideside-hook.[1] Note also that a shortside-hook is *only* defined when the football is scrimmaged near a hashmark (fig. 43, lower portion). Lastly, in the upper two diagrams in figure 44 note that a large area called *shortside square* is bounded horizontally by the line of scrimmage and vertically by the shortside hashmarks. However, this is not a zone in the traditional sense: first, the shortside square is manned only by the First Level end on the shortside; second, it only becomes operable in specific situations in covers-A -B or -C (see coverage section following).

Defining the Deep Zones. In figure 45, the perimeters of the deep zones are identified, also according to the field's landmarks, but these zones are unaffected by the positioning of the football between the hashmarks prior to the snap. The deep zones begin at a vertical depth of eighteen yards from the line of scrimmage, and when three deep zones will be manned the two outside zones, called *Deep 1/3*, begin immediately outside of each hashmark, the *Middle 1/3* between the hashmarks. On the other hand, when only two defenders are assigned deep coverage (i.e., the deep safety plus one Second Level defender), the Second Level defender *still drops off* to his assigned deep 1/3, however the safety adjusts his sprint forward in the direction of the *far* hashmarks, to his *deep 2/3* responsibility (fig. 45, lower portion).

PASS COVERAGES: MAX AND COVERS

While several of the mechanisms described in this section will be familiar to coaches, the individual coverages and, more importantly, their tactical implementation in the game situation are intended to provide a departure from the defensive thinking of the present time. However, this coverage system should not be viewed as a cavalier approach solving the problems of pass defense, for it is founded upon sound defensive principles—and it works! Unique characteristics of the system include:

- in max coverage receivers are allowed to get slightly deeper and behind pass defenders;
- all of the *traditional* zones are not occupied, but it is the deep zones that are sparsely filled, with the underneath zones *saturated* only in specific areas of the field, according to the offensive formation;
- much more combination coverage (i.e., max and zone within the same coverage) is employed;
- the system itself is less regimented, more automated.

Max Coverages

On passing plays, *max (basic)* best personifies the essential character of the 2-level Defense, an aggressive pass coverage in all phases, pass rush, receiver coverage, and end line enforcement. Yet the system is extremely simple for the defensive personnel to execute: each Second Level defender maxes his mirrored receiver, the deep safety patrols the end line, while the First Level swarms the quarterback. Universal rules govern each player's coverage responsibility in max; these are defined in table 5, and applications are illustrated in figure 46. Only two additional max coverages are included in the system each assigning double-coverage to designated offensive personnel. Since max coverage *never* necessitates any change in the Second Level's universal rules, it is the deep safety and the First Level ends who must effectuate any max-double; thus, up to three offensive receivers may be doubled (fig. 47). Each

Table 5. Summary of max pass coverage responsibilities: universal personnel rules.

MAX COVERAGES	DEFENSIVE PERSONNEL				
	SECOND LEVEL			DEEP	FIRST LEVEL
	LOU & ROSE	STRONG & BANDIT	GAEL	SAFETY	ENDS
"MAX" (BASIC)	= MAX # 1	= MAX # 2	= MAX # 3	= END-LINE COVERAGE	= 'CRASH'
"MAX/ DOUBLE" (IMMEDIATE RECEIVER SPECIFIED; USUALLY BY A OR B AREA DESIGNATION)	SAME*	SAME*	SAME*	= MAX-DOUBLE (ON THE SPECIFIED RECEIVER)	SAME
"MAX/ TIGHT CUSHION"	SAME	SAME	SAME	= END-LINE COVERAGE	= MAX-DOUBLE ONLY IF AN IMMEDIATE RECEIVER IN HIS C AREA**

* Soft max technique (i.e., traditional man-to-man pass coverage) must be utilized against immediate receivers *unless* that receiver has been specified for *double coverage*; this technique alteration must be disguised or delayed as long as possible prior to the snap.

** Note: in max coverages only other exceptions to ends' universal crash rule occurs in conjunction with cushion and dog stunts.

double coverage can be executed with *absolute concealment* prior to the play, and again, universal rules direct the specific responsibilities of the safety and the ends (table 5). In a "*max-double . . .* " the deep safety is assigned to double a *specific immediate receiver*, usually a wide receiver positioned outside the core in an A or B area (fig. 47); his double-coverage begins approximately ten to twelve yards from the line of scrimmage, according to the direction that the (designated) receiver has been steered by the Second Level defender. At the snap the deep safety must sprint towards this receiver, thereby eliminating his end line coverage, and thus a "max−double" call in the defensive huddle alerts Second Level personnel that unless it is their receiver being double-covered they must execute traditional man-to-man pass coverage (termed *max soft*), eliminating deep pass routes first. Appositely, a *max-tight cushion* has proven the superior mechanism for double coverage against tight ends and slotbacks: at the snap the jamming by the max defenders (the mirroring Second Level personnel and a First Level end) on these C receivers provides a safeguard should the ensuing play turn out *not* to be a pass but an off-tackle run or sweep. Also, in defending a C area receiver by means of tight cushion the deep safety's end-line coverage remains in force.

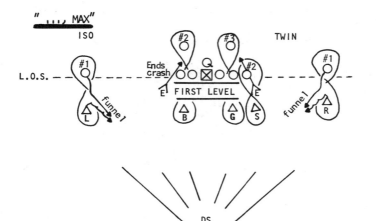

- No early-motion by mobile offensive personnel.
- Second Level defenders max their mirrored offensive personnel.

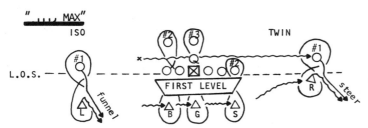

- Slotback jet-actions to twin on defensive right.
- Second Level remirrors accordingly; then, maxes <u>new</u> offensive personnel at the snap.

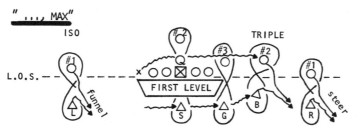

- Tight End jet-actions to triple formation on defensive right; Strong <u>usually</u> mirrors to the Tight End's side of the offense; thus, he ends up mirroring the Fullback (now #2) in this new formation.
- Second Level remirrors and maxes accordingly.

Figure 46 Max coverage: each Second Level defender maxes his mirrored mobile personnel; funnel and steer techniques used to assist deep safety in his end-line converage; the First Level attack and safety's end line (shown only in the upper diagram) are identical in max (basic).

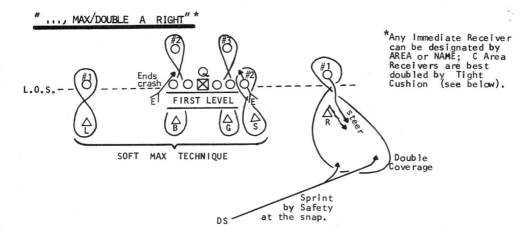

" ..., MAX/DOUBLE A RIGHT" *

*Any Immediate Receiver can be designated by AREA or NAME; C Area Receivers are best doubled by Tight Cushion (see below).

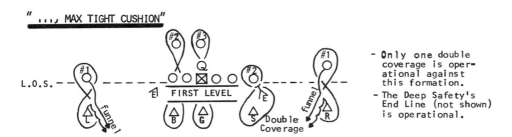

" ..., MAX TIGHT CUSHION"

- Only one double coverage is operational against this formation.
- The Deep Safety's End Line (not shown) is operational.

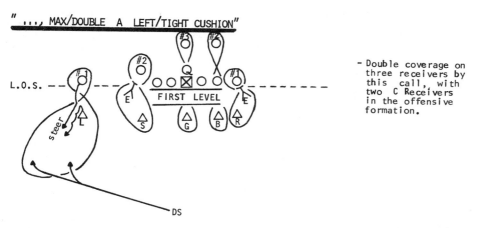

" ..., MAX/DOUBLE A LEFT/TIGHT CUSHION"

- Double coverage on three receivers by this call, with two C Receivers in the offensive formation.

Figure 47 Pass coverages where specific receiver(s) are double-covered, max/double (*receiver designated*) and max/tight cushion; note concealment before the snap of each coverage.

Cover Combinations

Since the early seventies the utilization of zone coverage as the primary defense against the pass has steadily eroded. As argued in chapter 1, however, its decline has *not* resulted from any conceptual defects in the zone mechanism. Employing the three-level model of defense, only three or four personnel are available for pass rush. To increase this number by blitzing weakens the model's effectiveness against the run while necessitating greater man-to-man pass coverage. Zone coverage in the 2-level model cannot remedy this dilemma; in fact, the defense's cover mechanisms are not intended as its primary *defense* against the pass (and neither is max coverage, for that matter). But, this system of zone coverage does offer viable alternatives.

- Maximal pressure against the quarterback is maintained as the primary (and only *absolute*) mechanism of pass defense when zone coverage is implemented.
- Saturation coverage is implemented only in the areas where a majority of the potential pass receivers are positioned.

Table 6. Summary of cover combinations: universal personnel rules.

COVERAGE VERIFIED[*] AT LINE-OF SCRIMMAGE	SECOND LEVEL PERSONNEL				
	LOU & ROSE		BANDIT & STRONG		GAEL
	TO SHORTSIDE	TO WIDESIDE	TO SHORTSIDE	TO WIDESIDE	
" COVER "	= DEEP 1/3	SAME	= SHORTSIDE HOOK[**]	= WIDESIDE HOOK	= MIDDLE HOOK
" COVER - A "	= REVERT TO "MAX"	SAME	= MIDDLE HOOK	= WIDESIDE FLAT	= WIDESIDE HOOK
- B "	SAME	= WIDESIDE FLAT	SAME	= DEEP 1/3	SAME
- C "	SAME	SAME	SAME	= WIDESIDE HOOK	= DEEP 1/3

[*] Only triple or quad immediate receivers wideside (visual) *verifies* Cover-A, -B, or -C; and when -A, -B, or -C is *not* verified, defenders revert to their universal cover rule. (Exception: any defenders isolated on an immediate receiver to the wideside—see text.)

[**] Exception: if mirroring a No. 2 receiver to the shortside = *shortside flat* (i.e. defender drops *directly* back into the flat, while the shortside end drops to hook—see corresponding footnote, table 6A).

- Built-in combination mechanisms permit max coverage to be implemented against any immediate receiver *isolated to one side* of the offensive formation (for example, a No. 1A receiver completely isolated near a sideline).
- Implementation of each mechanism is verified *visually* prior to the snap.
- For the most part, zone deployments are well concealed prior to the snap.

On the other hand, neither the explanation nor personnel rules governing cover are as straightforward as those of max coverage. Up to three rules for individual coverage personnel have been formulated in order for the system to operate (see tables 6 and 6A).

Cover. While there are always fine adjustments to be made, this *basic* zone coverage is governed by invariable rules: three defenders locate in the deep areas, Lou and Rose in the outside deep $1/3$, safety in the middle $1/3$, with four (of the five)

Table 6A. Summary of cover combinations: universal personnel rules (continued).

COVERAGE VERIFIED AT LINE-OF SCRIMMAGE	DEEP SAFETY	FIRST LEVEL ENDS	
		TO SHORTSIDE[*]	TO WIDESIDE
" COVER "	= MIDDLE 1/3	= SHORTSIDE FLAT[**]	= CRASH
" COVER - A "	= DEEP 2/3	= SHORTSIDE SQUARE	SAME
- B "	SAME	SAME	SAME
- C "	SAME	SAME	SAME

[*] Against a quarterback sprintout, end is *relieved* of *all* cover responsibilities; crash immediately.

[**] Exception: if a No. 2 immediate receiver locates outside the end (in Area B to the shortside) = shortside hook (i. e., end drops back directly into hook while the Second Level defender mirroring No. 2 drops into the flat—see footnote, table 6.).

underneath zones covered, that is, the wideside flat remains unoccupied (fig. 48). In cover the only coverage *decision* to be made involves the First Level end located to the *shortside* of the field; as a first principle, however, note that his crash responsibilities take priority over *any* cover assignment (i.e., the end is *automatically* relieved of all zone coverage responsibility and must crash):

- whenever the end (visually) defines *his field location to be wideside*;
- whenever a defensive end *must* align immediately inside of the offensive end, in tight;
- after the snap, anytime an end identifies a quarterback sprintout against his side of the defense, he must crash, contain and pressure the quarterback *immediately*.

Otherwise, in cover the end located on the shortside is assigned that flat. The only exception to this universal rule occurs when a *No. 2 mobile offensive personnel is located in the B area* well outside of the defensive end: against this offensive formation the Second Level defender mirroring the No. 2 immediate receiver (Bandit or Strong) is located in a more advantageous position to drop directly back into the shortside flat at the snap, and therefore the end assumes responsibility for shortside hook.

Cover-A, -B, or -C. By comparison, when either A, B, or C is verbalized following "cover" in the defensive huddle call, *major options* for several (but not all) of the defensive personnel are possible; the concept is explained in figure 49:

- First, will the A, B, or C mechanism called even be implemented? For this option is verified (visually) *only by the presence of triple (or quad) receivers to the wideside* of the offensive formation.
- Or will the A, B or C call simply be ignored? Without a triple formation wideside, coverage personnel simply revert to their universal cover rule.
- Finally, a max option is built into every cover-A, -B, and -C call: any Second Level personnel *isolated* to one side of the offensive formation mirroring an isolated receiver employs max coverage against his receiver (this adjustment eliminates the utilization, and often the wastage, of additional zone personnel).

Note particularly in figure 49, that if the offense threatens by positioning a majority of its receivers (i.e., a triple or quad) to the wideside,[2] the A, B, or C mechanism called is implemented; against an isolated No. 1A receiver *to the shortside*, however, max is employed. Conversely, if the offense does *not* assume a triple formation, the A, B, or C mechanism cannot be verified. Thus, all coverage personnel revert to "cover" (i.e., simply disregard the A, B, or C called), with one exception: in this instance, any Second Level defender isolated *to the wideside* mirroring an isolated receiver reverts to max coverage.

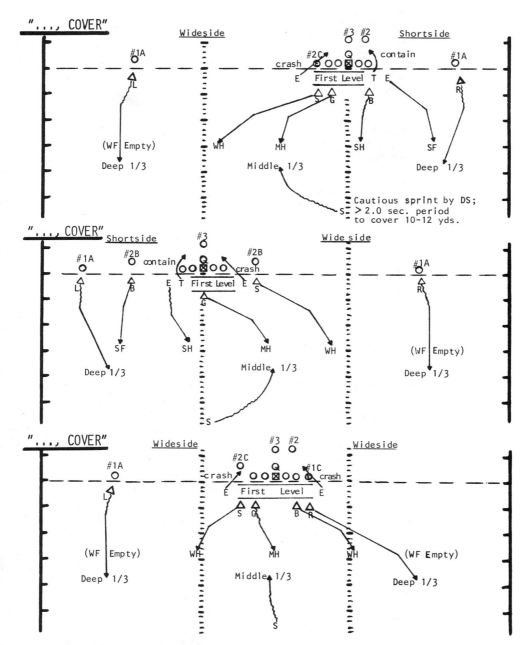

Figure 48 Cover pass coverage: the basic zone mechanism in the 2-level defense, spacing personnel across the field according to their target zones. (Key: shortside (S); wideside (W); middle (M); hook (H); flat (F).)

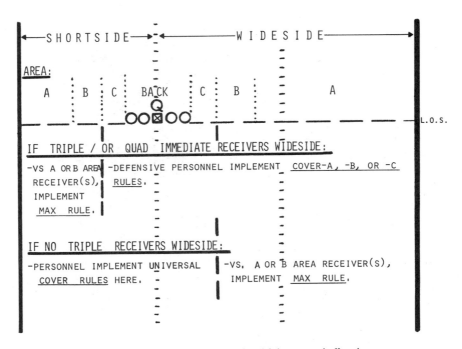

Figure 49 Verification of cover-A, -B, or -C: only a triple or quad offensive formation *to the wideside* verifies the implementation of cover-A, -B, -C (when called in the defensive huddle).

IMPLEMENTATION OF COVER-C (FIG. 50). Cover-C is the zone option most easily explained, particularly to describe Gael's *mental deductions* as to his choice of zone coverage (although the *mechanism* is identical for the A and B options). First, cover-C calls Gael, and *no other Second Level* personnel; therefore, when cover-C is called, Gael must select ONE of two coverage options, and his first option is critical to the safety of the entire defense, for it involves the wideside deep 1/3:

1. if the C option is implemented, Gael must *immediately* cover the wideside deep 1/3;
2. if the C option is not to be implemented, Gael will revert to his universal cover rule, (i.e., middle-hook responsibility, see table 6).

Second, a triple or quad receiver formation is required to *verify* the implementation of cover-C. Thus, *according to his mirroring* Gael must deduce the offensive formation, he cannot be peering over the entire offense moments before the snap to make this determination. Therefore:

- anytime Gael is mirroring an offensive backfielder, he immediately concludes there *cannot be a triple (or quad)*;

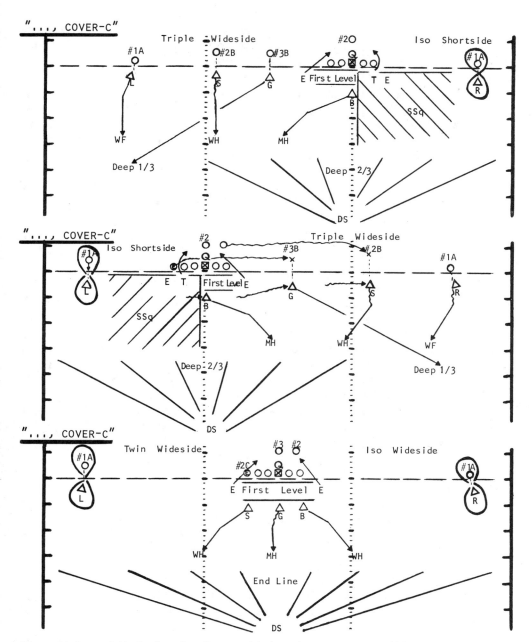

Figure 50 Cover-C Mechanism: the offense's triple formation (see upper & middle diagrams) verify Gael's wideside deep 1/3 coverage; without triple or quad receivers, the - C mechanism is simply ignored, "cover" implemented, except where personnel rule(s) dictate otherwise (see lower diagram adjustments by Lou, Rose, safety).

- however, the instant Gael mirrors an immediate receiver *wideside* (i.e., his No. 3 mobile player is positioned in the B or C area wideside) at the snap Gael implements cover-C, sprinting to deep $1/3$ wideside because the receiver formation *must be* a triple.

IMPLEMENTATION OF COVER-B (FIG. 51). Cover-B calls either Strong or Bandit, whichever of these defenders is mirroring his mobile offensive personnel *to the wideside*, and initiates a parallel deductive process: now this defender must decide whether to implement (wideside) deep $1/3$ coverage at the snap. Therefore, like Gael in cover-C, he must be able to quickly identify a triple *according to his mirroring*:

- in the first instance, to implement cover-B the wideside Strong or Bandit *must be mirroring his No. 2 in area B*, otherwise a triple is not possible;
- in cover-B, when this defender identifies his mirror as No. 2B, he merely locates No. 3 (i.e., the closest mobile offensive personnel to his inside):

a. if this player is an immediate receiver, the formation is a triple;
b. if this player is a backfielder, the offensive formation *cannot* include triple receivers.

IMPLEMENTATION OF COVER-A (FIG. 52). Verification of cover-A can prove more troublesome for Lou or Rose, whichever of these personnel is located *wideside*. In cover-A it is this defender who must decide whether to cover deep $1/3$ at the snap and, again, only triple (or quad) receivers to the wideside verify this action. Therefore, mirroring his No. 1A immediate receiver, Lou or Rose must discern the presence of both No. 2B and No. 3C immediate receivers to the wideside before implementing his A option. And occasionally, due to an offense's early-motion pattern, visual identification of a triple from the far sideline can prove disconcerting. (Note: this is one of the few instances where back-up *verbal* communication shouted by an adjacent Second Level defender may occasionally be required in implementing a *systems* decision.) Finally, whenever "Cover-A, B or C" is called, both Lou and Rose, whether wideside *or* shortside, *always must determine the offense's formation*: by rule, ONE of these personnel will execute zone coverage, while the OTHER must revert to max (review fig. 49, then examine figures 50-52 closely). This synchronization automates the underlying mechanism of the system's coverage combinations:

- *optimization of zone coverage* only in areas of the field where a majority of the potential pass receivers locate, as opposed to saturation coverage over the *entire* football field,
- thus, the First Level's pass rush capability is sustained even though zone coverage has been implemented.

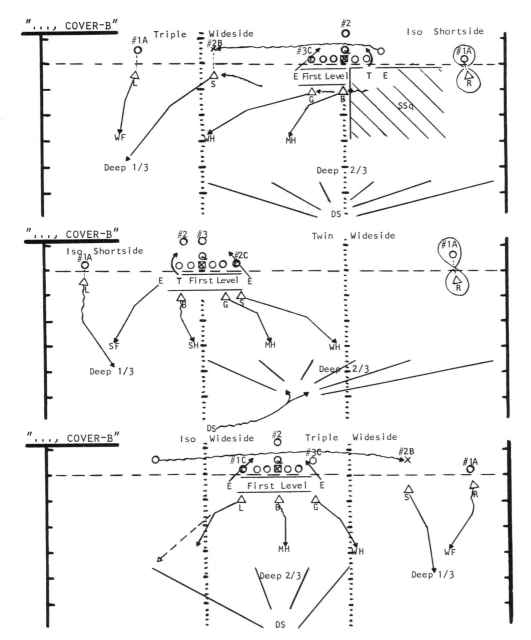

Figure 51 Cover-B Mechanism: the offense's triple formation (see upper & lower diagrams) verifies strong's (and on occasion Bandit's) wideside Deep $1/3$ coverage, the safety's Deep $2/3$ area, and the implementation *by rule* of zone coverage by other personnel; without triple or quad, the -B mechanism is ignored, "cover" implemented, except where rules dictate otherwise (see middle diagram).

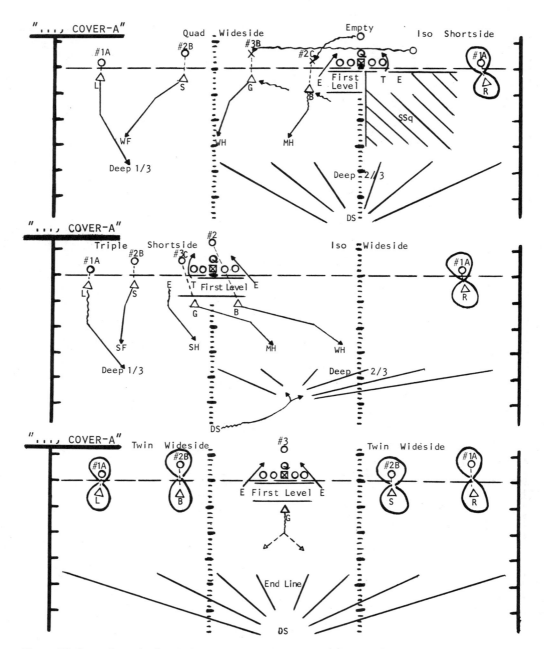

Figure 52 Cover-A mechanism: only an offensive triple or quad (see upper diagram) formation to the wideside verifies Cover-A implementation; a triple formation to the shortside (see middle diagram) does not; in the lower diagram, with no shortside defined, against this formation Cover-A essentially reverts *by rule* to "max," with the safety enforcing his endline.

By this mechanism, *isolated immediate receivers are max'd automatically.* In fact, if the point of scrimmage is defined as the middle of the field, *by rule* isolated No. 1A receivers and (possibly) wide No. 2B to *both* sides of the field would be max'd (compare the diagrams at the bottom of fig. 50-52).

> ### *Underneath Coverage with the -A/-B/-C Mechanism (fig. 53).*

When cover-A, -B, or -C is implemented against a triple formation, it should be appreciated that four Second Level personnel are now available to defend the three underneath zones to the wideside with the fourth, the *called* defender, sprinting to deep $1/3$ (fig. 53, top portion). On the other hand, if the A, B, or C mechanism is *not* verified (i.e., only iso or twin receiver(s) have positioned wideside), reverting to "cover" effectuates an equivalent mechanism *away from* the wideside (that is, to the shortside) where the majority of the potential receivers are now located. Inspecting figure 53 (top portion) note that the No. 1A immediate receiver to the shortside is max'd *by rule*. Therefore, implementing cover-A, -B, or -C, only the shortside No. 2 mobile offensive personnel (labelled the fullback [F] in fig. 53) can disrupt the precarious balance between a maximized pass rush and the optimized zone coverage. The defensive contingency against possible actions by this No. 2 is referred to as shortside square[3] and executed by the shortside defensive end.[4] This No. 2 personnel may initiate *one* of two basic actions (fig. 53, lower portion):

- movement *towards the wideside* away from the shortside end, or
- *towards the shortside*, directly at him.

Appreciate that if No. 2, by prealignment or through early-motion prior to the snap, locates as an immediate receiver either wideside (forming a quad wideside) *or* to the shortside (forming a twin shortside), either action is interpreted by the shortside end as *one* of these movements. Essentially, the shortside end should react *in the identical direction* to which this No. 2 offensive player moves when implementing the shortside square mechanism, specifically:

- *Movement wideside* by this mobile player (at the snap or prior to the play) = shortside end crash aggressively;
- *Movement shortside* = option to crash; note in figure 53 (lower portion) the specific instances when the shortside end *must* crash (i.e., to contain quarterback sprintout) *versus* pass defend on the shortside.

Finally, since it is such a large area, the end is permitted to roam in his shortside square, adjusting his actions according to the game plan and/or particular pass patterns. For example, if an offense is experiencing success passing to the isolated shortside (No. 1A) receiver or to wideside immediate receivers crossing to the shortside underneath, the end's coverage can be adjusted accordingly.

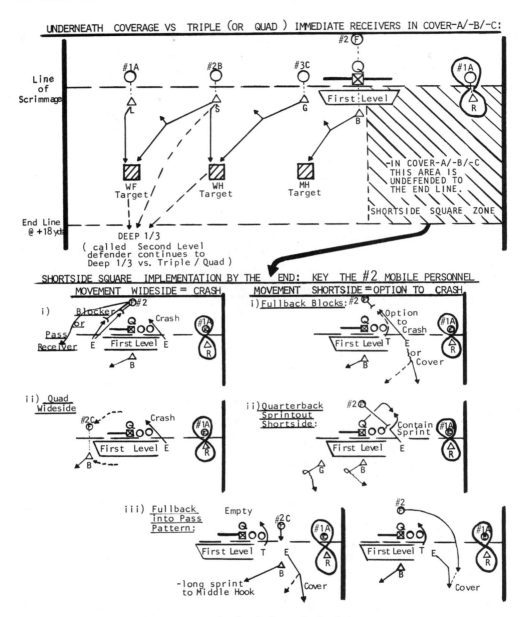

Figure 53 The underneath coverage mechanism in Cover-A, -B, -C: four defenders available to cover three underneath on the wideside; shortside square coverage by the First Level end on the shortside.

Max/Two-Deep and Cover/Two-Deep

To this point in the text, little mention of a second deep safety (or other personnel substitutions) within the present 2-level model has been made. This omission by the authors was both judicious and purposeful. Comprehension of this defense, and of its basic concepts and unique mechanisms is contingent upon the model's structure: two subunits (termed Levels) constituted in such a manner that each Level is *minimally dependent upon* the other. In order for the reader to best appreciate the internal operations and simplicity of the coverage system, five defensive personnel were allocated per Level, but this constituency is by no means a prerequisite. In fact, at the present time several model variations operate very effectively.[5]

- Every goal line defense is a two-level model (12, 13).
- Often, when additional deepbacks are substituted for linebackers in the three-level defensive model, various characteristics of the two-level model are manifested: an augmented pass rush, shadowing of receivers along the line of scrimmage, bump-and-run pass coverage, deepback(s) positioned up to twenty yards from the line of scrimmage.
- During the 1984 and '85 seasons the Chicago Bears popularized their 4-6 (+ free safety) two-level defensive model which dominated almost every statistical category in the National Football League.

Past this juncture in the text, the most imperative thing for the reader to understand about the present system relates to the *lack of effect* that any personnel substitution(s) have on the operation of the system per se. A second deep safety, specific goal-line adaptations, or suggested game-plan adjustments (see part IV) *never* alter the working model—neither the concept, the defensive mechanisms, nor the universal rules governing its operation. On the other hand, while the 5-5 (+ deep safety) deployment provides *optimal* flexibility for a two-level defensive model, appreciate that personnel substitutions impose specific restrictions upon the *system's* flexibility. For example, when a second deep safety is inserted into this defense:

1. A First Level tackle is substituted, in turn reducing the number of viable alignments for the First Level;
2. Specific delimitations are imposed upon the system itself for, obviously, positioning a second defender twenty-eight yards from the line of scrimmage is *not* a run defense adjustment.

First Level Alignments: Restrictions in Two-Deep. When a second deep safety is required for pass coverage, one of the defensive tackles is substituted, the specific substitution depending upon the game plan and the forthcoming defensive call (fig. 54).

SUBSTITUTION FOR LEFT DEFENSIVE TACKLE:

LINK   ALIGNMENTS

4-Link

RIP   ALIGNMENTS

(NO 4-RIP ALIGNMENT CALL:
ALIGNMENT NOT STRUCTURALLY VIABLE)

5-Link

5-Rip

SUBSTITUTION FOR RIGHT DEFENSIVE TACKLE:

LINK   ALIGNMENTS

(NO 4-RIP ALIGNMENT CALL:
ALIGNMENT NOT STRUCTURALLY VIABLE)

RIP   ALIGNMENTS

4-Rip

5-Link

5-Rip

AVOID SUBSTITUTION FOR NOSE:

-A new Alignment Call (a "44") provides the only viable
alignment for the personnel remaining in the First Level...

... and, all 4-Link and -Rip Alignments (above) achieve this identical
First Level alignment.

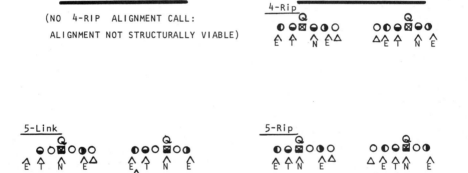

Figure 54 First Level alignments in ".../two-deep:" when a *second* deep safety
is substituted for *one* of the defensive tackles, viable First Level alignments restricted to 4- and 5-Alignment calls.

Appreciate that the nose should *not* be substituted in lieu of a tackle, for this would reduce the number of viable First Level alignments to *one*,—a 44-alignment—not even in the system (see diagram at bottom of fig. 54). A First Level end should not be substituted, for this would greatly weaken the defense's capability against an outside running play to that side, and substitution for *any* Second Level position would invalidate much of the Second Level's system of rules. By substituting for a defensive tackle, however, only *minor* accommodations are necessitated in the First Level.

1. Essentially, the defensive coordinator is limited to 4- and 5-alignment calls: both 5-link and 5-Rip are viable alignments with either defensive tackle substituted; however, 4-link is the only possible 4-alignment with the *left* tackle removed, and 4-rip with the *right* tackle substituted (fig. 54).

2. One minor rule adjustment must be implemented by the defensive end whose *adjacent* tackle was removed to accommodate two-deep coverage: he simply aligns tight (i.e., this end need not listen for a Link or Rip indicator as he would normally in 4- and 5-alignment calls). Note, though, that this minor adjustment does *not* compromise the end's universal rules in any way, particularly in covers: aligned tight, *by rule* he crashes, aligned loose to the shortside and possible only with specific 5-alignments (fig. 54), he implements either his universal cover or shortside square rule.

Max/Two-Deep: Increased Double-Coverage. In max coverage, the additional deep safety should be utilized primarily for double-coverage (fig. 55), not merely as an added *safety precaution* in max (basic); *one* deep safety can accomplish this latter function.

END LINE ENFORCEMENT BY ONE SAFETY, DOUBLE-COVERAGE BY THE OTHER. This combination is an excellent mechanism to employ against an offense which persists in isolating its best receiver to the wideside on either Lou or Rose, while maintaining a power-running formation in the core (see upper diagram, fig. 55). A variation of this combination also is illustrated in the lower diagram in this figure; in this instance the offense, after spreading the Second Level across the field, persists in isolating a back receiver against a specific Second Level defender.

BOTH SAFETIES INVOLVED IN MAX DOUBLE-COVERAGE. This mechanism may also be employed to double-cover both No. 1A receivers. A variation of this is illustrated in the middle diagram in figure 55, when an offense positions both its wide receivers to the same side; from their deep positioning at the hashmarks, the safeties experience little problem sprinting forward at the snap to *any location on the field* to implement their double-coverage.

One caution, however; when two deep safeties are present in the defense, the temptation will be for these personnel to prealign closer than twenty-eight yards deep;

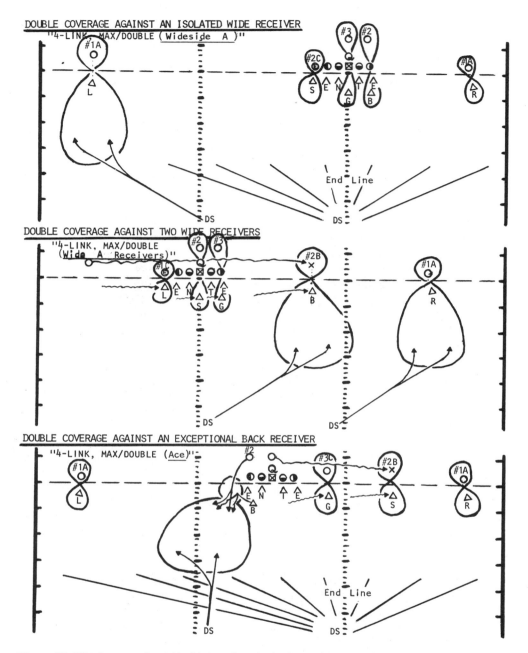

Figure 55 Effectiveness of max/double/two-deep for implementing a *specific* double coverage in conjunction with max (basic) (upper & lower diagrams), or for double coverage on *two* specific receivers (middle diagram). Note: two-deep cannot be read prior to the snap; requires no change in universal max rules. (The left defensive tackle has been substituted in examples.)

this is both imprudent and unnecessary. First, their *sprint* forward for double-coverage must only be slowed, the closer they position to the line of scrimmage. Second, one safety must still enforce the end line to *both* sides of the field, but if he prealigns closer than twenty-eight yards deep, end line enforcement to the far sideline becomes untenable. Third, with the decreased pass rush in max/two-deep (only four First Level personnel), the defense is further jeopardized and any preinversion by one safety (the one anticipating double-coverage) without the other permits the offense to read the mechanism.

Cover/Two-Deep: Increased Saturation Coverage. Whenever it chooses, an offense can protect its quarterback! Recognizing this offensive intention, the coordinator's most prudent response is to implement saturation zone coverage, for eight offensive blockers can stymie the First Level's pass rush, and without pressure most quarterbacks will dissect *any* man-to-man pass defense. Two-deep in conjunction with the system's cover mechanisms provides a range of zones equivalent to coverages presently available in most three-level defenses (14, 15): a three or four man pass rush, up to six underneath zones occupied, with the possibility of four-deep coverage (fig. 56). With two safeties in the defense, any Second Level player assigned deep 1/3 by the call now has an *option*: whether to continue dropping deep into this coverage area. In turn, coverage personnel *immediately* underneath these defender(s) may break off their zone drop as well, in effect creating three strata of zone coverage in that third of the field. Also note in figure 56 that both safeties (still) are assigned deep 2/3 coverage, that no alterations in their universal rules are necessitated; therefore, if one safety must commit to the deep 1/3 to his side of the field *early* in a pass play, the middle 1/3 remains covered.

Finally, in figure 57 three specific examples of two-deep coverage are illustrated, interchanging max-double (upper diagram) with cover (middle and lower diagrams) against an *identical* offensive formation and early-motion pattern. Comparing these examples, note the major shifts in the defense's pass coverage, from double-coverage against three immediate receivers (upper diagram), to zone saturation across the wideside of the field (bottom diagram). Particularly note the complementary alignment calls for the First Level, how in each instance the substitution of a *specific* defensive tackle involved tactical decisions. For example, in the middle diagram, by removing the wideside (left) tackle, the defensive coordinator created two alignment options in conjunction with cover:

1. "5-rip, cover" would have positioned the shortside end loose resulting in a six-under zone; against a twin shortside, this would have proven a prudent call.
2. However, the coordinator called "4-link," opting for a four-man rush, expecting only the iso shortside.
3. Compare this with the lower diagram in figure 57: in this instance the coordinator's "5-rip" call in conjunction with "cover-B" was intended to defend the *expected* triple to the wideside, thus, the 5-rip alignment positioned the shortside end for shortside square coverage.

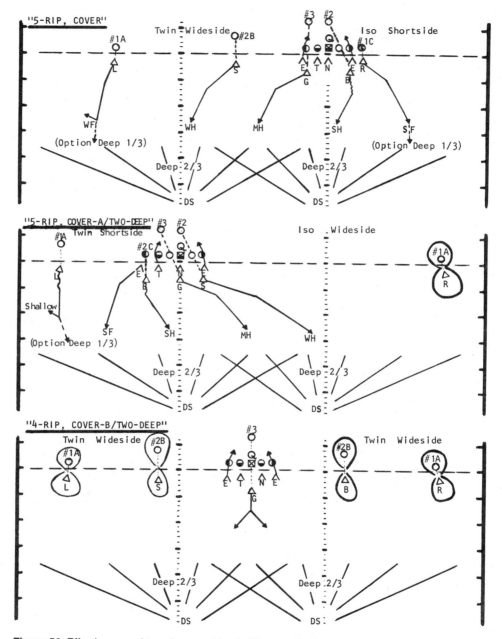

Figure 56 Effectiveness of two-deep combined with covers for saturating zones underneath, according to the offense's formation, whether call is verified or not; note in lower diagram, the coverage reverts essentially to max/two-deep. (The right defensive tackle has been substituted in examples.)

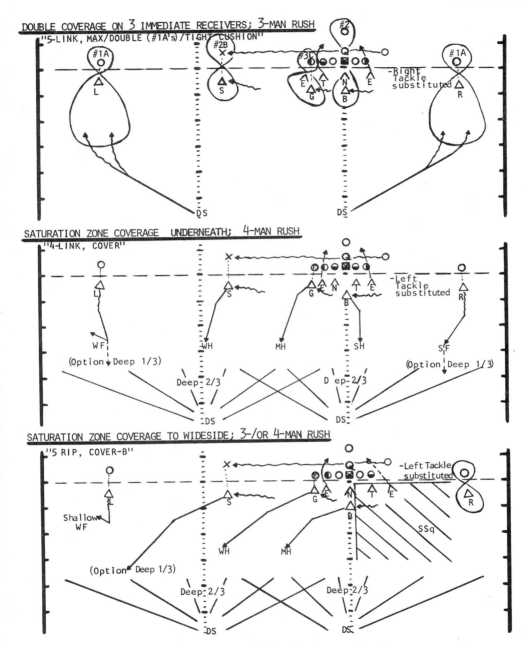

Figure 57 Substitution of second deep safety. Against this common offensive formation and early-motion, compare these coverage calls: I) that *cannot* be read prior to the snap; II) that are completely different pass defense mechanisms; III) that require *no* change in personnel's universal max, or cover rules.

PASS RUSH: CORE MECHANISMS

With the benefits of hindsight, erosion of the defense's pass rush would appear much simpler to analyze than to rectify. In the 1950s the offense's running attack, *not its passing*, remained the defense's primary concern. With the emergence of the linebacker unit, this *third level* simultaneously strengthened the defense's capability against the run and revolutionized its pass coverage against the *secondary* threat, the burgeoning pass offenses of that decade. Succeeding generations of coaches entrenched the three-level model. Thus, the pass arsenals of the eighties—possessing offensive weaponry and sophistication unimagined in the fifties—hold the advantage in both theory and practice. Pass rush provides an object lesson. Zone defense requires five (or six) defenders for underneath coverage, three (or two) must cover deep; therefore the defense's pass rush, by default, has been reduced to three linemen. But, three personnel cannot adequately pressure the quarterback, and in fact this was never intended *according to the original model*: the prototype of today's 34 Defense, the Okie 52, employed *five* defensive linemen (16). Utilizing four linemen in passing situations, the current compromise, assists only marginally compared to the coverage versatility that is lost, and the recent changes in offensive blocking technique and rules have placed the defense's pass rush at a further disadvantage. As a result, at the present time the three-level defense has been left one alternative: to *borrow* additional personnel from its other subunits at least once during every defensive series, although blitzing OR not blitzing—*either* scenario—often permits the offense to read the defensive coverage prior to the snap.

Against today's sophisticated blocking schemes, while technique and aggressiveness remain the physical requirements, at the systems level *leverage* has become the tactical prerequisite. The pass rush mechanisms incorporated into the 2-level Defense are a mixture of old and new (fig. 58), but it is their specific application within the system which manipulates the offense: *the threat of always five or more rushers, in combination with the pressures they may apply, forces the offense to make one of two basic choices.* With dropback passing (an elapse of $2^1/_2$ seconds before the quarterback's release of the football), at least two eligible receivers must be retained in the offensive core for blocking purposes; in turn, the number of receivers in the pass pattern is reduced to three, and this simplifies pass coverage for the defense. In addition, the *threat* of both First Level ends crashing discourages the use of moving pockets, semi-rollouts, and so on. On the other hand, if *more* than three receivers release, quick passing must be utilized (i.e., less than $1^1/_2$ seconds to release), for the quarterback will not have additional time in which to throw. Therefore, on defense, an offense's intentions may be read before the play. For example, the use of two offensive backfielders forewarn that most probably (if a pass is thrown) the receivers will run deeper pass routes, with the football being released two to three seconds after the snap; on the other hand, an ace (or empty) backfield indicates that receivers will run shallow routes, and for defending personnel to expect the football almost immediately.

FIVE-MAN PASS RUSH PRINCIPLE: I) MAN-BLOCKING SPREADS STATIC OFFENSIVE LINEMEN

II) ELIMINATES THEIR DOUBLE-TEAM BLOCKING

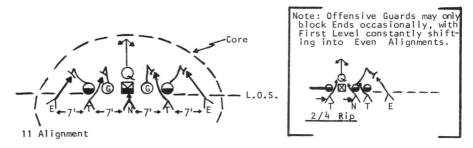

Note: Offensive Guards may only block Ends occasionally, with First Level constantly shifting into Even Alignments.

2/4 Rip

Core

L.O.S.

11 Alignment

OUTSIDE PASS RUSH PRINCIPLE: FORCES MOBILE PERSONNEL OUT OF THE PASS PATTERN TO BLOCK CRASHING DEFENSIVE ENDS

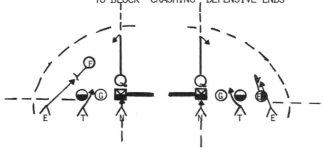

OVERLOAD PRINCIPLE: OUTNUMBERING THE OFFENSIVE BLOCKERS, BY FIRST LEVEL SHIFT TO 2- OR 4-ALIGNMENT JUST BEFORE SNAP, SECOND LEVEL STUNTING.

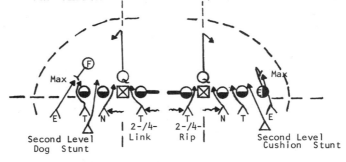

Second Level Dog Stunt

2-/4- Link

2-/4- Rip

Second Level Cushion Stunt

Figure 58 Reapplication of defensive leverage: principles.

5-Man Rush Principle

The substruction of the First Level prohibits defenders from aligning themselves further apart than seven feet.[6] First, this ensures that these personnel can always carry out their run defense responsibility, even in passing situations. Second, confronted by a First Level that is constantly shifting yet will stretch only to this finite limit, the offensive center-guard and guard-tackle gaps are forced to stabilize at two feet. Wider splits between these offensive linemen would reopen rushing lanes for the defense; narrower splits render man-on-man blocking impossible for no one would be positioned to intercept the crashing defensive ends (fig. 58, upper diagram). From this starting point, the inherent leverage of the First Level's pass rush develops. Numerically, it is difficult for the offense to double-team block the best pass rusher(s) without additional mobile personnel−eligible pass receiver(s)−remaining in the core. By contrast, the flexibility built into personnel alignment in the First Level permits the defense to muster its pass rush most advantageously: the nose against the offensive center or either of the guards; the defensive tackles against either the offensive guard or tackle to their side; the ends (aligned loose) against a physically smaller offensive backfielder. And First Level stunts increase the combinations that are possible employing these five pass rushers.

Outside Pass Rush Principle

With the exception of the 55-alignment, at least one defensive end always aligns loose, but, until the First Level shifts just prior to the snap, which end or whether *both* ends will align loose remains undeclared. Crashing from the extremity of the defensive core, and particularly with the adjacent defensive tackle (aligned open) confronting the offensive tackle, it becomes almost impossible for the interior guards or the offensive center to block the ends consistently. And this blocking pattern itself would open up sizable gaps in the wall of pass blockers. Thus, only an offensive backfielder or the tight end is positioned opportunely (fig. 58, middle diagram), and *this threat* further manipulates an offense. Again, the offense is obliged to retain additional mobile personnel in its core for blocking purposes; in turn, both the number and their location in the offensive formation permits the defense to read something of the offense's intention−dropback vs. quick passing. More strategically, the personnel that the offense withholds must be the physical equivalent of the defensive ends, or a mismatch will result to the advantage of the defense; therefore, except for the very talented backfielder, the versatility of these personnel in other phases of the offense may be restrictive (possessing reduced running speed because of their size, posing limited threat as pass receivers, etc).

Overload Principle

By the rules of the game the offense must remain stationary for one full second prior to the snap (and in practice most offense's remain pre-set for several seconds). On defense, however, movement is unrestricted. Therefore, once the offense has assumed its final set, it becomes a simple operation for the First Level to *overload* against one side of the offense, in a 2- or a 4-alignment. In combination with a Second Level stunt, all but the most proficient offensive blocking schemes will experience difficulty handling this overload, *even with the addition of mobile personnel* (fig. 58, lower diagram). On the other hand, it should be appreciated that this overload mechanism involves defensive risks and should not be utilized indiscriminately. If the offense executes a running play, not a pass, the defense's secondary mechanisms against the run are placed at a disadvantage. The reason for implementing this defensive mechanism in the first place is to take advantage of the additional mobile personnel blocking, increasing the defense's pass rush by a corresponding number of Second Level defenders. If, however, one of these offensive backfielders enters the pass pattern, in overload he immediately becomes the max responsibility of the defensive end to that side, and an end cannot provide as effective pass coverage as the Second Level.

Pass Block Mechanism

Increasingly, the quick pass has become difficult to defense because, as its proponents (17) claim, there is no consistent means by which to pressure the quarterback, even though his pass protection may be minimal. Accepting this as a given, the pass-block mechanism attacks the quick pass *inside the offensive core.* This simple mechanism is initiated by a tackle-end twist.[7] In passing situations, an ace backfield formation provides the most reliable indicator that a quick pass will be thrown. Therefore, when the quarterback executes only a three-step dropback action, then quickly sets up to throw, the defensive end is readied:

- he does not complete his twist inside *through* the offensive center-tackle area . . .
- rather, he penetrates as far as he can without contacting the offensive guard . . .
- anticipating the trajectory of the football, his leap is synchronized to the throwing motion of the quarterback . . .
- with arms extended he attempts to knock down the pass, in a motion similar to that of blocking a spike in volleyball.

To date in the development of the 2-level Defense, this mechanism has proven effective in game situations against smaller quarterbacks (small relative to the height of the ends), but not as the consummate technique for consistently blocking passes at the line of scrimmage. Rather, once one quick pass is deflected, the ends prove a considerable distraction to the quarterback, and in combination with coverage variations downfield the offensive completion ratio declines.

Notes

1. The wideside hook zone also is referred to as the *curl* (11). However, this term is not defined in this system, in order to simplify the rules by which zone coverage operates.

2. To the shortside of the field, the congestion resulting from triple or quad receivers makes these formations impractical in high school and college football, while maximizing the zoning potential of the defense.

3. Shortside Square is the terminology used throughout the text, for the technique is neither zone nor man coverage in any traditional sense.

4. Note: in the footnote in table 6A the shortside

end's *universal* rules require him to locate the No. 2 mobile offensive personnel whenever *any* cover is called.

5. Note: safety personnel may also be moved *closer* to the line of scrimmage, to free safety depth (see relevant sections in chapter 7).

6. By aligning *on* their offensive lineman, if First Level personnel would be split-out further than seven feet from each other, defenders must align shading the lineman's inside shoulder (see chapter 6).

7. Note: only from the 11-alignment may a *double* T.E.T. be executed.

References

1. JERRY SANDUSKY, *Developing Linebackers the Penn State Way* (West Point, N.Y.: Leisure Press, 1981), pp. 15-23.

2. Ibid., pp. 62-64.

3. STEVE WEIBERG, "Defenses haven't got a chance against Mississippi Valley's no-huddle offense." *U.S.A. Today*, October 19, 1984, p. 8C.

4. S. E. SULLINS, *Complete Book of Multiple Defense in Football* (West Nyack, N.Y.: Parker Publ. Co., Inc., 1978), pp. 180-181.

5. H. O. FRITZ CRISLER, *Modern Football: Fundamentals and Strategy* (New York: McGraw-Hill Book Co., Inc., 1949), pp. 184-185; 187-188; 208-211.

6. DANA X. BIBLE, *Championship Football* (New York: Prentice-Hall, Inc., 1948), pp. 154, 156, 159, 160.

7. Ibid.

8. JOHN F. BATEMAN and PAUL V. GOVERNALI, *Football Fundamentals: Basic Strategy and Teaching Methods* (New York: McGraw-Hill Book Co., Inc., 1957), pp. 131-133.

9. V-FIVE ASSOCIATION OF AMERICA, *The Naval Aviation Physical Training Manuals: Football* (Annapolis, Md.: U.S. Naval Institute, 1943), pp. 169-183.

10. PETE DYER, *Coaching Football's Split 4-4 Multiple Defense* (West Nyack, N.Y.: Parker Publ. Co., Inc., 1980), pp. 170-173.

11. SANDUSKY, *Developing Linebackers the Penn State Way*, p. 92.

12. SULLINS, *Complete Book of Multiple Defense in Football*, pp. 180-181.

13. ROBERT TROPPMAN, *Football's New Master Defense Guide* (West Nyack, N.Y.: Parker Publ. Co., Inc., 1983), pp. 151-154.

14. SULLINS, *Complete Book of Multiple Defense in Football*, pp. 32-42.

15. GAILORD BELLAMY, *Complete Guide to the Split-Pro Defense* (West Nyack, N.Y.: Parker Publ. Co., Inc., 1971), pp. 159-167.

16. GOMER JONES and CHARLES BUD WILKINSON, *Modern Defensive Football* (Englewood Cliffs, N.J.: Prentice-Hall, Inc., 1957), pp. 73-76.

17. CARL LOCKHART, "A single one-step, dropback short passing game," *Scholastic Coach*, 53: 28-30, 106, 1984.

Chapter 5
SHORTYARDAGE AND GOAL LINE ADAPTATIONS

For most players shortyardage and goal line situations appear reasonably similar because the immediate area of the football field to defend is relatively small. Both mentally and strategically, however, the circumstances of shortyardage, compared to goal line, are very dissimilar: each situation places either the offense or the defense at much greater risk; each occurs in discrete sections of the field; the crucial secondary and pursuit mechanisms of defensive team-play become inoperable on the goal line; and so on. Therefore, these two tactical situations must be clearly defined in order for defensive personnel to prepare mentally for the diametrical circumstances that each imposes. In the 2-level defensive system, *by definition*, goal line may not be instituted until the end zone's end line can replace the safety's end line. This only becomes possible once the point of scrimmage is inside the defense's own eight-yardline[1] (see footnote, table 7); however, once the safety has been substituted goal line is in force on *every* down, first through fourth. By contrast, over the other ninety-two yards of the field shortyardage situations must be *redefined* with each new opponent: for example, against one offensive opponent third down with less than two yards to go (for a first down) might be defined as shortyardage, against another only fourth down with inches to go would be, while against a third opponent the location of the football in the offensive as opposed to the defensive end of the field could provide an interacting factor influencing the defense's shortyardage posture. In other words, the arbitrary definition established for shortyardage against a specific opponent is always contingent upon the risks involved, *but never should the defense be placed at risk*. Shortyardage is entirely an offensive gamble, with much at stake should it fail and only minimal gain if a *first* down is gained. For defenders in shortyardage, this

Table 7. The shortyardage and goal-line personnel changes possible with the 2-level Defense; no system changes are required, however.

FIRST LEVEL PERSONNEL	TACTICAL SITUATION*	
	SHORTYARDAGE	GOAL LINE
5 DEFENDERS	5-5 (REGULAR) PERSONNEL (NO PERSONNEL CHANGE)	5-6 GOAL LINE PERSONNEL (DEEP SAFETY SUBSTITUTED FOR AN ADDITIONAL SECOND LEVEL DEFENDER, 'ROVER')
6 DEFENDERS	6-4 SHORTYARDAGE PERSONNEL (BANDIT SUBSTITUTED FOR AN ADDITIONAL NOSE)	6-5 GOAL LINE PERSONNEL (DEEP SAFETY SUBSTITUTED FOR AN ADDITIONAL NOSE)

* In shortyardage, the deep safety *must* remain in the defense to provide the endline; in goal-line (by definition, from the defense's 8-yardline to its goal-line the end zone's end line replaces the deep safety, thus an additional defender can be substituted into the First or Second Level.

should be their prudent approach, for the offense only assumes such risks when its chances of success appear certain. Contrast this approach with goal line, where the defense's security is threatened. The mental attitude of defenders in this situation becomes analogous to a life-and-death predicament, for in goal line they are placed in double jeopardy: the defense is not only endangered but must operate at a tactical disadvantage. In goal line, team-play all but disappears, for there is insufficient time for the secondary mechanisms of defense to function. By the time defensive pursuit normally would begin to operate, the offense has scored! In goal line, therefore, calculated gambles not normally considered become reasonable alternatives in each defender's determination to execute *his primary responsibility.*

SHORTYARDAGE ADAPTATIONS

This defense is a two-level model, and thus tactically well suited for shortyardage, being evolved from the Alabama 6-5 model (1). Therefore, independent of any personnel substitution (table 7), in many shortyardage situations only the *normal* defensive call need be made. In the 11-alignment (only) specific shortyardage adjustments can be implemented by adding "Shortyardage" to the "11" call in the huddle (fig. 59):

FIVE DEFENDERS IN THE FIRST LEVEL

(5-5 REGULAR PERSONNEL)
"11 SHORTYARDAGE,..."

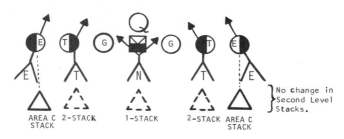

SIX DEFENDERS IN THE FIRST LEVEL

(6-4 PERSONNEL)
"11 SHORTYARDAGE,..."

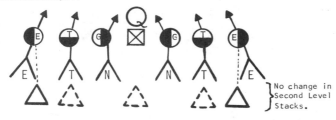

Figure 59 Shortyardage defense: adjustments in "11 Shortyardage" with five and six defenders in the First Level (see table 7).

- With the (normal) five personnel in the First Level, the defensive tackles align on the inside of their offensive tackles; this adjustment significantly improves defensive stability against running plays inside.[2]
- With the "11 Shortyardage" call and *six* defenders in the First Level (i.e., 6-4 personnel, see table 7), each nose assumes the *inside* alignment against his offensive guard; although this is a shrewd defensive gambit against inside running plays, it should be appreciated that retaining only four defenders in the Second Level is more precarious in the event of a possible pass.

Specific examples of shortyardage defense employing *five* and *six* defenders in the First Level are diagrammed in figures 60 and 61, respectively. Note that unless "11 Shortyardage" is explicitly called, there is absolutely no alteration in First Level alignments.[3] Note also that in shortyardage max is the preferred pass coverage but with the 6-4 personnel max is not possible. However, cover provides a viable alternative against high-percentage run situations (fig. 61).

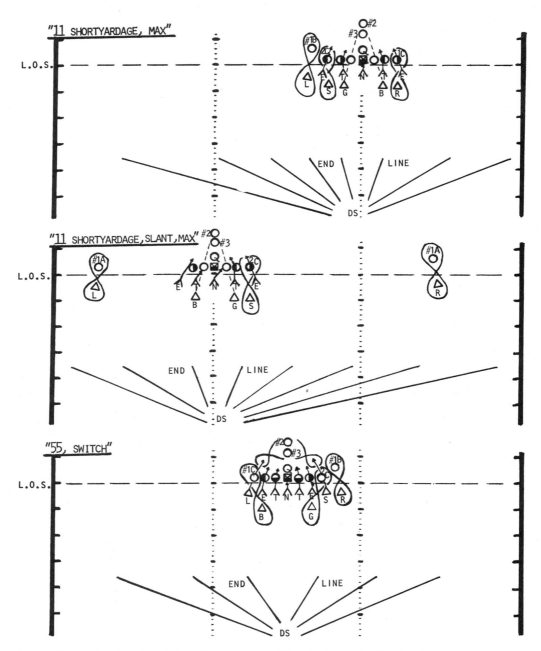

Figure 60 Shortyardage adaptation with 5-5 personnel (5 defenders in the First Level, no personnel substitution, no change in regular calls): in (11 shortyardage" there is no change in the tackles' gap assignment; however, they align *inside* against their offensive tackles; also note that max is the *preferred* pass coverage in shortyardage.

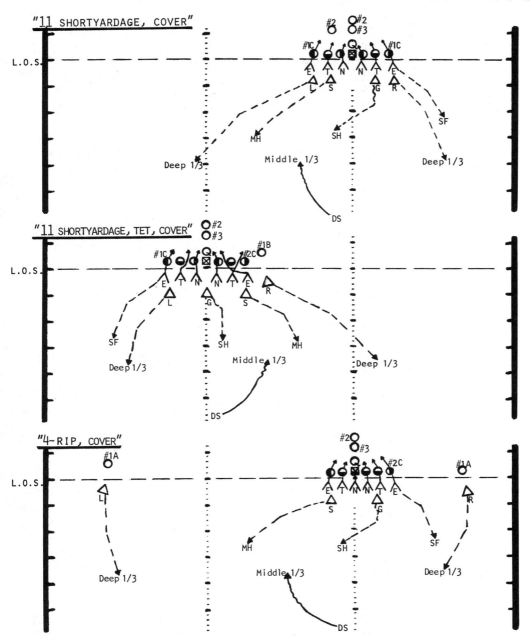

Figure 61 Shortyardage adaptation with 6-4 personnel (6 defenders in First Level, additional nose substituted for Bandit, no change in regular calls): in "11 shortyardage," *each* nose is responsible for a center-guard gap; however, in 2- and 4-alignments, extra nose aligns odd; also note that cover is the *practical* pass coverage (with Bandit out of Second Level).

GOAL LINE ADAPTATIONS

In goal line the expediency of the 2-level model becomes most evident. Once an offense has advanced to the defense's eight-yardline the deep safety may be substituted for a sixth defender either in the Second Level, the 5-6 goal line personnel (3), or for an additional First Level nose, the 6-5 goal line complement, with the entire system transferred *intact* (table 7).

With the addition of Rover (see symbol ▲ , figure 62) into the Second Level, the defense's response capabilities actually are enhanced inside its own eight-yardline.

- All First Level alignments and stunts remain operable; in addition, with an "11 Goal Line" call the defensive tackles also assume their *eagle* alignment and technique (this is *identical* to their shortyardage eagle adjustment, but is called in this instance by "11 Goal Line" to avoid any misunderstanding of the tactical situation).

- The zone coverages, particularly Covers-A and -B, prove most effective: with Rover, up to seven Second Level defenders crowd this constricted defensive area of the field (fig. 62, upper diagram).

- Rover also is available for double-coverage against an isolated No. 1A receiver (see middle diagram).

- In the core, varied pressures can be applied through Second Level stunting, with Rover's presence compensating for any structural weakness created (fig. 62, lower diagram).

At any point inside the eight-yardline the sixth defender may be added to the First Level, the 6-5 goal line personnel (a *second* nose in lieu of Rover's addition into the Second Level). Under these circumstances the penultimate advantage for employing the 2-level model is obvious: installation of the 6-5 adaptation is *not* a defensive remodeling, nor even a well-rehearsed auxiliary, it is *the* defensive system whose potency is actually maximized in goal line (fig. 63).

- The two nose defenders secure the two center-guard gaps, while opposing three offensive blockers (i.e., the center and both guards);
- Therefore, the tackles are matched against each other, likewise the ends, defensive versus offensive;
- Intact, the Second Level retains its basic flexibility and response capacity (fig. 63, middle and lower diagrams).

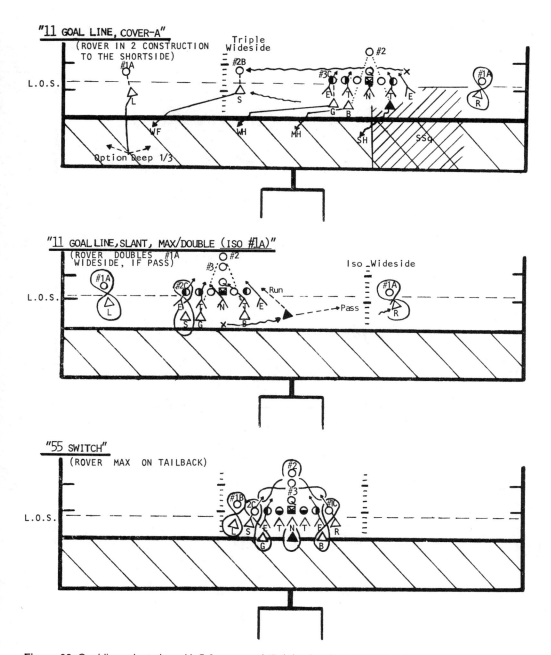

Figure 62 Goal-line adaptation with 5-6 personnel (5 defenders in the First Level, no change in regular calls, rover (▲) substituted into Second Level for deep safety): in "11 goal-line," tackles adjustment identical to "11 shortyardage" (see fig. 59); Rover stacked in the core (usually) and shifting (as necessary) to his final positioning just prior to the snap.

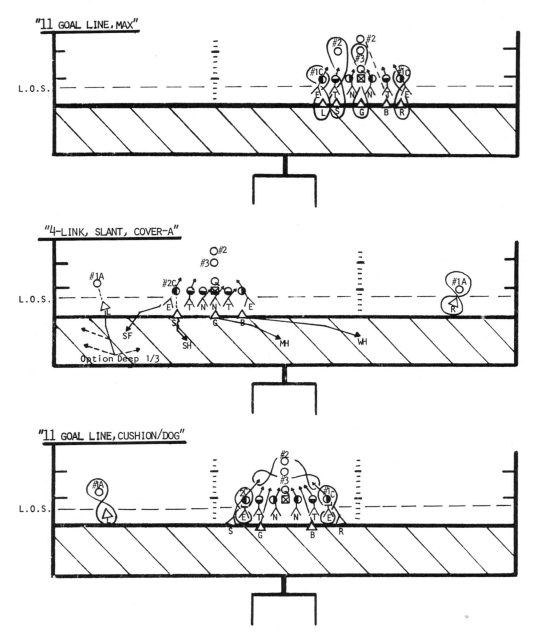

Figure 63 Goal-line adaptation with 6-5 personnel (6 defenders in the First Level, no change in regular calls, additional nose substituted into First Level for safety): in "11 goal-line" each nose is responsible for a center-guard gap; however, in 2- and 4-alignments, extra nose remains aligned odd.

Notes

1. On the other hand, as an offense penetrates deeper inside the defense's thirty-yard line, the safety is not positioned further back, into his own end zone, until the point of scrimmage reaches the eight-yardline (see final section, chapter 7).

2. As a historical note: this adjustment for defensive tackles was developed by the legendary head coach of the Philadelphia Eagles, Greasy Neale, and thus is referred to as the *eagle* alignment (2).

3. One minor qualification: with six personnel in the First Level, 33- and 55-Alignments may not be called.

References

1. PAUL BEAR BRYANT, *Building a Championship Football Team* (Englewood Cliffs, N.J.: Prentice-Hall, Inc., 1960), pp. 48-51.

2. NORM VANBROCKLIN, *Passing, Punting, Quarterbacking* (New York: The Ronald Press Co., 1961), pp. 28-29.

3. NILES H. NELSON, " 'The stopper' 5-5-1 flexible goal-line defense," *Athletic Journal*, 50(2): 78, 1980.

Chapter 6

RUN DEFENSE: TEACHING PROGRESSION

INTRODUCTION: INSTALLING A NEW SYSTEM

In football the acceptance of any new system, whether defensive or offensive, is always hampered by logistical necessity: no matter the viability of the system, it first must be installed, perfected,... coached. At present the division of labor on most coaching staffs is highly stratified, especially the established customs for coaching the line, linebacker, and deepback units of the three-level defensive model. Quite naturally, considerable inertia opposing change must exist. Ultimately, only one reality will dislodge staffs from their enthusiastic complacency with the 34 Defense: skidding defensive performance, escalating offensive point totals, and football games lost on defense. Still, when the decision is finally made to install the two-level model, a number of practical problems will be encountered. For example, this model is unconventional from several perspectives, and particularly from a coaching perspective. The present convention of one unit coach per level is *not* recommended; rather, defensive personnel in each level are coached by (up to three) different staff members rotating through programmed coaching cycles (see *Teaching Supplement*). If anything, more coaches and even greater staff coordination are required to accomplish this. And new techniques must be taught, an entirely new defensive position (the deep safety) installed, and so on.

While many coaches may disagree, in principle the so-called natural football player *cannot* exist; not, that is, without receiving many hours of meticulous systems coaching. The natural player is analogous to the fledgling aviator who eventually becomes an accomplished jet pilot, but not without rigorous, disciplined training.

Similarly, in defensive football even the most talented of athletes performing his function incorrectly attenuates the system; on the other hand, the "natural" is always in the right place, on time, and *then* executes with brilliance. Throughout part 3, therefore, the emphasis is placed on *integration*, upon the sequencing of precise skills and movement patterns required by personnel in order to operate the 2-level system. To achieve this, the major emphasis of each chapter is focused on team drills: game simulations involving several players in which each defender's primary and secondary responsibilities *within the system* can be perfected and coordinated. By comparison, all but the essential individual skills are summarized throughout part 3, for excellent references dissecting the fundamentals of defense are readily available, and abbreviated one and two-man drills abound. In this chapter, a teaching sequence is detailed for installing the run defense, and a corresponding progression in chapter 7 is detailed for pass defense. The duplication of information between these chapters is minimal, but the format adopted in this chapter is continued in chapter 7, and the reader is directed throughout to specific sections when the natural progression of an instructional sequence involves elements of pass defense. Therefore, coaches have the option of teaching the 2-level system in discrete units, run and pass defense separately, or of combining corresponding sections from both this chapter and chapter 7.

On defense, drills dissect each player's performance into component parts. By definition, *fundamental drills* compartmentalize the basic movements (agility, quickness and the physical skills of defensive football) while *team drills* build upon these fundamentals to include the cognitive and integrational components of positional play—key reading, play recognition, and secondary reactions. Fundamental drills involve limited participation—usually one defender, or two at most, performing individual skills; and team drills incorporate several defenders working through a programmed itinerary. In practicing fundamentals, specialized equipment is often required (a blocking sled, bags, tackling machine, etc.); but the team drill format rehearses the game itself, permitting each defender to focus upon discrete components of his positional play. At the present time an overabundance of fundamental drills are available to coaches; by comparison, only a meager volume of literature on team drills exists (1, 2, 3). For these reasons, in the following chapters detailed explanations accompany only the larger drill formats, and to implement these drills into the daily practice schedule the following suggestions are proffered.

- *Standardize the locations* on the field for each team drill. In figure 64 the minimum practice area is assumed, one-half a football field: many high schools have only one field for both practice and their games; at larger universities the defense is often restricted to an equivalent area when forced by the elements to practice indoors in a fieldhouse or covered facility. Whatever the situation, it is prudent to standardize a location for the various team drills. In figure 64 a field organization is suggested for *run* practices. (Note, in chapter 7 modifications are suggested to accommodate a *pass* practice.)

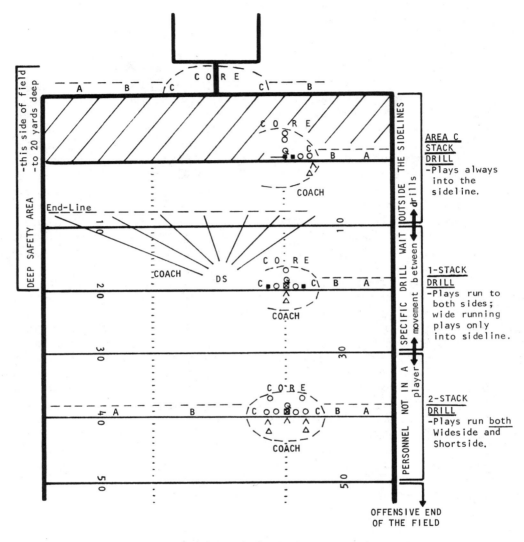

Figure 64 Field organization during the integration phase of a *run* practice. The defense's half of the field (including the end zone) is sectioned into three 20-yard divisions:

   I) the Area C stack drill, the goal-line stimulating the line of scrimmage;

   II) the 1-Stack drill employing the 20-yardline as the line of scrimmage;

   III) the 2-Stack drill, the 40-yardline as the line of scrimmage;

   IV) the deep safety drills to the wideside of the field from the end zone (its endline simulating the L.O.S.) out to the 20-yard line. Halfway through this phase of practice, these drills move in unison to opposite sides of the field.

- *Color-coded diagrams.* One diagram is worth many words of explanation, particularly in organizing team drills. Therefore, throughout chapters 6 and 7, figures diagramming the action sequences for each drill are included. It is suggested that these diagrams be either modified or copied directly onto large cards, that each diagram be color-coded (to better illustrate offensive actions, defensive reaction, etc.), and that a set of diagrams be stationed with each team drill for use in directing its practice.

RECOMMENDED TEACHING MODEL

Post-snap, each defender's actions are governed by offensive keys, the most immediate being recognition of the play and progress of the football. All actions must progress *according to a programmed sequence*: from primary, to secondary, to pursuit. Random movement cannot be permitted in the interests of defensive solidarity. Figure 65 illus-

Figure 65 The teaching model for the 2-Level Defense: throughout chapters 6 & 7, this model is modified according to the level, and by position in the level.

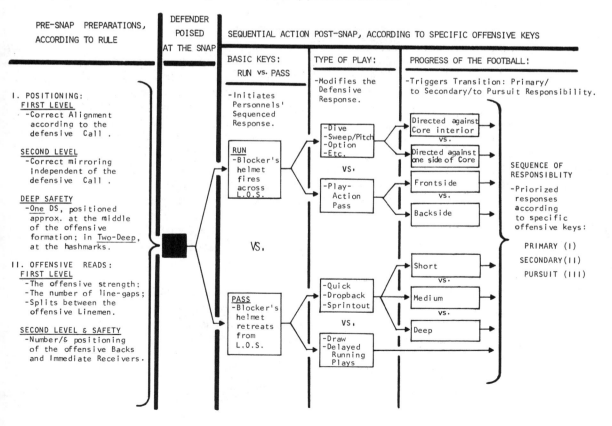

trates the basic teaching model followed throughout chapters 6 and 7 for sequencing defensive responsibilities according to specific offensive keys. The internal machinery of an offense—its personnel movement and patterns—are referred to as keys. On defense the transition from primary, to secondary, to pursuit responsibility is triggered by specific keys. Principally among these is the type of play (pass or run), and then the progress of the football against the defense. Each defender can quickly memorize his responsibilities, and this exemplifies the continuity built into the system. But memorization is not understanding, and even understanding does not guarantee recognition/reaction on the field. On defense, improved performance is achieved only through repetitive drill that simulates game conditions and provides feedback to players. The team drills outlined in these chapters are situation-oriented: each is designed to integrate a small number of defenders, with the coach providing immediate feedback at the conclusion of each drill sequence. The *ultimate* team drill is defensive scrimmage; only through constant refinement at *every practice* in fundamental and team drills, however, can the 2-level Defense operate with some semblance of solidarity when these groups are united.

RUN DEFENSE: FIRST LEVEL

Nose and Tackles: Fundamentals and Drills

Stance. The three-point stance (4, 5) is recommended for these First Level personnel: their power-move technique requires them to explode straight ahead with either foot (according to the blocker's actions); they also must lead-step to either their left or right when slanting and twisting. Therefore, a wide base is not recommended, (rather, it should be to shoulder width only), nor an exaggerated stagger between the heel of one foot and toe of the other. The body mass is extended forward, with the down hand placed well in front, arm and fingers extended, approximately eighteen inches back of the line of scrimmage. The non-supporting arm should not be resting on the thigh; rather, this arm is partially extended in front past the plane of the shoulders, readied to deliver an arm shiver (see technique). This stance *must be constant* so that the intended movement and technique post-snap will not be tipped. Finally, since it is preferable for First Level tackles (and ends) to have their *inside* hand down, it is recommended that naturally left-handed personnel play on the *right side* of the First Level.

Pre-Snap Shifting. This movement is executed with the player *already* in his three-point stance. Rapid shuffle steps laterally are used by the defender to reposition himself, but personnel never raise themselves up during this maneuver, maintaining an extended body position, the down hand skimming the top of the grass. The non-supporting arm also assists in this crabbing motion. Timing is all-important: the opponent's pre-snap cadence and the end's "link" or "rip" call (following single-digit alignments) must be well rehearsed over the preceding week of practice.

Positional Alignment. First Level nose and tackles align head-on with their offensive linemen, facemask to facemask (6). The exception to this is the inside eye-to-shoulder adjustment (7), by the nose in even or the tackles in open, termed the eagle adjustment. This is an automatic adjustment that these personnel must make in order to prevent the distance between them from exceeding seven feet and thereby creating a structural weakness in the core. The best way for the nose (in even) or a tackle (in open) to gauge the eagle adjustment is by observing the offensive line splits (rather than glancing at their teammate just prior to the snap). When the offensive line-gap to the inside exceeds two feet, the players should automatically align inside-eye because the distance between their (adjacent) teammate and themselves will be approaching seven feet.

Responsibility Sequence. In run defense, the following sequence must be executed rapidly by the nose and tackles:

> Primary (I): defend the offensive line-gap(s) assigned; this must be carried out.
>
> Secondary (II): provide immediate assistance to adjacent line-gaps to either side when the football threatens; however, do not *overreact*, vacating (I) responsibility too quickly.
>
> Pursuit (III): locate the football and execute tear, taking the correct pursuit angle to intersect the football; when the ball carrier is trapped, once the tackle is secured the second and third tacklers attempt to strip the running back of the football (8).

Techniques. Two techniques, power-move and slant, are summarized below, along with two secondary reactions, breakdown and tear. These are most important for the operation of this defense, but coaches will need to teach other basic (9, 10) and advanced (11) defensive techniques as well. From the head-on positional alignment, the nose and tackles may execute three directional movements: the charge forward, directly engaging the offensive blocker (the power-move), and the slant to the line-gap immediately inside or outside. Regardless of the direction, the defender's first step is critical. In the power move he must launch across the line of scrimmage *at* the blocker (according to the blocker's movement and actions). Slanting, his lead-step (not crossover) must be executed at approximately forty-five degrees directly into his assigned line-gap, before he moves forward across the line of scrimmage with his second step. The power-move involves two points of contact with the blocker: both hands strike blows on the upper arms of the blocker just below the shoulder pads, using the heel of each palm. A hard charge by both defender and blocker may also result in the defender's helmet making contact with the blocker; if so, this must be made just above the numbers, the defender *keeping the bend in his knees* and back bent well forward at the waist. At this point, it must be emphasized that the defender locks out by vigorously straightening both arms without drawing back (i.e., not losing ground back across the line of scrimmage). Against heavier offensive blockers the defender may not lock out completely, but separation from the blocker will be achieved, enabling the defender to see into the offensive backfield. By *pulling* on one arm or shoulder and *pushing* against the other, according to the direction of the block and path of the ball carrier, the defender can control the blocker. If the blocker grasps an extended forearm or elbow, by vigorously pulling down *through the blocker's thumb* the defender can quickly clear his arm, to begin pursuit or assist on the tackle. When slanting, simultaneous with his lead-step the defender drives his opposite arm and shoulder across his body (in a punching motion) so that his chest is never exposed to the offensive blocker directly across from him; with his head and shoulders well into the line-gap, the defender now can play whichever blocker comes at him:

1. with power-move technique if the adjacent offensive lineman (in the direction of the slant) blocks back on him; or
2. if the lineman on whom the defender initially aligned attempts to block him, by vigorously *recoiling* his inside arm and elbow against the blocker's shoulder and hand-fighting, the defender can lever past this blocker and secure the line-gap, his primary responsibility.

Exploding out of their stance, the most natural reaction for First Level personnel crossing the line of scrimmage *unobstructed* is to continue their penetration further into the offensive backfield. With the offensive line pass blocking, the First Level is *invited* to do so; on running plays, however, these personnel must breakdown immediately, shoulders squared to the line of scrimmage, when the offensive line fires *across the line* (fig. 65). Defenders must not continue to penetrate into the offensive core: *go only to the depth of the offensive blocking pattern* is an excellent rule for defensive personnel to follow in this instance. From this posture First Level personnel commence pursuit, initiated by tear: defenders must work *along* the line of scrimmage, seldom circling behind an offensive blocker nor being driven back off the line of scrimmage. In pursuit, the ordered arrangement of the First Level is critically important: one defender should seldom overrun another, and *never* overrun the football, always keeping the ball carrier *in front of him* while constantly adjusting his tear angle to the point of intersection with the football.

Key Reading. The nose and tackles read their basic key, run vs. pass (fig. 65), from the offensive lineman on whom they align; this lineman is referred to as their *key-man* (fig. 66). First Level personnel read *breakdown* (their initial response on runs) OR *throttleup* (their reaction to the basic pass key; see chapter 7) according to the movement of their key-man; often this may be the *only* key a defender comprehends until well into the play: therefore, in teaching key reading, this is the initial and most important key to which the First Level must react. In contrast, these personnel obtain *secondary* keys from the offensive linemen on either side of their key-man (fig. 66), referred to as their *key-triangle* (12). Along with the progress of the football, secondary keys *modify* a defender's basic read assisting him to identify the offensive play, but,

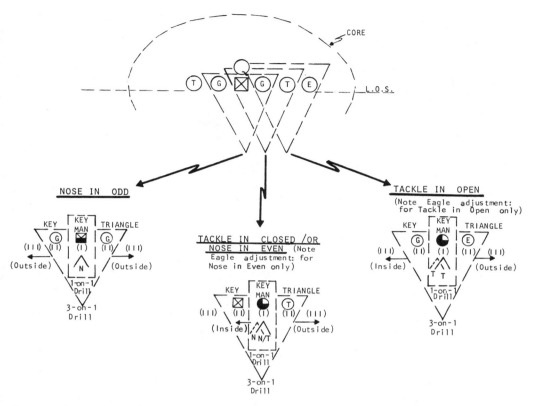

Figure 66 Key reading and the structure of key drills: setting up their key drills, the nose and tackles *define* their key-man on whom they align head-on (◖) or eagle (◐), their key triangle (for 3-on-1 Drills), the direction of the offensive center (inside vs. outside), shortside vs. wideside of the field.

secondary keys can be complex (13, 14) and require *constant* mental reprogramming and rehearsal for each new opponent. Therefore, each week during practice in key drills, secondary keys are altered according to the offensive system and blocking patterns employed by the upcoming opponent.

Drills

1. FUNDAMENTAL DRILLS. For non-specific drills for defensive linemen, see references 15-18.

2. GROUP DRILLS. In this classification three systems drills are detailed below, incorporating both the basic keys and secondary run keys. It is recommended that until defenders are well oriented in these drills, *live* contact be curtailed in order to maximize learning and avoid injury. Even, however, in lock-up drills, if a defender's performance is not technically correct—that is, if either his reactions or skills execution are incorrect—the personnel simulating the offensive blockers do not permit the defender to

win that play sequence. And the assistant coaching the drill provides *immediate* feedback on both correct and inappropriate actions by the defender after each play.

One-on-One Drill (fig. 67)

- Defender against his key-man only.
- Have the defender set up his own drill according to the location of the football, his positional alignment, wideside vs. shortside of field, etc.
- Emphasize the basic keys, run vs. pass, and the defender's break-down reaction on running plays.
- The one-on-one drill is the best format for practicing technique *with* primary (I) responsibilities.

Three-on-One Drill (fig. 67)

- The one-on-one format is enlarged to include the defender's key-triangle; again, the defender meticulously sets up his own drill.
- The three-on-one drill is the best format for practicing secondary run keys, and responsibility transition.
- Note that in figure 67, for purposes of simplification the secondary run keys have been reduced to three categories; against specific offensive systems or opponents these will have to be modified (see part IV).

Slant Key Drill (fig. 68)

- Three-on-one is the basic format for practicing slant technique in a systems-oriented drill (again, note that each defender should set up all his drills).
- However, slanting, his ability to read secondary keys is reduced because the offensive blocker *to the far side* of his key-triangle (i.e., away from the slant direction) quickly disappears from view once the play begins (fig. 68 top portion); thus, his key-triangle effectively is reduced to two offensive linemen.
- Therefore, there must be greater emphasis on carrying out primary (I) responsibility and locating the football on running plays in slant key drills.
- Also, because slanting increases the dynamics of line-play, each week the offensive blocking patterns must be *carefully detailed* for the First Level, then *thoroughly drilled* using these smaller group formats.

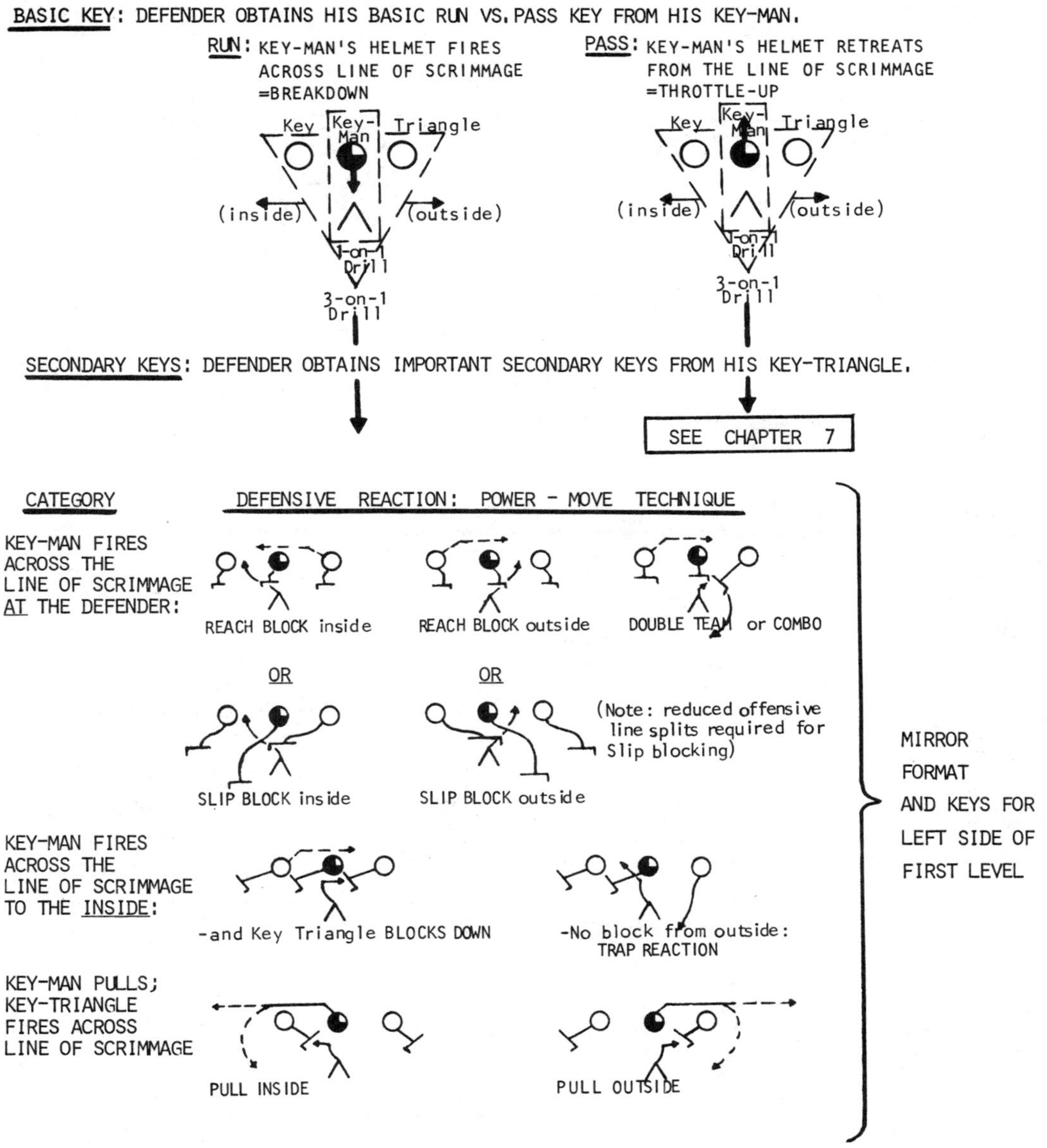

BASIC KEY: DEFENDER OBTAINS HIS BASIC RUN VS. PASS KEY FROM HIS KEY-MAN.

RUN: KEY-MAN'S HELMET FIRES
ACROSS LINE OF SCRIMMAGE
=BREAKDOWN

PASS: KEY-MAN'S HELMET RETREATS
FROM THE LINE OF SCRIMMAGE
=THROTTLE-UP

Key Key-Man Triangle

(inside)   (outside)

3-on-1 Drill

3-on-1
Drill

Key Key-Man Triangle

(inside)   (outside)

3-on-1
Drill

SECONDARY KEYS: DEFENDER OBTAINS IMPORTANT SECONDARY KEYS FROM HIS KEY-TRIANGLE.

SEE CHAPTER 7

CATEGORY	DEFENSIVE REACTION: POWER – MOVE TECHNIQUE

KEY-MAN FIRES
ACROSS THE
LINE OF SCRIMMAGE
AT THE DEFENDER:

REACH BLOCK inside   REACH BLOCK outside   DOUBLE TEAM or COMBO

OR   OR

(Note: reduced offensive
line splits required for
Slip blocking)

SLIP BLOCK inside   SLIP BLOCK outside

KEY-MAN FIRES
ACROSS THE
LINE OF SCRIMMAGE
TO THE INSIDE:

-and Key Triangle BLOCKS DOWN   -No block from outside:
TRAP REACTION

KEY-MAN PULLS;
KEY-TRIANGLE
FIRES ACROSS
LINE OF SCRIMMAGE

PULL INSIDE   PULL OUTSIDE

MIRROR
FORMAT
AND KEYS FOR
LEFT SIDE OF
FIRST LEVEL

Figure 67 Key drills for nose & tackles: one-on-one, defender against key-man only, emphasizing the basic keys; three-on-one, defender against key-triangle, emphasizing secondary keys and defender's transition from I → II → III responsibility (note: an offensive backfielder may be included in the drill format).

BASIC KEY: SLANTING, THE DEFENDER STILL OBTAINS HIS BASIC RUN vs. PASS KEY FROM HIS
KEY-MAN, HOWEVER...

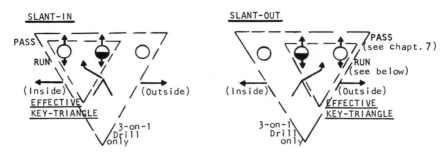

...SECONDARY KEYS ARE MORE DIFFICULT TO DISCERN BECAUSE THE DEFENDER'S EFFECTIVE KEY
TRIANGLE IS REDUCED.

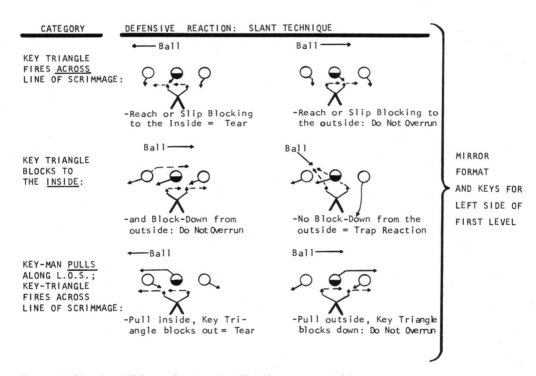

Figure 68 Slant key drill format for nose & tackles (three-on-one only): greater
emphasis on securing primary (I) responsibilities (i.e., assigned offensive line-
gaps) and locating the football; backfielder(s) may be included in drill. (Note:
the eagle adjustment is inadvisable when slanting, particularly outside.)

3. TEAM DRILLS. Cone Signal Drill (including Slants, T.N.T., and T.E.T.)

- see end of this section.
  Stack Drills
- see run Defense: First and Second Levels (final section of chapter).
  Half-Line Drills
- see chapter 7.
  Defensive Scrimmage.

Ends: Fundamentals and Drills Stance in Relation to Positional Alignment.

Aligned tight or loose an end may assume either the three-point stance (described in the last section) or a standing, two-point stance (19, 20). The three-point stance is preferable against run situations, and the two-point stance is mandatory when an end must execute a pass coverage responsibility. The only situation when a First Level end *must* assume a three-point stance is aligned tight immediately inside the offensive tight end, and the system automatically relieves him of any pass responsibility so that he can concentrate upon his primary run responsibility. Whether the end aligns tight against an offensive tackle or loose against the tight end or slotback (if either is present in the offense's formation), his positional alignment is always outside eye-to-shoulder. The common elements in both the two- and three-point stances involve the end's inside foot placement and initial step. Again, a wide base or exaggerated heel-to-toe stagger is not recommended, but the *inside* foot must be staggered slightly (particularly in the three-point stance); and his initial step always must be a lead-step with the *inside* foot.[1]

Pre-Snap Shifting. Shifting prior to the snap is *very restricted* for First Level ends. Initially, each aligns loose and in a two-point stance. From this vantage both have a clear view of the offense's formation: to make their link or rip call, and for the shortside end to locate the No. 2 mobile player to the shortside (*i.e.*, every time a cover is called). Therefore, if an end is to shift pre-snap, he only shifts from loose into tight as he is completing his link or rip call, and *only* then in 4- and 5-/55-alignments; otherwise, the end *remains* in loose, making only necessary minor adjustments.

Responsibility Sequence. For the overall integrity of the 2-level Defense, the First Level end to the play side (frontside) must execute a *crucial* primary (I) responsibility, while the other end on the backside executes an equally important trailer (III) responsibility.

Primary (I):	Containment. Anytime the football moves against the end's side of the defense, he must immediately contain the ball carrier (including quarterback sprintout) to the inside, compressing this area frontside as much as possible.
Pursuit (III):	Trailer. Anytime the football moves away from the end's side of the defense, he must immediately compress this

area backside, always *seeing the quarterback*, and trailing the ball carrier *at the depth of the football* to eliminate cutbacks and reverses (including the quarterback bootleg).

Secondary (II): By comparison, any secondary responsibilities are rather unstructured, for once an end loses his (I) containment on the frontside he is usually out of the play, particularly against sweeps and quick-pitches. He should, however, initiate pursuit as quickly as possible.

Techniques. From the perimeter of the core the two ends crash aggressively: force and contain the football; penetrate, squeezing both the frontside and backside running area; reduce the offense's timeframe to the minimum; and if trap blocked, create a pile deep in the offensive backfield. In loose, by aligning *outside* of the tight end or the offensive tackle to the split end side, an offense becomes almost powerless to stop this large, agile end from crashing (fig. 69, upper portion). Aligned tight, however, the capability of an end to apply this tactical pressure is reduced by a corresponding degree (fig. 69, lower portion):

- to the side of the split end, he may still crash aggressively with his adjacent First Level tackle closed, and a Second Level defender positioned directly behind him in 2-stack;
- on the other hand, with the tight end immediately on his outside, he must curtail his aggressiveness particularly in run situations.[2]

For these reasons, only two techniques are summarized below, crash and trailer. However, coaches will wish to teach other, traditional defensive end (21, 22) techniques, as well as supplemental outside linebacker techniques (23, 24, 25, 26).
The crash technique is critical in containing quick-pitches, sweeps and the quarterback sprintout. The end penetrates through the off-tackle area aiming at the near halfback, maintaining outside leverage on the football at all times yet forcing it directly, *never* permitting the ball carrier to cut up quickly inside (27). In tight alignment, however, this technique becomes more difficult to execute because the end's initial *crash angle* is reduced and because of the immediate blocking threat presented by the offensive tackle (fig. 69, lower diagram); with the tight end positioned on his outside as well, the First Level end must curtail his aggressiveness accordingly. Crash technique requires a three-step sequence beginning with the inside foot (fig. 69), with the length of each stride being lengthened in loose, shortened in tight, appropriately. For the most part ends are blocked *from the inside*: by their key-man immediately reach blocking them, by a backfielder or lineman trapping. An end must *maintain his feet*: this is critical, for once knocked to the ground his force-containment no longer can be adjusted to the ball carrier's movements. For this reason, arm shiver technique (28) is preferred, with the end playing *through* the head of blockers, disengaging as quickly as possible,

A. FIRST LEVEL ENDS ALIGNED LOOSE: THE 11-, 2-, & 3/33-ALIGNMENTS)

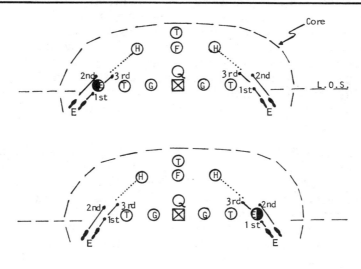

B. BOTH FIRST LEVEL ENDS ALIGNED TIGHT: 55-ALIGNMENT ONLY

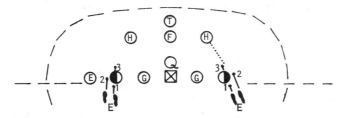

Figure 69 Crash technique by First Level ends: A) aligned loose;
B) aligned tight.

and always keeping his feet clear of the blocker. There are, however, two situations where shoulder technique should be employed.

1. When a trap blocker fires directly at the end *and* he reads off-tackle run, the *inside* shoulder technique (29) is preferred, with the end securing his outside leverage position on the football.

2. Aligned tight (in three-point stance), the tight end blocking down from the outside, the First Level end must step directly into this block with *outside* shoulder technique (30), using his forearm and free inside hand to fight through the head of the tight end, working out along the line of scrimmage but being alert for the ball carrier cutting back inside of him.

Trailer technique is a natural extension of crash. As the end is penetrating, it is critical that he reads on the move (see key reading, next section). When the near half-back or I-backs move away (against the far side of the defense) and no blockers threaten, the end must instantly *see* (and search) the quarterback, *locate the football*, throttle up, trailing at the depth of the football and *expecting* the ball carrier to cut back. Note that on reverses or the quarterback bootleg, the crashing end will encounter blockers almost immediately *before* he locates the football, indicating that he must execute primary (I) responsibility, and *not* progress to (III).

Key Reading. When an end is aligned tight and outflanked by the offensive tight end to his immediate outside, the offensive tackle becomes his key-man, the guard, tackle, and end his key-triangle (fig. 70, left-hand portion). When the end *outflanks* the offense in the core (see right-hand portion) the near halfback [(H) in fig. 70] is incorporated into his key-triangle. However, as the end crashes, his *basic* read, run vs. pass, must still be obtained from offensive linemen. Conducting crash drills, it is essential that the coach *constantly* ask the end at the completion of the play what he read . . . run? . . . pass? For only after constant repetition will the end read his key-triangle and not focus solely on the near back. When a back is not located in the *near* halfback position in the offensive formation, the end includes the *nearest* back, usually the fullback, or I-backs, in this expanded key-triangle (see specific examples in Crash Drills following). Finally, it again should be noted that, each week during practice, secondary keys must be altered in the crash drills, according to the offense of the upcoming opponent.

Drills

1. FUNDAMENTAL DRILLS. See references 15-18; emphasis on footwork drills (31) recommended.

2. GROUP DRILLS. In figures 71 and 72, formats are outlined for small group drills. Figure 71 outlines one-on-one and three-on-one drills similar to the formats outlined in the previous section, the end assuming an *outside* positional alignment against the offensive tackle and secondary keys altered accordingly. Again, carefully note the difficulty encountered in carrying out crash (I) responsibility when the offensive tight end *outflanks* a First Level end.[3] Figure 72 illustrates the drill format when the end *outflanks the offense* in the core, and this crash drill can be adapted for many different offensive formations and systems:

- the end aligned loose outflanking the tight end or a slotback, with one, two and three backs in the offensive backfield;
- loose *or* tight, the end outflanking the offensive tackle (to the split-end side), with limited backfield combinations.

END   ALIGNED   TIGHT   VS.   END   ALIGNED   LOOSE ...

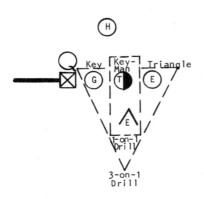

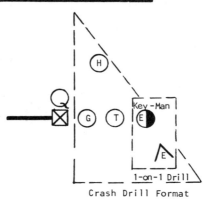

Crash Drill Format

AND   END   ALIGNED   LOOSE   OR   TIGHT   NO   TIGHT END   IN   THE   OFFENSE

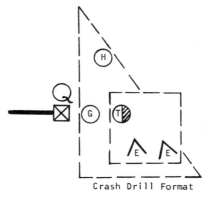

Crash Drill Format

-NOTE: IN EXAMPLES ABOVE, THE FIRST LEVEL
END <u>OUTFLANKS</u> THE OFFENSIVE FORMATION.

Figure 70 Key reading and the structure of crash drills for First Level ends.
(Note: end responsible for setting up these drills; see legend of fig. 66.)

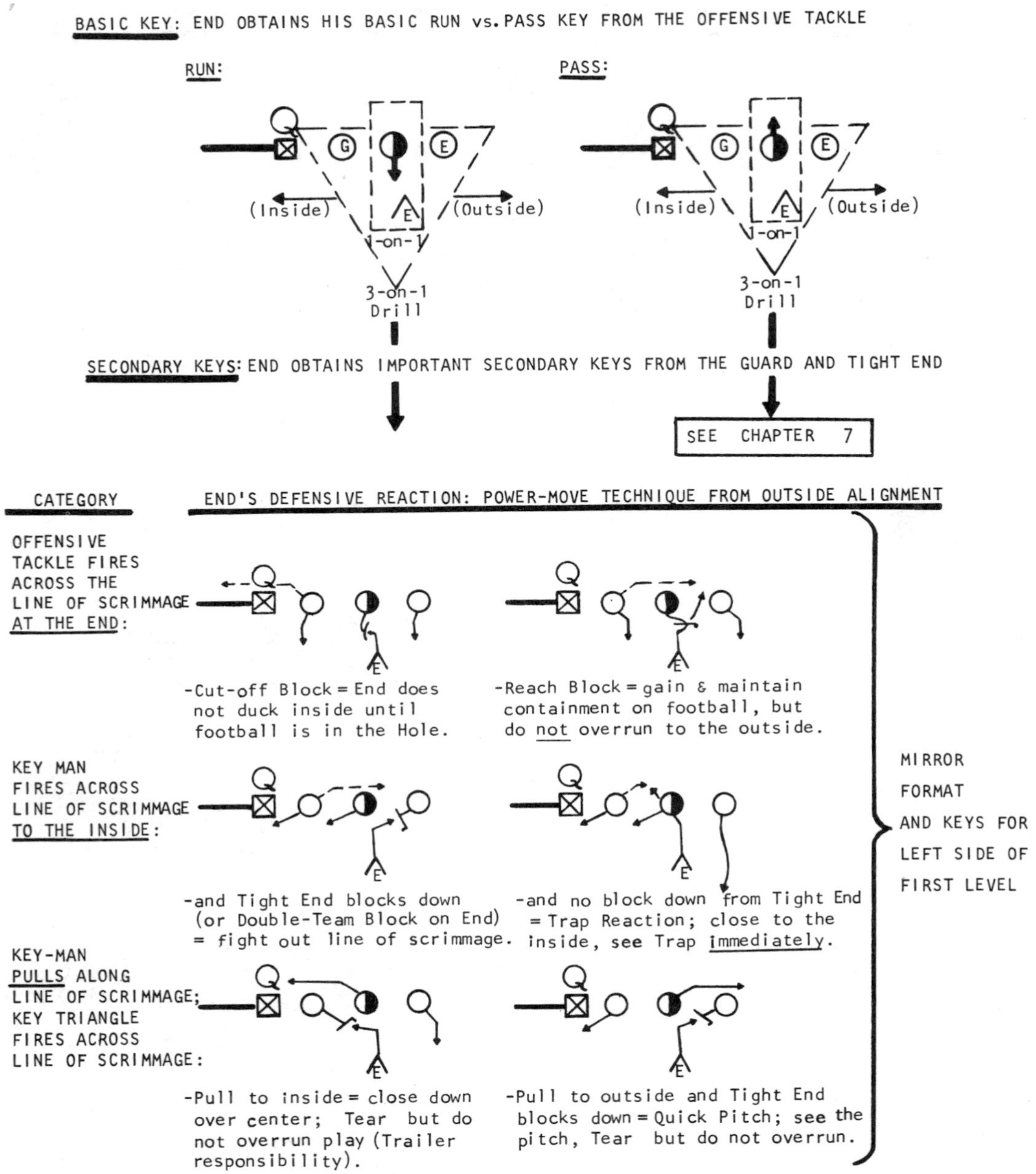

BASIC KEY: END OBTAINS HIS BASIC RUN vs. PASS KEY FROM THE OFFENSIVE TACKLE

RUN:

PASS:

(Inside)   (Outside)

(Inside)   (Outside)

3-on-1
Drill

3-on-1
Drill

SECONDARY KEYS: END OBTAINS IMPORTANT SECONDARY KEYS FROM THE GUARD AND TIGHT END

SEE   CHAPTER   7

CATEGORY

END'S DEFENSIVE REACTION: POWER-MOVE TECHNIQUE FROM OUTSIDE ALIGNMENT

OFFENSIVE
TACKLE FIRES
ACROSS THE
LINE OF SCRIMMAGE
AT THE END:

-Cut-off Block = End does
not duck inside until
football is in the Hole.

-Reach Block = gain & maintain
containment on football, but
do not overrun to the outside.

KEY MAN
FIRES ACROSS
LINE OF SCRIMMAGE
TO THE INSIDE:

-and Tight End blocks down
(or Double-Team Block on End)
= fight out line of scrimmage.

-and no block down from Tight End
= Trap Reaction; close to the
inside, see Trap immediately.

KEY-MAN
PULLS ALONG
LINE OF SCRIMMAGE;
KEY TRIANGLE
FIRES ACROSS
LINE OF SCRIMMAGE:

-Pull to inside = close down
over center; Tear but do
not overrun play (Trailer
responsibility).

-Pull to outside and Tight End
blocks down = Quick Pitch; see the
pitch, Tear but do not overrun.

MIRROR

FORMAT

AND KEYS FOR

LEFT SIDE OF

FIRST LEVEL

Figure 71 Key drills for First Level ends aligned tight (see similarity with the diagrams in fig. 67, also read legend for drill formats).

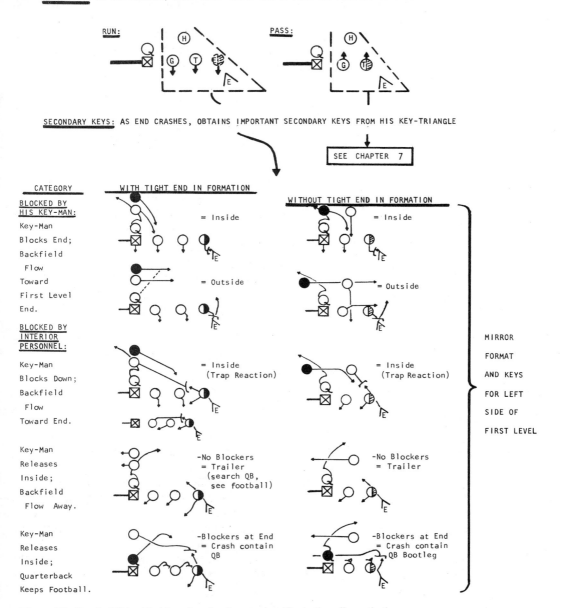

Figure 72 Crash drill for First Level ends when end *outflanks* the offense in the core. (Note: in the left-hand diagrams tight end may be replaced by a slotback.)

One-on-One and Three-on-One Drills (fig. 71)

- Emphasize the *basic* run vs. pass key, according to the offensive tackle's actions.
- In the three-on-one format, work on the tight end blocking down with the First Level end reacting out along the line of scrimmage, but not over-reacting to the outside (see technique section).

Crash Drills (fig. 72)

- Regardless of the specific drill format, the end must:
  - **a.** crash *under control*;
  - **b.** read his entire key-triangle to anticipate what may happen *before* it occurs;
  - **c.** maintain his feet.
- The crash drill format is principally for *run* defense, however, the *basic* pass key must also be interspersed throughout the drill.
- The end's *angle* and *depth of penetration*, according to the offensive keys, are the critical elements in force-containment; failing to *breakdown* soon enough and angling *too deeply into the backfield* must be avoided. When in doubt, the end must let the play *come to him* rather than over-penetrate.

3. TEAM DRILLS.   *Cone Signal Drill (immediately following).*
   Area C Stack Drills.
   The Crash Drill format *combined with* the Second Level (see run Defense: First and Second Levels, next section).
   Half-Line Drills (see chapter 7).
   Defensive Scrimmage.

Team Drill: First Level (only)

The nose and tackles are combined with ends in cone signal drills, and while its general format remains constant several personnel combinations are possible (fig. 73). These drills are non-contact, but, they serve to coordinate the initial phases of *run* defense for the First Level. A *live* quarterback and offensive center familiarize personnel with the next opponent's cadence, while the First Level rehearses its (pre-snap) shifting according to the game plan (fig. 73). On the snap the personnel in the drill execute their primary (I) responsibilities, including any First Level stunt(s) called (fig. 73, lower portion). Through each phase *fundamentals* are closely scrutinized by the coach: stance, shifting technique, post-snap movement (particularly personnel's *first step*), as well as overall coordination and timing. Including a *live* backfielder in the offense to simulate movement of the football is optional.

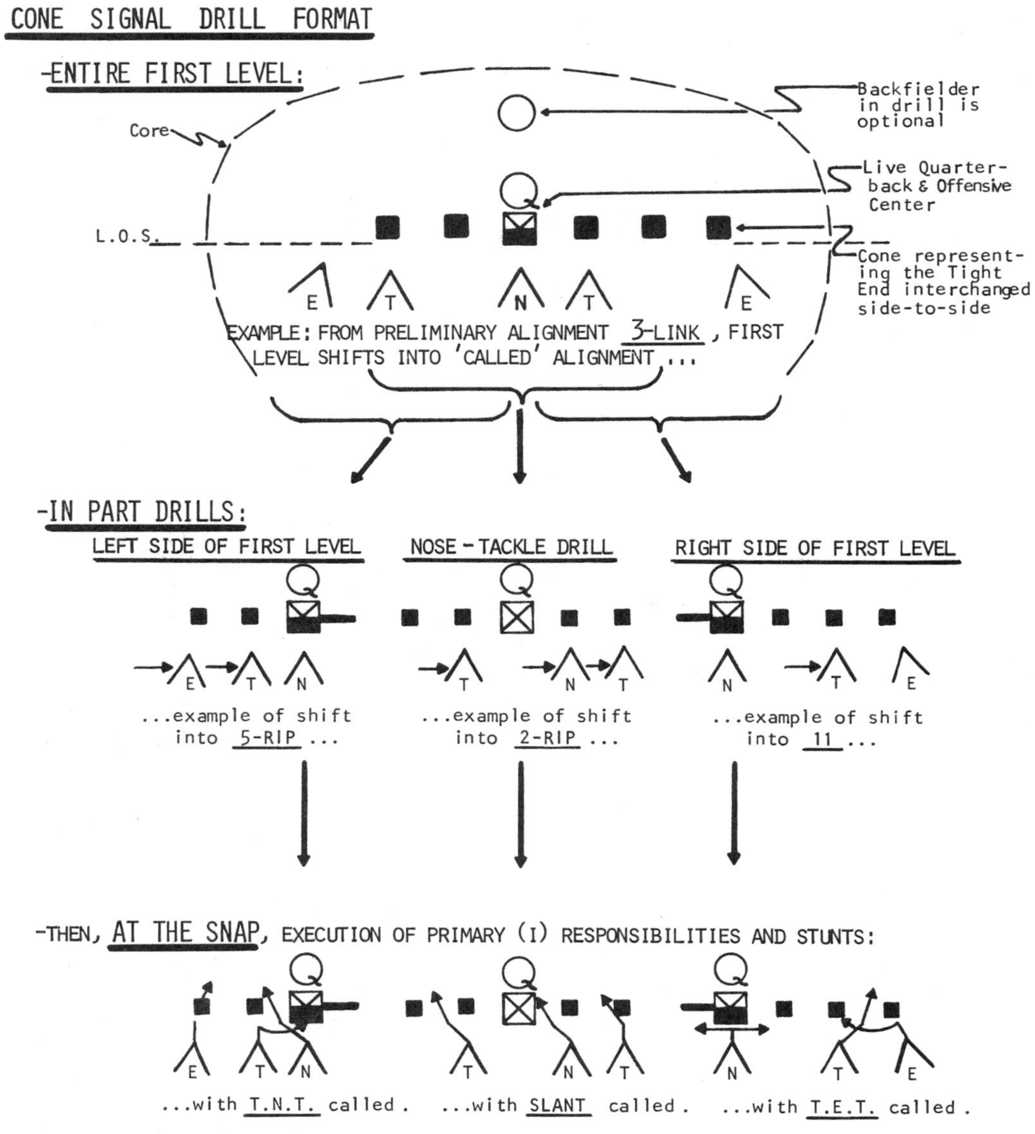

CONE SIGNAL DRILL FORMAT

-ENTIRE FIRST LEVEL:

Core

L.O.S.

Backfielder
in drill is
optional

Live Quarter-
back & Offensive
Center

Cone represent-
ing the Tight
End interchanged
side-to-side

E T N T E

EXAMPLE: FROM PRELIMINARY ALIGNMENT __3-LINK__, FIRST
LEVEL SHIFTS INTO 'CALLED' ALIGNMENT ...

-IN PART DRILLS:

LEFT SIDE OF FIRST LEVEL	NOSE – TACKLE DRILL	RIGHT SIDE OF FIRST LEVEL

E T N

T N T

N T E

...example of shift
into __5-RIP__ ...

...example of shift
into __2-RIP__ ...

...example of shift
into __11__ ...

-THEN, __AT THE SNAP__, EXECUTION OF PRIMARY (I) RESPONSIBILITIES AND STUNTS:

E T N

T N T

N T E

...with T.N.T. called .   ...with SLANT called .   ...with T.E.T. called .

Figure 73 Cone signal drills to coordinate team-play of the First Level: cones
simulate the offensive guards, tackles, and tight end(s), with the quarterback,
offensive center, and backfielder *live*; the First Level personnel in the drill execute their pre-snap shifting and post-snap (I) responsibility and stunts, as called
by the coach.

First Level Stunts: Coordination and Techniques

Slant. Coaches should appreciate that slanting is an *essential technique* to the 2-level defensive concept; however, the *mechanism* itself must be implemented with caution (individual technique is described earlier, see nose and tackle fundamentals). For the First Level to operate with maximum effectiveness, preemptive, coordinated movement is essential. The slant mechanism commits the nose and one tackle to a *predetermined* course of action; for this reason, in slant key drills significant practice must be spent on defenders' reaction when the offensive play is away from the direction of slant (fig. 68). Coordinating the slant mechanism and the various personnel combinations (fig. 30, 31), two coaching points must be emphasized.

- Relative to the *direction of slant*, it is critical that the *second* defender complete his slant: if he is picked off by blockers before securing his primary (I) line-gap, a breach is opened in the First Level between the two defenders.
- In the odd-numbered alignments (1, 3, 5) the nose and First Level tackle *away from* the tight end must slant in unison *toward* the tight end; in their cone signal drills practice must be spent identifying and communicating the location of the tight end to avoid mix-ups.

Twists. Like the slant mechanism, twists initiate preemptive movement in the First Level and are therefore essential to its operational effectiveness. The *twist mechanism* also must be implemented with caution, and for similar reasons. If either defender fails to secure his (I) responsibility, picked off by offensive blockers, the First Level will be breached.

T.N.T. (tackle-nose twist). To execute T.N.T.'s, the nose and tackle must be aligned adjacent to each other (fig. 31). Thus the First Level alignment call establishes which First Level tackle will twist behind the nose.[4] At the snap, the nose slants *immediately* outside, going first; the tackle momentarily engages his key-man, employing power-move technique. Then, *without drawing back*, the tackle disengages, stepping around the nose, and using him as a screen. Against running plays, with the offensive blockers firing across the line of scrimmage defenders must breakdown (not continue penetration), secure their assigned (I) responsibility, and locate the football. On passes, with the offensive line retreating from the line of scrimmage, the twist occurs deeper, on the offensive side of the line, and the nose in particular can throttle up, with his point of attack being directed at the *inside shoulder* of the adjacent offensive lineman (in his key-triangle). On the other hand, with four other First Level defenders rushing the passer, the tackle as he completes his twist to the inside should anticipate fullback draw before hitting the throttle.

T.E.T. (tackle-end twist). To execute the T.E.T., the tackle and end must be aligned open and loose, respectively, and, again, the First Level alignment call confirms which pair will twist (only the 11-alignment confirms *both*: in fig. 31, compare top right diagram with remainder of calls). At the snap the *inside* defender, the tackle aligned open, slants outside, going first, and must penetrate the off-tackle area because he now must assume quarterback containment vs. dropback pass action. The *outside* defender, the First Level end aligned loose, must crash for two steps (shortening each step substantially), engaging the tight end (if positioned in front of him and blocking), before twisting inside, going after the tackle has gone (the timing is similar to that of the technique explained in the preceding section). There is, however, one exception: if the offensive play is a quick-pitch, at the point in time when the First Level end would normally twist inside, if the ball carrier has advanced to the periphery of the offensive core the end may elect not to complete his twist.

RUN DEFENSE: SECOND LEVEL

Inside the defensive core *all* Second Level personnel must learn stack technique, and there are *five possible locations* at which stacks may be formed (fig. 74). Also, when a

Figure 74 The *nine* possible positions for Second Level mirroring defined by the 2-level Defense, and the limited number of techniques required.

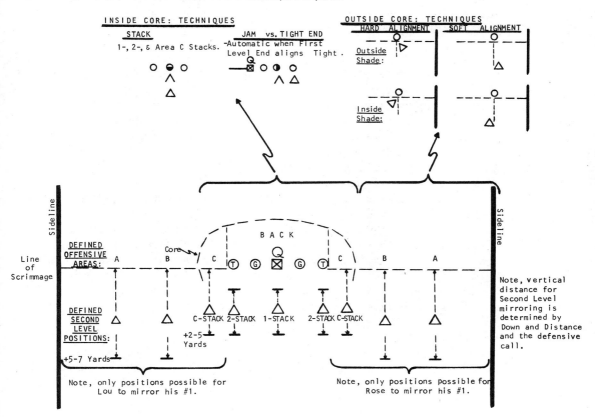

First Level end aligns tight the Second Level defender mirroring the tight end or slot-back automatically implements jam technique. In the core the subtle differences in stack technique relate to the actual location of the stack, not to the principles of the technique: in a 1- or 2-stack the Second Level defender is mirroring a backfielder, while in area C he is mirroring an immediate receiver. Note also in figure 74 that only Gael, Strong, and Bandit can form 1- and 2-stacks; whenever Lou and Rose locate in the core they *must be mirroring* a tight end. Outside the core, four locations are defined for mirroring immediate receivers, areas B and A to both sides of the offensive formation (fig. 74); and all Second Level personnel must perfect max and zone techniques (see chapter 7).

Stance. Stacked in the defensive core, *lateral* mobility becomes the most essential requirement for Second Level personnel. Defenders employ a two-point stance, feet parallel and shoulder-width apart, with minimal heel-toe stagger; body weight is forward over the toes, knees and waist bent slightly, with the arms forward, hands at the knees (but not resting on the knees) (32). The defender should feel comfortable yet able to move quickly in all directions, with a *clear view* of the offensive line and backfield immediately in front of him. By contrast, when a Second Level defender must jam the tight end or a slotback his *outside* foot is moved back (producing greater heel-toe stagger), widening both the stance and lowering the body's center of gravity accordingly (33).

Techniques. In the defensive core, Second Level mirroring incorporates two components. Each defender's *lateral* positioning is determined by the location of the mobile offensive player he must mirror. With early-motion, defenders move from one stack to an adjacent location, employing quick shuffle steps and always *keeping their shoulders squared* to the line of scrimmage in case the ball is snapped. Their *vertical* distance off the line of scrimmage (fig. 74) is determined by two factors. In general, when the offensive linemen *immediately in front of them* are covered by the First Level there is little need for a Second Level defender to crowd the line of scrimmage. On the other hand, as this offensive blocking threat increases according to the down and distance, the defender must move closer to the line of scrimmage; however, in longer yardage (i.e., passing) situations, Second Level personnel align up to five yards deep.

Against running plays in the core the Second Level's role is to provide *aggressive run-support* behind the First Level, and to accomplish this personnel must remain clear of blockers. On the other hand, they may not employ inappropriate movements to avoid blockers, for in so doing they open up a running lane (fig. 75). If the ball carrier, immediately behind a blocker, dives directly at a Second Level player, the defender must *fill* aggressively, stepping into the blocker and employing shoulder and forearm lift technique (34), keeping his hips and shoulders squared to the line of scrimmage, and playing through the blocker's head. Otherwise, if the football moves past the defender toward the outside, he must *scrape* immediately. This technique involves working down the line of scrimmage, employing shuffle steps to keep his shoulders squared and reduce his speed; while the ball carrier remains in the core, and thus inside defensive

1-STACK

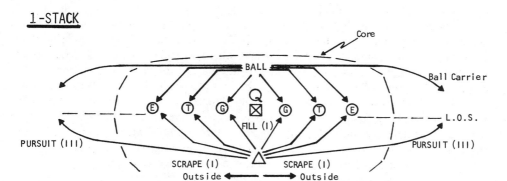

2-STACK

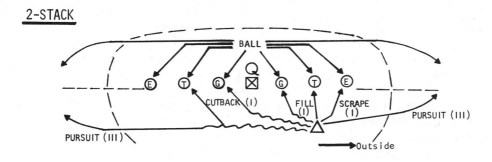

AREA C STACK

JAM

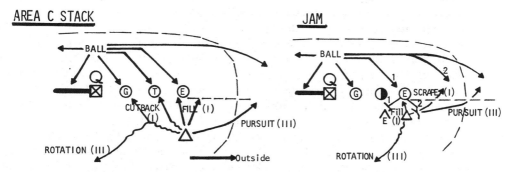

Figure 75 Second Level technique against the run: executing primary (I) responsibility fill and scrape immediately; however, play cutback cautiously, never overrunning the football; making the transition to pursuit (III), once the ball carrier escapes the core, turn and sprint continuing to play the football inside-out.

containment, the Second Level *always plays the football inside out*, expecting the ball carrier to cut up into the line of scrimmage at any point. While moving, the two-hand shiver is the best technique for shedding blockers rather than engaging them directly with forearm lift technique: the defender keeps his legs and body clear by locking-out the elbows on contact, drawing back as necessary in order to maintain his correct scrape angle, and keeping the feet moving (35). In contrast, when the football moves away from the defender toward the other side of the defense, he must *cautiously* implement *cutback*, a crucial responsibility in the overall defensive scheme against run. The Second Level defender must keep the football *well in front of him*, employing two-hand shiver technique to clear himself from blockers as he moves. By definition, *pursuit* is initiated *immediately* when the ball carrier moves out of the core. Frontside personnel must accelerate to catch up to (but *still* not overrun) the football, and their focus must shift to forcing the ball carrier to run *laterally* as much as possible into the sideline. The *deep* pursuit angle for Second Level personnel on the backside is termed rotation (fig. 36), and its timing requires that as the ball carrier is crossing the line of scrimmage frontside, these personnel be sprinting from the backside across the mid point of the offensive formation. Finally, when a Second Level player implements jam (fig. 75, lower right), he must be aware of several interacting factors which can affect both his technique and the execution of his defensive responsibilities. How great is the size and/or speed differential between himself and his Mirror? If this offensive player (the tight end or slotback) is successful blocking to the inside against the first-level end aligned tight (see sequence 1 in diagram), against sweeps this Second Level defender must be prepared to assume (I) responsibility for containing the football (36). In addition, the defender must be conscious of his mirror's release into the pattern on passing plays. Given these circumstances, therefore, often in jam, the Second Level defender must concentrate totally on his primary (I) responsibilities and all but ignore any plays away from him (i.e., cutback and rotational pursuit responsibility).

Interaction Of First Level Alignment And Second Level Stack Second Level stacks are structured independent of the First Level's alignment. However, in order to defend against the run there are situations when specific offensive linemen *must be covered* by the First Level in order to screen a Second Level defender (fig. 76). With two backfielders in the offensive formation, the creation of TWO 2-Stacks constitutes a sound defensive structure against the run (see upper portion); in turn, as the offensive Linemen immediately in front of the stacked defenders are covered by First Level personnel, they may align deeper (off the line of scrimmage), further strengthening the pursuit capability of the defensive core against outside running plays; the major concern for the Second Level with this core structure involves their key reading (see sections following). On the other hand, when an ace backfielder locates in the fullback position and the mirroring Second Level defender assumes a 1-Stack (fig. 76, lower portion) this affords both offensive guards and the tackles advantageous blocking angles. Therefore, the core defense against the run *must be strengthened* by aligning first-level defenders covering various offensive linemen.

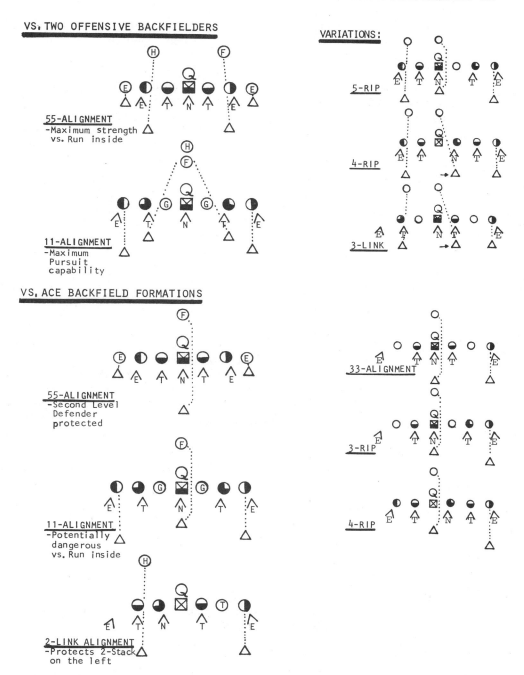

Figure 76 Structure of the core in run defense: interaction of First Level alignment and Second Level stacks *reinforcing* the core's strength vs. the run.

Responsibility Sequence: Run Defense   Mirroring an offensive backfielder in the core, run defense is defined as the Second Level's primary (I) responsibility, but in long-yardage situations their priority may be reversed.   On the other hand, outside the core, mirroring an immediate receiver, pass defense always is defined as the (I) responsibility for the Second Level, but, against outside running plays to their side, Second Level personnel must execute a crucial (II) responsibility, secondary containment (see conclusion of chapter 3).   Therefore, within their responsibility sequence the only uncertainty involves Second Level personnel mirroring an immediate receiver in area C: usually

- against a larger, slower tight end   (I)   =   run
             (II)   =   pass
- against a smaller, faster slotback   (I)   =   pass
             (II)   =   run.

It is recommended that in the defensive game plan these specific responsibilities be clearly defined for the Second Level, according to the offensive personnel, down and distance situations, and so on.

Key Reading.   Compared to that required of linebackers in the three-level defensive model, key reading in the present 2-level system is considerably simplified for the Second Level in the core, because these personnel are *not* assigned responsibility for defending a specific line-gap.   Similar to those of the inside linebacker, however, their keys are obtained from the offensive linemen and backfielder in the immediate vicinity of a stack, and the various combinations are illustrated in figure 77.   Their basic key, run versus pass, must be obtained from the offensive linemen; secondary keys are obtained by reading *through* the line into the backfield.   At the snap, it is imperative that the Second Level defender *see* the offense's forward surge (on running plays) or retreat (on passes), and *uncovered* linemen provide the most valid key in this regard:

- the rules of football state that on passes offensive linemen may *not* go over the line of scrimmage, downfield, before the pass is thrown; there-fore, if an uncovered center, guard, or tackle *remains on the line of scrimmage*, regardless of secondary keys or the backfield action the Second Level must play pass.

When the offensive line surges forward at the snap *with* uncovered linemen moving quickly off the line of scrimmage, Second Level defenders execute one of three actions: they may *fill* or *scrape* immediately, or *cutback* cautiously, according to the offense's secondary keys (see Drills section).   Stacked in area C mirroring the tight end, however, when this offensive lineman, also an *eligible* receiver, moves downfield, this does *not*

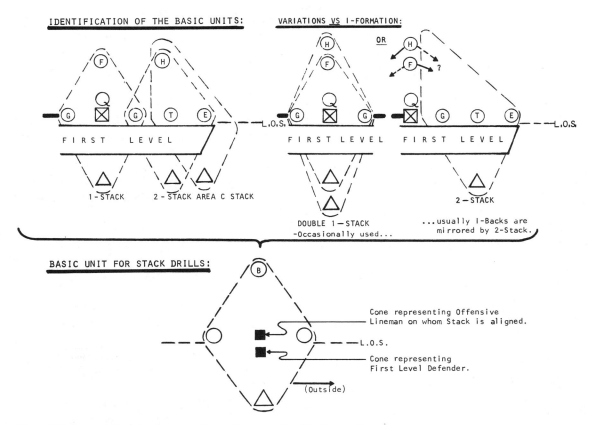

Figure 77 For each Second Level position in the core, identification on the *basic* unit for stack drills and key reading, according to the offensive formation.

automatically verify the basic run key. The subtle variations in each of these key reading situations require considerable stack drill practice in order to synchronize the reactions of Second Level personnel in the core.

Drills

1. FUNDAMENTAL DRILLS. Only a limited number of texts include basic movement drills that do not involve tackling (37, 38). On the other hand, literally *every* one of the many publications on linebackers, too numerous to reference, describe excellent tackling drills that incorporate basic movement and technique into a variety of drill formats.

2. GROUP DRILLS. In this section, five stack drills are detailed: a Basic Unit Drill, the three individual Stack Drills (*i.e.*, 1-Stack, 2-Stack, Area C Stack), and a modification of the Area C Drill jam *vs* tight end or slotback. The Basic Unit Drill

provides the format for introducing stack technique and fundamentals. In the individual stack drills these principles are adapted according to the location of the stack and the specific keys that personnel read, and the only major variation occurs when Second Level personnel implement jam technique. In learning individual stack technique, Gael, Strong, and Bandit rotate through the 1-Stack, 2-Stack and Area C Drills: on the other hand, Lou and Rose practice only the Area C Drills (see fig. 74).

Basic Unit Drill (fig. 78)

This drill incorporates the Second Level's basic key-reading unit (fig. 77); its purpose is to introduce the stack drill format and teach the principles of the stack mechanism (see pages 62-66). Before progressing to the individual stack drills (fig. 78, right side), Second Level personnel should understand and be capable of executing these *basic* techniques; practice time permitting, coaches are also advised to return periodically to this fundamental format in order to reinforce these basics.

Technique	The stack principle requires that First Level personnel prevent the offensive blockers (on whom they align) from firing directly at the Second Level stacked behind; thus, the immediate threat to the Second Level comes from *uncovered* offensive linemen.
	By varying their depth and stack location, making these *final* adjustments in concert with the First Level's shift just prior to the snap, then reacting quickly and correctly at the snap, Second Level players make it very difficult for the offense to block them effectively.
	The Basic Unit format is essentially a read-and-react and technique drill, requiring only that the inside/outside directions of the (simulated) offense be established by the Second Level defender when setting up his (own) drill.
Key Reading	In the Basic Unit Drill (and individual stack drills as well) the offensive linemen on either side of the stack remain *uncovered*:
	a. to provide the Second Level's basic read,
	b. to position blockers against whom the defender executes a *fill*, *scrape*, or *cutback*, according to his keys.
	On the other hand, both the First Level defender and the offensive lineman he covers (on whom the stack is aligned) are replaced by cones to *simplify* the drill, allowing the Second Level to focus more upon their basic and secondary keys.

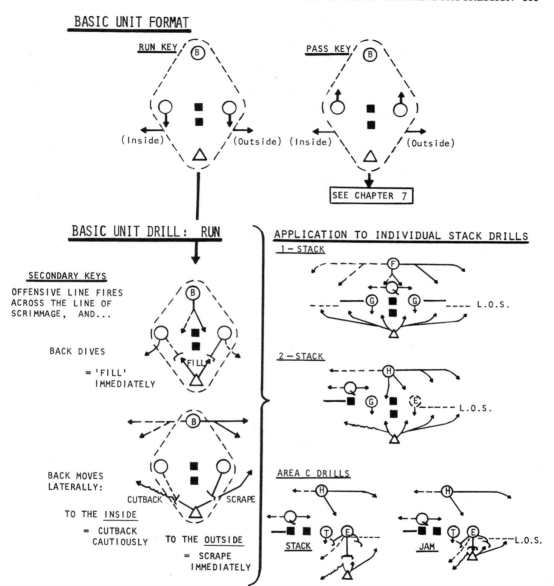

Figure 78 The basic unit stack drill and application of stack principle to 1-Stack (fig. 79), 2-Stack (fig. 80), and Area C (fig. 81). In these stack drills *uncovered* offensive linemen fire across the line of scrimmage (with pass keys interspersed) to give the basic read; then, according to secondary keys the defender executes fill, scrape, or cutback. (Inclusion of quarterback optional; for left side of defensive mirror format and keys).

Their basic key, run vs. pass, is always indicated according to the actions of the offensive linemen (fig. 78, top portion).

And there are three *main* secondary keys that the defender reads *through* the offensive line: specifically, when the near back dives (toward the line of scrimmage) or moves laterally, outside vs. inside (fig. 78, left side, lower portion).

In the individual stack drills secondary keys are modified according to the offensive blocking patterns, and the location of the stack.

1-Stack Drill (fig. 79)

For Gael, Strong, and Bandit, the 1-stack format simulates mirroring an ace (fullback) formation, with the center and First Level nose replaced by cones and the offensive guards left *uncovered*. With its location at the center of the offensive formation, note that the Second Level defender is always moving *both* frontside AND to the outside; thus, *by definition* he does not have cutback responsibility, only fill and scrape. For this reason the defender should not leave the interior of the core until the football has moved to the periphery and his *timing* becomes the critical factor in his transition from fill to scrape; operating this drill the ball carrier should be instructed to cutback on outside running plays when the defender is scraping outside too soon.

Technique With both guards uncovered, in the 1-stack the defender is very vulnerable.

Therefore, shoulder and forearm lift technique is stressed in this drill when the fullback dives over-guard behind the guard firing across the line of scrimmage.

Unless the running play is quick-pitch, the defender always should play *through* the head of blockers in this drill.

Key Reading Guard(s) *uncovered* provide the most reliable run (vs. pass) key for the Second Level; if these Blockers fire across the line of scrimmage at the snap, even before the defender *sees* the Quarterback hand-off the football he can yell: "run. . . . run. . . . " with absolute certainty.

However, in 1-stack secondary keys are more difficult to read.

a. It is the guards who execute the more sophisticated blocks (*i.e.*, pulling, false keys, etc.) in most offensive blocking schemes.

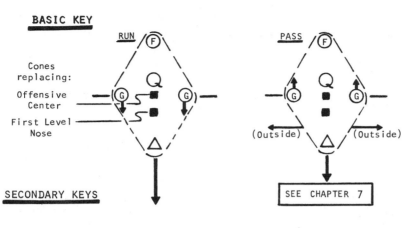

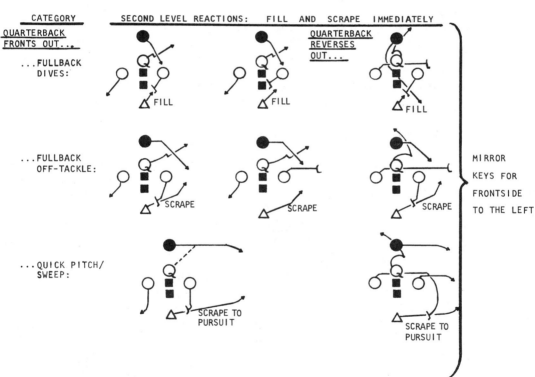

Figure 79 1-Stack Drill (Gael, Bandit, & Strong only align in 1-Stack): cones replace the offensive center *covered* by the nose, the guards remain *uncovered*; note variations in reads when half back is included in drill (see Cross-Key Drill), and when drill is adapted for a specific offensive system (see chapter 9).

  b. The Second Level defender tends to focus on the (ace) fullback in this drill and when a *second* back is included in the formation by not reading *through* the offensive line into the backfield the 1-stack defender quickly finds himself out-of-position (see next section).

  c. The time available for 'reading' is reduced, compared to the 2-stack and in area C where the defender is positioned further to the outside, away from the offensive center, initially.

2-Stack Drill (fig. 80)

In the 2-stack this situation is usually reversed: the basic (run vs. pass) key may be more difficult to read. Often the offensive guard immediately inside the stack is covered (i.e., in 1-stack usually one guard remains uncovered to confirm the basic run vs. pass key). On the other hand, there are only three directions in which the near back may move (fig. 80): reliable secondary reads are provided when the back dives or moves laterally to the inside. Positioned in 2-stack, however, the Second Level defender has *more time* to read and react. Thus he must be coached not to overreact to the outside (scrape) until the ball carrier moves out to him; or to the inside (cutback) when the football moves away, against the far side of the core. It should be noted also in figure 80 (lower half) that the 2-Stack Drill may operate with or without simulating the tight end, often an important variable when modifying the Drill's format during game planning.

Technique   In this drill, shiver technique should be emphasized: in game situations, the mobility of the 2-stack defender must not be restricted by engaging blockers with shoulder and forearm lift technique.

       The exception to this occurs when the near back moves immediately outside at the snap and the tight end blocks down on him (shoulder technique *through* the tight end, etc.).

       Also, in 2-stack the defender must *see* the football (handed off by the quarterback) as he fills.

Key Reading   The tactical location of the 2-stack provides straight forward, reliable keys, with two exceptions.

  a. When the near-back moves outside (fig. 80, lower portion) the defender must *see* his block on the First Level end before fully committing to scrape; without offensive linemen downfield a play-action pass is always a possibility, with the halfback avoiding the end moving into the flat.

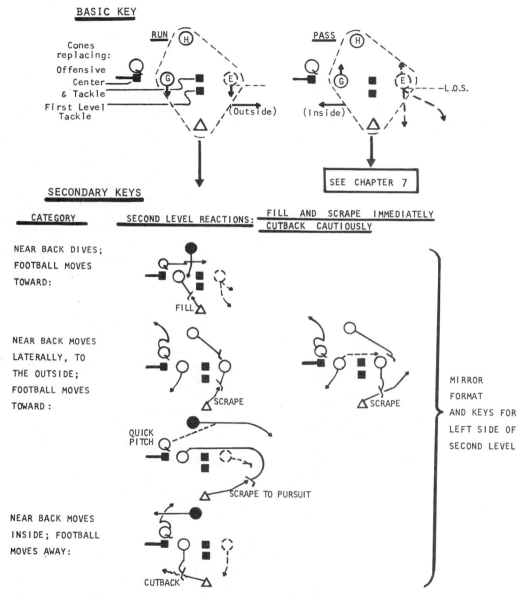

Figure 80 2-Stack Drill (Gael, Bandit, & Strong only align in 2-Stack): cones replace the offensive tackle *covered* by the First Level tackle, the guard and tight end (if positioned to that side of the offensive formation) remain *uncovered*; again note variations when a second back is included in drill format (see cross-key & I-Back drills, next section).

b. In addition, by employing a halfback in the formation an offense will invariably employ two backfielders, and this can complicate the defender's secondary reads (see Cross-Key Drill, next section).

Area C Drills (fig. 81)

Stack drill in area C is quite similar to the 2-stack in both location and technique: the basic run key is best verified by the offensive tackle or guard immediately inside, but often both of these linemen are covered. The near-back, however, is usually visible for secondary keys (fig. 81, top portion). On the other hand, in jam technique the Second Level defender is reduced to reading *only* the adjacent offensive tackle: seldom will he see much of the near-back, and with the First Level end aligned tight the offensive guard quickly disappears from his field of vision once the play begins. A fundamental difference in mirroring in area C lies with the *concentration* that the defender must focus on the tight end or slotback, because this player is an eligible receiver. When Lou or Rose mirrors the tight end (the No. 1C receiver to their side), there is no other Second Level player outside of them assigned secondary (II) containment; additionally, in jam this defender must assume primary (I) containment against outside running plays, a difficult assignment to execute.

Technique

When a large tight end is *not* a pass receiving threat: stacked, the defender should contact him vigorously *anytime* he releases off the line of scrimmage at the snap; in jam there will be contact on every play, and the defender should make down and distance adjustments, particularly against outside running plays.

When a smaller slotback is *not* a blocking threat: in jam the defender may be placed in a disadvantageous position for pass coverage, particularly in max; in long-yardage situations he may resort to aligning off the line of scrimmage.

Above are the two extremes; usually the tight end is both a blocking *and* a pass-receiving threat; in this instance these strategies must be combined according to the down and distance.

Key Reading

In both stack and jam, to obtain his basic key the Second Level defender must read his Area C receiver and the offensive tackle (fig. 81, top portion).

As a result, the secondary keys this defender is able to read may be reduced, and his most difficult read is the play-action pass (see chapter 7).

Also, mirroring in Area C, the defender sees much less of the football; therefore verbal identification of the play, run

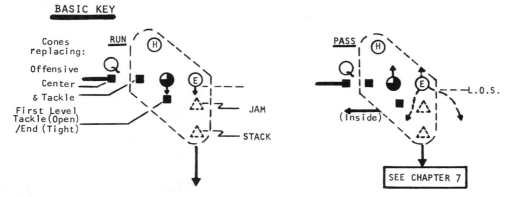

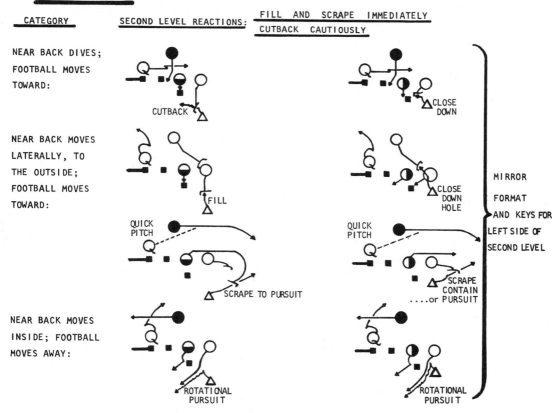

Figure 81 Area C Drills: Second Level personnel in *stack* (when First Level end aligned loose) and in jam (automatically when end aligned tight). With the offensive tackle seldom uncovered and the tight end (or slotback) an eligible receiver, the defender must *see* as far inside as possible.

vs. pass, yelled by a Second Level teammate (stacked in the interior of the core) will assist the defender with these decisions. But, this means of communication can only be practiced in the team drill format.

3. TEAM DRILLS. In this section, three additional drill formats are described which combine individual stack drills against specific offensive situations:

Cross-Key Drills: against *two* backfielders in the offensive formation,[6]

I-Back Drills: a *special*, two-back formation,

2-Stack + Area C Drills: the format for defending outside running plays and coordinating the switch stunt.

Additional *team drill* for the Second Level is detailed in the final section of this chapter: incorporation of specific First Level key drills within the stack drill format which provide the lead-up for full scrimmages. One caution, however: before progressing to these more complex formats Second Level personnel *must be proficient* at operating the individual stack drills, for their technique will be modified to some degree in these larger drills.

Cross-Key Drills (fig. 82).

Against two offensive backfielders, the two mirroring defenders (Gael and Bandit, or Gael with Strong) have three possible stack locations (fig. 82, top portion). Offensive plays are designed for these drills by combining the individual backfield patterns diagrammed in figures 79-81, with offensive linemen inserted into the drills as required to simulate blocking and keys; in game-plan preparation, the next opponent's *unique* backfield and blocking patterns are highlighted in these drills (see part IV). With the addition of the second backfielder, however, *no* changes in individual stack alignment or technique are required (fig. 82, middle portion) unless the paths of the backfielders cross (lower portion).

- When the near-back moves *to the inside*, stack technique always requires the Second Level defender to implement *cutback* (fig. 80, bottom diagram).
- With two backs in the formation, when the *near*-back moves inside the defender must immediately locate *the far backfielder*.
- And if the far-back is approaching towards him, on the move the defender switches his secondary key read to that back (fig. 82, lower diagrams), reacting accordingly—*i.e.*, he fills and scrapes immediately, or plays cutback cautiously.

CROSS-KEY FORMATS

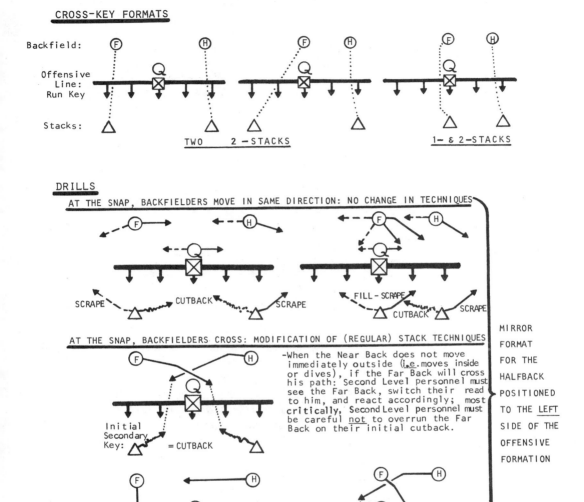

Figure 82 Cross-Key Drills: adaptation of individual stack techniques when backs *cross*.

However, to coordinate these simple adjustments first requires *disciplined* stack technique, as well as considerable cross-key practice and game rehearsal.

Technique

Appreciate that cutback is a backside responsibility, executed by the stacked defender (on the backside) moving *on key* through the center of the offensive formation; however, when two backs cross (on counters and reverse plays) this side of the defense becomes the frontside.

Thus, the critical technique in cross-key involves *how far* and *how fast* this Second Level defender proceeds through center. One factor in successful execution of cross-key is keeping free from offensive blockers: shiver technique should be employed, with quick shuffle, from a low football position.

Key Reading

A second factor in executing cross-key is anticipation. Only by *immediately* locating the far-back can the defender anticipate correctly:

a. if the far-back is approaching directly toward him, the defender must *retard* his cutback movement (never stopping the feet, however, nor raising himself up);

b. on the other hand, if the far-back is diving into the line of scrimmage, with the quarterback also moving in that direction, the (backside) defender must *accelerate through center* (fig. 82, lower left-hand diagram).

In contrast, with *both* backs and the football now to his side, the *frontside* Second Level defender (in lower left-hand diagram) must *search* the fullback to see if the quarterback handed-off the football before filling.

I-Back Drills (fig. 83)

When the halfback stacks behind the fullback, their "I" constitutes a *special* 2-back formation: from this alignment the fullback and halfback can execute unique backfield patterns (fig. 83) against which the Second Level requires considerable work. Defensively, *two* 2-stacks provide the best core structure against the I-formation. (A *double* 1-stack also may be employed, but has limited usage.) In figure 83 the basic backfield patterns run from the I-formation are illustrated:

- When the I-backs *split* in opposite directions at the snap, *or* move in *tight tandem* in the same direction, the Second Level is able to read and react to either pattern according to their individual stack techniques.

APPLICATION OF (REGULAR) STACK TECHNIQUES

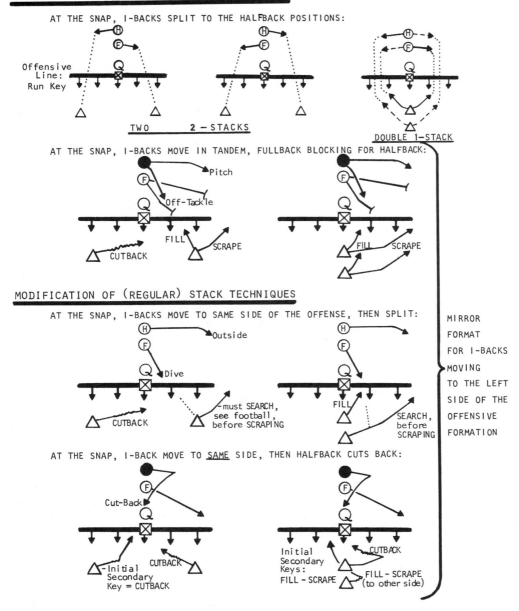

AT THE SNAP, I-BACKS SPLIT TO THE HALFBACK POSITIONS:

Offensive
Line:
Run Key

TWO 2 – STACKS

DOUBLE 1-STACK

AT THE SNAP, I-BACKS MOVE IN TANDEM, FULLBACK BLOCKING FOR HALFBACK:

Pitch

Off-Tackle

FILL

CUTBACK

SCRAPE

FILL SCRAPE

MODIFICATION OF (REGULAR) STACK TECHNIQUES

AT THE SNAP, I-BACKS MOVE TO SAME SIDE OF THE OFFENSE, THEN SPLIT:

Outside

Dive

CUTBACK

–must SEARCH,
see football,
before SCRAPING

FILL

SEARCH,
before
SCRAPING

MIRROR
FORMAT
FOR I-BACKS
MOVING
TO THE LEFT
SIDE OF THE
OFFENSIVE
FORMATION

AT THE SNAP, I-BACK MOVE TO SAME SIDE, THEN HALFBACK CUTS BACK:

Cut-Back

–Initial
Secondary
Key = CUTBACK

CUTBACK

Initial
Secondary
Keys:
FILL - SCRAPE

CUTBACK

FILL - SCRAPE
(to other side)

Figure 83 I-Back Drills: adaptation of individual stack techniques vs. I-back
formation, according to the backfield pattern of the two backs.

- In the lower diagrams in figure 83, however, the actions of the I-backs *after the snap* present considerable problem for the Second Level: when the backs move against the same side of the defense *then split,*
  a. the fullback diving, the halfback moving quickly outside, *or*
  b. the fullback moving outside, the halfback cutting back over center, even winding all the way backside.

Against these latter patterns, the Second Level defender in a 2-stack on the backside is again faced with the decision of *how far and how fast* to move through center, while the frontside defender in 2-stack must *search* before committing to fill or scrape. On the other hand, positioning in a double 1-stack (see diagrams, lower right) can provide a *short-term* solution, but only in certain situations: specifically, against long-yardage in max coverage, and in certain instances to defend against the triple-option. In a double 1-stack each Second Level defender can read and react *independently* to the fullback and the halfback; however, against most I-formation plays the double 1-stack has inherent weaknesses, particularly power running.

Technique The popularity of the I-formation is not accidental; offensively it incorporates several tactical advantages (39), and to defend against it techniques must be modified.

The *frontside* defender in a 2-stack must read through the offensive line, recognize run (vs. pass) and the offensive blocking pattern immediately, then *search* for the football before committing to his course of action, fill or *scrape.*

It is imperative that the backside cutback defender not overrun to the football, and remain clear of blockers by employing shiver and shuffle technique.

It should be appreciated as well, that against the I-formation the First Level must be employed advantageously:

a. aligned so that *potential blockers are covered*, allowing the Second Level personnel greater freedom of movement in the core;

b. the ends' crash containment frontside and trailer backside giving the Second Level critical time to read and search.

Key Reading In the I-Back Drills, two secondary keys must be stressed constantly:

a. immediate identification of the I-back pattern (according to fig. 83), particularly when both backs move in unison against one side of the defense, *then split*; on the move the Second Level must recognize the potential problems this action creates for them, and react accordingly.

b. as the I-backs move away in unison, the backside Second Level defender *must read the halfback*, retarding his movement if the halfback cuts-back, or accelerating through center as the halfback reaches the perimeter of the core, moving away.

2-Stack + Area C Drills (fig. 84)

From game analyses the running plays that *consistently* gain positive yardage "break...one to four yards outside the offensive end" (40). Therefore, practice time is well spent defensing off-tackle, sweep, and quick-pitch plays; this cannot be emphasized strongly enough to coaches. The absence of the First Level end (in the drill format) affords the Second Level the opportunity to practice jam exclusively. And, again, each week throughout the season these drills are modified, according to the next opponent's outside running game.[7] In the upper portion of figure 84, off-tackle plays are diagrammed; in the lower portion outside running plays. It is unnecessary to include all of the offensive players shown in these diagrams at the same time, but, these limited examples illustrate possible drill formats:

a. simulating a wide receiver in early-motion to the inside, blocking back on the Second Level on outside running plays, *or* only faking crack-back on off-tackle plays,

b. realigning a tight end/wide receiver formation into a slotback/split end formation by means of a simple interchange *before* the snap,

c. incorporating a deep safety into run defense (the *only* realistic format for these personnel other than scrimmage),

d. practicing the switch stunt.

Conducting these drills, it may be appropriate to intersperse an offense's *complementary* plays (quarterback bootleg, halfback option-pass, reverses, counters, etc.), which also threaten the perimeter of the core.

Technique   The *critical* technique involves the Second Level's jam, particularly against larger tight ends; as described earlier, this is similar to present outside linebacker play (41).

The defender in the 2-stack must learn when to scrape, and when to initiate pursuit:

a. scrape is possible only when the ball carrier is contained inside the core;

b. outside the core's imaginary perimeter and without containment, the defender must run the ball carrier laterally toward the sideline, and the timing of his transition, scrape-to-pursuit, is critical;

c. conducting these drills, the ball carrier should be encouraged always to bounce outside, and if he cannot outrun pursuit to cut back before reaching the sideline.

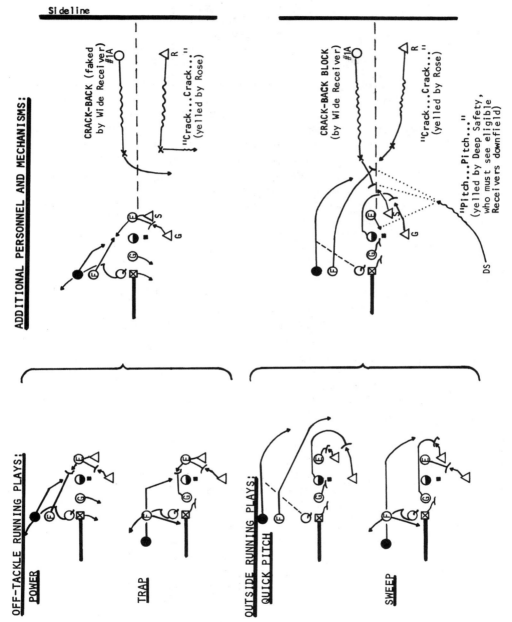

Figure 84 2-Stack + Area C Drills: off-tackle and sweep are two running plays that require constant practice. (Note: a wide receiver and deep safety also may be incorporated into this format).

174

Similarly, to simulate game situations for Lou and Rose, when they are not mirroring the tight end (No. 1C in the drill), insert a wide No. 1A receiver into the format (fig. 84).

Key Reading | For core defenders in these drills, keys are essentially unchanged from their individual stack drills; their most difficult read is play-action pass, discussed in the next chapter.

For Second Level personnel *outside* the core, pass defense remains their (I) responsibility, outside run containment (II), however their keys (also discussed at length in chapter 7) are less structured and more difficult to read. At this point, note that their secondary keys—*seeing* the quarterback handoff/or *hearing* the safety yell "pitch...pitch..."—are critically important for the execution of (II) and require constant rehearsal, according to the week's game plan.

RUN DEFENSE: FIRST AND SECOND LEVELS

Team drill combining First and Second Level personnel is achieved by incorporating specific First Level key drills into the appropriate stack format. Quite literally, the cones simulating both the First Level *and* the offensive personnel are removed from a stack drill, to be replaced by the (corresponding) First Level defender *live*, a player simulating the offensive lineman *live*, and the other linemen and back(s) transposed intact. This general format provides the basic and secondary keys for both the First and Second Levels, and any number of personnel combinations are possible. In this section, examples of these team drills are illustrated in photo sequences; the offensive action in each sequence combines various offensive keys and backfield patterns from the smaller group drills illustrated throughout this chapter.[8] Each week in their pre-game planning, however, the coaching staff selects only drill formats that replicate the next opponent's offensive system (see part IV). Before proceeding to this combined format, individual defenders must be well-schooled, through their smaller group drills, in the fundamentals and skills of their position. Though controlled, the larger numbers in these team drills prove confusing to the inexperienced player (although not nearly so confusing as *live* scrimmage) and lead to inappropriate reads and reactions. By the same token, these combined drills should be carefully scripted (42) to minimize confusion for the participants. Finally, anytime the First and Second Levels are combined, Second Level stunts should be practiced, whether a run or a pass defense practice is being conducted.

PHOTO SEQUENCE NO. 1

DEFENSE
*FIRST LEVEL ALIGNMENT: 11
SIMULATED (NOTE: IN ALL PHOTOS
CONES PLACED ON THEIR SIDE
INDICATE WHERE OTHER DEFENSIVE
PERSONNEL WOULD BE; CONES
STANDING REPRESENT OTHER
OFFENSIVE LINEMEN); LEFT END LIVE.
SECOND LEVEL: TWO 2-STACKS LIVE.
CALL: "11, COVER."*

OFFENSE
*FORMATION: I; TIGHT END (TO THE
DEFENSIVE) LEFT.
PLAY: TAILBACK DIVE INSIDE;
ISOLATION BLOCKING (BY FULLBACK).*

—uncovered (vs. "11") offensive guards fire
out at 2-Stack defenders; tight end blocks out
on First Level end, quarterback reverses
out...

... gives to tailback diving inside, fullback
lead-blocking.
—2-Stack defenders fill, taking on offensive
guards' blocks; First Level end crashes
through tight end...

... flattening his angle along the line of
scrimmage, keeping outside leverage on
tailback.

PHOTO SEQUENCE NO. 2

DEFENSE
FIRST LEVEL ALIGNMENT: 11 (SIMULATED); LEFT END LIVE.
SECOND LEVEL: TWO 2-STACKS LIVE.
CALL: "11, COVER."

OFFENSE
FORMATION: PRO; TIGHT END (TO THE DEFENSIVE) LEFT.
PLAY: CROSSBUCK, HALFBACK CARRYING OVER THE (DEFENSIVE) LEFT SIDE.

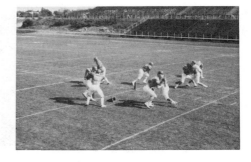

—uncovered (vs. "11") offensive guards fire out at 2-Stack defenders; tight end blocks out on First Level end, quarterback, reversing out, fakes to the fullback diving (to defensive) right...

...gives to halfback.
—the 2-Stack defenders crosskey and fill, taking on offensive guards ' blocks; First Level end crashes through tight end...

...flattening his angle along the line of scrimmage, keeping outside leverage on tailback.

PHOTO SEQUENCE NO. 3

DEFENSE
*FIRST LEVEL ALIGNMENT: 11
(SIMULATED); LEFT END LIVE.
SECOND LEVEL: TWO 2-STACKS LIVE.
CALL: "11, COVER."*

OFFENSE
*FORMATION: I; TIGHT END (TO THE
DEFENSIVE) LEFT.
PLAY: POWER OFF-TACKLE (TO THE
DEFENSIVE) LEFT.*

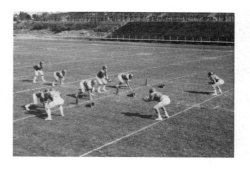

—Tight end (frontside) and backside
offensive guard (uncovered vs. "11") fire out
at 2-Stack defenders; quarterback reverses
out...

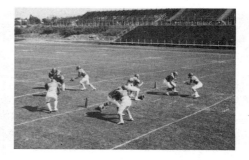

...gives to tailback following fullback
off-tackle;
—frontside 2-Stack defender scrapes...

...up, into off-tackle area; First Level end
takes on fullback's lead block, keeping
outside leverage on tailback.

PHOTO SEQUENCE NO. 4

DEFENSE
*FIRST LEVEL ALIGNMENT: 11
(SIMULATED); LEFT END LIVE.
SECOND LEVEL: 1-STACK AND AREA C
STACK LIVE.
CALL: "11, COVER."*

OFFENSE
*FORMATION: TIGHT END (TO THE
DEFENSIVE) LEFT; ACE.
PLAY: QUICK PITCH.*

—uncovered (vs. "11") frontside guard fires
out at 1-Stack defender; tackle reach-blocks
First Level tackle (simulated by cone lying on
its side); tight end attempts to reach block
crashing First Level end; quick pitch to ace
backfielder.

—Second Level defenders scrape...
...defender stacked in Area C through the
off-end area...

...defender in the 1-Stack has cutback; First
Level end crashing maintains outside
leverage on the ball carrier.

PHOTO SEQUENCE NO. 5

DEFENSE
*FIRST LEVEL ALIGNMENT: (NOT
SIMULATED BY CONES PLACED ON THE
FIELD); LEFT END ONLY LIVE.
SECOND LEVEL: LOU (AT BOTTOM) AND
ROSE (AT TOP OF PHOTO) LIVE (NO
OTHER SECOND LEVEL PERSONNEL IN
DRILL).
CALL: "..., MAX."*

OFFENSE
*FORMATION: TIGHT END AND FLANKER
(TO THE DEFENSIVE) LEFT; SPLIT END
RIGHT; I-BACKS.
PLAY: QUICK PITCH.*

—Pitch to the tailback, I-backs moving (to the defensive) left; immediate receivers release down field.
—First Level end crashes; Lou and Rose funnel wide receivers aggressively.

...seeing or hearing "Pitch... Pitch" (yelled by the deep safety), Lou commences his secondary (II) containment responsibility.
—Deep safety and Rose become responsible for halfback pass thrown to eligible receivers *continuing* downfield...

...if the First Level end does not contain the pitch he *must* force the tailback deep for Lou (in this example) to apply (II) containment.

PHOTO SEQUENCE NO. 6

DEFENSE
*FIRST LEVEL ALIGNMENT: 11
(SIMULATED); BOTH ENDS LIVE.
SECOND LEVEL: TWO 2-STACKS LIVE.
CALL: "11, DOG."*

OFFENSE
*FORMATION: TWO TIGHT ENDS; SPLIT
BACKS.
PLAY: DROPBACK PASS, BACKS FLARE.*

—Tight ends release (to be maxed by Area C
stack defenders, not in drill); backs flare
immediately, offensive line pass blocks.
—Both 2-Stack defenders elect to fire, First
Level end begins crash sequence...

...contact flaring backs, steer to the outside...

...both 2-Stack defenders continue their fire to
quarterback.

PHOTO SEQUENCE NO. 7

DEFENSE
FIRST LEVEL ALIGNMENT: (NOT
SIMULATED BY CONES PLACED ON
FIELD); LEFT END ONLY LIVE.
SECOND LEVEL: AREA C STACK
DEFENDER LIVE (I.E. NO 2-STACK
DEFENDERS MIRRORING THE I-BACKS IN
DRILL).
CALL: "..., CUSHION"

OFFENSE
FORMATION: TIGHT END (TO THE
DEFENSIVE) LEFT; I-BACKS.
PLAY: DROPBACK PASS, TIGHT END
RELEASING DOWNFIELD.

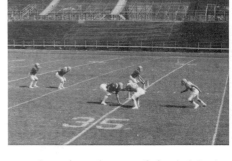

—just prior to the snap, C-Stack defender moves outside...

...up on the line of scrimmage outside *congested* off-tackle area...

...and at the snap crashes; I-backs split, quarterback drops back.
—First Level end maxes the tight end...

...funnelling him aggressively inside; C-Stack defender rushes the quarterback, keeping outside leverage (note: he is *not* responsible for screens, delays, etc., to fullback).

PHOTO SEQUENCE NO. 8

DEFENSE
FIRST LEVEL ALIGNMENT: (NOT SIMULATED BY CONES PLACED ON FIELD); LEFT END ONLY LIVE. SECOND LEVEL: AREA C STACK DEFENDER LIVE (I.E. NO 2-STACK DEFENDERS MIRRORING THE I-BACKS IN DRILL). CALL: "..., CUSHION."

OFFENSE
FORMATION: SLOTBACK (TO THE DEFENSIVE) LEFT; I-BACKS. PLAY: DROPBACK PASS, SLOTBACK RELEASING DOWNFIELD.

—Slotback positioned wider in area C...

...at the snap, C-Stack defender crashes (through uncongested C Area); First Level end maxes the slotback...

...steering him aggressively outside...

...C-Stack defender rushes the quarterback, keeping outside leverage (note: he is *not* responsible for screens, delays, etc., to fullback).

PHOTO SEQUENCE NO. 9

DEFENSE
*FIRST LEVEL ALIGNMENT: (NOT
SIMULATED BY CONES PLACED ON
FIELD); LEFT END ONLY LIVE.
SECOND LEVEL: ONLY AREA C STACK
DEFENDER LIVE (I.E. NO 2-STACK
DEFENDERS MIRRORING I-BACKS IN
DRILL).
CALL: "..., CUSHION."*

OFFENSE
*FORMATION: SLOTBACK (TO THE
DEFENSIVE) LEFT; I-BACKS.
PLAY: SLOTBACK WAGGLE, RELEASING
DOWNFIELD; DROPBACK PASS.*

—Slotback early-motion to the outside.
—first-level End and mirroring second-level
Defender loosen...

...when waggle-action takes end out *to the
limit* of his Area C
—he raises his outside arm
—yells "Yougottum....Yougottum..."
repeatedly.

...without turning his head/looking; keeps
signalling until the snap.
—Second Level defender continues to move
out with slotback (i.e., into Area B)...

...maxes slotback at the snap.

PHOTO SEQUENCE NO. 10

DEFENSE
*FIRST LEVEL ALIGNMENT: (NOT
SIMULATED BY CONES PLACED ON
FIELD); LEFT END ONLY LIVE.
SECOND LEVEL: AREA C STACK AND
2-STACK ON THE LEFT SIDE LIVE (OTHER
2-STACK DEFENDER ON THE RIGHT SIDE
NOT IN DRILL).
CALL: "..., SWITCH."*

OFFENSE
*FORMATION: TIGHT END (TO THE
DEFENSIVE) LEFT; I-BACKS.
PLAY: DROPBACK PASS, TIGHT END
RELEASING DOWNFIELD.*

—note C-Stack defender *cheats up* (by
constantly varying Second Level depth this
goes unnoticed).

—at the snap, I-backs split and tight end
releases.
—First Level end *and* C-Stack defender
crash in unison...

...2-Stack defender maxes tight end...

...fullback chooses to block First Level end
(who is *now* responsible for screens, delays,
etc., to this back); C-Stack defender comes
through cleanly.

PHOTO SEQUENCE NO. 11

DEFENSE
*FIRST LEVEL ALIGNMENT: 11
(SIMULATED); LEFT END LIVE.
SECOND LEVEL: 1-STACK DEFENDER
LIVE.
CALL: "11, MAX."*

OFFENSE
*FORMATION: TIGHT END (TO THE
DEFENSIVE) LEFT; ACE.
PLAY: PLAY-ACTION PASS.*

—quarterback reverses out; uncovered (vs.
"11") offensive linemen pass block.
—First Level end crashes; 1-Stack defender
scrapes (with fullback's action)...

...reading pass blocking and the fullback's
aggressive blocking against the First Level
end...

...the 1-Stack defender may throttle up to
provide secondary rush pressure; First Level
end must maintain his outside leverage on
the quarterback.

PHOTO SEQUENCE NO. 12

DEFENSE
*FIRST LEVEL ALIGNMENT: 11
(SIMULATED); LEFT END LIVE.
SECOND LEVEL: 1-STACK AND AREA C.
STACK LIVE.
CALL: "11, MAX."*

OFFENSE
*FORMATION: TIGHT END (TO THE
DEFENSIVE) LEFT; ACE.
PLAY: DROPBACK PASS, TIGHT END
RELEASING INSIDE.*

—quarterback drops back; fullback moves to block crashing First Level end; offensive line pass blocks; tight end releases inside downfield.
—1-Stack defender scrapes (with fullback's action)...

...C-Stack defender aggressively contacts tight end...

...funnelling him inside; reading pass blocking and the fullback's aggressive block against the First Level end, the 1-Stack defender may throttle up to provide secondary rush pressure.

PHOTO SEQUENCE NO. 13

DEFENSE
*FIRST LEVEL ALIGNMENT: 11
(SIMULATED); LEFT END LIVE.
SECOND LEVEL: 1-STACK AND AREA C
STACK LIVE.
CALL: "11, MAX."*

OFFENSE
*FORMATION: TIGHT END (TO THE
DEFENSIVE) LEFT; ACE.
PLAY: DROPBACK PASS, TIGHT END
RELEASING OUTSIDE.*

—Quarterback drops back; fullback moves to block crashing First Level end; offensive line pass blocks; tight end releases outside downfield.
—1-Stack defender scrapes (with fullback's action)...

...C-Stack defender also scrapes initially (with tight end's action)...

...then reading pass, aggressively contacts tight end, steering him further outside; 1-Stack defender may throttle up (seeing fullback's block) and the First Level end must maintain his outside leverage on the quarterback.

PHOTO SEQUENCE NO. 14

DEFENSE
*FIRST LEVEL ALIGNMENT: 11
(SIMULATED); LEFT END LIVE.
SECOND LEVEL: TWO 2-STACKS LIVE.
CALL: "11, MAX."*

OFFENSE
*FORMATION: PRO BACKFIELD, TWO
TIGHT ENDS.
PLAY: SEMI-ROLLOUT (TO THE
DEFENSIVE) LEFT; FLOOD LEFT,
HALFBACK INTO THE FLAT.*

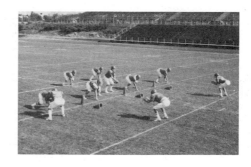

—uncovered (vs. "11") offensive guards pass block; backs move in unison (to the defensive) left; tight ends release downfield (to be maxed by Area C Stack defenders, *not* in drill); quarterback reverses out...

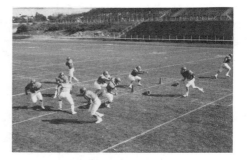

...begins rollout (to defensive) left.
—First Level end crashes; backside 2-Stack defender moves frontside *cautiously* to fullback; frontside 2-Stack defender scrapes...

...steering halfback into shallow flat...

...end pressures quarterback, keeping outside leverage.

Notes

1. Again, coaches should note that it is an advantage for the First Level end on the defensive right side to be naturally *left-handed*, since he works more with his left arm and shoulder, and always lead-steps with his *inside* left leg.

2. In such situations when a First Level end must align inside the tight end, switch may be called to reinstitute the crash from the outside perimeter of the core (fig. 32 and 62, lower diagram).

3. Only huddle calls "4-away" and "5-away" (when the directional indicator means *away from* the tight end) instruct the defensive end to align inside the offensive tight end.

4. Therefore, twists only should be called in conjunction with *single-digit* alignments.

5. On occasion in even-numbered alignments (2 and 4), a lighter Second Level defender may choose to stack "on" an offensive guard (behind the nose or closed tackle) rather than over center, where he is directly exposed to the block of the offensive center.

6. Cross-key principles can also be applied against Full House, Wishbone and Power-I formations, (*i.e.,* three backfielders, although these combinations are not covered in this section).

7. During some weeks, when preparing to play against triple-option teams, the quarterback-option will require the majority of time spent with this drill format; specific modifications are explained in a major section of chapter 9.

8. In the following photo sequences, to reduce confusion the only First Level personnel *live* is the end on the left. In addition, cones simulating other First Level personnel are positioned only in the 11-alignment. Implementing team drills in practice, additional nose, tackle and Second Level personnel would also be *live*.

References

1. GOMER JONES, *Offensive and Defensive Line Play* (Englewood Cliffs, N.J.: Prentice-Hall, Inc., 1961), pp. 150-159.

2. ROBERT TROPPMAN, *Football's Master Defense Guide* (West Nyack, N.Y.: Parker Publ. Co., Inc., 1969), pp. 141-142.

3. ARA PARSEGHIAN and TOM PAGNA, *Parseghian and Notre Dame Football* (Notre Dame, Ind.: Men-In-Motion, 1971), pp. 57-59; 65-67.

4. JOHN OLSON, "The battle for the line of scrimmage," *Athletic Journal*, 64(2): 14-17, 1983.

5. JONES, *Offensive and Defensive Line Play*, pp. 30-31; 116-117.

6. PAUL "BEAR" BRYANT, *Building a Championship Football Team* (Englewood Cliffs, N.J.: Prentice-Hall, Inc., 1960), pp. 35-37.

7. Ibid., pp. 32-33, 35, 37.

8. DONALD E. FUOSS, *Coaching the Offensive and Defensive Line Game* (West Nyack, N.Y.: Parker Publ. Co., Inc., 1972), pp. 225-226.

9. GEORGE H. ALLEN, *Complete Book of Winning Football Drills* (Englewood Cliffs, N.J.: Prentice-Hall, Inc., 1959), pp. 348-357.

10. FUOSS, *Coaching the Offensive and Defensive Line Game*, pp. 178-188.

11. JOHN OLSON, "The defensive Noseguard: advanced techniques," *Athletic Journal*, 64(3): 18-20, 1983.

12. FUOSS, *Coaching the Offensive and Defensive Line Game*, p.181.

13. JONES, *Offensive and Defensive Line Play*, pp. 152-155.

14. JULES YAKAPOVICH, *The Radar Defense for Winning Football* (West Nyack, N.Y.: Parker Publ. Co., Inc., 1971), pp. 33-69.

15. ALLEN, *Complete Book of Winning Football Drills*, pp. 346-365; 380-391.

16. JONES, *Offensive and Defensive Line Play*, pp. 9-20.

17. TROPPMAN, *Football's Master Defense Guide*, pp. 131-149.

18. *Illustrated Football Drills from The Coaching Clinic*, compiled by the editors of The Coaching Clinic (West Nyack, N.Y.: Parker Publ. Co., Inc., 1975), pp. 137-142; 143-148; 149-154; 241-244; 281-286.

19. PARSEGHIAN and PAGNA, *Parseghian and Notre Dame Football*, pp. 35-36.

20. FUOSS, *Coaching the Offensive and Defensive Line Game*, pp. 192-193.

21. TROPPMAN, *Football's Master Defense Guide*, p. 20.

22. JONES, *Offensive and Defensive Line Play*, pp. 132-133.

23. FUOSS, *Coaching the Offensive and Defensive Line Game*, pp. 190-197.

24. ESCO SARKKINEN, "Defensive end play," *Football Coaching*, compiled by the American Football Coaches Association; editor: Dick Herbert. (New York: Charles Scribner's Sons, 1981), pp. 134-137.

25. GARY SPERBER, "Ideas and drills for training crashing ends," *Illustrated Football Drills from The Coaching Clinic*, compiled by the editors of The Coaching Clinic (West Nyack, N.Y.: Parker Publ. Co., Inc., 1975), pp. 143-148.

26. JERRY SANDUSKY, *Developing Linebackers the Penn State Way* (West Point, N.Y.: Leisure Press, 1981), pp. 41-56.

27. ESCO SARKKINEN, "Defensive end play," *Football Coaching*, pp. 134-137.

28. SANDUSKY, *Developing Linebackers the Penn State Way*, pp. 59-60.

29. FUOSS, *Coaching the Offensive and Defensive Line Game*, pp. 192-194.

30. JONES, *Offensive and Defensive Line Play*, pp. 121-122.

31. GEORGE H. ALLEN, *Pass Defense Drills* (Menlo Park, Calif.: Addison-Wesley Publ. Co., 1968), chapter 4 pp. 51-72.

32. JERRY SANDUSKY, "Fundamentals and principles of Linebacker play," *Football Coaching*, compiled by the American Football Coaches Association; editor: Dick Herbert (New York: Charles Scribner's Sons, 1981), pp. 138-142.

33. LLOYD H. HELGESON, *Total Pass Defense* (West Nyack, N.Y.: Parker Publ. Co., Inc., 1978), pp. 83-84.

34. SANDUSKY, "Fundamentals and principles of Linebacker play," *Football Coaching*, p. 139.

35. SANDUSKY, *Developing Linebackers the Penn State Way*, pp. 59-60.

36. SARKKINEN, "Defensive end play," *Football Coaching*, pp. 135-136.

37. DONALD E. FUOSS, *Championship Football Drills for Teaching Offensive and Defensive Fundamentals and Techniques* (Englewood Cliffs, N.J.: Prentice-Hall, Inc., 1964), pp. 252-260.

38. SANDUSKY, *Developing Linebackers the Penn State Way*, pp. 69-83; 91-97.

39. JERRY HOWELL, *The Coach's Guide to Developing a Passing Attack* (West Point, N.Y.: Leisure Press, 1982), p. 134.

40. SARKKINEN, "Defensive end play," *Football Coaching*, p. 136.

41. GENE ELLENSON, *Coaching Linebackers and the Perimeter Defense* (West Nyack, N.Y.: Parker Publ. Co., Inc., 1972), pp. 55-60.

42. JIM YOUNG, "Arizona's game-week preparation," *Football Coaching*, compiled by the American Football Coaches Association; editor: Dick Herbert. (New York: Charles Scribner's Sons, 1981), pp. 22-25.

Chapter 7
PASS DEFENSE: TEACHING PROGRESSION

Installing the pass defense requires far less integration between the Levels than does installing the run defense. There are two distinct areas of coaching, rush and coverage, with pass rush being the principal role for the First Level, and coverage the responsibility of the Second Level and deep safety personnel. Only in specific instances do these areas overlap: Second Level stunting may be used to augment pass rush; the First Level ends are assigned limited pass coverage responsibility. Therefore, the organization of the football field for pass practices should be modified so these two coaching areas may proceed autonomously (fig. 85). It is strongly recommended that the goal line in the defense's end of the field be established as the line of scrimmage for all coverage drills, with the (simulated) offense working out from that end zone. In pass coverage particularly, defenders must know at all times where they are on the football field, and where certain actions and movements relocated them. With the goal line simulating the line of scrimmage, the yard stripes (counting out from the goal line) provide *numerical* feedback of vertical distance, the goalpost looming behind the offense an awareness of horizontal movement across the field. In addition, as coverage drills require the greater portion of the defensive end of the field (including the end zone, a forty yard block is allocated in fig. 85), when teams do not have a second practice area this field organization retains a twenty-yard strip for pass rush drills (i.e., between the thirty- to fifty-yardlines). During integration periods of practice, as required, First Level ends join the coverage drills at the goal line and vice versa. Specific Second Level personnel join the core drills near centerfield. In the first half of this chapter the fundamentals and drills of pass rush are presented, and (again)

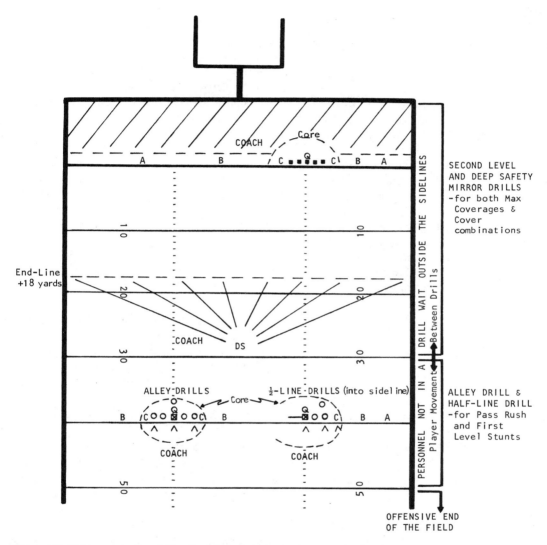

Figure 85 Field organization during the integration phase of a *pass* practice: pass coverage from the goal line (simulating the line of scrimmage) to the 30-yardline; core pass rush between the 30- and 50-yardlines. Throughout this phase of practice, in both sections of the field independently, the football is scrimmaged from one hashmark then moved to the other (with the alley and 1/2-line drills exchanging sides of the field.

organization and the teaching of *team drills* are emphasized, with individual skills and techniques being summarized. In the latter sections of the chapter a teaching progression for the installation of pass defense is detailed, with group and team drills for the various coverage personnel highlighted.

PASS RUSH

Nose and Tackles: Fundamentals and Drills

Stance, Positional Alignment, Pre-Snap Shifting. In theory, these First Level fundamentals should be performed *identically* prior to every play (see chapter 6) so that defenders can conceal their intended course of action at the snap. In practice, however, adjustments are possible, particularly in long yardage, as the necessity for a concerted pass rush increases. The base of the stance may be narrowed and the foot stagger exaggerated, "similar to (the stance) of a sprinter"(1) is the phrase commonly used in the coaching literature to describe this adjustment. Defenders may crowd the line of scrimmage to engage individual blockers immediately, before the offensive line has time to set up its pass blocking pattern. In long-yardage situations shifting may be canceled to allow each defender to concentrate on the snap count and the offensive lineman across from him.

Pass Rush Responsibility. When their *basic* key is pass, as the offensive line retreats from the line of scrimmage to pass block, the nose and tackles make the following adjustments in order to implement pass rush.

Primary (I): immediately defenders' assigned line-gaps *expand* to alleys, pie-shaped areas with wider frontage that extend back and converge at the quarterback. In pass rush, if a defender is blocked out of his alley he must work his way back, but the precise route varies according to the pass-action, dropback vs. sprintout (fig. 86).

Secondary (II): react to screen pass, draw and delayed running plays (see keys following).

Pursuit (III): as with the run defense, in pass rush pursuit commences *anytime* the quarterback runs outside the core (with the football), because containment has obviously broken down, and it serves little purpose for First Level rushers to penetrate further.

Key Reading. Increasingly, defensive pass rush has been thwarted by the variety of plays included in the offensive pass repertoire. When their basic read is *pass*, a number of options, both running as well as passing, confront the rush personnel (fig. 87, upper half) and even when their initial read is *run*, a variety of play-action and sprintout passes can eventuate (see lower portion). Therefore, in order to implement pass rush with consistency and effectiveness, against several of these options it is *secondary keys* which identify the play. At the systems level the 2-level Defense delimits these offensive options through its *primary* pass defense mechanism, concerted pressure by five First Level personnel. In turn, this greatly assists their key reading, particularly secondary keys: whatever option an offense has selected it may not delay, and almost

FIVE FIRST LEVEL PERSONNEL

- Five rushing Alleys

FOUR FIRST LEVEL PERSONNEL

- Four rushing Alleys

VS, DROPBACK-ACTION BY QUARTERBACK

- Note, if Quarterback drops DEEPER, key Screen (II) Pass.

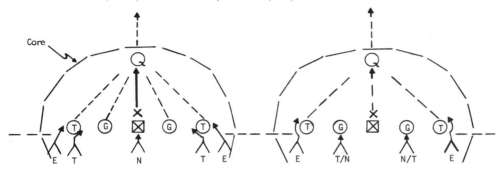

VS, SPRINTOUT-ACTION BY QUARTERBACK

- Note, if Quarterback runs OUTSIDE of core (with football), key Pursuit (III).

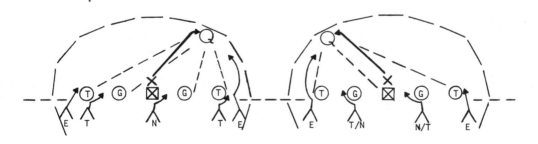

Figure 86 On passing plays the offensive line-gaps (defined for *run* defense) expanded to alleys, extending back from the line of scrimmage to perimeter of core and converging *at* the quarterback; note the route of each relative to the pass action of the quarterback.

immediately secondary keys become evident. For example, although several techniques as well as subtle variations in pass blocking are employed by the offense (2), against the five-man rush the most immediate secondary key is provided by the *depth* (from the line of scrimmage) at which the offensive line initially sets up its blocking pattern (3).

BASIC KEY: PASS   SECONDARY KEYS:

| CATEGORY | OF LESS IMPORTANCE IN READ | OF CRITICAL IMPORTANCE FOR READ |

-DEEP SET BY THE OFFENSIVE LINE:

Dropback Pass
-Note, 7 Blockers vs. First Level Rush.

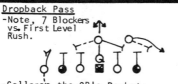

-Collapse the QB's Pocket;
-Do not let QB escape by rushing through ASSIGNED Alley (Tackles note, on T.E.T. must contain QB).

Screen Pass

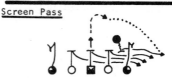

-An important Secondary Key for Screen can be:
   1st Deep-set by Offensive Tackle(s),
   2nd Backfielders moving UP, not to outside, amongst Linemen, OR
   3rd Retreat of QB through BACK OF CORE.

-SHORT SET BY THE OFFENSIVE LINE:

Quick Pass
-Note, Ace Backfield.

-Note, 3-Step Dropback by QB;
-Ace Backfielder (usually) fires TO THE SIDE the QB will throw to (to block First Level End).

Draw To Fullback/Delay To Tailback

-Note, UNCOVERED Linemen in Key Triangle (the Guards in these diagrams) short-set momentarily, then MOVE DOWNFIELD: Play Run immediately.

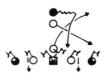

BASIC KEY: RUN

-AGGRESSIVE BLOCKING ON LINE OF SCRIMMAGE; ONLY SECONDARY KEYS AUTHENTICATE PASS:

Sprintout Pass

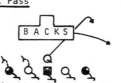

-Reach Blocking frontside & QB Sprint; immediately Defenders must seal seams between them.

Play-Action Pass

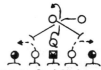

-QB fakes to Backfielders crossing (if 2 Backs) diving into Line of Scrimmage;
-Note, however, UNCOVERED Linemen DO NOT move downfield: Play Pass immediately.

Figure 87 Continuation of Figs. 67 and 68 to authenticate *basic* pass read: for first level rushers, an immediate secondary key is the *depth* at which the offensive line sets up.

1. Deep Set (fig. 87, top portion).   On dropback and screen passes, blockers establish their position *three yards deep* and to the inside of each defender (to eliminate the inside rush route).

2. Short Set (middle portion). By comparison, when the blockers set up quickly *less than three yards* from the line of scrimmage, leaving both the inside and outside rush routes open, quick passing or pass-action *runs* are more probable:

    •   if the blocker's head and shoulders are crouched lower (than normal) expect a cut-block (this block is employed on quick passes in order to lower defenders' hands);

    •   if the blocker is standing taller (than normal crouch), until the quarterback clears his backfielder(s), defenders should expect draw.

3. Aggressive Blocking (fig 87, lower portion). On sprintout and play-action passing, each defender's key-man usually attacks, attempting to control him *on the line of scrimmage*; this is the most difficult pass blocking pattern to read (because the initial read is run).

Finally, *anticipation* of passing situations and immediate *identification* of the specific play provide important assists for the defensive pass rush. Prior to the play, personnel must appreciate the implications of the down and distance situation, and the following guidelines should be adapted according to the specific tendencies of the offensive opponent. Potential passing downs include:

highest priority	third down and long yardage (more than seven yards)
second-order priority	second down and long yardage (more than seven yards)
	third down and medium yardage (more than four yards)
lowered priorities	in other tactical situations a run is more probable, according to the offensive tendency.

After the snap, as individual rushers identify the offensive play, by yelling "Quick...," "Screen...," "Sprint...," etc. they provide vital information for teammates who have not yet interpreted secondary keys; for example, hearing "Draw...Draw..." a defender initiating pass rush technique would *breakdown* (rather than continuing to *throttleup*) even though he had not read draw to that point in the play.

Techniques.   The individual pass rusher must be part artist and part bullock, aggressive and determined, but *always* under control and disciplined. His main focus must be to harass, obstruct, and even intimidate the quarterback. Causing fumbles and interceptions or sacking the quarterback may provide added incentive, but should never detract from unified First Level pressure. In the other areas of football, players are able to learn *all* of the basic skills of their position; in pass rush, however, it seems the average defensive lineman is best suited to only one or two techniques. From subjective observation, this varies according to two factors, all other things being equal:

- the player's *height*—whether he is taller or shorter than the opposing offensive personnel;
- his *foot quickness*—with slower feet a rusher is better suited to power techniques.

On the other hand, with hard work and coaching *all* defenders can develop into effective pass rushers, particularly with the 2-level Defense rushing five First Level personnel.

While there are a variety of basic techniques and finesse movements (4, 5, 6), a majority of coaches agree on the following essentials of pass rush:

- the defender must engage his blocker immediately, while the latter is still back pedaling, before he can reestablish a wide base of support and lower center of gravity;
- power technique is essential, particularly for the interior defenders (as opposed to the ends), whose alleys are narrowed, and their maneuverability restricted;
- on the other hand, the *same* technique cannot be employed repeatedly, and thus the (limited) techniques employed by the *average* pass rusher should complement each other.

INITIAL CONTACT.   Reacting to the first perceptible movement of the offensive line or the football, from his *sprinter's* stance the defender launches, accelerating with short, rapid steps, anticipating the blocker to set up deep, being alert for him to short-set, and engaging him before he can establish equilibrium.   This phase—making aggressive contact *before* the blocker is readied, on-balance, and set-up—is the most important in pass rush.

POWER TECHNIQUE: ARM-OVER/ARM-UNDER.   The nose and tackles must *collapse* the center of the quarterback's protective pocket, and this (suggested) rush technique is a natural extension of the power-move (described in chapter 6).   Again, initial contact is made by both hands striking the upper arms of the blocker just below the shoulder pads; and, again, if the defender's helmet inadvertently contacts the blocker this must be made just above the numbers by the defender charging low and hard.   At contact, the defender drives into the blocker, pressuring him, forcing the blocker to lean into the defender; at the same time the defender pulls down vigorously on one arm *to turn the shoulders*.   The pull-down may occur early in the charge, or be delayed, but when the defender feels one shoulder giving way he must accelerate his feet, *driving through the other shoulder*, quickly throwing the pulling arm over the blocker's helmet, and sprinting by him to the quarterback (this is commonly referred to as *swim technique*).   However, when the defender is unable to turn one shoulder because the blocker forcefully resists by rising up, *at that instant* the defender counters. Throwing the opposite arm *under* the blocker's (raised) shoulder and lifting forcefully, the defender drives by the blocker, leaning in as he levers through and bearing into the quarterback (this is most commonly referred to as *uppercut technique*). In employing this power sequence, therefore, First Level personnel have two *complementary* techniques: arm-over, driving through the blocker to the outside or inside; and arm-under, which also is executed to either side of the blocker. Force and leverage are applied wherever the blocker leaves himself vulnerable, but timing the appropriate move and countermove in the sequence requires hours of practice in order to refine and adapt this technique to suit the individual defender.

FINESSE TECHNIQUE. Several finesse movements also may be incorporated into pass-rush technique, including head faking, footwork, leverage application, and spinning off blockers (7, 8). Specific moves, however, must always be *suited* to the defender, according to his athletic abilities and stature. *Quick Arm-Over* is one technique that provides an excellent change-up to the power sequence, and also may be executed to either the inside or outside. The deception is to convince the blocker that power technique will (again) be employed; thus, the defender must charge close enough *to step on the blocker's toes* before aggressively clubbing the blocker on the shoulder with one forearm, simultaneously coming over the top with the other one, then stepping around the blocker and sprinting to the quarterback. The risk employing this technique occurs when the defender times his move *too early*, and the blocker reacts: off-balance, like a matador caught in mid-pass, the defender is driven out of his alley. Therefore, this finesse technique is employed most advantageously:

- by First Level ends who have more area in which to operate;
- sparingly by the interior personnel, and only when their blocker begins lunging forward at initial contact;
- with T.E.T. (tackle-end twist), by the First Level tackle to gain *depth* through the off-tackle area for quarterback containment.

TACKLING THE QUARTERBACK. With the quarterback's throwing action, First Level defenders directly *in the line of flight* extend their arms overhead; if an offensive blocker remains positioned between themselves and the quarterback at this point in the play, they should also leap as high as possible, especially against dropback passes, since these are thrown on a higher trajectory. On the other hand, if a pass rusher has an uncontested route to the quarterback, he must *make contact with the quarterback* and force him to throw under pressure, to absorb the rusher's hit as he releases the football. The only adjustment he makes is to tackle the quarterback high, and to pin his arms by coming down over his shoulders. It is most important that the rusher *completes the hit*. He *must never leap at this point. Repeated contact* with the quarterback will, if not on that play then later in the game, reap dividends for the defense.

Drills

1. FUNDAMENTAL DRILLS. For the defensive line, many sources feature nonspecific drills related to pass rush (see ref. 9-12).

Drills should emphasize stance and takeoff, footwork, and agility, including directional changes in which the player must accelerate and then quickly bring himself under control.

2. GROUP DRILLS. The four drills detailed below expand defenders' technique and key reading, from the one-on-one format in which fundamentals are stressed to the five-on-three Alley Drill, which integrates the nose and tackles' pass rush, pre-snap shifting, and stunting. It should be noted that when *pass rush* is practiced the three-on-one drill formats (see chapter 6) result in player inactivity and standing around; thus, only the three-on-one Slant Key drill is recommended when the defensive game plan calls for considerable stunting. Otherwise, the three-on-three Alley Drill is superior for pass rush purposes.

One-On-One Drill (continuation of fig. 67, with the addition of *pass keys* adapted from fig. 87)

> Defender against his key-man, with each player setting up his own drill (see chapter 6).
>
> A format to work on pass rush fundamentals exclusively: *live*, drills operate best against offensive linemen (not defensive personnel simulating pass blockers, where lock-up and thud should be used); First Level personnel require *extensive* practice in the one-on-one format.
>
> Primary (I) responsibility is practiced employing this format: in isolation any secondary keys become too obvious; as well, a *live* quarterback (i.e., replacing a cone target) only is included in format to key the defender's arm extension reaction *on the throwing motion.*

Slant Key Drill (continuation of fig. 68, with the addition of *pass keys* adapted from fig. 87)

> The three-on-one format has *limited* usefulness solely as a pass rush drill: two of the three players simulating the offense merely give the basic pass key on *every* sequence.
>
> However, this format can prove useful:
>
> **a.** if the defensive game plan entails substantial slanting; or
> **b.** more usually, any pass keys that are *essential* should be interspersed into the Slant Key Drill during *run* practices (see chapter 6).

Alley Drill: Three-On-Three (fig. 88, a continuation of fig. 73)

> This drill is an extension of one-on-one operating within the Cone Signal Drill format (fig. 73): the *uncovered* offensive linemen are still simulated by cones, while *covered* linemen now are *live* (fig. 88). Operating *live*, three-on-three operates best against offensive linemen (not defensive personnel simulating the offensive blockers).

BASIC FORMAT

FIVE-MAN FIRST LEVEL: 11-ALIGNMENT

DROPBACK-ACTION
BY QUARTERBACK

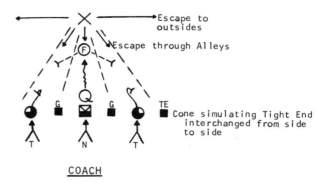

Escape to
outsides

Escape through Alleys

TE
Cone simulating Tight End
interchanged from side
to side

COACH

FOUR-MAN FIRST LEVEL: 2-ALIGNMENTS

SPRINTOUT-ACTION
BY QUARTERBACK

2-Rip

COACH

2-Link

COACH

Figure 88 Alley Drill: 3 on 3. An extension of 1 on 1 pass rush drill to integrate
the nose and tackles within the cone signal drill format (see Fig. 79): the
covered offensive linemen are now *live*; the quarterback also is *live*; inserting
an offensive backfielder into the drill is optional. (Note that the drill has two
basic formats employing five- and four-man First Level personnel.)

This format integrates the nose and tackles performing their pass rush
fundamentals, with screen and draw reactions interspersed (the keys adapted
from fig. 87); however, pre-snap shifting and stunting should not be included
because of the limited number of offensive blockers (see five-on-three drill
following).

In this format, only the *essentials* of team rush are practiced: technique, with each defender working through his alley according to the pass-action by the quarterback (fig. 88); immediate transition to (II) and (III) responsibilities, keyed by the quarterback handing-off (to the backfielder in the drill) *or* escaping to the outside or through an alley.

Alley Drill: Five-On-Three (fig. 89, a continuation of fig. 73)

In the five-on-three format all offensive positions are *live* (fig. 89); executing *mainly* pass offense (as opposed to running plays), the drill should progress lock-up to thud, but seldom *full* contact unless working against offensive line personnel.

The nose and tackles execute pre-snap shifting (with the coach making the ends' link or rip call) and First Level stunts; however the offensive blocking pattern must be carefully *scripted* according to the alignment and stunting called (and diagrammed on color-coded cards accompanying each drill).

Personnel make the transition from primary (I) responsibility through pursuit (III) according to the *limited* secondary keys that can be executed by the offensive personnel in the drill (i.e., they adapt appropriate keys according to fig. 87). During many plays it is important that the quarterback, after executing the dropback-action, readies to throw, then attempts to escape to the outside or through an interior alley to key First Level pursuit.

3. TEAM DRILLS.

Half-Line Drills

Drill format to integrate the nose, tackle, and end to either side of the First Level (see next section).

Stack Drills (see final section of chapter 6)

Appreciate that the *combined* stack drills provide the best format for run defense where First and Second Level integration inside the core is critical: however:

a. pass plays and keys must be interspersed between running plays in order to discipline defensive personnel to read their keys, not guess.

b. preparing for a strong passing team, coaches may elect to practice against particular aspects of the opponent's *total* pass offense, employing the stack format: draws and delays, screen passes, sprintout and play-action passes in particular require extensive First Level involvement and integration.

Defensive Scrimmage.

BASIC FORMAT

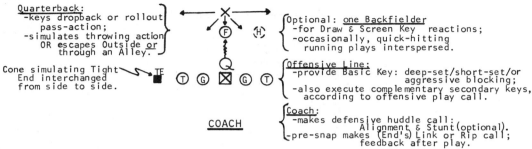

Quarterback:
-keys dropback or rollout
  pass-action;
-simulates throwing action
  OR escapes Outside or
  through an Alley.

Cone simulating Tight
End interchanged
from side to side.

COACH

Optional: one Backfielder
-for Draw & Screen Key reactions;
-occasionally, quick-hitting
  running plays interspersed.

Offensive Line:
-provide Basic Key: deep-set/short-set/or
                        aggressive blocking;
-also execute complementary secondary keys,
  according to offensive play call.

Coach:
-makes defensive huddle call:
                Alignment & Stunt (optional).
-pre-snap makes (End's) Link or Rip call;
                feedback after play.

VARIOUS COMBINATIONS

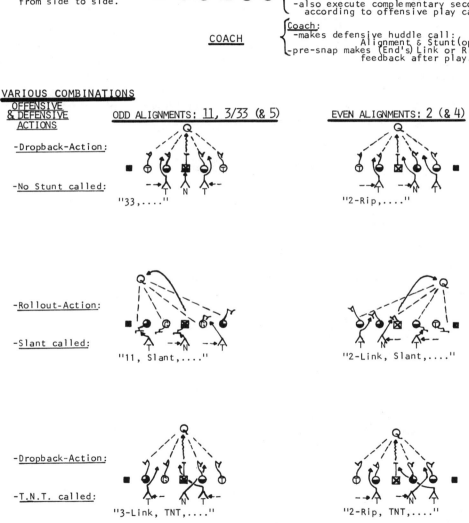

OFFENSIVE
& DEFENSIVE
ACTIONS

ODD ALIGNMENTS: 11, 3/33 (& 5)

EVEN ALIGNMENTS: 2 (& 4)

-Dropback-Action:

-No Stunt called:

"33,...."

"2-Rip,...."

-Rollout-Action:

-Slant called:

"11, Slant,...."

"2-Link, Slant,...."

-Dropback-Action:

-T.N.T. called:

"3-Link, TNT,...."

"2-Rip, TNT,...."

Figure 89 Alley Drill: 5 on 3. For practicing pre-snap shifting and First Level
stunts in conjunction with pass rush technique and First Level teamwork.

Ends: Fundamentals and Drills

As summarized in table 8, First Level ends have three areas of responsibility within the 2-level Defense. In this section only pass-rush responsibilities are detailed, their critical role being containment and pressuring of the quarterback through the outside alleys (fig. 86). The offense must believe that both ends will be crashing on every play. And outflanked to both sides (by the ends) and with the nose and tackles committed to pressuring the offense through the interior, as stressed repeatedly, these circumstances *force* an offense to make adjustments when passing.

Stance, Positional Alignment, Pre-Snap Shifting. Without a pass coverage assignment the end's stance is optional, two-or three-point, except when the end is aligned tight *inside* the offensive tight end. In passing situations, when the end chooses a three-point stance, he must, like the nose and tackles, adopt the *sprinter's* stance, mentally preparing to throttle up at the snap. However, on every play the end's actions prior to assuming his final alignment and stance should be invariable:

- initially, aligning loose in a two-point stance, reading the offensive formation, timing his link or rip call;
- then, simultaneous with the call (if one is necessary just prior to the snap) making his final adjustments, including aligning tight, assuming the three-point stance.

Table 8. The areas of responsibility for the First Level ends in the 2-level defensive system.

POSITIONAL ALIGNMENTS	AREAS OF RESPONSIBILITY FOR FIRST LEVEL ENDS		
	VS RUN (see Chapter 6)	PASS RUSH (This Section)	PASS COVERAGE (Section Following in Chapter)
END OUTFLANKING THE OFFENSE IN THE CORE: 'LOOSE' OR 'TIGHT'	-PRIMARY (I) CONTAINMENT VS SWEEPS AND PITCHES,	-PRIMARY (I) CONTAINMENT OF QUARTERBACK (VS DROPBACK- & SPRINT-ACTION),	MAX COVERAGE[*]: -IN 'DOG' -AND 'CUSHIONS' IN 'COVERS'[**]: -SHORTSIDE FLAT
END OUTFLANKED BY THE OFFENSIVE TIGHT END: 'TIGHT'	-'TRAILER' (III) PURSUIT,	-SECONDARY (II) RESPONSIBILITY: REACT TO SCREEN OUTSIDE CORE; CONTAIN DRAW INSIDE CORE,	(OR SHORTSIDE HOOK WITH #2B RECEIVER) IN 'COVER'; -SHORTSIDE SQUARE IN 'COVER-A/-B/OR -C',

[*] To avoid a first-level End aligning 'tight' AND inside the offensive Tight End, the Defensive Coordinator should NOT call '4-Away', '5-Away' and "55" Alignments with 'Dog' and 'Cushions'.

[**] Aligned 'tight' AND outflanked by the offensive Tight End, automatically the first-level End is relieved of *all* 'Cover' responsibility.

The purpose of this ritual is to conceal when the end will *not* be crashing.

Key Reading. When their *basic* key is pass, an ends primary (I) responsibility is quarterback containment. An end is relieved of this crucial (I) responsibility only when another defender is assigned quarterback containment by the huddle call; specifically,

> the (adjacent) First Level tackle *is assigned* containment by "T.E.T". (tackle-end twist) and "tight cushion" calls, automatically *assumes* containment in covers when the end does not crash;
>
> "cushion" *assigns* quarterback containment to the Second Level defender mirroring the tight end or slotback.

Against the run, specific secondary (II) responsibilities are difficult to define for the First Level ends: however, in pass defense an end is assigned two important (II) responsibilities: screen passes to his side, draw and delayed running plays inside. Pursuit (III) responsibilities for the ends are identical to run defense, with backside pressure on sprintouts from the trailer end being particularly effective. The end's *basic* pass key is verified only by the interior, offensive linemen in the end's key-triangle retreating from the line of scrimmage and setting up to pass block. By contrast, there are a number of secondary keys for the end to read, depending upon his positional alignment and the specific offensive personnel in his key-triangle.

- The depth at which the linemen initially set up, particularly the offensive tackle when the end is aligned   tight (fig. 90, upper diagrams).
- The initial movement of the near backfielder, particularly if the backfield flow is *toward* the end (see middle and lower diagrams).
- The pass-action executed by the quarterback: the end must see the football as he crashes (fig. 90, lower diagrams).
- Any delayed actions occurring later in the play, such as interior linemen moving outside to form screen blocking, short-set by the offensive line initially followed by uncovered linemen moving downfield, and so on.

Techniques. The tight alignment provides a starting point for the ends' pass rush, and their technique (as described in the preceding section) is identical. The major differences for the ends involve their wider, outside alleys and critical (I) responsibility of quarterback containment. In tight, the only additional technique suggested is an *Upfield Move* executed at the snap for securing outside leverage on the quarterback. Aligned outside of the offensive tackle, the end sprints to a spot approximately four yards deep behind the tackle: the end must arrive first, keeping his inside shoulder low, sprinting by the blocker's outside shoulder and bearing-in on the quarterback. This

BASIC KEY: PASS

OBTAINED ONLY
FROM OFFENSIVE
TACKLE & GUARD
IN KEY TRIANGLE

CATEGORY

-DEEP-SET BY
 OFFENSIVE LINE;
 DROPBACK-ACTION
 BY QUARTERBACK:

-SHORT-SET BY
 OFFENSIVE LINE;
 3-STEP DROPBACK
 OR SEMI-ROLLOUT
 BY QUARTERBACK:

BASIC KEY: RUN

-AGGRESSIVE
 BLOCKING ON
 LINE OF
 SCRIMMAGE.....

SECONDARY KEYS:

READ ACCORDING TO THE DEPTH OFFENSIVE LINE SETS UP, THEN THEIR
SUBSEQUENT ACTIONS (SEE FIG. 87); INITIAL MOVEMENT OF THE NEAR-
BACK AND FLOW OF THE BACKFIELD

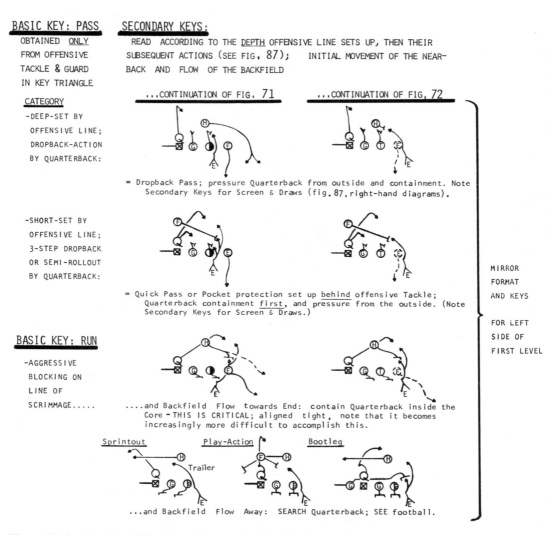

...CONTINUATION OF FIG. 71   ...CONTINUATION OF FIG. 72

= Dropback Pass; pressure Quarterback from outside and containment. Note
  Secondary Keys for Screen & Draws (fig. 87, right-hand diagrams).

= Quick Pass or Pocket protection set up behind offensive Tackle;
  Quarterback containment first, and pressure from the outside. (Note
  Secondary Keys for Screen & Draws.)

....and Backfield Flow towards End: contain Quarterback inside the
Core - THIS IS CRITICAL; aligned tight, note that it becomes
increasingly more difficult to accomplish this.

Sprintout   Play-Action   Bootleg

Trailer

...and Backfield Flow Away: SEARCH Quarterback; SEE football.

MIRROR
FORMAT
AND KEYS

FOR LEFT
SIDE OF
FIRST LEVEL

Figure 90 Continuation of Figs. 71 and 72 to authenticate *basic* pass read for
First Level ends. (Note: only against running plays does the presence of the
tight end or a slotback pose a potential threat.)

upfield move is best employed against slower blockers, forcing the offensive tackle to
backpedal and set up quickly.

Aligning further to the outside in loose, a different combination of factors
confront the First Level end. Foremost, *initial contact* is delayed, particularly if an
offensive backfielder has been assigned to block the end. Also, the end is usually
larger, and if he is fully accelerated by the point of contact, often the back's only chance
is to cut block; unlike grappling with an agile offensive tackle, this block should cause

only momentary delay because the back must leave his feet. Far too often, however, the cut block succeeds in toppling the end because he is not reading *through* his key-triangle, focusing too quickly only on the quarterback, never actually *seeing* the cut. Therefore, despite the greater risk of injury, ends should practice *live* against the cut block: as the blocker throws himself across the legs of the rusher, the rusher presses down with both hands on the blocker's back, simultaneously clearing his feet (13). With his wider alley, the end may move around or step over the blocker; however, he must immediately regain his outside containment even if his arrival at the quarterback is delayed a split second.

Finally, aligned loose or tight, the First Level end has two important secondary (II) responsibilities. With depth of penetration the likelihood of an end overrunning a draw or delayed running play increases; however, crashing from loose the hand-off from quarterback to running back, often occurs before the end is engaged by his blocker. On the other hand, to disrupt a screen pass the end must position himself in the blocking wedge as it forms, and this requires first recognition, then breaking-down, and reversing direction (on screens to the outside). Otherwise, once the pass is completed all First Level personnel must commence pursuit immediately, *deepening* their angle to the point of intersection accordingly. However, First Level personnel, and the ends in particular, seldom sacrifice aggressiveness and pressure because a screen or draw play *might* occur.

Drills

1. FUNDAMENTAL DRILLS. See references 14-17; emphasize stance, take-off, and throttleup *on key* from two- and three-point stances, aligned both tight and loose.

2. GROUP DRILLS. The two pass rush formats for ends are outlined in figure 90. The left-hand diagrams, a continuation of their Key Triangle Drills (from fig.71 in chapter 6), requires the end to align tight; however, One-On-One Drill is the most practical for working on pass rush fundamentals (with the three-on-one format there is excessive standing around by the personnel simulating the offense). In the right-hand and lower diagrams in figure 90, a continuation of their Crash Drills (from fig. 72), the end must align *outflanking* the offensive formation; while this format requires more offensive personnel to operate, when a First Level end is working *independently* cut blocking should be practiced, with both the speed and intensity of the drill carefully monitored by the coach.

3. TEAM DRILLS. The main difference between the two formats listed below, the Half-Line and Crash Drills, is the inclusion of the tight end and I-backs in the latter drill while the split end and near-halfback are included in the former. Thus, Half-Line is the format for integrating the ends into pass rush, with running plays interspersed, particularly draws, sprintout, or quarterback escape (from the pocket). On the other hand, Crash Drill provides the format for practicing run defense (vs. offensive power formations, see chapter 6) *with pass keys interspersed*. The *common* element between these drills is the First Level end's always *outflanking* the offensive formation regardless of the format.

Half-Line Drill (see fig. 91, a continuation of fig. 73)

This drill is an extension of the Cone Signal Drill, with all offensive personnel *live*, including the quarterback and near-back (positioned as a halfback); a tight end usually is not included in the formation.

Simulating the offensive patterns and blocking on passing plays (with runs interspersed), the drill should progress lock-up to thud, but seldom employ *full* contact; the exception to this involves cut blocking against the First Level end (i.e., this block cannot be performed *live* at half speed, and thus must be carefully scripted so the end always is *alerted by his keys* to anticipate the block — see possible situations in   fig. 91).

First-level personnel execute pre-snap shifting, with the end making the link or rip call, and stunting (see examples in fig. 91); the offensive blocking must be carefully scripted according to the alignment and stunt called (and diagrammed on color-coded cards accompanying each drill).

This is also the best format for performing pass-block vs. quick passing, at the completion of the end's twist inside in T.E.T. (see example in fig. 91); note, in T.E.T. the First Level tackle is now assigned quarterback containment as his (I) responsibility.

It is important that the quarterback, after executing the pass-action, readies to throw, then attempts to escape to the outside or through an interior alley.

(Specific Second Level personnel also may be included in this drill format, however the end's *coverage* responsibilities should be emphasized more when these personnel are scheduled, particularly dog stunts and covers — see next section.)

Crash Drill (primarily for run defense, see format fig. 72)

The tight end and two running backs (I-backs preferred) are included in the offensive formation; *run defense* is emphasized with pass plays only interspersed.

However, Crash Drill provides an excellent format to prepare for a *passing* team's complementary running plays: sprintout, sprintout draw, and delays that break outside, as well as screens and specific play-action passes (bootleg, etc.).

Crash Drill also provides an additional format for practicing Second Level stunts in which First Level ends are involved; however, this should be limited to the cushions. (Note, the Mirror Drills detailed through the last sections of this chapter provide the *best* format for integrated pass *coverage* drill.)

Defensive Scrimmage.

OFFENSIVE AND
DEFENSIVE ACTION

THE DRILL'S FIVE ALIGNMENT COMBINATIONS, INCLUDING
PRE-SNAP SHIFTING, FIRST LEVEL STUNTING

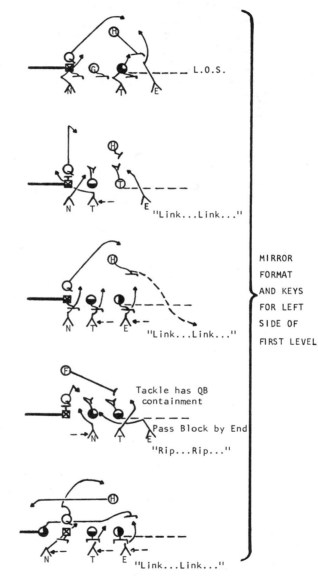

SPRINTOUT-ACTION
With Cut Block by HB;
     Delay Draw to HB;
     QB Escape to outside.

NO SHIFT: "11, SLANT,..."

DROPBACK-ACTION
With Screen;
     HB Draw;
     QB Escape.

SHIFT INTO: "3-LINK, TNT,..."

SPRINTOUT-ACTION
With Cut-Block by HB;
     Delay to HB;
     QB Escape outside.

SHIFT INTO: "5-LINK,..."

QUICK PASS-ACTION
With QB pump-faking;
     QB escaping, inside
     or to outside.

SHIFT INTO: "2-RIP, TET,..."

BOOTLEG ACTION
With Cut-Block by Guard;
     QB Escape outside.

SHIFT INTO: "4-LINK, SLANT,..."

L.O.S.

"Link...Link..."

MIRROR

FORMAT

AND KEYS

FOR LEFT

SIDE OF

FIRST LEVEL

"Link...Link..."

Tackle has QB
containment

Pass Block by End

"Rip...Rip..."

"Link...Link..."

Figure 91 Half-Line Drill. Continuation of Fig. 73, for integrating the end with
the tackle and nose to one side of the First Level: format for practicing pre-snap
shifting, pass rush technique, and stunts.

PASS COVERAGE

In the remainder of this chapter the techniques and drills for installing the pass coverages of the 2-level Defense are presented in three sections. First is a short section detailing the ends' limited coverage responsibilities (see table 8). Essentially a continuation of the preceding section, this completes their critical role within the system. Next, the two major areas of pass coverage are presented: the techniques and responsibility of the Second Level, followed by the teaching progression suggested for deep safety personnel. At the conclusion of each of these sections various Mirror Drills, the *team format* suggested for integrating pass defense (along with Pass Skeleton, Scrimmages, etc.) are detailed.

Ends: Fundamentals and Coverage Responsibility

As summarized in table 8, ends are assigned possible max responsibility only in dog and cushions. In dog, the end must max the *first* offensive backfielder running a pass route outside the core to his side. However:

- if *no* back enters the pass pattern to the end's side, he is free to execute his primary (I) pass rush responsibility;
- if the near-back blocks, the end must crash *through* this potential receiver to the quarterback, ensuring that a screen or dump pass is not thrown to him late in the play.

In cushions, the end must max the tight end or a slotback; again, however:

- if no receiver is positioned in the end's C area, he is free to execute his (I) pass rush responsibility;
- if one of these receivers locates immediately in front of the end and then blocks, again the end must crash *through* this potential receiver to eliminate late screen or safety-valve passes.

The First Level ends must learn *three* basic pass coverages: max vs. an offensive backfielder; max vs. an immediate receiver; and shortside zone-drop. In general, these fundamentals are similar to the coverage techniques currently employed by outside linebackers, and the reader also is referred to references 18-20.

Stance, Positional Alignment, Pre-Snap Shifting. Prior to the play, there must be no change in the end's alignment ritual, but, when the coverage responsibility called in the huddle is verified at the line of scrimmage the end must remain in a standing, two-point stance. (Note to coaches: when reviewing game film, check carefully that when the ends outflank the offensive formation in the core their choice of stance *appears* to be random.)

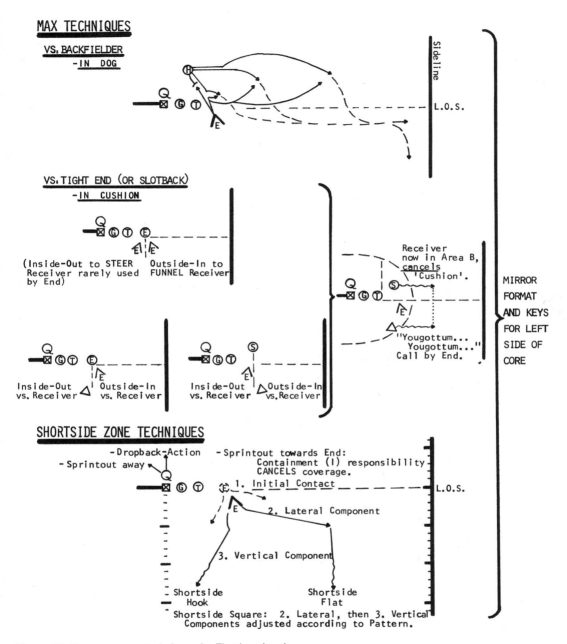

Figure 92 Pass coverage techniques for First Level ends.

Coverage Techniques. As a *general rule* of pass defense, receivers coming from the offensive core are *steered*: that is, they are forced to the outside, toward the sideline, by the defender's positioning and technique (21, 22). This principle is illustrated in figure 92.

MAX VS. BACKFIELDER IN DOG (upper diagram). The near-back may execute one of three actions at the snap:

- If he sets-up immediately and blocks, the end must crash *through* the halfback, maintaining outside leverage on the quarterback at all times.

- Since the end is constantly crashing, if the halfback moves at a forty-five degree angle towards the end, the halfback (usually) will move to the outside around the end early in this pass route. Meeting the back *as deep as possible* in the backfield and forcing him to commit early is the key to steering in this instance: the back should never be permitted to turn upfield around the offensive tackle, moving at full speed (23).

- In dog, however, when crashing *too* aggressively the end may overrun the near-back when the halfback (or tailback in I-formation) sprints laterally at the snap, swinging out of the backfield. With this action the end must break-down, and immediately tear outside parallel to the line of scrimmage, even retreating, until he has regained his inside-out positioning on this backfielder.

- At this point the end can anticipate two options: for the back to break further outside into the flat (i.e., flare route, see next section) or initially break outside then turn upfield immediately (i.e., flare and up). The end should defend against the latter possibility, particularly *to the wideside*, and react to the first option.

In each instance the end must attain and maintain an inside-out positioning, steer the back laterally (using his hands as necessary), and by 1 $1/2$-seconds into the play have secured a very tight relationship with his receiver (also see photo sequence No. 6, in chapt. 6).

MAX VS. TIGHT END OR SLOTBACK IN CUSHIONS (middle diagrams, fig. 92). Against a stationary immediate receiver on the line of scrimmage, a defender's alignment establishes which direction he will force the receiver to release off the line, *steer* him to the outside or *funnel* the receiver to the inside (these alignments and techniques are explained in detail in the next section). Seldom, however, should a First Level end shade the tight end to the inside because of his critical containment responsibilities, unless this receiver splits out considerably from the offensive tackle. Therefore, for the most part, in implementing cushion technique ends funnel their receiver, and this is directly opposite to their technique in dog. A second imperative concerning the implementation of cushion specifically: in the defensive game plan this coverage should be employed against tight ends, and only rarely against a fleet slotback unless the First-Level ends possess sufficient speed; "tight cushion" with its double-coverage (i.e., end plus mirroring Second Level defender) is usually reserved for these smaller, speedier receivers.

- In cushion technique, at the snap the end employs arm shiver technique (in case the offensive play is run, not pass) fixing his hands securely on the tight end.

  a. If this receiver releases inside, in funnelling him the end stays even with the receiver and very close while moving downfield; he can prevent the tight end from cutting back to the outside by his body positioning, and can anticipate any inside cuts according to the depth and timing of the pattern.

  b. On the other hand, if the tight end releases outside, the First Level end steers him aggressively to the outside, allowing the end only to break-out, or out-and-up, and the defender's positioning and anticipation are similar to those described for the dog stunt.

- In tight cushion, the First Level end has double coverage, with the mirroring Second Level defender stacked behind him (fig. 92). Therefore, when the end funnels the receiver he assumes *outside* and *short* coverage responsibility, the deeper defender assuming *inside* and *deep* coverage. And the First Level end may play more aggressively initially as the receiver releases off the line of scrimmage, then cutting underneath in front of the receiver as he moves downfield, anticipating the pass. Conversely, when the First Level end initially steers the receiver he assumes inside and short coverage, the Second Level defender outside and deep (see double-coverage technique, next section).

- Finally, a cushion (either tight cushion or cushion) is called off by the end yelling "Yougottum..." while at the same time waving his *outside* arm in the air, pointing to the outside. Thus, the Second Level defender directly behind can both *see* and *hear* the call-off, for the end should not look back at this point, so close to the snap. The end may choose to call-off a cushion *at any time*; however, the usual reason is that in his judgment the receiver to be cushioned has relocated (via early-motion) outside the perimeter of his C area (also see photo sequences No. 7-9).

SHORTSIDE ZONE DROP-OFF (fig. 92, lower diagram). Zone technique involves three *sequenced* components: initial contact, lateral movement, and a vertical drop to zone depth.

- Initial Contact. When the tight end or a slotback is contacted, particularly when both defender and receiver are *on* the line of scrimmage, his release is delayed, disrupting both the pattern's timing and the receiver's pass route. Also, the receiver should be steered if his release is outside, since most zone drops proceed from inside to outside, and this initial action is similar in both max and zone coverage.

- Lateral Component. Disengaging from the receiver, the end moves (almost) parallel to the line of scrimmage, toward the near sideline, employing a shuffling action (or *short* sprint); as he moves, the end reads both the quarterback and pass pattern shortside. The lateral distance covered is dependent upon two factors: i) the end's read, and ii) his specific zone assignment (in shortside square the distance varies; with shortside hook the lateral component becomes negligible - examine lower diagram in fig. 92).

- Vertical Component. Planting the outside foot, drop-stepping directly back with the inside foot, the end backpedals to target depth (and, again, the vertical component in shortside square can be quite variable, compared to flat and hook depth).

Approaching his shortside target, the end's pattern read should be completed, therefore, he may concentrate on the quarterback's eyes and break on the throwing action. Unless the pass is deep (over fifteen to eighteen yards), in zone the football must be caught *in front of the underneath coverage*, with these defenders always playing the football *through* the intended receiver, particularly on curl and hook routes. Finally, unless a pass route is very shallow, the zone defender must prevent any receiver from crossing through his zone *from the outside to the inside*: whenever possible *collision* a crossing receiver and alert the zone defender immediately inside by yelling "Man across...."

Pass Read. In the next section, pass pattern *recognition* is analyzed in more detail; at this point, to summarize:

- prior to the play, ends visually scan the offensive formation from inside to outside to determine the link or rip call (if one is required according to the alignment called);
- in their pass coverage, ends move from inside the core to the outside;
- therefore, as a general principle their pass read also should proceed from *inside to outside* as they move (24).

There are two defined phases in the ends' pass read. Prior *to the snap* each must verify his coverage responsibility at the line of scrimmage. Specifically:

- when "dog" was called in the huddle, the location of the near-back in the backfield set,
- when a cushion was called, the presence (or absence) of an immediate receiver in his C area,
- when *any* cover was called, the location of the No. 2 receiver to the shortside (only) to confirm: shortside square with -A, -B, or -C verification, or shortside flat (or hook) in cover.

Then, *after the snap* the end must read the pass pattern according to the receivers in his immediate area of the field, specifically:

- if a max responsibility has been designated, his receiver's individual pass route within the pattern, *when* the receiver will make his final break, *what* direction to anticipate, the probable reception area.
- However, in covers the shortside end reads through No. 3 to No. 2 or through No. 2 to No. 1, always inside *to* outside. The exception to this occurs in shortside square: No. 3 cannot be in his field of vision (i.e., for this coverage to be verified), No. 2 is (usually) an ace fullback, with a No. 1A receiver split to the near sideline; practically, therefore, the end only can read No. 2 (review fig. 53).

Drills

1. FUNDAMENTAL DRILLS. Several texts detail drills for practicing *linebacker* zone-drop technique and playing the football, as well as a number of individual man-coverage drills that are applicable for First Level ends (references 25 - 27).

2. GROUP DRILLS. In practicing an end's *individual* pass coverages, it is recommended that both the Crash Drill and Half-Line formats be employed (respectively, with and without a tight end in the offense, *but with the First Level end always outflanking the formation*). The drills in figure 93 illustrate a number of these formats, but to prepare the ends for a specific pass offense these drills must be adapted according to *exact* formations, early-motion patterns, secondary keys, pass patterns, even down to the idiosyncrasies exhibited by specific personnel in that offense. When pass defense is emphasized it is advisable to intersperse *run keys*, particularly the quarterback sprintout. In addition, when a Second Level defender joins these drills: if mirroring in a 1- or 2-stack, script dog stunts; when stacked in area C, script cushions; with the Second Level defender mirroring a No. 2B receiver (shortside), script cover; and so on (fig. 93).

Coverage Drill: Crash and Half-Line Formats (figure 93, a continuation of fig. 72 and 91)

- This drill is an extension to the ends' pass rush (i.e., Half-Line Drill, fig. 91) and run defense (Crash Drill, fig. 72) formats; to minimize confusion for the end, as few offensive players as possible should be employed (only an offensive tackle for basic pass vs. run key), and only *one* Second Level defender scheduled at a time.
- The drill should seldom employ *full* contact, but with limited players in the drill, again, it is the best format for the ends to practice against cut blocking *live*; this must be carefully scripted so that an end always is *alerted* by secondary keys to anticipate the cut.

PASS COVERAGE VERIFIED: "COVER"

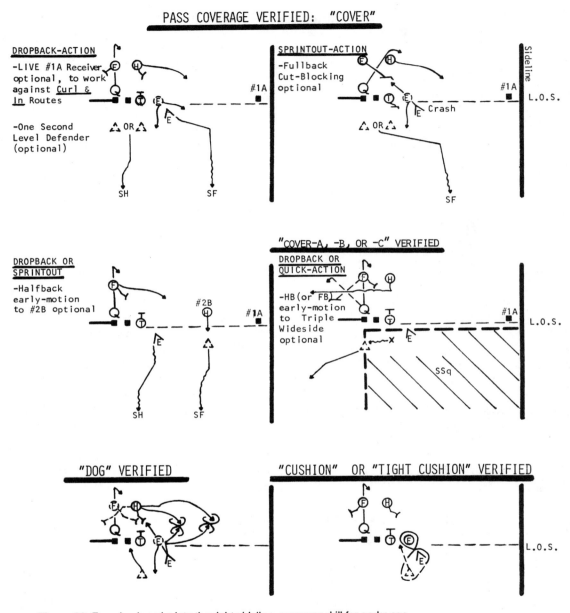

Figure 93 From haskmarks into the right sideline, coverage drill for ends: continuation of Figs. 91 and 72, format for practicing coverage techniques and reading secondary keys, according to the pattern; note, a Second Level defender *regularly* scheduled into drill. (From the left hashmarks, mirror these drill formats.)

- An important objective of this drill is to force the end to make tactical decisions:

    a. pass vs. run (according to the offensive tackle),
    b. then with a pass read, coverage *vs.* crash,
    c.then in coverage, correct technique according to the pattern.

- Therefore, individual plays must be carefully scripted, keys progressed from simple (fewer secondary keys) to more complex, decisions sequenced from basic to multiple. The color-coded cards directing the offense must be carefully prepared to accomplish this.

3. TEAM DRILLS.

- Preceded by appropriate individual and group drill, participation in specific Mirror Drills is scheduled on a limited basis and according to the end's progress to that point (see sections following).
- Pass Skeleton, with regular offensive personnel replacing the defensive personnel operating in the mirror format.
- Pass Scrimmage (defensive unit): it is advisable to carefully script the offense's patterns according to the coverage, in effect manipulating the scrimmage *in favor of* the defense.

Second Level: Fundamentals and Coverage Responsibility

Whether defenders are located in the core or outside, there are only two basic alignments that Second Level personnel can assume (table 9A): mirroring their mobile offensive personnel *stacked* behind a First Level defender, and when they are *not stacked* (i.e., with no offensive or defensive personnel positioned between receiver and defender). Combined with the tactical situation on the field, each positional alignment modifies their pass coverage fundamentals (see footnotes, table 9A). When the Second Level players are *stacked*, their coverage techniques are quite similar to the fundamentals presently employed by linebackers; these are summarized in the first part of this section (also see references 28-30). On the other hand, when *not stacked*, and particularly when mirroring in areas B and A, much of the Second Level's technique is similar to deepback fundamentals, detailed in the latter half of the section (also see references 31-33); included in this latter part are the coverage modifications when a Second Level defender aligns in Area C in jam against the tight end (note: the more critical implications pertaining to run defense are discussed in chapter 6). In addition, the Second Level implements only a limited number of pass coverages (see table 9B). They have three max coverages with *one* universal rule governing their receiver assignment, and three stunts (executed in conjunction with max); however, personnel must be positioned in the defensive core in order to be involved. In cover, by rule each Second Level defender is assigned a main underneath zone, with rotational principles

A.

DEFENSIVE RESPONSIBILITY	SECOND LEVEL STACKED		IN AREA C*		SECOND LEVEL NOT STACKED	
	IN 1-Stack	IN 2-Stack	STACKED	JAM	IN AREA B	IN AREA A
VS RUN (see chapter 6; Stunts this Section)	= PRIMARY (I) RESPONSIBILITY				= SECONDARY (II) CONTAINMENT OF RUN	CONTAIN-OUTSIDE
VS PASS (This Section)	= SECONDARY (II) RESPONSIBILITY**		= PRIMARY (I)		= PRIMARY (I) RESPONSIBILITY	

B.

MAX COVERAGES

"MAX (BASIC)"
– WITH STUNT (OPTIONAL); "DOG"=BLITZ INSIDE
"CUSHION"
"SWITCH" } = CRASH

"MAX/DOUBLE (Receiver Designated)"
"MAX/TIGHT CUSHION"

COVER COMBINATIONS

"COVER"
–APPLY UNIVERSAL ZONE RULE (SEE TABLE 6).
(EXCEPTION: MIRRORING #2B RECEIVER SHORTSIDE = SHORTSIDE FLAT (OR BANDIT/OR STRONG)

"COVER-A"/ -B"/OR -C" VERIFIED
–ROTATION PRINCIPLE: ADJUST ONE ZONE TO THE WIDESIDE. (EXCEPTION: THE SECOND LEVEL DEFENDER 'CALLED' TO DEEP 1/3)

–APPLY UNIVERSAL RULE: EACH DEFENDER MAX'S HIS MIRRORED OFFENSIVE PERSONNEL (SEE TABLE 5). (NO EXCEPTIONS TO RULE EVEN WITH 2 DEEP SAFETIES; ONLY TECHNIQUE VARIED ACCORDING TO THE COVERAGE AND GAME PLAN)

–ADJUSTMENTS

VS SPRINTOUT SHORTSIDE: ROTATION PRINCIPLE, ADJUST ONE ZONE SHORTSIDE.
WITH TWO DEEP SAFETIES: ACCORDING TO GAME PLAN, THE SECOND LEVEL DEFENDER 'CALLED' TO DEEP 1/3 HAS OPTION ONLY: DEEP 1/3 COVERAGE OR REMAIN IN HIS UNDERNEATH ZONE.

Table 9. Area of Responsibility (A) and summary of pass coverage responsibility (B) for Second Level defenders in the 2-level defense.

* In effect, mirroring in Area C (vs. Tight End or Slotback) run or pass can assume Primary (I) responsibility depending upon the tactical situation.

** Similarly, pass defense often assumes Primary (I) importance for Defenders in the core depending upon the tactical circumstances at the time.

These situations must be clearly defined in the Game Plan (i.e., down/&distance, score, time, weather, etc.).

governing his adjustments, one zone to the wideside or shortside according to the call; in all, three universal rules must be implemented.

Second Level: Stacked.

STANCE AND POSITIONING. In defined passing situations only minor adjustments are necessitated in either stance or positional alignment; stacked in the core, Second Level defenders usually align at a maximum depth of five yards off the line of scrimmage. However, there can be exceptions:

- according to specific game plan adjustments, such as mirroring a fullback who is principally a blocker.
- when a Second Level defender finds himself exposed (to offensive blockers) because of the First Level's alignment on that particular play (fig. 76).

On the other hand, when a Second Level defender is involved in a stunt, he should definitely align further from the line of scrimmage rather than closer: crowding the line may give away the stunt, and if the play is not a pass the defender gives himself less chance to compensate for any First Level miscues.

COVERAGE TECHNIQUES. Stacked in the core, Second Level defenders must learn four basic techniques (fig. 94). Each requires modification from week to week according to the offensive opponent and the game plan requirements, but, there is considerable overlap when a defender is *not stacked* and outside the core (see section immediately following).

- Two max techniques must be implemented depending upon the stack location: in 1- and 2-Stacks, max against an offensive back moving out of the backfield; in Area C, max against a tight end or slotback, and occasionally max-double when tight cushion is verified.
- Locating inside the core, zone-drop technique is quite variable, although Strong, Lou, and Rose must drop off the furthest distances (fig. 48-57).
- Verification of dog requires the Second Level defender to fire inside through the interior of the core; cushion and switch impose crash responsibilities and technique on stunting Second Level personnel.

MAX VS. BACKFIELDER (fig. 94, upper left-hand diagram). Although the defender in this figure is positioned in a 2-stack, the coverage techniques are similar for 1-stack, and the *principles* applicable when a Second Level defender is stacked in area C (middle diagrams). Reading the offensive personnel that comprise his basic unit (review fig. 77), with a pass key the stacked defender employs *scrape* tech-

MAX TECHNIQUE.....

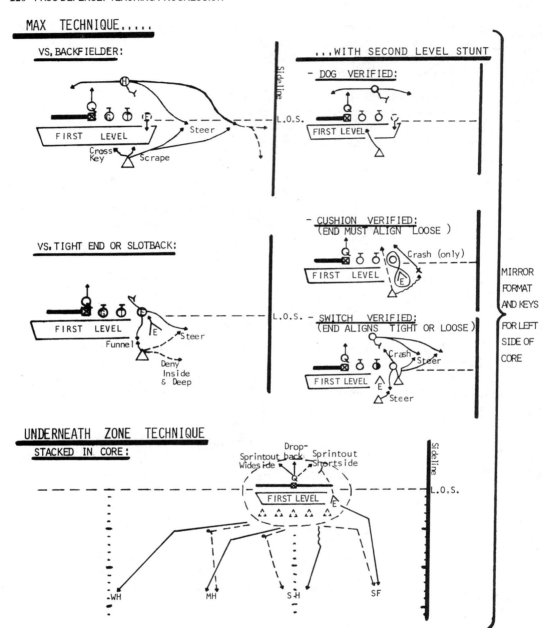

Figure 94 Continuation of Figs. 78-81, pass coverage technique for stacked Second Level personnel in core.

nique when his mirrored backfielder moves immediately outside at the snap. Working to the outside, the defender intercepts the back as he crosses the line of scrimmage, securing an inside-out position to *steer* him further outside. By his body position (and use of hands as necessary) the defender prevents the receiver from cutting-back to the inside over center, but this technique becomes more difficult in the open field for a Second Level defender (than for the First Level end who contacts the near-back much sooner and in a more confined area). Once steered to the outside, the defender anticipates his receiver's outside routes according to the pass pattern (also see photo sequence No. 14, in Chapter 6). If, the backfielder cuts-back over center (not shown in diagram), the defender must:

- delay the receiver as he cuts inside (using his hands as necessary),
- immediately drop-step with the inside foot and run with the receiver downfield,
- compress the reception area to the inside, although it becomes almost impossible to funnel the receiver at this point.

On the other hand with the basic pass key, if his mirrored back moves immediately to the inside at the snap crossing the center of the offensive formation, the stacked defender initiates cross-key (see fig. 82 and drills at end of this section).

Finally, if at the snap the backfielder sets up and pass blocks, the Second Level defender may initiate either of two actions: *fire*, which, however, by this point will provide only secondary pressure, (also see photo sequences No. 11-13), or *drop-off* to assist on any inside pass routes over center. With either action the defender has responsibility for screen and delayed passes thrown late in the play to his receiver; therefore, it is imperative that Second Level defenders *are never predictable* executing either action (when reviewing game film, this is another point coaches must examine closely). To assist this process, as well as to avoid Second Level defenders literally standing around in max (if their back blocks with regularity on passes), the dog stunt initiates a preemptive fire by stacked defenders (fig. 94, upper right-hand diagram). Unless the backfielder dives into the line of scrimmage directly at the stacked defender, he is freed to fire through the sixth line-gap in odd-numbered alignments or according to the *overload* in 2- and 4-Alignments (also see photo sequence No. 6).

MAX VS. TIGHT END OR SLOTBACK (fig. 94, middle left-hand diagram). Stacked in area C, reading the offensive personnel in his basic unit (review fig. 81), when the basic key is pass and his mirror releases *outside* the Second Level defender may initiate two techniques:

1. Scrape immediately, contact the receiver with inside-out position, *steering* him further outside; this technique is employed when the tight end is expected to run an outside route into the flat area (also see photo sequence No. 13).

2. Move laterally in order to maintain the three-to-five yards between receiver and defender, establish an inside positioning to deny the inside and deep pass routes; this coverage technique is preferred when the tight end or slotback may turn upfield running deep, or attempt to cut back over center.

On the other hand, if at the snap the tight end releases to the *inside*, the stacked Second Level defender must step up and, employing shiver technique, contact the end just as he would *any* offensive blocker, firing out at him. Reading pass simultaneously, the defender follows up by aggressively *funnelling* the tight end inside, then anticipates the pass route and reception area according to the pattern (also see photo sequence No. 12).

Finally, if at the snap the tight end (or slotback) pass blocks, the Second Level defender may (again) either fire or drop back to assist in pass coverage; with either action he remains responsible for screen and delays thrown to his receiver late in the play, so his actions must *never be predictable*. The cushion stunt in particular is designed to take advantage of a tight end who blocks the crashing First Level end *with regularity* on passes (fig. 94, middle right-hand diagrams): the mirroring Second Level defender is freed to crash, assuming the force-containment responsibilities and technique of the First Level end, while the latter defender maxes the tight end (also see photo sequences No. 7 and 8).

UNDERNEATH ZONE TECHNIQUE (fig. 94, lower diagram). Zone-drop technique is sequenced according to its three components, as outlined in the last section.

- *Initial Contact* is (usually) made with the tight end or slotback mirroring in area C, and then the receiver is steered. In 1- and 2-stacks, initial contact with one's mirrored offensive backfielder is not possible, but the Second Level defenders must *delay* their zone drop to defend against possible draws and delayed running plays.
- Independent of the stack location, from inside the core the *lateral component* becomes even more variable. With only a *short* distance to his target area, the defender employs shuffle technique; with a longer distance, particularly in crossing to the wideside of the field, he may sprint for a few strides. In employing either technique, however, the defender must move (almost) parallel to the line of scrimmage to target *before* deepening,[1] reading the quarterback and the pattern as he moves.
- Planting the outside foot, drop-stepping with the inside foot, the defender backpedals to target. However, the *vertical component* varies according to the pass pattern and proximity of receiver(s): in zone, short- and medium-depth passes must be caught *in front of* the underneath coverage, and any receiver attempting to cross through a zone at medium depth, from outside to inside, must be *collisioned* (and the adjacent Second Level personnel alerted).

The only major adjustment in zone technique occurs when the quarterback sprints *shortside* (fig. 94, see dashed lines in lower diagram). The shortside end *must crash*, thus, a shortside zone is opened. To compensate, underneath coverage personnel rotate one zone to the shortside by breaking off their lateral movement *on key*. With the proximity of the sideline, however, the quarterback has limited area in which to maneuver, so underneath personnel must guard against over-rotation. Against sprintout to the wideside, *minimal* rotation is necessary because the First Level end on the wideside is never assigned to a zone, and with verification of cover-A, -B, and -C, the underneath coverage already is rotated *one* zone to the wideside.

Pass Read. As summarized in the preceding section (and detailed in the section following), there are *two* phases to reading. *Prior to the play*, Second Level defenders must verify their coverage according to the huddle call; in addition, by reading the offensive formation often specific pattern(s) can be anticipated, particularly *quick* passes with an ace-backfield formation. *After the snap*, their read is influenced more by the type of coverage.

- In max, the pass-action and the receiver's route *within the pattern* enable the defender to anticipate the final cut and probable reception area.
- In covers, reading the quarterback and the pattern *from inside to outside* indicate which receiver to anticipate and his route.

Drills

1. FUNDAMENTAL DRILLS. There are a number of movement and ball drills appropriate for Second Level personnel stacked in the core; these are essentially inside linebacker drills for practicing both man-to-man coverage and zone-drop technique (ref. 34-36).

- Adapting various zone drills, it is recommended that particular attention be paid to the *lateral* component of each personnel's drop technique; that is, ensuring that personnel move into their target area *before* commencing their backpedal.

2. GROUP DRILLS. Continuing the *individual* stack formats from chapter 6, specifically the 1-stack, 2-stack, and area C Stack Drills (fig. 79, 80, and 81, respectively), in game preparation only the most important pass route(s) run by the mirrored offensive personnel should be incorporated. In these *individual* stack formats, pass keys and routes should be interspersed, but unless the coach deems it essential they should seldom provide the main focus for these *run-oriented* drills.

3. TEAM DRILLS. On the other hand, continuing the *combined* stack formats detailed in chapter 6, specifically the Cross-Key, I-backs, and 2-Stack + Area C formats (fig. 82, 83 and 84, respectively), pass defense must receive greater emphasis because a

high degree of coordination between Second Level defenders is required in both run and pass defense. In figures 95 and 96, only a few of the basic routes run by various offensive personnel are diagrammed; in game preparation detailed patterns should be highlighted, particularly the *final leg* of each pass route as the receiver makes his final cut to the reception area.

Cross-Key Drills (see upper portion of fig. 95, a continuation of fig. 82)

- This drill is a continuation of the cross-key format when the *basic* read is pass and (at least) one of the backfielders moves downfield on a pass

Figure 95 Continuation of Figs. 82 and 83, cross-key and I-backs format: basic pass routes for the stacked defenders to recognize and react to both max (solid lines) and covers (dashed lines).

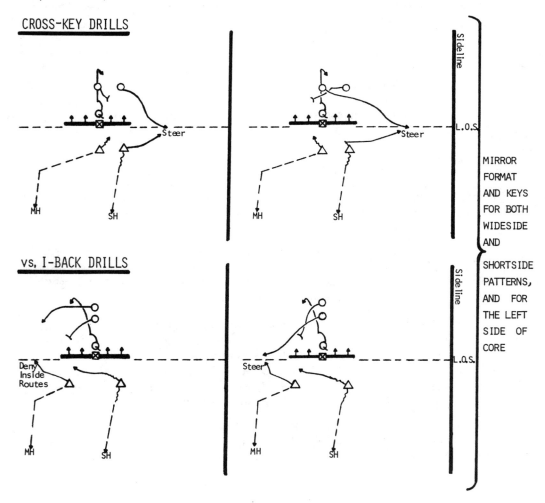

CROSS-KEY DRILLS

vs. I-BACK DRILLS

MIRROR FORMAT AND KEYS FOR BOTH WIDESIDE AND SHORTSIDE PATTERNS, AND FOR THE LEFT SIDE OF CORE

2-STACK + AREA C STACK

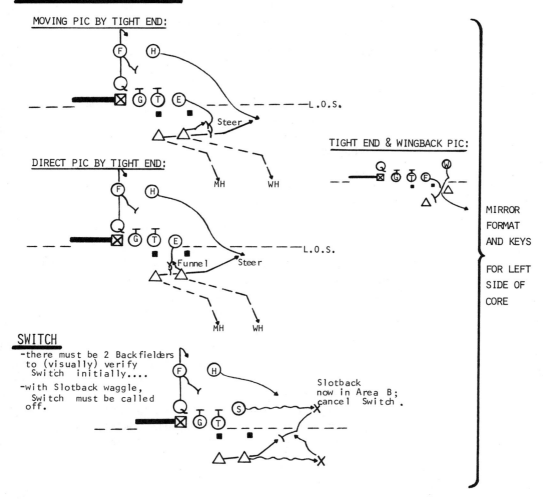

Figure 96 Continuation of Fig. 84, the 2-Stack + Area C format: defensive problems which require considerable practice:

— zoning receiver(s) coming out of the backfield,

— zoning or max coverage against tight end *PIC* when back comes out of the backfield,

— cancellation of switch (see lower diagram).

route; also, cross-key provides a realistic format for practicing screens and draws.

- The backs need not cross on every play (compare left- and right-hand diagrams); specific pass plays are designed by combining the individual backfield actions from the 1- and 2-stack Drills, with offensive linemen inserted as required to simulate a specific opponent's pass blocking system and keys.

- Either a max or a cover is designated before every play (including runs, see fig. 82) so that defenders can react accordingly when their *basic* key is pass. Stunting should be very limited, or disregarded.
- Inserting passes into Cross-Key Drills serves several important purposes:
  a. foremost, pass keys must be scripted into *all* drills that primarily practice *run* defense;
  b. always, *play-action* passes should be employed (with quarterback faking) so defenders must *search* for the football;
  c. an important objective is to further coordinate the two stacked defenders *to react correctly and in unison* to secondary keys (see explanation of cross- key in chapter 6).

I-Backs Drill (see lower portion of figure 95, a continuation of fig. 83)

- This drill is a continuation of the I-back format when the *basic* key is pass; (at least) one of the backfielders moves downfield on a pass route, with screen and draw plays also highlighted.
- Again, only play-action passes should be scripted, with the defenders' secondary read being critical:
  a. are the I-backs moving *in unison*, or do they *split*, and....
  b. the important implication of both reads for their subsequent coordinated action and coverage (see text accompanying I-Back Drills in chapter 6).
- Either a max or a cover is designated prior to every play (including runs) so that defenders can react accordingly when their *basic* key is pass. Again, stunting should be very limited with this format.

2-Stack + Area C Drill (see fig. 96, a continuation of fig. 84)

- There also are a number of pass situations employing the 2-stack *and* area C stack combination which must be coordinated, particularly:
  a. in cover, zoning back(s) coming out of the backfield, so-called *banjo* technique (37);
  b. in max, when the immediate receiver in area C attempts to *pic* the 2-stack defender to his inside (upper and middle diagrams);
  c. cancellation of switch (lower diagram).
- When the First Level end is not present in the drill, the Second Level defender mirroring the tight end (or slotback) usually aligns *in jam* (figure 84); in passing situations this defender may be scripted *in stack*,

to create greater congestion in the area (but this is optional and varies with the coverage and pass pattern).

- In simulated passing situations, various cover calls or, in max, switch can provide an appropriate defensive adjustment against an offense that persists with a pic-action against the 2-stack defender. However...

  .... in zone considerable coordination is required for the Second Level defenders to pick-up the receivers entering the pass pattern...

  .... with a switch call initially verified (*i.e.*, two backfielders visually verify switch), a slotback or tight end waggle into area B *automatically* cancels the switch...

  .... and note that even with cancellation, the pic-action by the outside receiver may still be executed.

- Note that in that figure 96 (upper-righthand diagram), employing a tight end and wingback formation the pic-action by the wingback is similar (and appropriate to intersperse into this format as a special game preparation).

Three additional team formats through which stacked Second Level defenders should progress:

Mirror Drills

Both the *individual* Stack Drills and these combined formats (fig. 95, 96) are incorporated into this larger format in which Second Level personnel continually move from inside the core, and *stacked*, to outside of the core *not stacked.*

Pass Skeleton

Essentially the Mirror Drill with *live* offensive personnel, complete pass patterns, but limited contact between offensive and defensive personnel.

Pass Scrimmage

Defensive unit practice.

Second Level: Not Stacked

When no other personnel (either defensive or offensive) are positioned between a Second Level defender and the immediate receiver he is mirroring, the defender obviously cannot secure the protection and advantage of the stack alignment. On the other hand, different responsibilities are presented the defender when he is *not stacked*: locating outside the core mirroring in Areas B and A, pass defense must be his primary (I) concern and often *in jam* in area C this will be the case as well (see table 9A). Therefore, *not stacked*, Second Level personnel have several positional alignments that they may assume according to their pass responsibility, always the *primary* determinant of coverage technique. In this section the implications of the defender's initial stance and positioning against an immediate receiver (fig. 97) are carried through to completion of the coverage both in max and cover.

Stance and Positioning. In fig. 97, the positional alignments for Second Level personnel are defined. Mirroring in area C inside the core, the defender has fewer alignment options (the implications for stance and positioning are discussed in chapter 6 and the section preceding), compared to outside the core in areas B and nearer to the sideline in A.

ALIGNMENT DEPTH: HARD, MEDIUM, OR SOFT. Descriptive terminology is used to define the depth at which the Second Level aligns.

> Hard: as the name suggests by aligning on the line of scrimmage and within one yard of his mirror the defender may initiate immediate and aggressive action at the snap from this alignment; therefore physical contact with the receiver is possible, bump-and-run max technique, etc.

Figure 97 According to the pass coverage called (in the huddle), the determinants of coverage technique for Second Level personnel *at the line of scrimmage*: specific combination of factors dictate coverage technique to be employed.

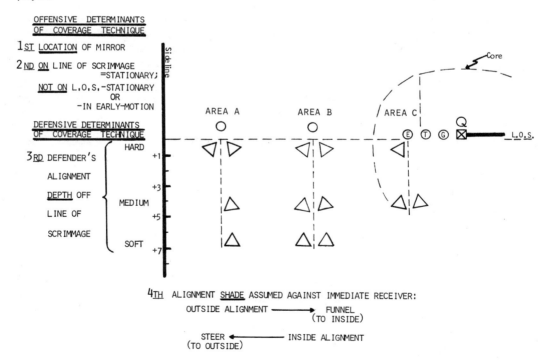

Soft: by contrast both the name and the alignment, approximately seven yards off the receiver, are less aggressive, more *reactionary*; therefore, Deep $1/3$ coverage, max-soft (i.e., man-to-man) technique, etc. are executed from this depth.

Medium: by initially aligning three-to-five yards from his mirror, the defender is positioned either to initiate contact for bump-and-run or to immediately backpedal at the snap; the speed and ability of the receiver, coupled with the defender's specific coverage responsibility, determine his actions and technique.

ALIGNMENT SHADE: INSIDE OR OUTSIDE. Unrestricted, an immediate receiver is free to run pass routes shallow or deep, to the inside and outside. On defense, therefore, the *combination* of positional depth and shade against the receiver is critical in order to limit these options; that is, by virtue of his alignment the defender positions himself advantageously should the receiver move to his depth and in his direction. (However, this technique for channelling receivers can place the defender at a disadvantage, particularly in max, should his receiver move oppositely.) To deny the area inside, the Second Level defender must shade his mirror *to the inside*, and his positioning *on* the receiver varies with his alignment depth (fig. 97). Similarly, to deny outside routes the defender must shade *to the receiver's outside*; again, depth is the primary factor determining the degree of shade he assumes on his receiver, but the proximity of the sideline provides an interacting variable (in area A only). Within five yards (approximately) of the sideline at medium-to-soft depth, the defender need only shade inside, because the area to the outside is out-of-bounds; this principle particularly applies in zone coverage.

Two general guidelines govern stance and body posture as Second Level defenders constantly move across the field, mirroring in different areas, aligning against various receivers, and varying their positional depth and shade.

First: when stacked inside the core minimal heel-to-toe stagger is recommended (see chapter 6); moving to the outsides, however, the feet should be staggered with the inside foot up, outside foot back, and body weight forward. This guideline is independent of the defender's shade, with one exception: aligned outside shade *on* the line of scrimmage (i.e., aligned *hard*, with minimal distance separating defender and receiver) the inside foot must be placed well back (see technique in the section following).

Second: the closer the defender mirrors his receiver (particularly when aligning at hard-to-medium depth), the more he should lower his center of gravity, by lowering the hips and widening the stance (however, the feet should never go past shoulder width).

In constantly varying their positional alignment prior to the snap during the quarterback's cadence a supplemental problem for the Second Level arises: to disguise their coverage technique. This becomes especially important at medium-to-soft alignment depth; on the other hand, when defenders are aligned at hard depth on the line of scrimmage the defender's intentions, *but never the coverage* (i.e., max vs. cover), become obvious. Finally, there is only one tactical situation when Second Level personnel outside the core are severely restricted in their choice of positional alignments: mirroring an immediate receiver in early-motion (fig. 97, left-hand margin). Usually the defender trails this receiver at *medium* depth, employing shuffle technique, and then at the snap channels the receiver in the *same* direction; what the defender must prevent, particularly in max, is the receiver cutting back behind him (footnote, table 10).

The Interaction of Directional and Coverage Technique. Table 10 summarizes various technique combinations, according to the defender's alignment depth and positional shade at the snap. Each combination is comprised of a directional and a coverage variable, but only these specific combinations are recommended.[2] *Directional technique* varies with the alignment depth and shade, and determines what

Table 10. According to the pass coverage called (in the huddle), combination of factors determining specific coverage technique against stationary[*] immediate receivers.

DIRECTIONAL AND COVERAGE TECHNIQUE COMBINATIONS:

		ALIGNMENT SHADE	
		INSIDE	OUTSIDE
DEPTH	HARD	- STEER. - DENY **INSIDE** & SHALLOW - TO - MEDIUM PASS ROUTES. - UNDERNEATH ZONE COVERAGES; BUMP-&-RUN MAX TECHNIQUE.	- FUNNEL. - DENY OUTSIDE &
ALIGNMENT	MEDIUM	↑ EITHER COMBINATION ↓	↑ EITHER COMBINATION ↓
	SOFT	- DENY **INSIDE** & MEDIUM - TO - DEEP PASS ROUTES. - DEEP 1/3 ZONE COVERAGE (WITH UNDERNEATH COVERAGE, ONLY AS A CHANGE-UP); MAX-SOFT TECHNIQUE.	- DENY OUTSIDE &

AREA C TECHNIQUES

THESE TECHNIQUES REQUIRING OUTSIDE SHADE RARELY EMPLOYED NEAR A SIDELINE.

[*] When the Immediate Receiver is in early-motion, medium depth alignment (usually) is employed with the Defender trailing slightly behind the Receiver to prevent him from cutting-back behind the Defender at the snap.

area(s) downfield the defender will deny his mirror by positioning. For example, aligned at *soft* depth, physical contact with any receiver will only be incidental; it must be *positional* factors, initial alignment and then the defender's movements throughout the play, which place him always in position to deny specific pass routes. By contrast, aligned at *hard* depth, physical contact provides an additional means by which to channel an immediate receiver, and at *medium* depth both techniques, direct contact vs. positional denial (with any contact being incidental), are possible (table 10, middle row). On the other hand, *coverage technique* varies directly with the pass defense called. In max, technique is determined by the end line coverage, whether one or two deep safeties are in the defense, whether single or double coverage has been assigned. In cover, each Second Level is assigned a specific underneath zone or Deep $1/3$ responsibility, and its location and distance always dictate individual coverage technique.

Directional Techniques. In fig. 98 both the inside and outside directional techniques are illustrated: aligned at hard-to-medium depth, *steer vs. funnel* technique; and aligned at medium-to-soft depth, *positional technique* for denying specific pass routes. In general, these directional techniques are applied during the initial coverage phases in both max and zone; in addition, independent of direction, these combinations share common *principles* of technique.

- The Second Level defender denies the receiver specific areas or pass routes downfield according to his initial positional shade (fig. 98).

- The defender always positions himself to *see* the quarterback in his peripheral vision (the exception is when aligning close to the line of scrimmage and shading *well inside* his mirror, the defender must turn his back to the quarterback, a disadvantage of the steering technique - examine upper left diagram).

- As the defender aligns closer to his mirror, he assumes a more *obvious* shade against the receiver. Compare the upper and lower diagrams in fig. 98: on the line of scrimmage, even the defender's shoulders and stance are rotated according to the direction of his shade; by comparison, aligned at seven yards depth, it is actually the defender's initial backpedal direction which establishes his shade.

- The closer a defender aligns to his mirror, the more he can employ collision techniques; note, however, that forcefully *pushing-off* a receiver should be employed only with underneath zone coverage and only when the defender must break contact immediately, *never in max.*

- As a defender aligns further from his mirror, the more he must react to the receiver, allowing the latter to close the distance between them, and to make the first move; continually, the defender adjusts *to the receiver* until either contact is initiated or coverage per se commences (fig. 98, middle and lower diagrams).

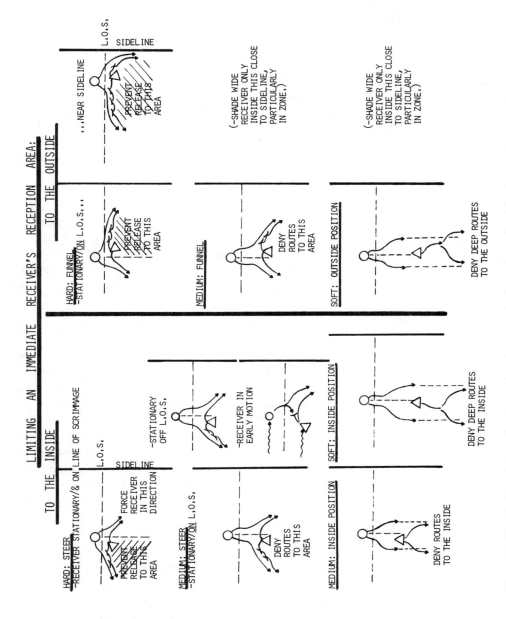

Figure 98 Directional techniques for Second Level personnel. (Examples to the defensive right *only*.)

Coverage Techniques. Pass coverage itself is the natural extension and follow-up to intelligent directional technique, and must be continuous with it. In max, each Second Level defender assumes coverage on his mirror, now his assigned receiver by rule (see table 5) according to his alignment depth and shade at the snap. On the other hand, with underneath zone responsibility, alignment depth and shade are established so that following initial contact, the defender is already proceeding to target; and with Deep 1/3 responsibility, Second Level personnel must align at medium-to-soft depth in order to facilitate their drop to deep coverage. Therefore, *not stacked* Second Level personnel must learn five coverage techniques; each is executed in accordance with the defender's positional alignment (at the snap) and preemptive directional technique. Three of these are identical to their core techniques and require only minor adjustments when mirroring outside the core.

> Max Technique—aggressive bump-and-run technique; there must be end line coverage.

> Max-Soft Technique (new)—traditional man-to-man pass defense; must be employed when there is no end line coverage, with defenders aligning at medium-to-soft depth initially.

> Max-Double Technique—the two defenders involved in the double-coverage always start and remain at different depths:

>> vs. area C receivers in tight cushion, the First Level end on the line of scrimmage, and the Second Level personnel mirroring the tight end or slotback;

>> vs. immediate receivers in areas B or A in max-double (receiver designated), the mirroring Second Level defender underneath, with deep safety coverage on top beginning at twelve yards downfield.

> Underneath Zone Technique—identical to drop-off technique in the core, with two modifications:

> directional techniques play a much more important role; mirroring outside the core usually positions Second Level personnel closer to target, therefore the lateral component of their zone drop varies accordingly.

> Deep 1/3 Technique (new)—at the snap, immediate drop-off to Deep 1/3; Strong, Gael, and Bandit by rule move only to the wideside of the field, while Lou and Rose drop only into Deep 1/3 to their side of the field.

1. Max Technique.

Aligned at *medium* depth (fig. 99, middle diagram), directional technique cannot be as aggressive; however, eight-to-fifteen yards downfield, max technique requires that

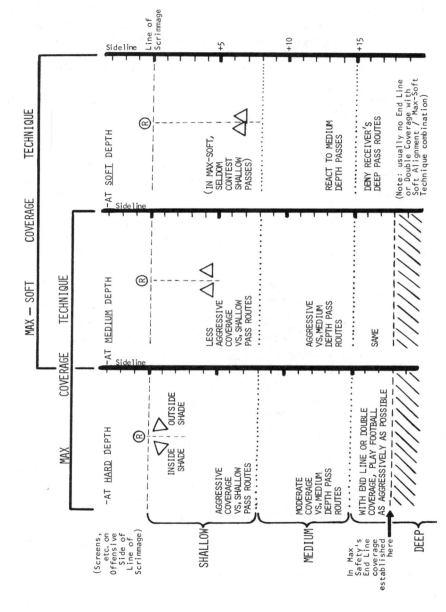

Figure 99 Max techniques for Second Level personnel (on the defensive *right* only), according to their pre-snap alignment (see Fig. 97) and the max coverage called (in the huddle); coverage *continuation* employing max and max-soft techniques as an extension of their directional techniques.

234

the defender establish a tight relationship with his receiver—*at his hip*, to the side he initially shaded (or at the other hip, if the defender has been unsuccessful in maintaining this initial positioning). By comparison, positioned on the line of scrimmage, aligned *hard* (diagram on left), the defender runs with his receiver much earlier (because the receiver must sprint to clear the line), crowding the receiver as they move together downfield; from this prealignment tighter coverage on the receiver occurs over the initial five-to-seven yards. Throughout, the defender concentrates on the receiver's torso (not the head, arms or lower body), and his footwork is *critical* because (by the rules of the game) a pass defender has very restrictive use of the hands. He must avoid crossing the feet to change direction, always drop-step opening up the hips toward the direction of movement; he must *react* to the receiver and force him to run, and until the receiver commits along his intended pass route the defender must stay under control, combining running and gliding technique. Also, with max technique the defender reads through the receiver: *funnelling* his receiver, the defender reads both the quarterback and the pass pattern inside; *steering*, however, with his back to the quarterback, the defender only can read the pattern to the outside. Finally, in max coverage the defender must anticipate and beat the receiver to the reception area, stepping underneath (in front of) the receiver to do so. The defender does not "knock the football to the ground," however, as many texts describe (38, 39) and which is more difficult to accomplish. If the defender cannot intercept, he needs only to tip the football (at its highest point) up and over the receiver, keeping it airborne for the deep safety closing-in behind to run under (see *Enforcement Sequence* for Deep Safety).

2. Max-Soft Technique

This technique must be employed when there is no endline coverage by the deep safety (fig. 99, right-hand diagram). Otherwise, max-soft technique is employed only as a change-up. In the 2-level defense, max-soft is the nomenclature designating traditional man-to-man coverage with Second Level personnel aligning five-to-seven yards off their receiver, this distance being adjusted according to the speed differential between defender and receiver. The *new* skill required for execution of max-soft (and also for Deep $1/3$ coverage) is the backpedal: this skill enables the defender *at any instant* to plant the rear foot and move either forward or laterally in either direction. Backpedalling is not running backwards (that is, with body erect, weight well back); rather, by staying low and bent at the waist the player keeps the body's center of gravity well forward. Executing max-soft, the defender should maintain his backpedal as long as possible, and at $1-1/2$-seconds after the snap he should have established tight coverage *behind* the receiver. It is imperative that the defender deny the *deep* pass routes because a pass completion behind the defender usually means a long gain for the offense. Therefore, the defender may reasonably contest medium-depth passes, but must play through the receiver to the football. There is, however, less immediate need for Second Level personnel to contest shallow passes: these are short gains for the offense, and on the very next play the defender could be executing max technique with the receiver set up for the interception.

3. Double-Coverage Technique

Mirroring the tight end or a slotback in area C, verification of tight cushion assigns the Second Level defender the *deep* coverage responsibility, commencing at approximately five to seven yards downfield, with a First Level end underneath. On the other hand, in areas B and A max double assigns a Second Level defender to the underneath responsibility when it is his mirror that has been designated for double-coverage, with deep safety coverage on top beginning at twelve yards downfield (see final section of chapter). In learning double-coverage, therefore, it is the *principles* of this technique that personnel must understand; specifically, according to their coverage assignment the adjustments to be made in their max techniques. Foremost, throughout the double-coverage the two defenders *must remain staggered*, one deeper than the receiver at all times (see max-soft technique), the underneath defender moving aggressively in front of the receiver nearing the reception area (see max technique), *never allowing the receiver to split them* and outrun the deep coverage. Second, it is the underneath defender who establishes *his* shade to one side of the receiver, thereby denying the pass routes both *underneath* and *to that side*; thus, the defender assigned deep responsibility *adjusts* his coverage accordingly, to deny both the *deep* routes and passes thrown to *the other side*.

4. Underneath Zone Technique

As a general rule, outside the core the Second Level personnel assigned underneath zone responsibility shade their mirror so that, at the snap, each defender can channel his mirror *along with him* as he moves laterally towards his zone; this adjustment allows the defender to sustain initial contact and to steer or funnel his mirror more effectively (fig. 100, upper diagrams). On the other hand, when a defender's target is located directly behind where he is positioned (at the snap), effectively there can be no lateral component in his zone drop (there can be only the vertical component); therefore, the defender shades to the inside to collision his mirror should he attempt to run a crossing route through the zone. A second general rule effecting only the lateral component of underneath coverage pertains to *inside* receivers crossing to the outside in front of a defender...*across his face.* Underneath defenders move laterally according to the widest receiver in their immediate zone area; therefore, when an inside receiver (tight end, slotback, wingback, or running back) moves to the outside, crossing in front of a defender,[3] he widens his zone drop accordingly. Third, the further that Second Level personnel mirror from the heart of the core (i.e., from their 1- and 2-stack alignments), the more adjustments and variability are possible in underneath zone coverage. Again, however, these mainly influence only the lateral technique component.

5. Deep 1/3 Zone Technique

There are enough skills common to both the Deep 13 and max-soft technique often to disguise these coverages over the initial stages of a pass play. Assigned either

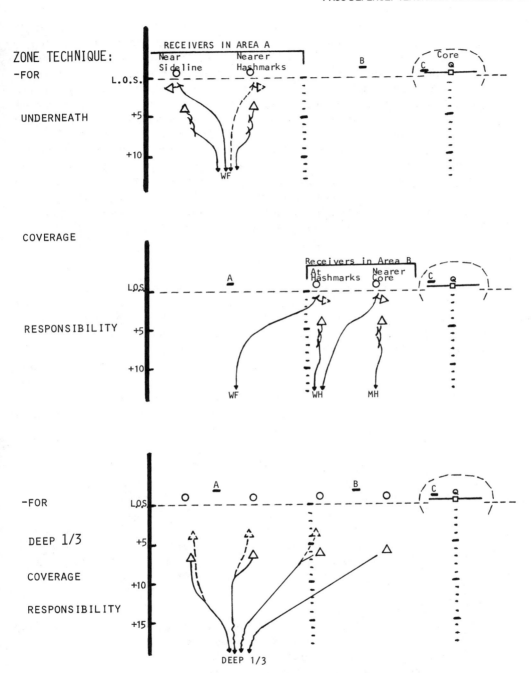

Figure 100 Zone techniques for Second Level personnel: coverage continuation according to the cover called, and their pre-snap depth and shading.

coverage, the Second Level defender must align medium-to-soft, with the precise depth dictated by the speed of the wide receivers to his side; on the other hand, with Deep $1/3$ responsibility the defender usually shades *to the outside* (unless his mirror aligns close to a sideline−see fig. 97). At the snap, the defender initiates Deep $1/3$ coverage employing backpedal technique; however, there are obvious differences between max-soft and deep-zone technique, which are difficult to disguise even for veteran personnel. In zone coverage, utilization of (any) directional technique must be curtailed: Deep $1/3$ coverage formally begins *only* when the Second Level defender reaches the zone. Therefore, at the snap personnel must proceed *immediately* to the approximate-center of the zone; in fact, some coaches (40, 41) recommend that deep coverage personnel turn and sprint for several strides, rather than backpedal the entire distance. On the other hand, once defenders are located in Deep $1/3$, coverage technique against any receiver entering the zone is similar to max-soft: the defender must establish a relationship directly *behind* the receiver, always denying the deep pass routes by playing through the receiver to the football when a pass is thrown.

Pass Read: Pattern Recognition. Mirroring an immediate receiver, only in area C (i.e., mirroring the tight end or a slotback) are Second Level personnel able to obtain their basic read, pass vs. run, according to the offensive tackle and guard to that side of the center (fig. 81). Therefore, as their mirror splits out from the offensive core, Second Level personnel switch to an *alternate read*, as defined in fig. 101.

- If their mirror *releases downfield* at the snap, personnel initiate pass coverage, their primary (I) responsibility when mirroring outside the core (review table 9A).
- However, if their mirror *blocks:*
  a. aggressively to the inside at the snap,
  b. against the Second Level defender after initially releasing downfield, *or*
  c. as a continuation of early-motion from the outside, *cracking-back* on the First Level end, personnel should *cautiously* initiate their secondary (II) responsibility, outside run containment; that is, a defender must see the quarterback hand-off the football or hear "pitch...pitch..." before crashing (see final section of chapter 3).

When pass is read, according to his coverage responsibility each defender must quickly diagnose *specific* receiver routes within the pattern: in max, the pass route of his assigned receiver; in cover, which receiver will enter his zone area. It is the pattern of the offensive action and movement that can provide meaningful, predictive

IMMEDIATE RECEIVER STATIONARY:

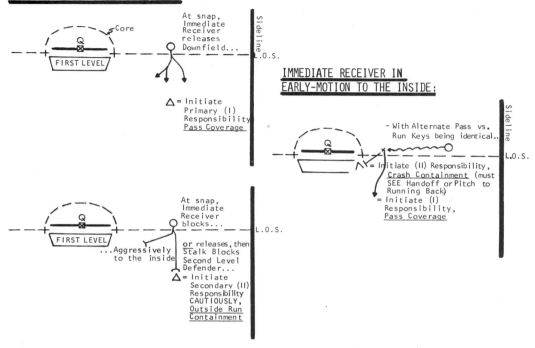

Figure 101 Alternate pass vs. run read for Second Level personnel mirroring outside the core (their location prevents them from obtaining their *basic* key, from interior offensive linemen).

information, seldom individual pass routes: however, there are so many possible pattern combinations (fig. 102) that these must be simplified for defensive purposes.

In table 11, a minimum number of *universal* patterns[4] are defined according to the pass-action and reception areas. Offensive passing can be reduced to four types of actions: quick, straight-dropback, play-action and sprintout. In addition, defined according to the reception area, dropback and play-action may be classified together even though the backfield actions differ (table 11, left-hand column). While the pass-action in itself manipulates the defense (sprintouts, for example, force defensive rotation, play-actions delay the underneath coverage, etc.), from the standpoint of their pass read it is the *number of steps* taken by the quarterback that provides *predictive* information for defenders: the distance downfield of the intended throw is read according to the time taken by the quarterback to set up.

Independent of a specific pass-action, the further receivers maneuver downfield the more time is required, and offenses *buy time* by incorporating additional steps and movement into the quarterback's set-up (42), although there are exceptions such as screen passes. Teaching *pattern* recognition, therefore, pass defenders read the *depth* of

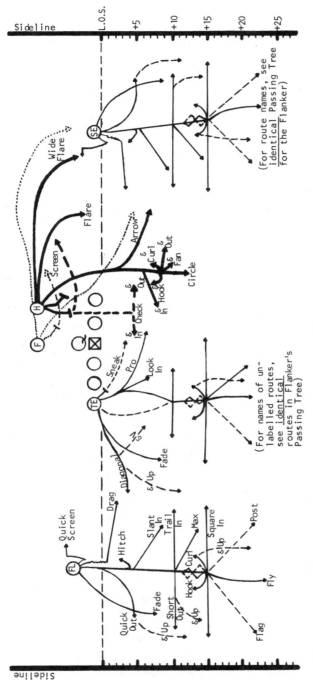

Figure 102 The passing trees for immediate receivers [flanker (FL), tight end (TE), and split end (SE)] and backfielders [fullback (F) dotted routes and halfback (H) thickened lines]; note that several receiver positions are *not* shown; also that label are the most common nomenclature for these pass routes, some routes have as many as four different names.

Table 11. Universal pass patterns defined according to the quarterback's pass-action and the reception areas.

QUARTERBACK'S PASS-ACTION	RECEPTION AREA		
	TO FRONTSIDE*	OVER MIDDLE	TO BACKSIDE
QUICK : (1-3 STEP DROP/ 1.5 SECONDS TO RELEASE)	- QUIK - PIC - CIRCLE	- PRO	- ISO (SEE INDIVIDUAL PASSING TREES)
DROPBACK : (5-7 STEPS/2.5 SECOND RELEASE) -STRAIGHT DROP-ACTION -PLAY-ACTION, BOOTLEG	- FLOOD - CURL	- HOOK AND CROSSING	
SPRINTOUT : (QUARTERBACK MOVING OUT OF BACK AREA)	- SEAM	ROUTES	- THROWBACKS (IE, TIGHT END SCREEN, IN & POST ROUTES TO A BACKSIDE RECEIVER, ETC.)

* For this Table note: when the Quarterback's pass-action is Straight Dropback, Formation *Strength* is interpreted as the 'Frontside'; similarly, 'Backside' and offensive Weakside terminology may be used interchangeably (*only* in this Table).

the reception area accordingly—shallow, medium, or deep. At the same time, according to their defensive location—on the offense's frontside, on the backside, or over the middle (see headings for table 11)—defenders moving into a reception area also can anticipate the *final leg* of specific receiver route(s). Offensive coaches (43, 44, 45) are in agreement on five strategies by which to attack modern pass defenses (detailed in chapter 8). Therefore, as Donahue and Smith (46) explain, their versatile pass offense at U.C.L.A. is actually built upon a *very limited number* of basic patterns. And even though several adjustments are possible within a given pattern, according to the attack strategy the complementary receiver routes are always organized in a highly predictable manner. In turn, defensively it becomes possible to reduce the maze of individual pass routes (fig. 102) to a finite number of *universal* patterns (fig. 103 to 106).

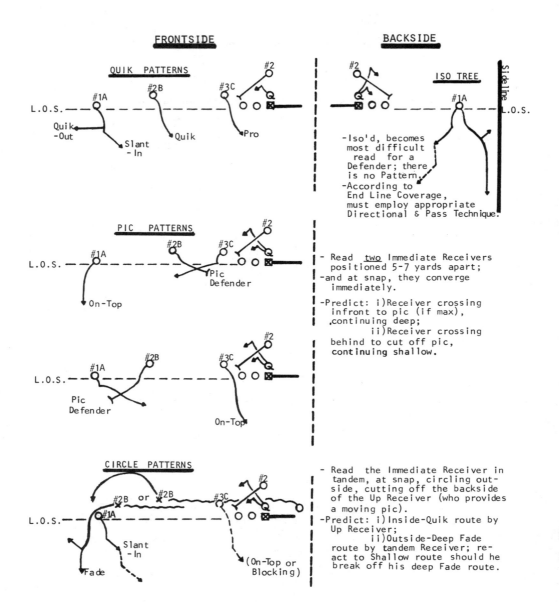

FRONTSIDE

BACKSIDE

QUIK PATTERNS

#2

#1A   #2B   #3C

L.O.S.

Quik
-Out

Slant
- In

Quik

Pro

ISO TREE

#2

#1A

Side line

L.O.S.

-Iso'd, becomes
  most difficult
  read for a
  Defender; there
  is no Pattern.
-According to
  End Line Coverage,
  must employ appropriate
  Directional & Pass Technique.

PIC PATTERNS

#2

#1A   #2B   #3C

L.O.S.

On-Top

Pic
Defender

- Read two Immediate Receivers
  positioned 5-7 yards apart;
-and at snap, they converge
  immediately.
-Predict: i)Receiver crossing
  infront to pic (if max),
  .continuing deep;
       ii)Receiver crossing
  behind to cut off pic,
  continuing shallow.

#2

#1A   #2B   #3C

L.O.S.

Pic
Defender

On-Top

CIRCLE PATTERNS

#2

#2B or #2B   #3C

#1A

L.O.S.

Slant
- In

Fade

(On-Top or
 Blocking)

- Read the Immediate Receiver in
  tandem, at snap, circling outside, cutting off the backside
  of the Up Receiver (who provides
  a moving pic).
-Predict: i)Inside-Quik route by
  Up Receiver;
       ii)Outside-Deep Fade
  route by tandem Receiver; react to Shallow route should he
  break off his deep Fade route.

Figure 103 Examples of quick pass patterns (see Table 11).

242

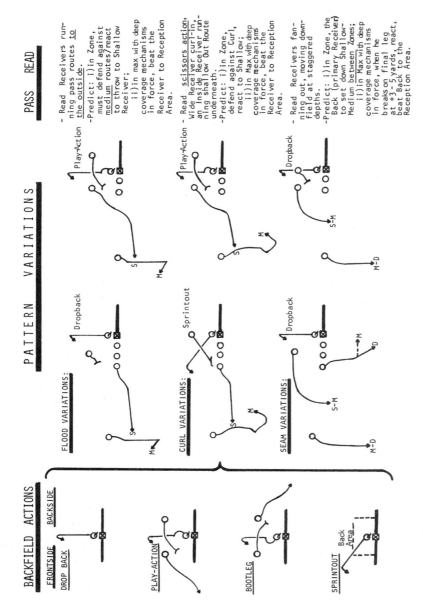

Figure 104 Examples of universal frontside patterns: flood, curl, and seam, according to the receiver depths shallow (S), medium (M), and deep (D).

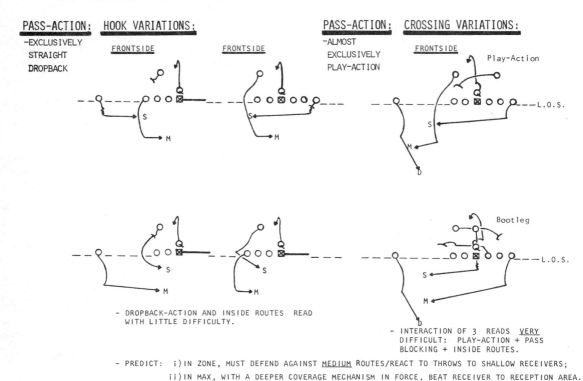

PASS-ACTION: HOOK VARIATIONS:

-EXCLUSIVELY
STRAIGHT
DROPBACK

PASS-ACTION: CROSSING VARIATIONS:

-ALMOST
EXCLUSIVELY
PLAY-ACTION

- DROPBACK-ACTION AND INSIDE ROUTES READ
  WITH LITTLE DIFFICULTY.

- INTERACTION OF 3 READS <u>VERY</u>
  DIFFICULT: PLAY-ACTION + PASS
  BLOCKING + INSIDE ROUTES.

- PREDICT: i) IN ZONE, MUST DEFEND AGAINST <u>MEDIUM</u> ROUTES/REACT TO THROWS TO SHALLOW RECEIVERS;
           ii) IN MAX, WITH A DEEPER COVERAGE MECHANISM IN FORCE, BEAT RECEIVER TO RECEPTION AREA.

Figure 105 Examples of hook and crossing patterns over the middle.

For purposes of reading, this number should be reduced to *as few as possible* and categorized according to the pass-action and reception area (as suggested in table 11). That is, while offensive systems, formations, and individual receivers and their routes vary greatly, from week to week throughout a season the attack strategy, quarterback set-up and final leg of each route in a pattern provide a common focus. To learn effectively in the time available, defensive personnel must have these *universal* variables already compartmentalized. For example, in fig. 104, several variations of flood, curl and seam are illustrated, yet the *universal* elements are clearly distinguishable.

- In each example the pass-action immediately identifies these as $2^1/_2$ second passes (in contrast to quick passing—examine fig. 103).
- Reception areas are frontside (as opposed to over the middle—examine fig. 105).
- Flood is characterized by primary receivers running *outside* routes, in order to saturate the frontside areas.
- Curl is unmistakable: the wide (No.1A) receiver, initially driving deep,

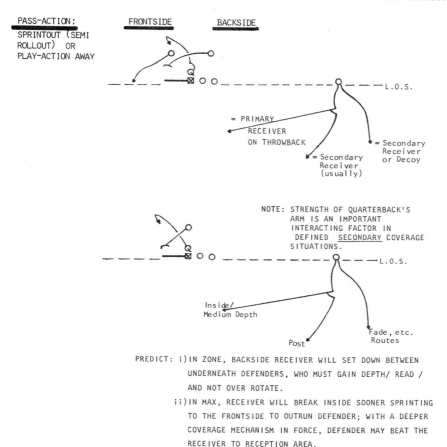

Figure 106 Universal throwback pattern: read play-action away, inside and medium-depth pass route run by backside wide receiver.

curls-in at twelve-to-fifteen yards; the complementary scissors-action of a receiver from the inside running his outside route shallow underneath, in order to expand the passing lane quarterback-to-wide receiver.

• Seam is identified by the receivers fanning out immediately, then moving downfield, with the individual routes staggered at various depths.

Finally, while there are many variations of the universal patterns defined in figs. 103-106, independent of the specific pass being executed defenders should apply *constant* principles in reading the pattern; as explained in the previous sections, their pass read proceeds inside to outside (47). Specifically: Gael reads No.3 to No.2 to the side of the offense he is moving; Strong and Bandit read No.2 to No.1 and, if possible, see No.3 as well; pre-snap both Lou and Rose always identify No.3 in the offensive formation, post-snap they must see the No.2 receiver to their side (unless iso'd, or *steering* with their back turned to the quarterback and pattern inside).

Drills

1. FUNDAMENTAL DRILLS. For Second Level personnel not stacked, operating outside the core, directional movement and agility drills are most appropriate and have substantial carry-over to all phases of their play. Ball drills should emphasize tipping and interception, but defenders should *never* catch the football like offensive receivers (i.e., with their backs to the quarterback, by cradling the football, etc.—see Lollipop Drill below).

An excess of deepback drills are available throughout the coaching literature (see ref. 48 - 50); even an entire text (51) has been devoted to this critical aspect of coaching. Following is one suggested format specifically adapted for the 2-level Defense, combining many of the requisite fundamentals and skills.

Lollipop Drill (fig. 107)

- Only one Second Level defender at a time operates in the drill; however, the offense progresses through three formats.

  Initial Sequence: no football (or quarterback) in drill, nor receiver (cone on sideline at T simulates the receiver being mirrored).

  - Stress initial alignment, backpedal (without a *live* receiver, directional techniques are not possible), and the six directional movements (pre-called by coach).
  - In-season, this format may be curtailed or eliminated entirely.

  Progress To: *live* quarterback and football *poorly* thrown (i.e., high, low, wobbly, etc.).

  - Continue alignment and backpedal sequence, with addition of ball skills.
  - On the throwing action of the quarterback the defender breaks from his backpedal, executing his directional movement accordingly:
    a. intercept the football at its highest point; stress that personnel must turn (often in mid-air) facing the quarterback to intercept, catch with arms extended, in the hands and fingers, never with the body, *or*
    b. tip high passes that are not catchable up-and-over (for the deep safety, see Group Drills).

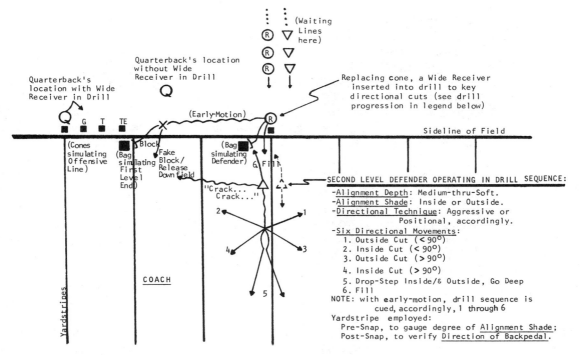

Figure 107 Progression of the Lollipop Drill (example to the defensive *right* only: directional movements and fundamental skills required by Second Level personnel.

  I.   Without football (and quarterback)—stress alignment and movement skills, particularly footwork.

 II.   With football thrown (quarterback *live*)—continue; include ball skills, tipping, and interception.

III.   With addition of receiver—progress to coverage skills.

Final Format: addition of a *live* receiver (replacing cone); simulation of an offense with the *live* quarterback moving in behind the center cone.

- Continuation of alignment and movement skills, according to the individual pass routes run by the receiver; begin at three-quarter speed, progress to full speed.

- Stress directional techniques, and coverage of the final leg of each pass route; in this drill run only the basic pass routes (i.e., final cut to reception area, with minimal jukes).

- In addition, with a *live* receiver, both the alternate run keys and early-motion keys can be included in this drill sequence (see fig. 107 for details).

- In-season this final sequence of the drill becomes the main format for Lollipop.

2. GROUP DRILLS. Excellent small group drills for deepback personnel are also detailed throughout the football literature; for the most part these involve two or three players operating in drills that are systems-oriented yet accord fundamental movement and coverage skills the *major* emphasis (ref. 51).

Applied to the 2-level defense, it is suggested that group drills focus upon *end line enforcement* in order to practice both the defensive skills and coordination required between the Second Level defender and deep safety. Two drill formats have been adapted to simulate this critical portion of the pass defense, Beaten Outfielder and Down-Out-Down drills; it is recommended that these be included in the practice schedule *daily* (fig. 108).

Beaten - Outfielder Drill (fig. 108)

According to the organization of the football field outlined in fig. 85, from the five-yardline (at the hashmark) the offensive receiver (starting ahead of a Second Level defender) breaks downfield on a fly, post, or flag route, with the defender taking the correct angle in hot pursuit; the pass is arc'd by the quarterback (located behind a simulated offense in the end zone) over the defender to the receiver.

- Hearing the safety's "ball...ball..." call while reading the receiver's eyes and hands, the defender times his head turn and leap, thrusting his hands in the air:
  a. to screen the receiver when the football is thrown high overhead (thus, *turning back to the football* is mandatory to avoid an interference penalty),
  b. to tip the football *up*-and-*over* for the safety closing from behind,
  c. to intercept.
- This *pincer-action* between Second Level defender and deep safety is coordinated so that the pass receiver absorbs the safety's hit, while the Second Level defender underneath is safeguarded; by design, his preservation becomes the responsibility of the safety (see final section of chapter), and both these coverage skills and enforcement of the end line require constant practice.
- Often in this drill:
  a. the quarterback purposely *underthrows* the receiver; the defender must recognize and react accordingly when the receiver comes back to the football.
  b. by pre-arrangement (between receiver and quarterback), the receiver will break-off his deep route, running a medium-depth inside or outside route.

Down-Out-Down Drill (fig. 108)

Standing just inside the end zone on the goal line (which simulates the line of scrimmage), the offensive receiver aligns within five to seven yards of the sideline;

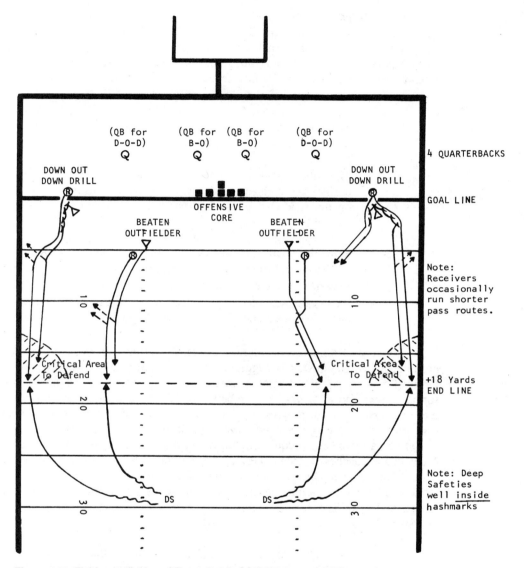

Figure 108 Field organization of Down-Out-Down Drills (near sidelines) and Beaten-Outfielder Drills (at the haskmarks): With four groups operating and a quarterback throwing, if the receiver does not break off his pass route early, the football is arc'd to him at the endline.

immediately across the goal line, a Second Level defender aligns at *hard* depth, assuming either an inside or outside shade on the receiver, according to the directional technique to be employed. Primarily, the pass receiver runs a deep fade route with the quarterback's arc'd pass dropping along the sideline; however, specific routes in the wide receiver's passing tree should be interspersed (for example, see fig. 103, upper right-hand diagram). Also, in this drill (only) offensive receivers are permitted unrestricted use of the hands, including illegal tactics—initially releasing off the line of scrimmage, and throughout the coverage pushing and grabbing the defender. (Note that defenders are *not* allowed similar license and must operate within the rules.)

- Similar to Beaten Outfielder, hearing the safety's "ball...ball..." call while reading the receiver's eyes and hands, the defender times his turn inside and leap accordingly, to screen the receiver, tip the football, or intercept.
- The critical field area to defend is shown in fig. 108, near the sideline, at fifteen-to-eighteen yards and deeper, since this may be the only area on the field (being the furthest distance) where the safety's *arrival* (coinciding with the arrival of the football's) may be delayed. Thus, close coverage by the Second Level defender, pinning the receiver along the sideline, requires constant practice and refinement.
- In addition, often the quarterback's pass should be purposely *underthrown*, to cue recognition and reaction by the defender.
- And again, safeguarding the Second Level defender from *the hit* at the end line is the responsibility of the safety (see section following).

3. TEAM DRILLS: THE MIRROR FORMAT. With appropriate fundamental and group drill (as lead-ups) it is suggested that the *team* portion progress: from Mirror Drills (fig. 109), to Pass Skeleton, then to live Scrimmages. Therefore the mirror format is intended to *bridge the gap* between these fundamentals and their integration into the system, with progressively larger numbers of defensive personnel being involved (i.e., the entire Second Level and deep safety personnel, with First Level end(s) being included as required). Installing the system's pass coverages, the major problem for coaches to overcome may appear somewhat surprising: initially, players experience considerable difficulty switching from max *into* zone (however, interchanging back to a max coverage seldom proves a problem). Therefore, from the outset, in the various Mirror Drills it is the covers that are emphasized, with max interspersed.

- According to fig. 85, the defensive end of the field out to the thirty-yard-line (including the end zone) is reserved for the Mirror Drills during pass practices. The goal line provides the most practical facsimile of the line of scrimmage in these drills, for several reasons:
  a. Field markings beginning on the defensive side of this line provide *exact* feedback of movement depth, the goalpost a spacial awareness of horizontal movement.
  b. Therefore, cones defining the underneath zones are positioned quickly and always with precision (see illustration in fig. 109).

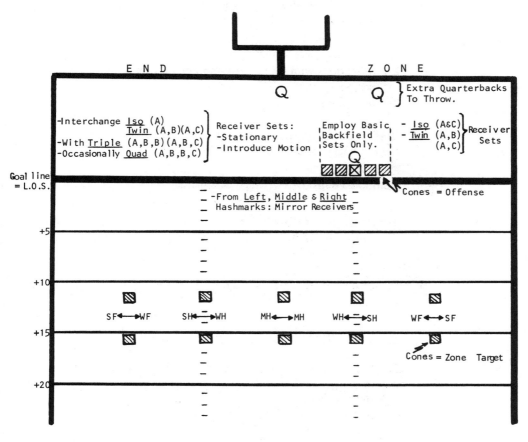

Figure 109 Drill format and underneath coverage for cover-A/-B/-C: progression.

    c. The end zone itself has diagonal markings (or no markings at all) to demarcate the *offensive area of play* back of the simulated line of scrimmage; extra quarterbacks locate just inside the dead-ball line (see diagram), one throwing shortside to any isolated receiver, the other throwing to the far sideline

    d. Behind the end zone in the vicinity of the post provides a central area for organizing the simulated offense — for its huddle, where the coach is stationed with color-coded card diagrams, etc.

    • Independent of the number of defensive personnel operating in a specific drill, the mirror format progresses through three stages (fig. 109, bottom portion).

Stage One: with the point of scrimmage always on or near one hashmark (*i.e.* until defenders are proficient in all phases of coverage, wideside *vs.* shortside should remain obvious), defenders mirror:

1. static offensive formations,
2. formations with single early-motion, players simulating offensive personnel used.
3. then multiple early-motion, etc.

- Besides mirroring, precise shading and depth alignments across the field (whether stacked or not stacked) are assumed by Second Level personnel.
- Additional objectives of Stage One include:

1. pre-snap, verification of cover-A,-B, or -C, *or* revert to cover,
2. and reading the implication of the final offensive formation, according to each defender's coverage responsibility.

- In season, Stage One is employed *briefly* to review game plan particulars.

Stage Two: technique provides the main focus for this stage:

1. Following (appropriate) alignment and directional technique, executing the components of the zone drop, and target accuracy (note: usually in this stage, at the snap the simulated offensive personnel proceed downfield only far enough to cue these defensive actions);
2. *At* target depth, reading the quarterback's eyes, breaking on the throwing motion, and ball skills (note: at least three footballs to be thrown);
3. And one optional drill, to be performed *live* prior to deep safety personnel joining Stage Three, executing the quick pass routes against both max and the underneath zone coverages.

Stage Three: correct technique, pass reading, as well as coverage of the final leg (of receiver routes) provide the important focus for this stage, and *many* variations may be incorporated.

1. Generally, $2^1/_2$ second passing with deeper patterns are emphasized (thus, deep safety personnel are scheduled into this stage, accordingly).
2. Receivers moving downfield:

- may execute the entire pattern at full speed *or* at reduced speed;
- may *freeze* at predetermined points throughout the pattern, affording coaches the opportunity for detailed instruction, etc.

   3. Indicated on every pass pattern diagrammed, up to three footballs may be thrown to the receivers designated, with the *main* quarterback (positioned behind the offensive center cone−fig. 109) always throwing to the end line to key the safety.
   4. Stunts involving Second Level core personnel with First Level end(s) may be practiced; it is *equally important* for core personnel, in max when their mirror pass blocks (i.e., does *not* enter the pattern), to carefully rehearse what actions the Second Level defender(s) should take (see pages 221 and 222).
   5. Throughout this final stage, the patterns executed by the simulated offense should progress:

- from simple to complex (additional receivers out, more pass-actions, etc.),
- from universal to specific (the variations expected in the upcoming game),
- unique game plan adjustments in coverage, etc.

Deep Safety: Fundamentals and Coverage Responsibility

From several perspectives the deep safety is an entirely new defensive position, not merely another deepback, or a free safety positioned absurdly deep. At the snap deepbacks must *react*, but, one of the major difficulties in coaching the deep safety position is to train personnel *not to react* or commit prematurely to an inappropriate course of action. With end line or Deep $2/3$ responsibility (i.e., responsibility for only two-thirds of the end line) it is impossible for a safety to become involved in *any* play before $1^{1}/_{2}$ seconds (and usually more) have elapsed. Over this period the safety must complete his *read sequence* (fig. 110), and many of the fundamentals and techniques for this position were developed expressly to curb his reflex actions. For example,

- while deepbacks assume a semi-crouch, readied to spring at the snap, the deep safety, standing and relaxed, commences rhythmic bouncing lightly on the toes (similar to the footwork of a boxer).
- while deepbacks are drilled constantly in agility and directional dexterity, the safety must be trained to advance methodically from his commanding depth tracking the football, before initiating a definite course of action. Any sudden directional change means that the safety committed too soon and in the *wrong* direction−a cardinal error of this position.

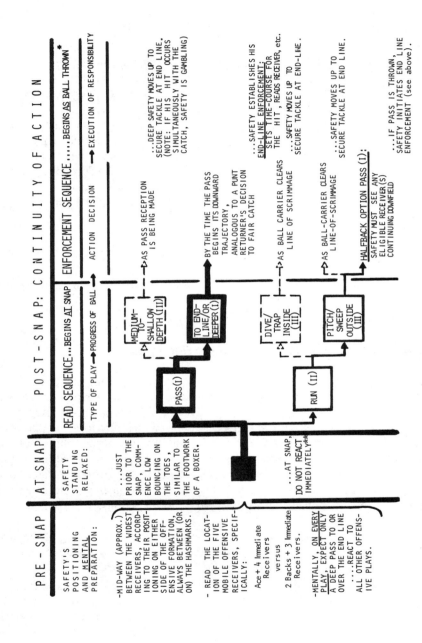

Figure 110 Flow-chart of the deep safety's decisions and responsibilities (i.e., I→II→III): on *every* play, his reading involves the elimination of keys that do not verify primary (I) responsibility, end-line enforcement; this *negative approach* to pass reading, eliminating keys, slows his natural instincts to react.

According to fig. 110, although the safety has four areas of responsibility (see boxes) only one is defined as being primary (I) (follow solid lines), and his *read sequence* initiates a process of eliminating keys in order to identify this type of offensive play: deep passes thrown to or over the end line. When the deep safety finally initiates a course of action, termed *enforcement sequence*, it is cued only by the quarterback's releasing the football on passes. Finally, the mental set of the safety is diametrically opposed to that of the deepback: *on every play* he must practice patience, expecting only a deep pass and mentally sorting through various offensive keys for verification. The safety may not read and react instinctively, and even when recognizing the offensive play he may anticipate, yet delay enforcement.

Interaction of Read and Enforcement. By definition, the deep safety's read sequence begins at the snap; however, an offense's formation, and particularly the positioning of the wide receivers, affords an important preliminary read (fig. 110, left-hand column). Strictly defined, enforcement begins only when the safety initiates a decisive course of action; but again, anticipatory movement always precedes the main action phase. Therefore, while enforcement *by definition* follows read, in practice both sequences proceed simultaneously, with the safety spontaneously repositioning according to his ongoing read of the offense, until fully committed *on cue* to enforcement. The read sequence involves only cognitive processing of (visual) information, enforcement only technique and the physical skills of the position, but throughout every play both sequences constantly influence each other. The model of their interaction is summarized in fig. 110.

FUNDAMENTALS OF ENFORCEMENT. *First*: at the snap, when twenty-one players on the field instantly accelerate, the twenty-second cannot just stand and watch. Therefore, to provide a specific reaction for safety personnel, that is in no way directionally oriented, yet permits limited mobility, the safety begins light bouncing on the toes just prior to the snap. This motion is like that of a tennis player anticipating his opponent's next shot, or that of a boxer's shuffle-and-glide action.

Second: post-snap, over the initial stages of the play the *direction* of the safety's glide is critical: it must be mainly lateral and only minimally forward, traversing a banana-shaped route (fig. 111). That is, according to his ongoing reading of the offensive play, the safety, gliding under control but gradually accelerating, maintains his depth *to the last possible instant*, then sprints forward to intersect the football: there can be only one point of intersection, and the safety must meet the football *head-on*. If the safety must ever regain depth in order to make his play, this most critical fundamental has been violated.

Third: commencing enforcement *on cue*, the deep safety has essentially only two choices: either to enforce primary (I) responsibility when a medium-to-deep pass becomes airborne, or (III) responsibility, which includes *all* other types of plays (i.e., against shorter passes and all running plays). Against all other plays (i.e., III responsibilities), the safety must without fail secure the tackle.[5] Enforcing (I) responsibility, his courses of action are very restricted: to make the hit on the intended receiver (*by far* the preferred decision), or attempt the interception. And the safety

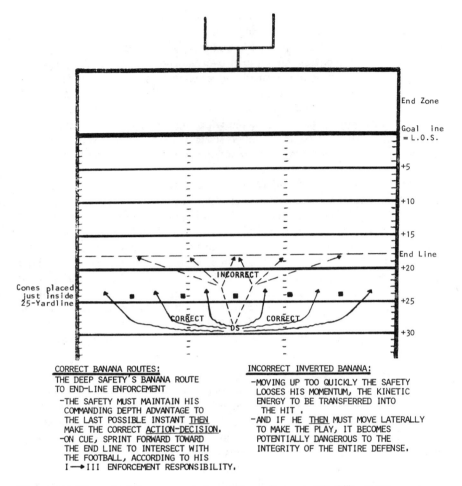

CORRECT BANANA ROUTES:
THE DEEP SAFETY'S BANANA ROUTE
TO END-LINE ENFORCEMENT

- THE SAFETY MUST MAINTAIN HIS
  COMMANDING DEPTH ADVANTAGE TO
  THE LAST POSSIBLE INSTANT <u>THEN</u>
  MAKE THE CORRECT <u>ACTION-DECISION</u>.
- ON CUE, SPRINT FORWARD TOWARD
  THE END LINE TO INTERSECT WITH
  THE FOOTBALL, ACCORDING TO HIS
  I → III ENFORCEMENT RESPONSIBILITY.

INCORRECT INVERTED BANANA:

- MOVING UP TOO QUICKLY THE SAFETY
  LOOSES HIS MOMENTUM, THE KINETIC
  ENERGY TO BE TRANSFERRED INTO
  THE HIT .
- AND IF HE <u>THEN</u> MUST MOVE LATERALLY
  TO MAKE THE PLAY, IT BECOMES
  POTENTIALLY DANGEROUS TO THE
  INTEGRITY OF THE ENTIRE DEFENSE.

Figure 111 The safety's banana route to end-line enforcement: in drills, cones
are placed just inside the 25-yardline to force safety personnel to move through
the row of cones, *then* up to the endline.

must make his decision *before* the football reaches the apex of its flight and begins its
downward trajectory. This is analogous to a punt returner's decision of whether or not
to fair catch, but the safety has less time to make this decision because of the flatter
trajectory of most deep passes compared to punts.

    Fourth: with his decision to make the hit, the safety no longer focuses on the
airborne football, enforcing primary (I) responsibility *only on the intended receiver*,[6]
setting his timing to the hit, and adjusting his route according to the receiver's
movements as he closes. Reading the eyes and hands, as the receiver looks back and
extends to make the catch the arrival of the football signals the hit; at this point the
safety cannot be concerned if his hit will occur a moment early, and his freedom to

proceed *as scheduled* must be guaranteed (this is not, however, license to commit flagrant pass interference or very late fouls). Through his peripheral vision the safety also must be aware of Second Level defenders closing in: to play the football aggressively these personnel must have *absolute confidence* that their safety does not roam about aimlessly, making indiscriminate hits. As an unwritten convention, therefore, whenever possible the safety works to the far side of the receiver away from the closest Second Level personnel by tackling *through* the receiver's exposed torso at the numbers.

READ SEQUENCE. With the exception of a double-coverage assignment, in all max coverages deep safety personnel will have end line responsibility. Without exception, in cover-A, -B, or -C the safety will implement a Deep $2/3$ responsibility:

- *to the shortside* with coverage verification (i.e., a triple or quad formation to the wideside), or
- without this visual verification, Deep $2/3$ *to the wideside*.

And in cover-A, -B, or -C/two-deep, *anytime* two safeties are in the defense, end line verification becomes even simpler: each safety automatically assumes the Deep $2/3$ to the side of the field in which he aligned. In implementing these end line responsibilities there are two distinct phases in the read sequence:

> *Preliminary Read*—the safety's analysis of the offensive formation prior to the snap (fig. 110, left-hand column).
>
> *Elimination of Offensive Keys*—assuming always that the play will be a pass to or over the end line, the safety's mental processing of information during the play to identify this type of pass and where it will bisect the end line.

Preliminary Read: in addition to (visually) verifying his coverage before the snap, the safety often can formulate tentative predictions based upon his analysis of the offense's *final* formation. Are there sufficient mobile personnel remaining in the offensive core (two backfielders and a tight end) to permit the quarterback time to throw deep if they block? Essentially, this prediction involves recognition of that offense's tendencies as dictated by formation of $2\frac{1}{2}$-second passing employing maximal pass protection, versus quick passing with four immediate receivers spread along the line of scrimmage and ace backfield. And predetermination of which receiver(s) threaten the end line *most immediately*, is imperative—invariably in spread formations these are wide receivers.

Elimination of Offensive Keys: at the snap, safety personnel must expect a deep pass and mentally initiate a process of eliminating those offensive keys which do not verify this expectation. A safety must see the entire field and read from the outsides into the middle third of the field. With experience, a safety learns that at the last possible instant he is able to sprint forward to enforce the middle third of the field—in fact, he can move up to the end line anywhere inside the field's numbers - distances of ten to twenty yards—while the pass is still airborne. This process of elimination involves a disciplined format that safety personnel dare not ignore.

- Generally, when any receiver moving downfield cuts sharply (at ninety degrees) this receiver can be eliminated as a deep threat, particularly if the safety has recognized the total pass pattern by that point.

- A safety must *eliminate* non-meaningful keys, *not react to them*; for example, seeing a quick pitch, the safety must continue searching for keys to verify a deep pass, and may react up only *on cue* (i.e., the ball carrier crossing the line of scrimmage).

- The safety must use peripheral vision to see a composite of the offense's movement pattern, similar to the coach's X's-and-O's perception in the press box above the play.

- The safety dare not focus on the quarterback, even when he drops straight back, or sprints out in clear view, and never on play-actions. On passes the quarterback will always reappear with the football, becoming the obvious center of attention at the line of scrimmage (with blockers surrounding him, and rushers clawing to get at him).

- Finally, on passes to the end line, the safety's transition from read to enforcement, from mental integration to physical action, involves a gradual commitment, a building of momentum:

  at the snap, mentally eliminating the offensive possibilities, starting with the various seam patterns, while gliding slowly (i.e., covering only a short distance);

  as the moment of his action-decision approaches, accelerating his glide (according to his reading of the play);

  as the pass rush closes in on the quarterback, never fully committing *until cued* because unpredictable events always are happening in football—seemingly trapped quarterbacks manage to escape, sure interceptions bounce crazily off helmets and hands, offensive personnel make brilliant individual efforts when least expected, and so on.

Additional Pass Coverages. Only by two coverages calls (max-double and cover) are safety personnel *not* assigned an end line responsibility (that is, the entire end line or a Deep 2/3 responsibility). Compared to end line enforcement, the critical differences in each of these coverages occur *at the snap*, with safety personnel moving immediately to implement the specific coverage responsibility.

DOUBLE-COVERAGE TECHNIQUE. Because of his starting depth it becomes virtually impossible for any receiver to get deeper than the safety against double-coverage. At the snap the safety sprints towards the line of scrimmage, his objective being to link up ten-to-twelve yards deep. However, if the safety is to cover this distance (often decelerating as he approaches) within the time that the receiver moves only ten to twelve yards downfield, the Second Level defender must employ *aggressive* directional technique (see preceding section). And it is imperative that the receiver be fully committed along his pass route by the time the safety assumes coverage on top. As he approaches, by reading the pattern and the quarterback the safety can link up with the duo moving downfield (the Second Level Defender steering *or* funnelling his mirror), positioning himself to deny both the deep pass and ones thrown to the side away from the Second Level defender. Smooth transition into double-coverage becomes the responsibility of the safety; therefore he cannot be sprinting forward and then suddenly reverse direction. Prior to initiating coverage on top the safety must have read the pass pattern, predicted the receiver's route, and adjusted his coverage accordingly. Finally, with a single deep safety in the defense, effective double-coverage can be implemented against the No.1A receiver *only to the shortside*. To double-cover the No.1A isolated on the far sideline, it is recommended that a second deep safety be employed, while the safety positioned at the shortside hashmarks enforces a (normal) end line.

DEEP ZONE TECHNIQUE. In cover, at the snap the deep safety must move up immediately, to the approximate center of the Middle 1/3 zone (review fig. 45). Again, this involves a short sprint forward, reading the pass pattern and quarterback while on the move, gradually decelerating and adjusting his Middle 1/3 coverage according to the receiver entering that deep zone. The safety must establish his position *behind* the receiver, always denying the deep pass by playing through the receiver to the football when a pass is thrown.

On the other hand, in cover/two-deep (i.e., two deep safeties), automatically *both* safeties implement Deep 1/3 responsibility (review fig. 56 and 57: against dropback passing this adjustment provides saturation coverage underneath). Against the sprintout, however. cover/two-deep unavoidably creates indecisions: for the frontside safety, the question of whether he should abandon the disciplined format of his read sequence and rotate up into his threatened outside-third prematurely; for both Lou and Rose, with the quarterback sprinting, whether they should implement Deep 1/3 or flat coverage. To alleviate any indecision, a *zone roll* (fig. 112, lower diagrams) may be instituted into the defensive game plan in conjunction with cover/two-deep calls (*only*):

- *on cue*, the deep safety to the sprint-side moves up immediately into Deep 1/3 coverage on the frontside;
- the other safety (to the backside of the quarterback's sprint) follows, rotating up into Middle 1/3;
- the backside Lou or Rose implements Deep 1/3 coverage;
- the frontside Rose or Lou automatically inverts into his frontside flat.

As coaches will discover, the two safeties rolling up frontside from their commanding depth *behind* saturation coverage underneath provides a powerful zone mechanism to combat sprintout quarterbacks. And for the safeties their fundamentals (moving up into

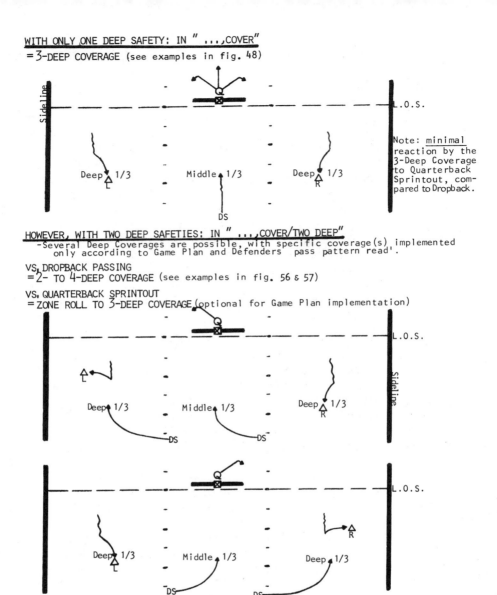

Note: minimal reaction by the 3-Deep Coverage to Quarterback Sprintout, compared to Dropback.

Deep 1/3   Middle 1/3   Deep 1/3

L.O.S.

DS

HOWEVER, WITH TWO DEEP SAFETIES: IN " ...,COVER/TWO DEEP"
    -Several Deep Coverages are possible, with specific coverage(s) implemented only according to Game Plan and Defenders' pass pattern read'.

VS. DROPBACK PASSING
= 2- TO 4-DEEP COVERAGE (see examples in fig. 56 & 57)

VS. QUARTERBACK SPRINTOUT
= ZONE ROLL TO 3-DEEP COVERAGE (optional for Game Plan implementation)

L.O.S.

Deep 1/3   Middle 1/3   Deep 1/3

DS   DS

L.O.S.

Deep 1/3   Middle 1/3   Deep 1/3

DS   DS

Figure 112 In "cover" (only), various deep coverages with one and two deep safeties in the defense: specific combinations are implemented only according to game plan, and keyed by the offensive pass pattern.

either Middle 1/3 or an outside Deep 1/3) are identical to deep zone technique described above.

Conversion from Deep- to Free-Safety. Finally, a number of tactical situations can arise in which *deep* personnel in the defense are unwarranted; to this point only goal line adjustments have been analyzed (chapter 5). First, when an offense continues its advance inside the defense's own thirty-yardline (but before it reaches the eight-yardline), safety personnel do not retreat into their end zone in order to align twenty-eight yards deep. Second, specific offensive receivers may warrant double-coverage, but, with deep safety personnel being required to sprint toward the line of scrimmage at the snap, this can be read by the quarterback, or it may be necessary against particular receivers to apply the double-coverage sooner. Both these situations are rectified by prealigning safety personnel closer to the line of scrimmage. Third, crisis situations can arise where increased rush pressure becomes more imperative than any *deep* coverage. Fourth, against a specific set of receivers, individually the Second Level may absolutely dominate each receiver; or the quarterback's ability to hit his receivers may be extremely limited. Fifth, occasionally the field conditions (strong winds in the face of an offense, heavy rain, and the like) may nullify an opponent's passing game, making an end line unnecessary. In each of these situations it may be desirable to realign the deep safety as a free safety (or even remove this player from the defense entirely at certain points). The various calls in the 2-level system that accommodate this conversion and corresponding technique adjustments are summarized in table 12.

Table 12. Conversion of deep- to free-safety: coverage calls and adjustments.

NUMBER OF SAFETY PERSONNEL ON-THE-FIELD	(IDENTICAL) COVERAGE 'CALLS'	ADJUSTMENTS	ADVANTAGES AND TECHNIQUES
TWO SAFETIES*	'...MAX/TWO-DEEP'	-2 Deep On-Top; -4-Man, First Level Rush; -Tight 'max' by Second Level.	-Little Difference in both technique and pass coverage presently in use with the 3-Level Defensive Models: tight man-to-man coverage underneath, with 2 Deep Zones On-Top.
	'...MAX-DOUBLE(S) /TWO-DEEP'	-The regular comb-inations possible (see chapter 4), Safeties pre-aligned accordingly; -4-Man Rush.	- Little Difference in both technique and and combination coverage that are presently in use with the 3-Level Models.
	'...COVER /TWO-DEEP'	-Regular 5 and 6 Underneath, and 2 - 4 Deep Zones possible; -Also 'Roll' to 3 Deep optional.	-Absolutely no difference in both tech-nique and zone coverages presently in use with 3-Level Defensive Models (ie. saturation underneath, with Deep Zones filled On-Top accordingly).
ONE SAFETY*	'...MAX(SOFT)'	-Second Level fun-nels Receivers in to Free Safety; -5-Man Rush.	-Coverage support in the middle area of the field more immediate/implemented shallower, the closer the Free Safety pre-aligns to the L.O.S.; however against deep outside pass routes max-soft technique must be implemented (ie. no deep help). Therefore, pass rush pressure is critical.
	'...MAX-DOUBLE'	-Regular max-double implemented (see chapter 4), with Safety pre-aligned accordingly; -5-Man Rush.	-Max-double against a particular offensive Receiver; max-soft technique by Second Level (except Defender involved in the double-coverage).
	'...COVER-A'/-B' -C'	-For saturation coverage under-neath, best in run situations; -best vs pass situations.	-Major advantage: Safety in Deep Zone On-Top can provide assistance for Lou /or Rose (ie. if either is isolated on a wide #1A Receiver); however, these coverages are dangerous versus (expected) deep pass patt-erns without End-Line Enforcement.

* Pre-aligning from 8-12 up to 18 yards deep from the line-of-scrimmage employing Deep Zone /& max technique, adapted accordingly (ie. End-Line Enforcement impossible aligning at Free Safety depth).

When the safety *cannot*, because of field position, or *will not*, according to game plan, prealign at the deep position, the player on the field moves to free-safety depth, from eight-to-eighteen yards off the line of scrimmage.   In general, the major disadvantage with this conversion is that it further isolates Lou and Rose, now with no end line behind them; however, several compensatory adjustments are possible, as summarized in table 12.   The best of these is to also substitute a second free-safety personnel into the defense, appreciating that this adjustment both weakens the core against the run (i.e., with removal of a First Level tackle) and reduces its pass rush.   As compensation, now with two free-safeties in the defense, this adjustment allows most of the pass coverages and techniques *presently employed* by the three-level model of defense to be duplicated (see upper half of table).   On the other hand, leaving only one safety in the defense, aligned at free-safety depth, involves greater risk against the pass but maintains the status quo of the core (table 12, lower half).   In max coverage, Second Level personnel must align at medium-soft depth and employ max-soft technique; however, in cover-A, -B, or -C the safety is still capable of providing assistance deep to help Lou or Rose, isolated on a wide receiver.

Drills

1.   INDIVIDUAL DRILLS.   As recommended for the Second Level (at the end of the preceding section), basic movement and agility drills are also most appropriate for deep safety personnel, with substantial carry-over to all phases of their play (see ref. 48-51).

Two drill sequences, *Enforcement* and *Read* are outlined below. It is recommended that portions of each sequence be scheduled into *every* practice, according to the progress of the deep safeties to that point or the game plan for that week.

Enforcement Drills (fig. 113)

- In drill sequence fundamentals leading up to the safety's end line enforcement are developed.   The *key* fundamentals include the safety's action-decision, then the hit.
- Similar to a baseball outfielder who must judge the trajectory and distance of flies at the crack of the bat, the safety must gauge the landing area of the pass *at launch-point*; this requires repeated practice in judging passes thrown to and over the end line.
- To maximize teaching effectiveness, the (simulated) pass receivers in these drills must aggressively contest for the football without fear of personal injury; therefore, at the hit the following *rules* apply:
  - *live* hits are made only on (simulated) pass receivers carrying hand-held air dummies;
  - otherwise, the safety initiates a *bear-hug tackle*, not driving

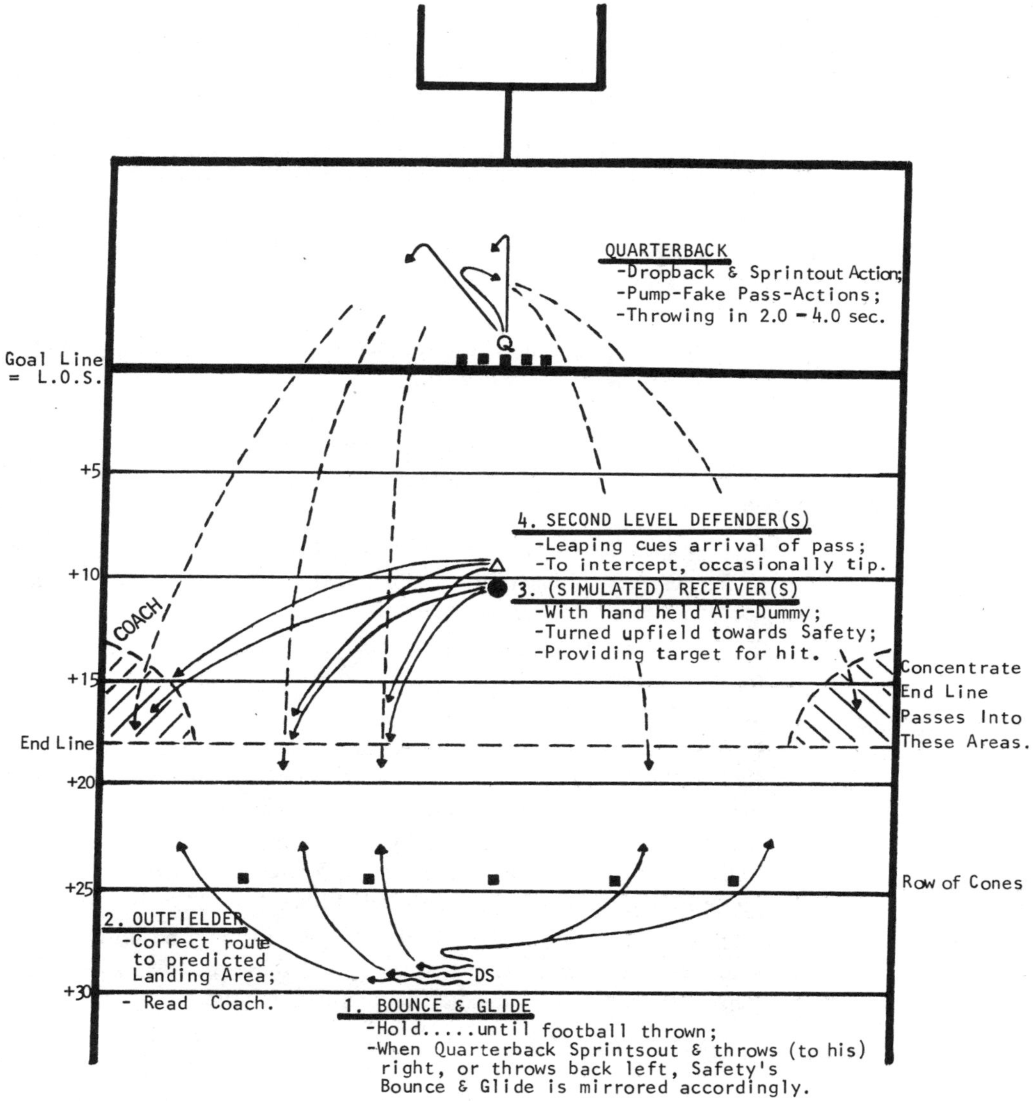
QUARTERBACK
-Dropback & Sprintout Action;
-Pump-Fake Pass-Actions;
-Throwing in 2.0 - 4.0 sec.
Q
Goal Line = L.O.S.
+5
4. SECOND LEVEL DEFENDER(S)
-Leaping cues arrival of pass;
-To intercept, occasionally tip.
+10
3. (SIMULATED) RECEIVER(S)
-With hand held Air-Dummy;
-Turned upfield towards Safety;
-Providing target for hit.
COACH
+15
Concentrate End Line Passes Into These Areas.
End Line
+20
+25
Row of Cones
2. OUTFIELDER
-Correct route to predicted Landing Area;
- Read Coach.
+30
DS
1. BOUNCE & GLIDE
-Hold.....until football thrown;
-When Quarterback Sprintsout & throws (to his) right, or throws back left, Safety's Bounce & Glide is mirrored accordingly.

Figure 113 The deep safety's enforcement drill sequence against endline passed (– – →): four phases are suggested (corresponding to the phases described in text) building the drill sequence, from the safety's bounce & glide pre-snap, to completion of the hit *live* (against a simulated receiver (●) moving/holding target air-dummy.

through the receiver at contact, supporting the receiver from falling if necessary, etc.;

or employs *two-hand touch* when the safety sees two or more players (the receiver and Second Level defenders) precariously positioned in the landing area.

Phase 1: Bounce and Glide Drill

- With the (simulated) quarterback dropping back or sprinting out....looking off the safety....pump-faking his pass-action prefatorily....finally launching the football....
- the safety continues *low* bouncing, barely off the toes, gliding according to his read, maintaining bounce and glide until the launch-point.
- A number of pass reads may be incorporated to expand the safety's peripheral vision (see Read Drills following).
- Note that on misplayed enforcements this simple technique is often at fault—the safety travelling too far, too quickly, to recover in time.

Phase 2: Outfielder Drill

- Continuous with his bounce and glide, at launch-point the safety sprints along the appropriate route (around and through the row of cones) according to his *prediction* of the landing area.
- The safety must *not* continue to (visually) track the football on its downward flight once he has:
  1. predicted the landing area, and
  2. finalized his action-decision to make the hit (vs. interception).
- Rather, the safety reads the coach, standing to one side just in front of the end line (fig. 113), holding up one to five fingers of one hand in front of his chest (which the safety must count and yell out as he closes to the landing area); *live* pass receiver(s) also can be inserted into this phase for the safety to read (see Read Drills following).
- The majority of end line passes in this phase should be thrown to the sidelines (fig. 113, hatched areas) since these involve the safety's longest sprints, and his most difficult enforcements.

Phase 3: The Hit

- Assuming the safety's action-decision is to make the hit, this phase can be scaled down into smaller areas of the field for lead-up drills:
  1. with two stationary receivers spread fifteen to twenty yards apart...
  2. holding air dummies at waist level...
  3. the safety running from three-quarter to full speed, from twenty yards back towards them...
  4. the quarterback throwing to one receiver or the other, timing this *cue* so the safety can break on the throwing action/initiate enforcement...
  5. finally, the intended receiver raising the air-dummy to chest level (visually) signals the arrival of the football. (Note: receivers never

attempt to actually catch a pass when holding an air-dummy; rather, they give the safety his *cue*, a target to hit through, always face the safety, and protect themselves.)

- Thereafter, this drill can be expanded: over larger areas of the field, to include receivers running abbreviated routes, until expanded completely to the entire defensive area of the field (fig. 113).

- Expanding this format, many innovative *live* hitting drills can be incorporated, for both deep safety personnel and the offensive receiver corps.

Phase 4: Addition of Second Level Defenders

- As soon as possible Second Level personnel should be included in the enforcement sequence:

    to provide a peripheral read (as the safety focuses upon the receiver he must also see Second Level defender(s) closing in);
    to purposely tip the football up and over the intended receiver (so the safety closing in from behind can react);
    to simulate the positional variations and confusion that three, four, and sometimes five players create going for the football at the end line.

- In these situations: the Second Level defender(s) leaping for the end line pass *cue* the arrival of the football; also *on cue* the (simulated) receiver raises the air-dummy.   The safety must move up between players to make the hit; on intercepted passes "bingo...bingo..." call is yelled and defenders initiate transition to run back.

- An overriding objective of *all* enforcement drills is personal safety, avoiding incidental injury to key personnel.   One simple rule accomplishes this: at the end of each drill sequence *everyone is standing*, no one is on the ground.   Thus, at crucial points of collision, teammates hold each other upright: receivers prevent defenders from tumbling, and the safety in particular, by his approach and then his hit (through the receiver), can prevent pile-ups.

Sequence Of Read Drills (fig. 114)

- This sequence of drills with *live* receivers is a continuation of enforcement, integrating these physical skills with the safety's pass pattern read; however, the hit is deemphasized in Read Drills (i.e., without the protective air-dummy, a bear-hug or two-hand touch is employed).

- Progressively, the safety is forced to employ peripheral vision, to read over a wider portion of the field: initially, pass routes for one and two receivers thrown to the middle-third or an outside-third (fig. 114, upper

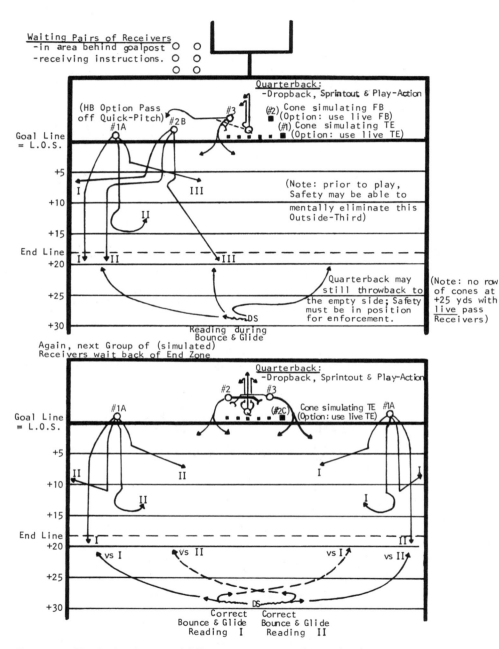

Figure 114 The deep safety's read drill sequence: patterns threatening the middle-third and one outside-third (upper diagram), or *both* outside-thirds (lower).

diagram); then, the addition of specific backfield actions, particularly play-actions and bootlegs; finally, patterns encompassing the entire defensive area (see lower diagram), even the inclusion of *trick* passes (halfback option pass, flea-flicker, etc.).

- Progressively, more complex patterns (than I, II, III, etc., shown in fig. 114) are included, particularly during game-plan preparation; however, the principles of reading, integrated with enforcement, remain constant:

  1. mentally eliminating those offensive keys which do not verify an end line pass;

  2. pattern identification according to the universal *patterns.*

- Unfortunately, in these Read Drills safety personnel obtain only limited preliminary reads (during pass skeleton and defensive scrimmage, where offensive formations, down and distance, etc., are simulated more closely, pre-snap reading proves more meaningful).

- Two tactical situations should be avoided in these drills.

  1. Quick passing: it becomes a waste of time in these safety-oriented drills unless receivers *threaten* deep.

  2. Patterns where *more than one* receiver actually runs a deep route: without a concerted pass rush *plus* Second Level coverage, these patterns prove unrealistic.

- Four phases also are recommended for the Read Drill sequence; in each, drill modification and coaching innovation are encouraged, according to the progress of personnel to that point. And during practice, as safety personnel *physically* review the movement skills of enforcement, appropriate Read Drills should be interspersed to reinforce the interconnection of their read *directing* these physical actions.

Phase 1: Without (Simulated) Receivers

Before *live* receivers are simulated in these drill formats, reading the coach (counting the number of fingers he holds up, etc.) provides a focus for the safety's read without distracting his attention completely from the physical skills of enforcement (see Phases 1 and 2 in preceding section).

Phase 2: Simple, Two-Man Patterns

With receivers simulated *live*, safety personnel must expand their field of vision. Every practice, as lead-ups to Phases 3 and 4 (below), only the *basic* routes are run by receivers (i.e., flood, curl, etc.–fig. 114, upper diagram).

Phase 3: Universal Patterns

Then, these basic patterns are expanded to include more receivers, utilize the entire defensive area, etc.; however, the basic *mechanism* of each pattern (flooding, curl, iso, throwback, etc.) must remain clearly discernible (fig. 114, lower diagram). As well, the fakes and jukes of the receivers running these patterns should be minimized (it still is preferable to employ defensive personnel to simulate the offensive receivers for this reason through Phase 3).

Phase 4: Game-Plan Variations

This stage (usually) involves pass skeleton, employing offensive receivers to simulate an opponent's pass offense as closely as possible. For this reason only limited individual drill can be performed by safety personnel in this final stage; however, *individual* work is accomplished by the coach positioning himself behind the safety, directing, talking, and giving immediate feedback after every play (see Team Drills following).

2. GROUP DRILLS. Beaten-Outfielder and Down-Out-Down are recommended as the drill formats for incorporating Second Level coverage with end line enforcement (see fig. 108 and accompanying text). For safety personnel, however, these drills afford *minimal* pattern reading: the intended receiver and his pass route are predetermined by the drill, blatant hits against exposed teammates are never allowed, even their row of cones must be removed from the field (in the interests of safety). Therefore, these smaller drills provide worthwhile practice only when the focus for safety personnel is limited to movement and the physical skills of enforcement:

- its sequencing, from bounce and glide through to the *timing* of the hit,
- at launch-point, judging the landing area quickly, yelling "ball...ball..." repeatedly to signal that the football is airborne and at the apex of its trajectory.
- refocusing immediately upon the receiver, adjusting enforcement according to his actions,
- finally, moving through the players converging at full speed, to the receiver, avoiding collisions prior to contact, and pileups afterwards.

3. TEAM DRILLS. No position is as accessible to the coach during practice as that of the deep safety. In addition, for the more involved Mirror Drills (see preceding section), Pass Skeleton, and live scrimmages, the coach will have in hand the detailed script for each unit of work. Therefore, the coach is able to (verbally) direct the safety, particularly his *visual focus* during the safety's pre-snap read, then provide extensive feedback following each play (as safeties seldom need to join the defensive huddle, the coach calling most of their coverages, with appropriate directives, according to the script for that practice). However, once a drill sequence or simulated play is under way, the coach should *stop talking*: it becomes too confusing for the safety to read, move, and try to listen. Moreover, throughout the practice week in preparation for an opponent, the coach should gradually reduce the amount of information interchanged, so as to allow safety personnel to make their mistakes and learn by them in practice.

Mirror Drills

Deep safety personnel join the Mirror Drills in Stage Three, when deep pass routes are incorporated within this format (see preceding section).

Pass Skeleton

Essentially a continuation of Stage Three, with offensive receiver personnel being inserted and tactical situations simulated (down and distance, complete pass patterns, etc.), safety personnel continue to employ bear-hug or two-hand touch on contact in their end line enforcement.

Pass Scrimmage

Defensive unit practice with full contact and tackling; for the deep safety, however, *live* is optional (this is a decision to be made by the coaching staff).

Notes

1. In deepening immediately, at a forty-five to sixty degree angle from the line of scrimmage, three difficulties are encountered: defenders must turn their back to the quarterback; if they then begin their backpedal prematurely, the underneath zones will be *compressed* horizontally; and by these actions, the quarterback is able to read zone coverage immediately.

2. For example, one ill-advised combination might be: to assign *hard* alignment, outside shade, and aggressive funnelling, and then assign that Second Level defender Deep 1/3 zone coverage.

3. *Across the face* is a unique phrase to differentiate this zone adjustment from *collision* (i.e., the technique for delaying outside receivers crossing to the inside).

4. Defensive coordinators will need to supplement this list, according to the offensive opponent and/or game-plan specifications.

5. And there need be only one qualification—or caution—regarding his various courses of action. On quick pitch and sweep plays, as Second Level personnel move up to execute their (II) responsibility (outside run containment), by yelling "pitch...pitch..." the deep safety assists their reaction, but he must continue to search for eligible pass receivers moving downfield. The possibility of the halfback option-pass now becomes his (I) responsibility until the ball carrier has crossed the line of scrimmage.

6. Continuing to focus on an *accurately* thrown pass, and not seeing the intended receiver as well as the Second Level defenders in the reception area, is another critical fundamental of end line enforcement that *must not be violated.* Coaches will only need to observe this cardinal error one time: the safety crashing directly into teammates at full speed, the catch being made by the receiver with an open field ahead, and one or two defenders seriously injured on the play.

References

1. GIL ROMAINE, "Defensive line play versus the passing game," *Football Coaching.* Compiled by the American Football Coaches Association, ed., Dick Herbert (New York: Charles Scribner's Sons, 1981), p. 191.

2. NICK METROKOTSAS, *The Complete Book of Offensive Line Play* (West Nyack, N.Y.: Parker Publ. Co., Inc., 1977), pp. 131-171.

3. THE CANADIAN AMATEUR FOOTBALL ASSOCIATION, *Coaching Certification: Level III* (Ottawa, Canada: Fitness and Amateur Sport, 1980), pp. 128-129.

4. JOHN OLSON, "The defensive noseguard: advanced techniques," *Athletic Journal*, 64(3): 18-20, 1983.

5. ROMAINE, "Defensive line play versus the passing game," *Football Coaching*, pp. 192-193.

6. OLSON, "The defensive noseguard: advanced techniques," pp. 18-20.

7. ROMAINE, "Defensive line play versus the passing game," pp. 192-193.

8. LLOYD H. HELGESON, *Total Pass Defense* (West Nyack, N.Y.: Parker Publ. Co., Inc., 1978), pp. 52-56.

9. DONALD E. FUOSS, *Coaching the Offensive and Defensive Line Game* (West Nyack, N.Y.: Parker Publ. Co., Inc., 1972), pp. 198-205.

10. ARA PARSEGHIAN and TOM PAGNA, *Parseghian and Notre Dame Football* (Notre Dame, Ind.: Men-In-Motion, 1971), pp. 52-54.

11. HELGESON, *Total Pass Defense*, pp. 59-62.

12. GOMER JONES, *Offensive and Defensive Line Play* (Englewood Cliffs, N.J.: Prentice-Hall, Inc., 1961), pp. 162-167.

13. JERRY SANDUSKY, *Developing Linebackers the Penn State Way* (West Point, N.Y.: Leisure Press, 1981), p. 59.

14. GARY SPERBER, "Ideas and drills for training crashing ends," *Illustrated Football Drills from The Coaching Clinic*. Compiled by the editors of The Coaching Clinic (West Nyack, N.Y.: Parker Publ. Co., Inc., 1975), pp. 143-148.

15. GEORGE H. ALLEN, *Pass Defense Drills* (Menlo Park, Calif.: Addison-Wesley Publ. Co., 1968), pp. 201, 206, 212.

16. DONALD E. FUOSS, *Championship Football Drills for Teaching Offensive and Defensive Fundamentals and Techniques* (Englewood Cliffs, N.J.: Prentice-Hall, Inc., 1964), pp. 140, 232, 258, 305, 309.

17. ROBERT J. BRIGHAM, "Factorizing drills for linemen," *Illustrated Football Drills from The Coaching Clinic*. Compiled by the editors of The Coaching Clinic (West Nyack, N.Y.: Parker Publ. Co., Inc., 1975), pp. 223-226.

18. SANDUSKY, *Developing Linebackers the Penn State Way*, pp. 34-36; 64-66.

19. HELGESON, *Total Pass Defense*, pp. 102-115; 167-174.

20. GENE ELLENSON, *Coaching Linebackers and the Perimeter Defense* (West Nyack, N.Y.: Parker Publ. Co., Inc., 1972); chapter 3: pp. 37-93.

21. HELGESON, *Total Pass Defense*, pp. 106-108.

22. S. E. SULLINS, *Complete Book of Multiple Defenses in Football* (West Nyack, N.Y.: Parker Publ. Co., Inc., 1978), pp. 166-177.

23. HELGESON, *Total Pass Defense*, pp. 167-171.

24. THOMAS FEY and JOSEPH KIMBALL, "Presenting your pass defense concepts," *Athletic Journal*, 65(7):32-33, 1985.

25. SANDUSKY, *Developing Linebackers the Penn State Way*, pp. 83-97.

26. ALLEN, *Pass Defense Drills*, pp. 98-113; 126-128; 136-137.

27. ELLENSON, *Coaching Linebackers and the Perimeter Defense*, pp. 32-36.

28. SANDUSKY, *Developing Linebackers the Penn State Way*, pp. 34-36; 64-66.

29. ELLENSON, *Coaching Linebackers and the Perimeter Defense*, pp. 37-93 (see relevant sections on inside linebacker play).

30. FUOSS, *Championship Football Drills for Teaching Offensive and Defensive Fundamentals and Techniques*, pp. 248-252.

31. HELGESON, *Total Pass Defense*, pp. 83-91 and 155.

32. HAL DYER, "Defensive backfield techniques," *Athletic Journal*, 43(9): 48-50 and 100, 1974.

33. JACK BURGETT, "Cornerback technique in two-deep, zone underneath," *Athletic Journal*, 66(4): 30-31, 1985.

34. SANDUSKY, *Developing Linebackers the Penn State Way*, pp. 69-72; 83-90.

35. FUOSS, *Championship Football Drills for Teaching Offensive and Defensive Fundamentals and Techniques*, pp. 260-265.

36. FLOYD "BEN" SCHWARTZWALDER, "Syracuse line-backer drills," *Illustrated Football Drills from The Coaching Clinic*. Compiled by the

editors of The Coaching Clinic (West Nyack, N.Y.: Parker Publ. Co., Inc., 1975), pp. 155-162.

37. ELLENSON, *Coaching Linebackers and the Perimeter Defense*, pp. 44, 143.

38. DEWAYNE DEWEY KING, *Jericho: a Modern System of Pass Defense* (Englewood Cliffs, N.J.: Prentice-Hall, Inc., 1963), pp. 200-203.

39. JOHN W. DURHAM, *Game-Tested Football Drills* (West Nyack, N.Y.: Parker Publ. Co., Inc., 1980), pp. 167-169.

40. ALLEN, *Pass Defense Drills*, pp. 54-65.

41. HELGESON, *Total Pass Defense*, p. 88.

42. BILL WALSH, "Controlling the ball with the passing game," *Football Coaching*. Compiled by the American Football Coaches Association, ed., Dick Herbert (New York: Charles Scribner's Sons, 1981), pp. 85-86.

43. TERRY DONAHUE and HOMER SMITH, "U.C.L.A.'s passing attack: successful patterns and adjustable routes," *Athletic Journal*, 65(2):8-13, 1984.

44. TOM OLIVADOTTI, "Defensive analysis of pass offense," *Scholastic Coach*, 54(1):48-49 and 69, 1984.

45. WALSH, "Controlling the ball with the passing game," pp. 85-93.

46. DONAHUE and SMITH, "U.C.L.A.'s passing attack: successful patterns and adjustable routes," pp. 8-13.

47. OLIVADOTTI, "Defensive analysis of pass offense," pp. 48-49 and 69.

48. PARSEGHIAN and PAGNA, *Parseghian and Notre Dame Football*, pp. 68-73.

49. ELLENSON, *Coaching Linebackers and the Perimeter Defense*, pp. 217-226.

50. CHAMPIONSHIP BOOKS, *Championship Drills for Football. Vol. II: Defensive Drills* (Lake Mills, Iowa: Graphics Publ. Co., Inc., 1982), pp. 50-61.

51. ALLEN, *Pass Defense Drills*.

CHAPTER 8

ANALYSIS OF OFFENSE: BASIC MECHANISMS

INTRODUCTION: THE MACHINERY OF OFFENSE

The media has popularized the artistry of offense in mechanical terms, characterizing successful passing attacks as "air service" and power-running teams as "juggernauts," and calling sophisticated multiple offenses "well-oiled." Throughout this final part of the text this inelegant analogy is retained, not, however, because of any exterior similarities between football offense and machines but, rather, because of the offense's internal machinery. Portraying the football offense as intricate machinery best conceptualizes how it must operate—a highly structured mechanism requiring precision timing and movements by its integral parts, the offensive personnel. To this point, these mechanistic elements have been emphasized only with regard to key reading.

The greatest defensive challenge is to unite a group of young men who, individually, may not be the equal of their offensive counterparts, yet on the field function as the *superior* tactical unit. Whenever the physical disparity between the defensive personnel and their opponents is not insurmountable, then superior coaching must offset the difference. To accomplish this, however, an intimate understanding of the offense's *machinery* is prerequisite for formulating a viable game plan, and each week in season the compressed time frame imposed upon defensive preparations makes this even more imperative. Essentially, football coaching follows a spiral course of pre-game preparation → in-game implementation → post-game evaluation; this dynamic process and its interrelationships are illustrated schematically in figure 115. To assist the coach, these final chapters provide information and detail procedures for implementing the 2–

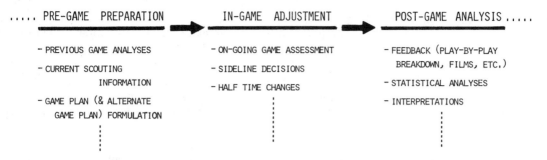

Figure 115 The dynamics of football coaching: from pre-game preparations through in-game adjustments to post-game analysis, this cycle is repeated from game to game, throughout a season - even carried over from one season into the next.

level Defense in the game situation. This chapter details various methods of offensive evaluation, what other texts categorize under scouting; in this chapter, however, offensive mechanisms are dealt with only in *general* terms−first running, then passing, examining the specific advantage(s) which each offensive maneuver hopes to gain. In chapter 9 the evolution of offensive football is traced beginning with the T formation in the 1940s, which marked the advent of the modern era (see also table 1 and accompanying text). In this final chapter, the major systems of offense are analyzed in terms of their specific machinery, the *principles of leverage* by which the defense is manipulated. In addition, with each systems analysis the most successful plays are highlighted; ultimately, these were incorporated into the versatile multiple offenses which have evolved in the eighties.

There are no ultimate formula's for devising defensive strategy. On occasion, in fact, what proved successful on the field should not have, according to chalkboard theory: the will and determination of well-coached athletes simply *made it happen*. Defense is as much emotion and verve as X's and O's. The aim is to achieve equanimity between textbook recipes and that gut feeling which every coordinator must fall back on when it's decision time on the field, before a crucial play or series of downs. The purpose of the final two chapters is to refine the coach's analytical ability and instincts. Three general areas are examined: strategy planning pre-game, in-game adjustments, and post-game analysis. To begin with, the following principles are suggested as general guidelines, to be observed when carrying out any offensive analysis.

First and Foremost, Prioritize What Your Opponent Does Best. Even though a multiple system may be employed, most offenses cannot execute a *multitude* of running and pass plays with equal facility. And even if it were possible, coaches must still make tactical decisions in order to prepare their game plan. Initially, then, the coaching staff should decide:

- what plays must be defensed-their opponent's most successful plays, the ones most frequently run, or the system itself (see chapter 9),

- which offensive personnel must be stopped-the quarterback, a running back, or specific receiver(s),
- where the opponent's tactical strengths lie-in long yardage, on first downs, capping off scoring drives, etc.

Defensing what your opponent does best presumes that offense then will be forced to run plays less suited to its style of attack, or to utilize less skilled personnel. And while this theory is not infallible, its premise at least can provide a viable starting point for strategy planning(1).

Evaluate Personnel Match-Ups. Equally important, as a point of departure, are the coaches evaluation of how their defensive personnel measure up in comparison to the offense's. Ultimately, football is reduced to a series of one-to-one confrontations, blocker against tackler, receiver against pass defender. A realistic appraisal at which positions the defense is physically mismatched must influence both the game strategy and how the system of defense will be manipulated in the finalized game plan.

Observe the Laws of Compensation. On the other hand, given the range of most offensive systems, there are limits to how much eleven defenders can compensate in order to counter a specific offensive threat or cover a particularly vulnerable sector on defense—reinforcing one area of the defensive structure may, in turn, weaken another. And the important corollary to this principle, overcompensation—bastardizing the system to too great an extent—is as imprudent as inadequate planning. It is best to implement the defensive system in full measure, yet understand and stay within its inherent limitations.

Finally, information and detail for planning defensive strategy is obtained from four main sources. Three of these provide valuable background, and the fourth provides the most current data on the upcoming opponent. Reviewing previous game plans proves very useful as a starting point. Second, post-game summaries from the most recent meetings (with the upcoming opponent) provide further insight and information, particularly the statistical analyses (see final section of this chapter). Third, a *critical* examination of previous game film is essential, remembering that the opposing coaching staff is appraising similar footage; thus, critiquing strategy should be the focus of this reevaluation. Lastly, with this background as refresher, the opponent's scouting reports over their last two to four games[1] provide the most vital information for defensive planning; even better, of course, league rules permitting, is a film exchange of each team's latest games.

ANALYSIS OF OFFENSE PRIOR TO THE SNAP

At the tactical level, several pre-snap analyses should be carried out. First, the formations that an offense employs must be evaluated, for each alignment structure embodies inherent strengths and weakness. In addition, the offense's placement of specific personnel within the formation should be carefully examined. For example, placement of the offenses's best receivers to the same side in a spread formation increases the probability that any pass thrown will be in their direction; positioning an ineffectual blocker at tight end reduces the outside running potential of a power formation, and so on. The individual personnel matchups must also be closely evaluated, and this is particularly crucial given the mirroring mechanism that the present 2-level Defense employs. For example, if Gael is more of a linebacker type, a specific triple formation may force him to mirror a much faster receiver; if so, personnel substitutions will have to be made appropriate for the down and distance. In this section a simple *numerical rating* method is suggested as the basic analytical tool by which to evaluate formation; in the next chapter this methodology is applied to the various systems of offense.

Formational Evaluation

From the perspective of defense, at the heart of every formational analysis lies the defensive strategy for countering the personnel alignments of the offense—its mechanisms for quickly relocating defenders according to the offense's concentration of blockers and potential pass receivers. Since the 1940s several mechanisms have been incorporated into the systems of defense to accomplish such adjustments—the Monster defenses of the 1960s (2, 3); interchanging linebackers according to formational strength (4, 5); rotational mechanisms involving the deepback unit (6, 7); and so on. In run defense, traditionally the major consideration has been the location of the tight end (8); until the early seventies offensive structuring was so static in nature that this concept alone was sufficient for defining formational running strength, with few anomalies. In the 2-level Defense, Second Level mirroring is the mechanism by which the number of defenders in the core is matched *automatically* to formational strength. However, although equalization of personnel proves sufficient against the majority of formations, tactical situations can arise where this mechanism still leaves the defense at a disadvantage.

- First, the location of *superior* offensive personnel must influence core structure—when it is obvious these blockers will dominate any defender, the core structure must be strengthened at these areas.
- Specific formations complement the running game more than others: formations with *two* tight ends or a large tight end and a wingback enhance the run potential; I-backs can move *immediately* against either side of the core, adding up two blockers at the point of attack; etc.
- Various systems of blocking incorporate advantages: double-team blocking at the point of attack, two blockers against one defender; trapping, whereby an additional blocker (a backside lineman) pulls and blocks at the point of attack frontside; etc.
- Unusual formational manipulations can result in a running gap being undefended unless defensive adjustments are quickly implemented *before* the snap (see fig. 26 and accompanying text).

- More and more, early-motion is being employed to bring an additional blocker to the point of attack *at* the snap.
- The hashmarks—creating wideside *versus* shortside—remain an important defensive factor, often influencing an offense's play selection; the defensive coordinator must be aware of the opponent's tendencies in this regard because the *location* of the football will often dictate the core alignment.

These as well as other unique formational considerations (see chapter 9) must be analyzed by coaches in preparing their run defense. In planning strategy against a specific opponent, the following numerical rating can provide a basis upon which to expand this evaluation (fig. 116).

1. In the core, the offensive personnel aligned in an area (e.g., in fig. 116, the *potential* blockers on one side) *plus* any additional personnel who may augment the blocking pattern at the point of attack are assigned specific numeric values, ranging from....

   - a value of 0.5, assigned to inferior blockers or those poorly positioned to execute their designated task, to....
   - a maximal of 2.0 points, assigned only to a *very* superior all-star.

2. The numeric assignment given specific offensive personnel is based upon a corresponding rating value of 1.0 points for each defender located in that area of the core. Why a constant value of 1.0 per defender?

   - personnel rated *less than* 1.0 by their own coaches would not be starting (or, by this point-scale, the defense is really in trouble);
   - towards the higher end of this scale, rating any defender *above* 1.0 can mislead coaches badly in the planning stages.[2]

3. Numerically, therefore, when the total point value assigned the offense by this method (see examples in fig. 116) exceeds the totaled value for the defense, additional structural adjustments (other than mirroring) should be considered when formulating the core structure.

In pass defense, before the snap, mirroring automatically relocates coverage personnel directly across the line of scrimmage from the eligible pass receivers *independent* of an offense's formation; therefore, seldom should this mechanism of adjustment ever prove a major concern in the overall planning of strategy. On the other hand, planning pass defense several formational variables require careful analysis.

- First, the personnel matchups are even more critical than in run defense, because Second Level personnel can be isolated at any time by specific formations: considering the coverages planned *vis-à-vis* the abilities of the various receivers, will specific defenders be equal to the

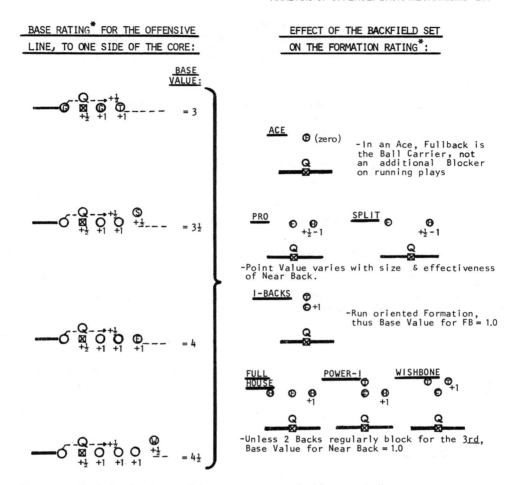

Figure 116 Basis for planning run defense strategy: a method for numerically rating offensive formations.

tasks asked of them, or should personnel substitution be made? Or would alternate coverage mechanisms, in the first instance, prove the superior adjustment within the global plan (considering both pass *and* run defense)?

- Equally important decisions involve the depth alignment and shading to be assumed by the Second Level against individual receivers. In table 10 and accompanying text, *general* alignment principles are explained; depending upon the situation on the field, however, in defensing a specific formation or against a particular receiver these guidelines may be deemed inappropriate or even place the defender at a disadvantage in certain coverages.

- To varying degrees defenders' actions *during* a play are predicated upon their pre-snap read of the offensive formation *in relation to* the tactical circumstances of that play. Against all but the most sophisticated pass offenses (where pre-snap cues may be minimal), this anticipatory process can often dictate directional technique as well as the degree of aggressiveness in technique execution; however, the interaction of formation with field situation should be *precisely defined* by the coaching staff in the planning stages.

Countering Formation Strength And Tendencies

Prior to the snap, a limited number of mechanisms and adjustments are possible within the 2-level defensive system to counter an offense's formational strengths and probable actions (table 13). To offset any potential advantage, however, the countermeasures planned for the three areas of defense—run defense, pass rush, and pass coverage (left—hand column)—must be selected *with caution*: occasionally the specific adjustment needed to reinforce one area will weaken another to too great a degree.[3] Additionally,

Table 13. Before the snap, the mechanisms and adjustments within the 2-level system for reinforcing run defense, pass rush, and pass coverage.

	FIRST LEVEL	SECOND LEVEL	DEEP SAFETY
INSIDE THE CORE			
RUN DEFENSE:			
MECHANISMS	- 4- /& 5-ALIGNMENTS - PRE-SNAP SHIFTING	- LOCATION OF STACKS	N/A
ADJUSTMENTS	- EAGLE Adjustment	- DEPTH Adjustment (in Stack)	N/A
PASS RUSH:			
MECHANISMS	- 11- /& 3-ALIGNMENTS - OVERLOAD Mechanism (from 2- /4-Alignments)	N/A	N/A
ADJUSTMENTS	- WIDER Alignment by Ends (in 11- to 3-Alignments)	N/A	N/A
OUTSIDE THE CORE			
PASS COVERAGE:			
MECHANISMS	- REGULAR 5 - GOAL LINE 5	5 6 (+ Rover)	1 -
	- REGULAR 4 } (- One - VARIATION* 4 } Tackle)	5 6 (+ Rover)	2 (+ Second Safety) 1
	- SHORTYARDAGE 6 } (+ Second - GOAL LINE 6 } Nose)	4 (- Bandit) 5	1 -
ADJUSTMENTS	- 2-POINT STANCE (Involved in Pass Coverage, End(s) must assume 2-Point Stance)	- DEPTH & SHADING Adjustments. - SHIFTING (to Final alignment during Quarterback's Cadence)	

*Variation popularized by the Chicago Bears Defense.

outside the core all but the most subtle changes in alignment become impossible to conceal from offensive scrutiny; for this reason, the range of possible adjustments is substantially greater *inside* the core. For the most part, the mechanisms summarized in table 13 involve *positional manipulations*, in several instances requiring personnel substitution as well; on the other hand, the adjustments outlined in table 13 involve *positional fine-tuning*, alignment variations to be implemented by individual defenders independent of the mechanism called.

First Level. To defense the run, particularly against offenses that operate power-oriented systems or have superior blocking linemen, the 4- and 5-alignments move the ends into tight, concentrating the First Level personnel in the center of the core (fig. 117, upper diagram). On the other hand, the 2- and 4-alignments may be planned to position the nose over one of the offensive guards (in even) reinforcing that side of the core (see middle diagrams, 2-rip example). Pre-snap shifting incorporates a mechanism for both effecting the alignment call and, in concert with Second Level movement, confusing an offense's blocking pattern. There are only two basic adjustments that various First Level personnel may implement: aligned loose, an end improves his *leverage* against sweeps, quarterback sprintout, etc., by splitting wider to outflank specific offensive formations; the nose or a tackle improves core stability by the eagle adjustment anytime the distance between (adjacent) First Level defenders approaches seven feet. These adjustments may be planned (fig. 117, 11-alignment), or implemented independently by these personnel according to the tactical situation (fig 117, bottom diagram).

Some of these pre-snap manipulations, geared primarily to reinforce run defense, also can augment the First Level's pass rush. For example, in the upper diagram (fig. 117) the "55" call will improve pass rush if various First Level defenders *dominate* the interior linemen on whom they align (not, however, the case in *this* example) because this alignment makes any double-team blocking difficult on passes. An end splitting wider in loose is actually moving further from the quarterbacks' pocket; thus, this planned adjustment, in order to complement pass rush at the same time, must take advantage of a less agile offensive tackle, or isolate that end on a smaller blocking-back. There are few absolute rules for determining the most advantageous combinations against a specific opponent, and in fact, from week to week through the season the mechanisms and adjustments planned should be varied:

1. unless the defense will physically dominate, the manipulations implemented against the last opponent will probably not prove as effective in the upcoming game (assuming the offense has done its homework);

2. in constantly employing the same approach, a defense becomes *highly predictable*, to its ultimate disadvantage in post-season play, when teams are most evenly matched.

Second Level. In planning strategy for the Second Level, by far the most important considerations are the placement of stacks and the physical capacities of the personnel in each stack. To strengthen the run defense of the core, in every example in

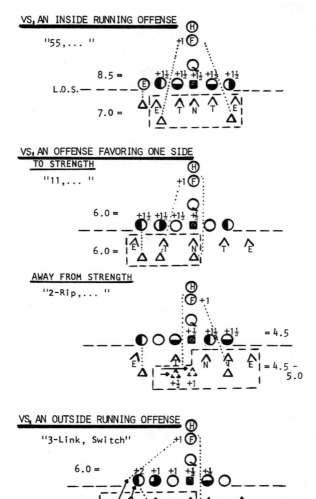

Figure 117 Examples of mechanisms and adjustments within the 2-level system to reinforce the structure of the core, according to the numerical ratings and run potential of the offense.

figure 117 note that the *number of defenders* in a threatened area is increased by locating additional stack(s) in those areas, that the *core structure* is reinforced by stacking at the most threatened gaps. To back up the First Level by this mechanism, obviously linebacker types are preferred in these various stacks; but in passing situations, although the mechanisms remain constant, speed, not size, becomes the primary prerequisite at these positions. Therefore, unless the interior of the Second Level (Bandit, Strong, and

Gael) can perform *both* functions, substitutions should be planned accordingly, with the power of the stacks providing a measure of security for the defense should an offense run in long-yardage situations. Of secondary importance in planning run defense is the depth adjustment for each defender in his stack: 2 1/2 to 5 yards off the line of scrimmage, and in area C the walkaway adjustment (fig. 117, lower diagram). Two interactions influence these individual stack adjustments-the tactical situation (usually in passing situations stack alignment is deepened) versus the degree to which a specific stack location exposes the Second Level defender (should the football be run directly at him, the defender must be positioned to fill immediately).

Personnel substitution is also the primary pre-snap mechanism to consider when planning pass defense (table 13, lower third). In addition to each defender's pass covering ability, the *number* of Second Level personnel may be altered, increased from the regular *five* defenders to *six* with the addition of rover, or reduced to *four* (by removal of Bandit). The addition of rover usually is planned as a situational substitution for goal line (see chapter 5), to defense the triple option (see chapter 9), in zone coverage to saturate underneath, as a special max-double coverage, and so on. On the other hand, removing Bandit from the Second Level should be reserved exclusively for high-percentage run situations since cover provides the only practical pass defense in conjunction with this complement of personnel. Since both the personnel substituted *and* intentions of the defense conveyed by specific substitution cannot be concealed from the offense, in the planning stages coaches are advised to concentrate more upon the actual pass coverages, particularly their concealment. With every coverage there are positional adjustments that Second Level personnel must implement pre-snap so as to gain the advantage post-snap: combinations of depth alignment hard through soft, in conjunction with shading (inside vs. outside). However, if individual adjustments become patterned or blatantly obvious, this permits both receivers and the quarterback to read the coverage. Pre-snap, therefore, both subtle concealment and shifting during the quarterback's cadence (from a preliminary into the required alignment) should be planned.

Deep Safety. Prior to the snap, only two considerations related to safety personnel need to be planned, but both are vital to the integrity of the defense (table 13, right-hand column)—the number of safeties on the field in given situations, and their depth adjustment. The number of safeties in the defense should be varied throughout a game, interchanging two-deep with the (usual) single safety, with depth adjustments (from deep- to free-safety) planned accordingly. The poorer a quarterback's range and throwing accuracy, the more this *latter* option can be planned, with wind, rain, and field conditions providing interacting factors to consider before actually implementing the free-safety adjustment. On the other hand, the more an offense relies upon passing and the potency of its attack, the more frequently substitutions and depth variations should be planned.[4] The only instance when safety personnel *must make* positional adjustments occurs inside the defense's thirty-yardline when an opponent continues to advance. Prior to the snap, personnel never retreat into their own end-zone area; therefore, when they are unable to align uniformly twenty-eight yards deep, specific adjustments become dependent upon the coverage called (table 12 and accompanying text).

ANALYSIS OF OFFENSE AFTER THE SNAP

The ultimate objective of defense is to have sufficient numbers of personnel in position *to make the play*: to swarm the ball carrier at the point of attack on runs, to pressure the quarterback on passes, and when a throw is on target to disrupt the catch. However, all three of these areas of defense cannot be *maximized* at the same time during the same play, because the resources of eleven defenders can be stretched only so far. Therefore, strategy and planning should essentially be viewed as the process of making tactical judgments: specific manipulations of the system for maximizing personnel effectiveness, without leaving one area of defense at risk. (And this latter point cannot be over emphasized-from the opposing perspective, offensive coaches plan when and where a specific adjustment places the defense in jeopardy—with insufficient personnel to make the play or those close at hand mismatched.) The analysis of offense has two major components. Pre-snap the *positional potential* of the defensive system is maximized through advantageous deployment of personnel, as discussed in the last section. By contrast, post-snap analysis must focus on the *internal operations* of the system:

> considering the offensive probabilities in any given situation, with each defender carrying through his *programmed* primary (I) $\rightarrow$ secondary (II) $\rightarrow$ pursuit responsibility sequence, will sufficient defenders be positioned *to make the play*?

These judgments by coaches lie at the heart of defensive strategy, and from week to week the only *new* element that should influence this process during the planning stages involves specific offensive keys. Small adjustments of the system based upon a *unique set of recognition* factors are acceptable, given sufficient practice time to perfect such nuances; however, major systems alterations are strongly discouraged, particularly on a weekly basis. In order to enable coaches to gauge which run defense and pass coverage mechanisms are best employed, in this section a *general* analysis of offense is presented: what the various running plays and pass patterns are trying to achieve; how each attempts to manipulate either the defensive system or the individual defender(s) operating within the system. Similar analyses of *specific* offensive systems are presented in chapter 9.

Analysis Of Run Offense

Each offensive running play exhibits distinctive characteristics because of the internal "machinery" required to operate that play. For purposes of analysis, these characteristics have been reduced[5] to four recognizable features:

- *Timing*, the immediacy or delay with which the ball carrier hits the line of scrimmage,
- *Location of the hole*, where the ball carrier attempts to penetrate,
- *Pattern of Blocking*, the structured movements of the *other* offensive personnel, particularly the linemen,

- and *Backfield-Action*, the least reliable feature as far as the defense is concerned.

The essential interrelationships between these characteristics are shown in table 14, grouped according to four descriptive classifications (left-hand column)-traditional speed versus power running plays, combinations of speed and power (the best example being triple options), as well as runs which *by design* hit very late ("delayed" plays).

Speed Running Plays. To gain the advantage by employing this type of running play, the ball carrier must hit the hole in the *shortest* elapsed time. This timing factor of speed plays dictates man-blocking and backfield-actions with minimal complexity. Tactically, these plays attempt to gain advantage by three means. First, speed plays operate best where one First Level defender is overmatched, and by man-blocking a momentary advantage is gained for the offense. Second, by the ball carrier moving quickly into this crack in the defense, positive yardage may be gained *before* the secondary mechanisms of defense converge. And third, by employing spread formations, the defense's pursuit capabilities can be fragmented to a much greater degree. On defense,

Table 14. Analysis of run offense: hole designation, speed of the back into the hole, and complimentary blocking patterns.

TIMING ....Back's Timing in Hitting-the-Hole At The Line-of-Scrimmage	HOLE DESIGNATION AND BLOCKING PATTERN		
	INSIDE*	OFF-TACKLE	OUTSIDE
SPEED: - Specific Hole Designated; - Back into Hole Immediately.	DIVES - AREA BLOCKING. - QUICK TRAPS.	(Seldom run - see Text)	PITCH - REACH & SLIP BLOCKING.
TRIPLE OPTION - Combination; - Hole not Designated.	DIVE OPTION - BOTH AREA AND DOUBLE-TEAM BLOCKING TO INSIDE OF HOLE	QUARTERBACK OPTION (No Blocking at Hole Required)	PITCH OPTION (Only Lead Blocker in open field)
POWER: - Hole Designated; - Back must wait for Blocker(s) in front to proceed through Hole.	- Almost exclusively from the I-Formation. TAILBACK DIVE - FULLBACK LEAD BLOCKING.	- Almost exclusively, from the I-Formation FULLBACK LEADING TAILBACK, from Pro /or Split-Backs, HALFBACK LEADING FULLBACK.	SWEEP - From Pro /or Split-Backs. - Linemen Lead Blocking.
DELAYED - General Area Designated, or - Back finds a Hole; - Play intentionally hits later than Power.	COUNTERS TAILBACK 'SEARCH' DRAWS & SPRINT DRAWS -FALSE KEY Blocking and FINESSE (ie. Blockers Turn on Defenders, not required to drive them off Line-of-Scrimmage; Shallow-Set initially, faking pass blocking; etc.)		REVERSES (Note: Delays occasionally hit wide, however Backs are coached to turn Upfield much sooner)

*Inside Plays hit between the offensive Tackles.

this type of run is quickly recognized due to the reduced complexity of both the plays themselves and the offensive keys. When planning defensive strategy, an opponent's quick-hitting plays should be *expected* at points along the line of scrimmage where a particular First Level defender is overmatched. Pre-snap, the 2-level system has two compensatory mechanisms that can be implemented:

1. plan alignment calls which position First Level teammates immediately beside this defender;[6]
2. plan Second Level stacks closer to or immediately behind this defender, thereby maximizing the defense's secondary response capability.

Post-snap, the mechanisms planned should emphasize *movement* in this area of the core, as opposed to the personnel in the area remaining static and only reacting. The First Level defender targeted would participate in more slanting and twists; not on every down, but stunts specifically designed to vary his directional charge in given situations, first to the inside, then outside. In addition, dog stunts might be planned to blitz through this area of the core as change-ups.

Power Running Plays As the name suggests, power running plays are designed to *outnumber* the defenders at the point of attack. Therefore, the moving of blockers through the hole ahead of the ball carrier lends these plays distinctive characteristics (table 14). Invariably, formational alignments feature (at least) one tight end and two running backs (or there would be insufficient personnel in the core—in both size and numbers—in the first place). Power running plays hit up to a second later than speed plays, requiring the hole to be held open longer; in turn, this has necessitated greater complexity and play variations. In the backfield, the amount of criss-cross action by the backs (fig. 80, 81) must be *carefully* analyzed. During the week of practice, to prepare, how much Cross Key (fig. 82) and I-Backs (fig. 83) drill will be required? To hold open the hole, blocking patterns have become particularly complex and numerous: for example, in figure 118 many (but not all) of the blocking patterns that have evolved for opening the off-tackle hole are analyzed. Power plays have proven particularly successful in running off-tackle; hitting further outside defensive pursuit has been elevated to such a technical art that wider sweeps are not sure gainers as in the past (9), and when offenses attempt to power through inside, the defenders already positioned usually prove too numerous to *guarantee* a high success ratio. For the defense, reading power running is more difficult; in planning, therefore, coaches should—and this is perhaps the best suggestion the authors will give throughout all of part IV: −*expect* off-tackle power, always prepare for an opponent's power runs (fig. 118) whether rated a threat or not, and plan to defense off-tackle power *without stunting* (coaches should specialize the pre-snap alignment, however, only employing stunting against power running *as a last resort*).[7] Pre-snap, the 2-level Defense has several mechanisms to reinforce run defense in the C Areas. The system's *basic* pre-snap mechanism involves stacking on the tight end, according to the outside running threat:

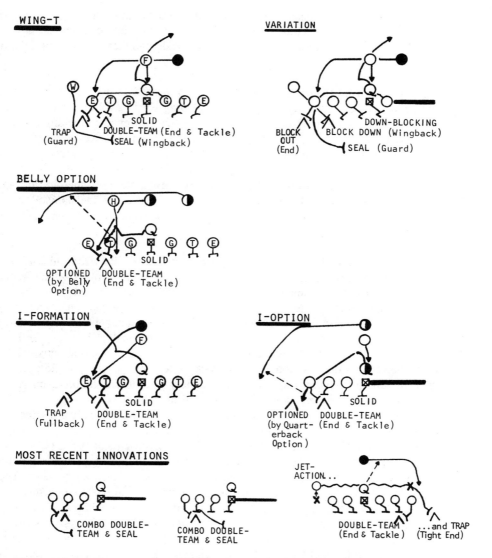

Figure 118 Double-team and trap blocking patterns that have evolved to open and *hold open* the off-tackle hole sufficiently to allow additional blockers and the ball carrier through (see complete systems in chapter 9).

1. the loose alignment of the First Level end is adjusted, outside eye-to-shoulder on the tight end for greater emphasis in contacting the tight end, or aligned further outside for greater emphasis on crashing, meeting particular power plays deeper in the backfield;

2. the mirroring Second Level defender is adjusted, walkaway (wider and deeper)

against speed backs, expecting them to bounce outside when finding the off-tackle area too congested, or head-up with the tight end against larger backs, expecting them to power through off-tackle and then *cut back* into the heart of the core.

Other pre-snap mechanisms include planning a 2-stack to be located adjacent to the tight end stack and, as judged necessary, planning First Level alignments which *completely* hide Second Level defenders from any direct offensive blocking threat (fig. 76 and accompanying text).   Post-snap, the secret to stopping specific variations of off-tackle power is repetitive group and team drill, and scrimmage *live*, replicating the upcoming opponent's plays *as precisely as possible*. In addition, the First Level's charge may be sacrificed, according to how vulnerable defensive personnel are to trap blocking.   As a last resort plan switch (primarily a run defense mechanism) or cushion (secondarily a run mechanism); *however, plan these Second Level stunts carefully* (see footnote 7).

Combination Running Plays: Speed And Power.   Between quick-hitting dives and the power sweep, there is a range of offensive running plays which feature both speed and power mechanisms, variable timing factors, but generally more basic blocking patterns than many complex power runs.   One such example is analyzed in this section, the triple option mechanism (10, 11); offensive systems which feature other combination plays (such as quick traps, isolations, etc.) are analyzed in chapter 9.   Options are unique in several ways (see table 14 for comparisons).   One distinctive characteristic of power running, the double-team block, is featured in many triple options; however, the complementary trap block immediately outside the double-team is *not a requirement*, permitting this power-dive mechanism to hit very fast (fig. 119).   The football also can move outside very quickly, and the option-pitch, unlike a sweep or quick pitch play, requires only one blocker (and in some models no one; fig. 119) in front of the pitchman, allowing this mechanism to hit with even greater speed (with few blockers to wait for).   From the defensive perspective, the majority of running plays combining speed and power are quickly recognized because of their uniqueness.   Therefore, since the defense knows immediately *how* it is being manipulated, coaches should appreciate that the major problem in defensing specific combinations lies principally in the restrictions forced upon the defense, the extent to which their system must be attenuated and/or bastardized in order to defense these plays.   For example, the fourth generation of option football is emerging (see chapter 9), but, since the development of the second-generation models (i.e., the Wishbone triple option), man-to-man principles have been *forced upon the defense* in both pass coverage (12) and its run defense (13) in order to strategically counter *all* of the option and companion plays in these series.   In turn, when the offense runs a play that is *not* in their combination series, these restrictions inhibit the response capability of the defense, and this has increasingly proven true as complementary passing attacks have gained sophistication.   Various mechanisms and adjustments within the present system to defense *specific* combination plays and series are examined individually in chapter 9.

MODEL OF VARIOUS SECOND- AND THIRD-GENERATION TRIPLE OPTIONS:

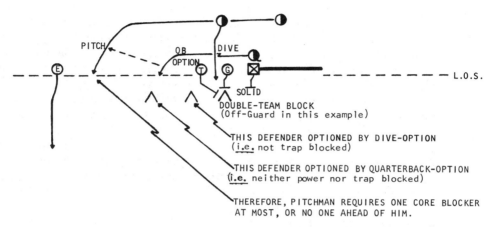

Figure 119 A model illustrating the speed and power components of the option mechanisms: at the present time, fourth-generation models are emerging (see chapter 9).

Delayed Running Plays. Several types of plays may be included in this fourth classification, runs which are purposefully *delayed* (table 14, lower portion): counters, reverses, draws and, in the eighties, the emergence of the tailback search. Although these plays seem dissimilar, they share several common characteristics. By design they hit *slower* than power. Often a hole is not designated only the general area, or in execution the opportunistic running back will see an opening elsewhere and be gone. Delays are highly complex, finesse-oriented plays in which the timing of the machinery, both in the backfield and on the offensive line, is critical. One distinctive characteristic of this classification is the false key: for example, counters and reverses feature *misdirection*, backs and line appearing to block in one direction while the football is actually moving against the other side of the defense; draws and tailback search feature *pass-action*, the line initially short-setting and appearing to pass block, while the quarterback, dropping back, is actually carrying the football to the running back before handing off. All delayed plays are designed to operate during the defense's transition to secondary (II) responsibilities, by taking advantage of core defenders who overreact or proceed too rapidly through their (I) and (II) responsibilities:

> a defender believing that he has executed his primary (I) responsibility proceeds rapidly to secondary (II) only to find this action premature, placing him out of position to make the play, or more often, allowing his offensive blocker to gain a positional advantage.

By the same token, delayed plays are always in imminent danger of losing yardage *without* this overreaction, because the football remains behind the line of scrimmage well after the snap: one offensive miscue, even one defender not reacting according to plan, brings these plays quickly to a halt. To defense delays, strategy should be coordinated at three levels. First, *in planning*, choices must be made by coaches as to which plays in the offense's multiple repertoire to concentrate on; once this limited selection is made, however, only small adjustments should be made to counter any particular delay unless it is rated as a consistent threat, and then only within the overall strategy being planned. Second, when the key to defensing this type of play lies in eliminating secondary (II) errors, then *in practice* repetitive drills and scrimmage must replicate each play as closely as possible, down to the individual details which tip the play. Finally, *at the systems level* delays are best handled by solidifying secondary (II) mechanisms: only when each defender gains absolute confidence that teammates will execute their (II) responsibility will every defender operate within the system of defense with rigid discipline. By contrast, when even one defender fails to complete the (II) responsibilities required of his position, discipline begins to erode: other defenders, almost unconsciously, make small adjustments in their responsibility hierarchy to compensate...it is then that specific delays may catch these defenders overreacting or out of position.

Analysis Of Pass Offense

As in all phases of its operation, the machinery of offense also dictates that certain components of the passing game mesh more compatibly than others (review table 11 and accompanying text): some patterns operate much more effectively when combined with a particular pass-action, and in turn, certain combinations of action with pattern favor specific reception areas as primary targets. Compared to run defense, however, pass coverage must cope with two confounding factors. By its very nature, passing allows more of these basic components to mesh together making pass defense *less predictable*. In addition to the pattern and the primary receiver's talent, by design most passes also incorporate secondary receiver(s), who must be open should the quarterback find his primary receiver covered. In their efforts to reduce the almost limitless possibilities of the passing game, both defensive (14, 15) and offensive (16, 17, 18) coaches are in general agreement on five attack strategies that the offense has at its disposal (Table 15, right-hand column). In most instances three of these—vertical stretching, horizontal stretching, and isolating—are utilized as the predominant operational modes; although the remaining two strategies may be applied less frequently, however, they can result in sizable gains through catching a defense off guard. In planning pass coverage, therefore, it is the *incorporation of specific components* that provides the basis for analyzing an opponent's underlying attack strategy and for determining which manipulation that pass offense is attempting. In this section, an analytical model is proposed to assist coaches in this process (see headings atop table 15). To begin with, three more general evaluations are suggested before applying the model, because each, independently, will influence the final strategy and coverages planned.

    Evaluate the quarterback: Both the starting and backup quarterbacks should be evaluated, particularly when their style and talents vary greatly. Often the backup proves more effective coming off the bench, because the defense is ill prepared. Evalu-

Table 15. Analysis of pass offense: model relating the pass-action, pass pattern, and (primary) reception area for analyzing an offense's attack strategy.

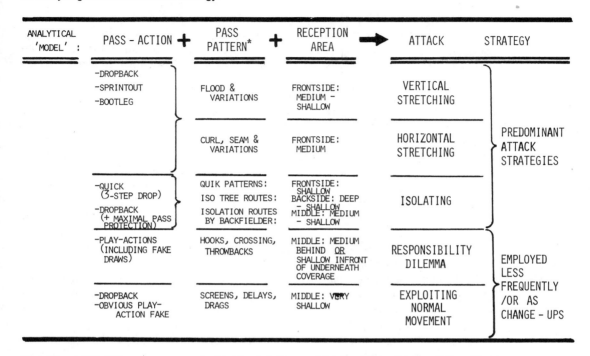

ANALYTICAL 'MODEL' :	PASS - ACTION ➕	PASS PATTERN* ➕	RECEPTION AREA ➡	ATTACK	STRATEGY
	−DROPBACK −SPRINTOUT −BOOTLEG	FLOOD & VARIATIONS	FRONTSIDE: MEDIUM − SHALLOW	VERTICAL STRETCHING	PREDOMINANT ATTACK STRATEGIES
		CURL, SEAM & VARIATIONS	FRONTSIDE: MEDIUM	HORIZONTAL STRETCHING	
	−QUICK (3-STEP DROP) −DROPBACK (+ MAXIMAL PASS PROTECTION)	QUIK PATTERNS: ISO TREE ROUTES: ISOLATION ROUTES BY BACKFIELDER:	FRONTSIDE: SHALLOW BACKSIDE: DEEP − SHALLOW MIDDLE: MEDIUM − SHALLOW	ISOLATING	
	−PLAY-ACTIONS (INCLUDING FAKE DRAWS)	HOOKS, CROSSING, THROWBACKS	MIDDLE: MEDIUM BEHIND OR SHALLOW INFRONT OF UNDERNEATH COVERAGE	RESPONSIBILITY DILEMMA	EMPLOYED LESS FREQUENTLY /OR AS CHANGE - UPS
	−DROPBACK −OBVIOUS PLAY- ACTION FAKE	SCREENS, DELAYS, DRAGS	MIDDLE: VERY SHALLOW	EXPLOITING NORMAL MOVEMENT	

*See Figure 103-106 and accompanying text for definition and details of these "Univeral" Pass Patterns.

ate each quarterback's throwing accuracy, range, hang-time (to adjust deep safety enforcement on longer passes), and arm strength, particularly on quick-outs. Evaluate quickness and speed: on dropbacks, each quarterback's setup time; on sprintouts, the run threat each presents and ability to throw on the run. Evaluate throwing action: when the support−hand comes off the football through the throwing action, when the jersey numbers become exposed (to the intended receiver), and the quickness of the release from that point; these factors can provide important visual key for pass defenders to break-on. Does a quarterback focus immediately on his primary receiver, or *look off* the defense? And on runs and play-actions is the quarterback adept at faking? If so, an *obvious* play-fake almost invariably signals screen. One of the important uses of scouting is to chart the frequency of the starting quarterback's throws downfield: to favorite receivers, reception areas, or even to one side (of the formation). In addition, the most frequent pass-actions should be established in order to adjust core alignments and rush pressure most advantageously. Establish how each quarterback reacts to pass rush and pressure: will he still step up into the pocket to throw or bail out early−does he have courage? Finally, can a quarterback improvise−find secondary receivers, scramble out of the pocket (quite distinct from bailing out early)? And the most intangible quality of all to defense: is the quarterback a leader, a winner? Evaluate this only in the fourth quarter, in very close games, and always according to his teammates' reactions (do they look to him?).

Evaluate the wide receivers: With its plethora of formations and maze of early motions, the offense can now isolate against any pass defender it wishes; therefore, rate each wide receiver as superior, average, or inferior. Essentially, this rating determines which receivers can be covered effectively in one-on-one matchups, in turn, reducing the number of substitutional and coverage mechanisms that must be planned. Receiver speed should exert the greater influence on the rating, assuming that all receivers move and catch adequately; catching ability and pattern movement are secondary factors to consider in this regard. Interacting factors also must be evaluated: the likely matchups throughout the game (receiver vs. a specific defender), an offense's favorite patterns. On the other hand, statistical breakdowns of scouting reports often indicate that it is not so much one specific receiver (when all are rated equally) but rather *their positioning* in the formation that is significant: by location, a receiver is aligned closer to a favored reception area, or in position to run a particular route. And, finally, receiver ratings must also be influenced by intangibles, particularly game experience and the ability to make the *clutch* catch.

Evaluate the core receivers: Besides their running threat, tight ends and backfielders also represent a substantial pass threat; therefore in game planning two additional factors should be evaluated. First, the extent of their participation in the passing game: slower tight ends used primarily as blockers allow their Second Level mirror considerably more lattitude for walkaway adjustments. A backfielder employed primarily for blocking purposes permits the defense to plan more overloading (i.e., 2- and 4-alignments + dog). Some systems invariably block the fullback *to the front side* (to ensure the quarterback's protection), and this key can *greatly* facilitate defensive planning. Other offenses now substitute (almost) their entire receiving corps, which can simplify planning, run vs. pass defense, in specific situations. Second, combined with these receivers' speed and abilities, their release into the pass patterns directly influences where Second Level stacks must locate. Backfielders may release either by moving through the interior of the offensive line or by releasing immediately to the outsides; to counter various possibilities, the 1-stack *centrally* locates a Second Level defender, but against the run the 1-stack generally provides *less* of a positional advantage. On the other hand, a 2-stack places a Second Level defender at a disadvantage in max if his mirror releases out the far side of the formation. And this tactical juggling can be confounded by the amount of crossing-action a particular backfield will utilize. With the First Level end aligned loose (and crashing), a tight end's release must be sharply to the inside or, quickly stepping around this defender, wider to the outside. Therefore, first analyze if either release tips the play for the mirroring Second Level defender to read: often inside release signals off-tackle or sweep, outside release tips pass. In addition, a crucial evaluation involves the offense's tendency to throw crossing routes (fig. 105): when a tight end releases inside and has the speed to outrun his Second Level mirror, in max this *absolutely controls* the width and depth to which this defender can walkaway.

Vertical Stretching. Referred to as the hi-lo strategy (see table 15), this offensive manipulation is designed primarily to attack a specific area of zone coverage underneath; against max coverage hi-lo breaks down into one-on-one, can receivers beat their defenders. At least two receivers are required in the pattern to accomplish vertical stretching, and in figure 120 its operating principles against zone coverage are illustrated: flooding the frontside flat, one receiver runs his route behind the flat defender, the other moving in front. Therefore, the defender must make a choice, and his zone rules dictate that he must defend against the deeper of the two receivers and *react up* if the pass is thrown in front. Analyzing this attack strategy, vertical stretching is independent of the quarterback's action as long as it incorporates more than 2 seconds for receivers to run their routes; on the other hand, it is best identified when the *pattern* receivers on one side of the formation move to set depths downfield, medium and shallow usually, then slide parallel to the line of scrimmage and to each other.

In planning max coverage, increased pressure against the quarterback provides a tactical element that can tip the balance in the defense's favor: these are 2 1/2-second patterns, therefore the pass rush has a viable chance to pressure or even reach the quarterback. As well, vertical stretching threatens the deep safety minimally, as receivers run out or inside routes primarily, therefore, one personnel on top is sufficient. (Occasionally safety personnel may even be removed if the threat of mismatching vs. the Second Level is also minimal in favor of an extra pass rusher.) Finally, in max with the minimal threat deep, Second Level defenders in turn can play their coverage very aggressively. On the other hand, planning zone coverage increased saturation underneath is *not* the best mechanism to combat this attack strategy: two-on-one and three-on-two advantages may still be created, and saturating, in turn, diminishes the pass rush. Much better is to plan three strata of zone coverage in the threatened area, that is, to the side of the formation with two or more immediate receivers. This may be accomplished by planning the -A or -B mechanism in conjunction with cover/two-deep (fig. 120, lower diagram): This defensive response also maintains a degree of rush pressure, four First Level defenders by the appropriate 4- and 5- alignment calls.

Horizontal Stretching. This pass strategy as well is designed primarily to attack zone coverage, specifically the areas *between* adjacent defenders. Horizontal stretching usually attacks underneath (table 15). However a single deep safety is also vulnerable to this attack in max; only his initial depth, combined with an effective pass rush, provides the measure of safety once the wide No. 1A receivers running deep fade routes along both sidelines get behind Lou or Rose (which is not all that difficult when aggressive directional technique is employed). Several pattern combinations are possible in employing this attack mode. The most common, variations of curl and seam, are diagrammed in fig. 121 to illustrate its working principles: two and three receivers move downfield, into the medium-depth areas, equidistant between defenders underneath; at that point they may slide either inside or to the outside. And horizontal stretching is usually independent of the pass-action as long as its timing (>2 sec.) permits receivers to move downfield.

EXAMPLES OF VERTICAL STRETCHING: FLOOD VARIATIONS

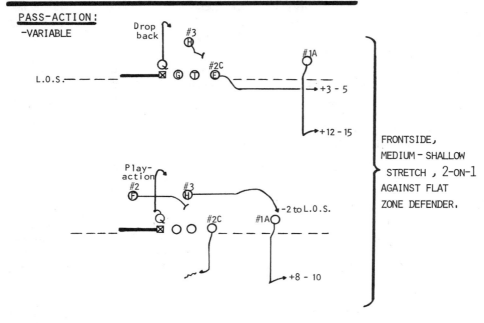

FRONTSIDE, MEDIUM-SHALLOW STRETCH, 2-ON-1 AGAINST FLAT ZONE DEFENDER.

FOR ZONE COVERAGES: PLAN THREE STRATA OF DEFENSE

"..., COVER-B/TWO-DEEP"

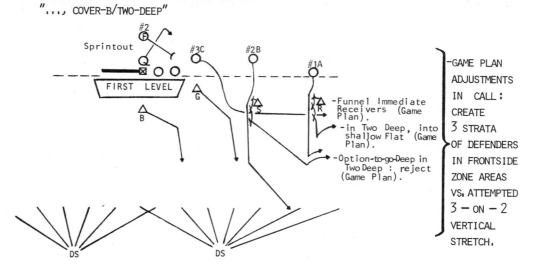

-GAME PLAN ADJUSTMENTS IN CALL: CREATE 3 STRATA OF DEFENDERS IN FRONTSIDE ZONE AREAS VS. ATTEMPTED 3 — ON — 2 VERTICAL STRETCH.

Figure 120 Pass attack strategy: vertical stretching.

EXAMPLES   OF HORIZONTAL STRETCHING: CURL ,   SEAM   & VARIATIONS

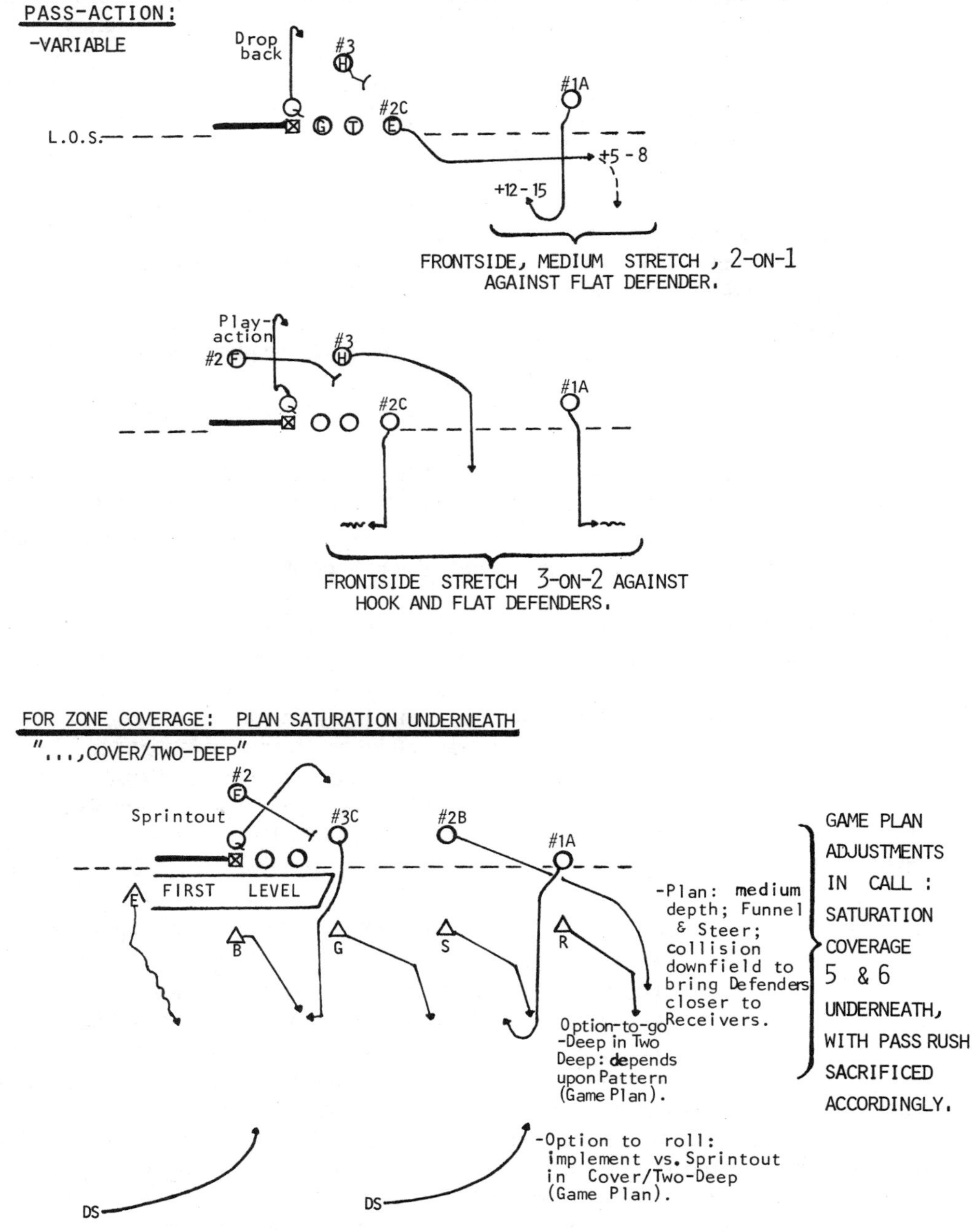

PASS-ACTION:

-VARIABLE

Drop back

#3

#2C

L.O.S.

#1A

+5 - 8

+12 - 15

FRONTSIDE, MEDIUM STRETCH , 2-ON-1
AGAINST FLAT DEFENDER.

Play-action

#2

#3

#2C

#1A

FRONTSIDE   STRETCH 3-ON-2 AGAINST
HOOK AND FLAT DEFENDERS.

FOR ZONE COVERAGE: PLAN SATURATION UNDERNEATH

"..., COVER/TWO-DEEP"

Sprintout

#2

#3C

#2B

#1A

FIRST   LEVEL

E

B

G

S

R

-Plan: medium
depth; Funnel
& Steer;
collision
downfield to
bring Defenders
closer to
Receivers.

Option-to-go
-Deep in Two
Deep: depends
upon Pattern
(Game Plan).

-Option to roll:
implement vs. Sprintout
in Cover/Two-Deep
(Game Plan).

DS

DS

GAME PLAN
ADJUSTMENTS
IN CALL :
SATURATION
COVERAGE
5 & 6
UNDERNEATH,
WITH PASS RUSH
SACRIFICED
ACCORDINGLY.

Figure 121 Pass attack strategy: horizontal stretching.

With some patterns this pass strategy becomes immediately recognizable, and therefore, both max and covers may be planned: for example, curl is unmistakable and pass defenders quickly predict the final leg of each route (fig. 121, upper diagram). On the other hand, seam may not provide a reliable read soon enough (middle diagram); in this instance, against horizontal stretching, saturating the underneath coverage provides the best pass defense to decrease the distance between the defenders underneath, specifically "cover" in conjunction with "two-deep" (fig. 121, lower diagram).

Isolating. The threat of an offense's isolating mechanisms, in combination with its vertical and horizontal attacks, forces the defense to make coverage choices on every play: zoning the entire field (with its inherent disadvantages), combination coverage according to formation (usually forcing at least one pass defender to cover man-on-man), or blitzing the quarterback. Therefore, in analyzing this attacking strategy the various isolations that an offense executes provide the key to defensive planning (table 15):

- quick passing, featuring its distinctive pass-action and shallow routes (fig. 103);
- mismatching, isolating a speed receiver against a slower linebacker in a sparsely filled zone area underneath or in man-to-man assignment;
- mismatching, isolating a superior wide receiver against an overmatched deepback with minimal zone or double-coverage assistance available.

Planning strategy against these various isolating mechanisms, the choice that is *not* recommended is zoning the entire field (i.e., cover and its variations); this wastes personnel when only one area of the pass defense may require reinforcing. On the other hand, the coverages incorporated into a game plan, specific zone combinations (choices: -A, -B, and -C) and double-coverages (choices: max-double, tight cushion, a special inserting rover), must be integrated within the overall pass defense strategy. That is, seldom should an offense's iso attack be defended by coverage mechanisms that fragment the comprehensive strategy planned. It is much better to plan specific adjustments within each coverage:

- disrupt specific iso routes by aggressive jamming, then funneling and steering of receivers;
- within the selected combinations and double-coverages, plan for defenders to *overplay* their receiver, according to the iso routes expected.

Responsibility Dilemma. Employed in conjunction with these three pass strategies, specific backfield-actions can provide the offense with a supplementary attack mode (table 15). Operating best against zone coverage, play-action is designed to delay the underneath defenders momentarily moving to their zone. By diving a back into the line, ball-faking and aggressive blocking, a responsibility dilemma is created for these defenders: whether to drop normally to their underneath assignment or, respecting the possible run, delay? Analyzing play-action, in the game plan include any which potentially could expose a hook or flat zone area. Within the pass coverages planned, however, only small adjustments should be implemented in any coverage to defense specific threats. On the other hand, at the systems level there is one set of circumstances which may be exploited, but the coverages must be planned with care:

- since play-actions require 2 $\frac{1}{2}$ second patterns, pass rush has a viable chance to pressure the quarterback....
- and pressure is implemented best in conjunction with max, implemented *automatically* with Second Level stunts....
- in turn, for core personnel max eliminates any responsibility dilemma created by play-action (with the elimination of zone assignments).

To the defense's disadvantage, however, often play-action involves criss crossing by the backs, and in max specific crossing-actions can place the pass defenders at a disadvantage (see fig. 95 and accompanying text). During planning, one key to defensing play-action is determining the offense's tendencies from scouting reports; during practice, the key to recognizing play-action is replicating these passes (and runs off the identical actions) as closely as possible, down to the individual details which tip each play.

Exploiting Normal Movement. Employed less frequently but nonetheless a threat, screen and short delay patterns to backs and ends are designed to take advantage of the defense's *normal* movement on passes (table 15). Against zones, before the pass is thrown the underneath coverage is given time to drop well off the line of scrimmage; in max, it is the defenders who drift back (after reading their mirror's initial blocking-action) being exploited. By this point in the play as well, pass rushers have advanced well into the offensive core area. The hallmark of this type of play features straight dropback with very obvious (mechanically poor) play-action faking by the quarterback to heighten these *normal* defensive responses. Therefore, an open area along the line of scrimmage is created where the offense attempts to dump the football off to the receiver; these are high-percentage pass completions with a likelihood of gaining positive yardage, particularly in the case of screens with blockers leading the receiver downfield.

In defensive planning, these ultrashort passes often appear as major threats; when they are placed in proper perspective, however, the defense's jeopardy is minimal *unless* the defense is *caught unaware*. The offensive risk increases with these plays, particularly the chances of netting minimal or negative yardage. Not only are these plays used sparingly, therefore, but they are often used very predictably by an offense: for example, on third-and-long, deep in its own end, screening only into the near sideline, and so on. Since screens and short passes are thrown in front of the coverage, each defender must execute his responsibilities according to a disciplined sequence. In zone, they must keep the receiver *in front of and inside* the coverage, by defender(s) on the outside containing the receiver while underneath defenders and the pursuit (from the inside) *complete the triangle*, trapping the receiver. In max, tight coverage combined with increased pressure can be planned: the pass rush forcing the offense to declare its intentions earlier, with each pass defender *clamping tight* onto his assigned receiver, tackling immediately (if the reception is made), or even knocking down the pass.

DYNAMICS OF IN-GAME ANALYSIS

In addition to game preparation and plan formulation, the ability to analyze and adjust tactically *during the game* is another requisite coaching skill. And while the general approach is identical to analytical procedures detailed to this point (and in chapter 9 following), the process itself is substantially altered by the situational constraints of the game. In the planning stages *time* is available for decision-making—even for debate; by comparison, the breakneck pace of the game imposes time constraints, and arbitrary decisions must be made on the spot, often without preliminaries. Superimposed upon this process is the prevailing *emotional climate*; when decisions become most imperative on the field, a crisis situation is usually fast approaching. This section explores the process of in-game analysis both on the sidelines and over halftime, the latter providing a short respite from these pressures; also, at the end of the chapter some suggestions are proffered regarding specific post-game evaluations. Presented in chronological sequence, the schematic illustrated in figure 115 (see introduction, part IV) is the model followed in examining this on-going adjustment process.

Alternate Planning

In the *final* analysis it is the offense that dictates the action during the game; therefore, on defense, alternate scenarios must be anticipated so as to avoid rash decisions or miscalculation in the heat of battle. In-game situations constantly arise that require an immediate defensive response, and it is therefore the authors' firm conviction that, on defense particularly, a coaching staff *must prepare for change*. Coaches must appreciate that the game plan, per se, is a *preliminary* document very necessary to the conduct of practice, to focusing players' mental awareness, and as a point of departure at game time—but it is not etched in stone. The defensive plan always influences the outcome of a game, but *never* with twenty-twenty foresight, especially when two teams are evenly matched. Given that the essence of football is dynamic, it follows that coaches must prepare for the game itself, over and above game planning. Each week, by Thursday's practice the defensive plan must be well advanced. From the tactical perspective, there is little a defensive staff *should do* at that point to interfere with preparations already in progress: a sound, well-integrated plan thoroughly practiced and rehearsed is far superior to afterthoughts introduced late in the week. Following Thursday's scrimmage, with all but final adjustments set, what should coaches be discussing informally, or thinking about, particularly when trying to sleep on the nights before a game? Some staffs suppose that further analysis at this time is counterproductive: construed as second-guessing, with its negative connotation. Accepting the change hypothesis, the authors would suggest this to be the coach's *most productive* time, when his mental faculties have an intense, singular focus—the opponent. And this thought process should be viewed as highly positive: mental images flash possible scenarios followed by instant evaluations and then storage in short-term memory (or rejection outright). Using the game plan as a starting point, although the details seldom need to be formalized, short notes to oneself and discussion amongst staff members tend to crystalize the essential alternatives that may confront the defense. During the game, when the opposition acts—as they *must* when things go badly for them on the field—this informal planning pays substantial dividend.

Sideline Adjustment

The average football play lasts five to ten seconds; between plays approximately thirty seconds is available, independent of official time-outs. To coach effectively on the sidelines, procedures must be formalized in order to complete play analysis, communicate this information, and then implement any adjustment within these time constraints. Random behavior or emotional outbursts on the sideline only disrupt the regimen necessary to expedite this process; coaches must stay calm and make decisions as quickly as possible. Accurately evaluating what happens on the field is the first stage of the adjustment process. Each member of the staff is assigned the responsibility of analyzing specific areas of the defense: systems analysis (usually) is the responsibility of the defensive coordinator and one or two experienced coaches in whom he has confidence, with technical corrections handled by each unit coach. This involves a highly coordinated effort; therefore, to facilitate this process the following three stages (19) are recommended: protocols instituted for recording the progress of play; procedures established for information communication; then opportunities defined when adjustment may be implemented.

Recording The Progress Of Play. With pencil and clipboard, on an appropriate chart each defensive call is recorded along with the tactical situation at the time, the offensive play run and its success or failure. Knowledgeable persons, such as a manager or a backup player, should be employed for this clerical purpose, never coaches. At the end of each defensive series, during halftime or at any point in the game, these accumulated data can be used to determine the offense's plan of attack and to pinpoint where the defensive weaknesses under attack might be.

Information Communication. Many football games have been lost because of a failure of communication at a crucial point. Therefore, two separate lines should be formalized: between members of the coaching staff, and with player personnel. Immediately following every play and defensive series it is recommended that the former takes precedence over the latter, with communication facilitated by phone lines (i.e., to the press box), and by coaches being uninterrupted until each hasty conference has concluded. On the other hand, player-coach communication is facilitated by a *structured* bench organization: the defensive personnel are assigned to specific bench areas, with players sitting with *their backs to the field* during these interactions (they are not spectators and, if needed suddenly, will be called). As in all sideline communication these are formalized and two-way with players imparting to their coach as much detail and information as possible about their "defensive world" on the field.

Adjustment Opportunity. During the game only four opportunities may be categorized as appropriate times to make adjustments, and the *amount* of information exchanged is restricted by their time frames, which vary greatly. Therefore, it is again recommended that each opportunity be formalized with limits clearly defined for each exchange.

1. Following offensive plays. With two communication links to be completed within thirty seconds (or less), this exchange must be oriented towards the *next* call and limited to systems discussion. The most *imperative* link, between the coordinator and the defensive signal-caller (on the field), cannot be maintained through direct verbal means; therefore, hand signals and/or messenger service (via personnel substitution with the call) are the usual means employed. This link, in itself, seldom breaks down; invariably, miscommunication results from a breakdown in the staff interchanges preceding it. Coaches vacillate in their decision-making, engage in non-systems discussion, even desert their phone linkup with the game in progress.

2. During official time-outs. This opportunity is very similar to the above, being essentially for signals communication and systems discussion; however, a period of one minute is guaranteed. The format also is identical, coaches' communication preceding instruction of signals. Unfortunately, the time factor itself can be a cause of communications breakdown. Inexplicably, other coaches and non-coaching personnel often become involved in these one-minute conferences, monopolizing valuable time: remember, *many* opinions are not needed—only the *correct* one(s)!

3. Following every defensive series. Most importantly, these opportunities afford a substantially longer time period (until the defense must return to the field). Therefore, the coaches' communications can include related analysis as warranted (matters technical, mental, statistical, etc.). On the other hand, with the time period so variable, discussions must be prioritized, particularly during the unit conferences with player personnel that follow: the most urgent issues must always be addressed first. These bench periods also afford an opportunity to implement *minor* changes in the game plan when necessary.

Half Time Adjustment

This fourth opportunity guarantees the only time frame long enough to implement *major* change(s) that require lengthy explanation. Therefore, a team's half time ritual must ensure maximum usage of this period. By isolating themselves initially, coaches can review the statistical summaries of the first half to determine the offense's successful plays and players, and to assess the offensive strategy; a growing number of teams also view specially prepared video highlights of the first half to assist this evaluative process. Whatever the format, discussion must never get bogged down or deal with irrelevancies: overview, then assessment of the first half is the order of business. Next, speculations and forecasts regarding the upcoming half are proffered, with (basically) two options considered—the offense continuing its present plan of attack (always more likely), or redirecting its attack against other area(s) of the defense. In concluding this short meeting, succinct objectives and the necessary adjustments for the second half are finalized: no changes in the game plan, or as few as possible is always the best decision (but is not always possible). On the other hand, if major changes *must* be implemented, it is critical how these are introduced over the half time.

In meeting with players, three general formats are possible: coordinator talking to the entire defense, coaches meeting individually with their unit personnel, or some combination of the above, a brief overview by the coordinator preceding smaller group meetings. Which format is selected depends upon the adjustments being implemented, as well as the physical setting (often visitor dressing areas are cramped, lacking even a blackboard). Whatever venue is selected for these player-coach meetings, it is recommended that the information covered be summarized under three main headings:

1. First, always, an overview highlighting the first half, then an assessment; in close games coaches should dwell on the positive aspects of the defense's play, critique only the major errors, and correct but not harp on smaller mistakes.

2. This summary should conclude *logically* with the defensive adjustments for the second half; however, any departures from the game plan should be introduced by referring back to a previous plan. For example, the coach might begin:

   > "We're going to reactivate the strategy we used to stop State U. two weeks ago..."

   > "We're going to incorporate that State U. mechanism into the huddle calls in the second half. It worked perfectly two weeks ago..."

   Coaches should always introduce changes in the middle of a game via *prior association*: what is familiar, what proved successful in the past, what the defense knows and feels comfortable with.

3. Conclude by focusing (or refocusing) mental awareness: highlight the defensive objectives for the second half (or reiterate the original game objectives). And always, stress aggressiveness, emphasize tackling and turn-overs—make something happen!

Post-Game Analyses

With the game concluded, hindsight rumination or a postmortem cannot change a performance or the final outcome for the better; a team can only learn from the greatest teacher of all, experience. Therefore, all post-game analyses should serve as teaching aids for improvement of performance, but the time available must dictate the extent of these evaluations. Following are the obvious and not-so-obvious analyses that should be conducted before the game preparations (for the next opponent) progress too far.

Game-Film Analysis. For viewing *in private* on the morning after (to give coaches an evening's respite from the pressure), separate videos of the defense, offense, and specialty teams are prepared from the game; with more staff members, additional cassettes should be made available (given the expense of film, this may not be as practical). While each staff develops its own procedures, a general format is recommended which includes:

- the head coach and coordinators previewing each unit's video, to overview and prepare summary critiques;
- each coordinator and assistants viewing their unit video, making more detailed notations;
- finally, each assistant on his own evaluating and grading[8] personnel.

This format frees the head coach and coordinators to begin planning for the next opponent with a current knowledge of the operational status of their units, while detailed analysis of the game film is completed by the other coaches, assistants who will meet with players during the week to make individual corrections during practice. By this format as well, the repeated viewing of the game film allows coaches the chance to dissipate pent-up emotions carried over from the game. To their critical eyes game film is *never* error-free, yet coaches come in many varieties of temperament. Therefore, *in private*, early on a Saturday or Sunday morning with lots of coffee...nonproductive and even negative behavior which players should seldom witness may be vented, enabling the staff to proceed positively with the crucial preparations at hand. It is shortsighted in any case not to build into this process a period for cascading their emotions, when a staff of five to ten proud men have placed their hearts, souls, and egos, to say nothing of their livelihoods on-the-line.

Analyzing film, the individual performances, personnel matchups (particularly mismatches), and the operation of the system are examined, with game statistics (see sections following) employed as the *objective criteria* by which successful execution is gauged. For example, if the offense accumulated close to 500 yards over the course of the game, something went wrong defensively, and *first* the cause(s) must be determined.

1. Analysis of Individual Performance. Begin with fundamentals, technique, positioning, movement on the field, and transition from (I) $\rightarrow$ (II) responsibility, evaluating by position whether or not a defender did his job. Next, personnel matchups are scrutinized according to the three areas of defense: in run defense and their pass rush, were First Level personnel able to hold their own, or did inferior technique or physical size result in mismatches? In pass defense,

individual performance is best evaluated in max coverage, one-on-one: again, were fundamentals at fault, or were Second Level personnel lacking speed, size, or some other physical attribute? Finally, when giving feedback, coaches should remember that it is equally important to reinforce error-free execution as it is to critique technical faults.

2. Analysis of the System. The essential *advantage* conferred by any football system is its positioning and movement of personnel; therefore, when technical error or physical mismatch is not the cause of breakdowns, the application of the system—the game strategy and the tactics employed—*must* be at fault, and these coaching errors are especially difficult to ferret out. With the 2-level defensive system, however, there are a number of sensitive indicators.

In run defense :

- Were the defenders with primary (I) responsibility for the running areas out of position too often; did personnel assigned (II) responsibility make too many of the tackles?
- Were ball carriers trapped, hemmed in by well-positioned defenders chocking off the running lanes, or did shoestring tackles have to be made at the last moment?

In pass rush :

- Were pass rushers positioned to fill each alley, or could the quarterback run out of his pocket through gaping holes (between First Level rushers)?
- Was the quarterback throwing off his *back* foot because the center of his pocket collapsed?

In pass defense :

- A key indicator is whether the quarterback was able to throw on a *flat* trajectory, or did most passes have to be arc'd over well-positioned defenders?
- Was the offensive strategy to run specific Defender(s) deep downfield on (almost) every play? If substitutions were not planned (accordingly), were these defender(s) fatigued late in the game (see evaluation of fourth quarter statistics, last section)?

3. Finally, from the film analysis, as a major cause of error it can be determined whether defenders were reading their offensive keys *incorrectly*.

Statistical Analysis. Game statistics provide the *objective* criteria by which performance is gauged, beginning with the most important of all, the final score. And while this may be the only statistic that counts, several others prove important bellwethers: if a team is winning its games yet losing statistically, before long the scores will also reflect these warning signs. In this final section various statistical categories are analyzed from the defensive standpoint.

TOTAL OFFENSIVE YARDAGE: Many games are won even though the opposition dominates this statistical category. (There can be several reasons for this—yards gained long after the final outcome was decided, protracted offensive drives that fizzled out before the goal line, and so forth.) By implication, therefore, total yardage in itself need not be considered crucial; however its two components, the running and passing totals, provide important insights. Foremost: did the defensive game plan achieve its goals, and if not, why not? For example, if the plan was to shut down a strong running attack, or prevent middle-depth passing, or whatever, these sub-totals provide a very objective measure of success.

PLAY FREQUENCY AND SUCCESS. By the same token, *where* the offense experienced success running and passing can provide important feedback for the defense. Often game plans are designed to stop a specific running back or receiver. Charting the play frequency and the yardage gained by these personnel quickly evaluates the defensive performance; then, according to this (objective) valuation, reason(s) for success or failure can be probed.

ANALYSIS BY DOWNS. Third downs provide the pivotal point during each four-down series: over the course of a game the defense must prevent a first down from being achieved *at least* 50 percent of the time on third downs (i.e., only three plays then punt permitted). Conversely, the crucial analysis in first-and-ten situations involves the yardage given up: allowing more than four yards (average) on first down makes it very difficult for the defense tactically because a series of third-and-short yardage situations minimize the offensive jeopardy, in fact, often manipulates the defense to the greater degree.

TIME OF POSSESSION. This statistic provides a general indicator of the *appropriateness* of the defensive tactics. As the time of possession by an offense mounts, it becomes clear that the opposing defense is permitting series of first downs to be made, and this has direct implications regarding the defensive strategy: not aggressive enough in certain situations, perhaps overly aggressive in others. Whatever the reasons, when figures for the time of possession swing decidedly in the opponent's favor, careful analysis is warranted.

TURNOVERS. In analyzing interceptions and fumble recoveries by the defense, two factors are of significance: foremost is the number of turnovers *relative to* the interceptions and fumbles given up by one's own offense; of lesser importance, is the *net* yardage exchanged. Turnovers deny an offense the use of its most consistent gainer, the punt. When the opponent is denied the chance to punt, this translates into an immediate gain by the defending team of thirty to fifty yards, even without considering field position or advancement of the football after the turnover. Therefore, as a rule of thumb, the defense must create at least an *equal number* of turnovers as its offense gives up on the theory that this tends to equalize the yardage swings over the course of a game. On the other hand, when and where a crucial turnover occurs can influence the outcome of the game itself, and this criteria obviously overrides this more general rule of analysis.

Strategy Analysis. On the crucial issues of strategy and decision-making, how should a staff critique *itself?* If subjective criteria are continually invoked for this purpose, coaches are in danger of reinforcing their own bias, *particularly after a win*—merely patting themselves on the back but never really analyzing the larger implications of specific game decisions, both the successful adjustments and those blown.[9] On the other hand, objective conclusions need to be tempered by consideration of the extraneous factors that influence the outcome of all football games: field conditions, the injury situation, facing your league's best (or worst) team, the vagaries of luck, and so on. The five analyses following introduce a degree of objectivity into the evaluation of coaching performance; four consider the opponent's offensive stats by quarters (of the game), while the fifth analysis examines the course of the game itself.

TO EVALUATE THE GAME PLAN: FIRST-QUARTER STATISTICS. Compared with the defense's first-quarter performances in previous games, the offense's statistics over the early going in a game provide an empirical basis for evaluating the game plan strategy. While there are no ultimate criteria, in general when a defense experiences either an exceptional or a poor opening quarter a prime consideration should be the plan itself.

TO EVALUATE IN-GAME ADJUSTMENT: SECOND-QUARTER STATISTICS. Comparing the offense's second versus their first quarter statistics, valid conclusions regarding the defense's in-game adjustment may be drawn from either of the following:

1. the defense's game plan was *at fault* in the first place; however, the statistical picture was much improved through the end of the first quarter to halftime in favor of the defense;

2. when the game plan, based upon first-quarter stats, was judged *satisfactory*, and successive offensive adjustments were countered by an ongoing readjustment on defense.

In both instances, tactical competence in-game may be judged (unless the turn of events was unduly aided by extraneous factors).

TO EVALUATE THE HALFTIME PROCESS: THIRD-QUARTER STATISTICS. Elements of both strategy planning and in-game adjustment are inherent in the process and procedures of halftime; therefore, a staff may objectively evaluate its performance *over halftime* according to results of the third quarter and any changes therein (by statistical comparisons with the first half).

TO EVALUATE PHYSICAL CONDITIONING: FOURTH-QUARTER STATISTICS. Very simply, if the starting defense has out performed an offense *for three quarters*, any sudden decline in their statistical dominance in the fourth quarter (independent of score and final outcome) can indicate a lack of *physical* conditioning. One caution, however; this conclusion should never be based upon a single game's performance, but when this statistical trend becomes evident over several games coaches need look no further than the physical preparedness of their personnel.

TO EVALUATE DECISION-MAKING: FIRST-AND-TEN ANALYSIS. Based upon the current statistics for a league or conference, the expectancy of points (20, 21) can be calculated according to where an offense takes possession of the football first-and-ten on the field (Table 16). Since all teams operate under identical playing conditions, rules, and officiating, the league's scoring expectancy allows coaching staffs to analyze their decision-making more objectively[10]: according to field position (where the opponent took possession throughout the game), a defensive staff can determine if the *average* points scored were less or more than expected. Then, applying this criterion in grading their decision-making during each defensive series, the staff can backtrack to determine cause and effect: when scoring was *less* than expected analyzing tactically correct calls and the strategy behind each; when scoring was *more* than expected their tactical errors or any breakdowns in their decision-making process.

Table 16. The computed point value of field position.*

FIELD POSITION		SCORING EXPECTANCY
TAKING POSSESSION OF THE FOOTBALL, 1ST - AND - 10 BETWEEN THESE YARDLINES....		.........THE POINT VALUE EXPECTED** (ACCORDING TO INITIAL FIELD POSITION):
OFFENSE'S GOAL LINE	0	+ 0.9 POINTS
	10	+ 0.2 ··
	20	− 0.3 ··
	30	− 1.1 ··
	40	− 1.6 ··
CENTERFIELD	50	− 2.4 ··
	40	− 3.2 ··
	30	− 3.7 ··
	20	− 4.3 ··
	10	− 5.8 ··
DEFENSE'S GOAL LINE	0	

* Adapted from reference 20 (with permission), this statistical analysis is based upon 46 games, including 6,738 plays, during the Canadian (Professional) Football League's 1978 season.

** For example: Team A's offense takes possession of the football at Team B's 35-yardline; therefore, it would be expected that Team B's defense would give up 3.2 points (the *average* point value given up in the CFL in 1978 starting from this field position).
On the other hand, Team B's defense would only be expected to give up (*on average*) 1.1 points if, every time, Team A takes possession between its own 30-40 yardlines.

Notes

1. Performance of offensive (and defensive) units continually goes in cycles; an individual cycle can accelerate suddenly, or evolve gradually over an entire season. While the latest scouting report provides tactical information, it gives little hint of the opponent's cyclical status.

2. Various mechanisms are available to the offense for negating the effects of even the most superior of defenders: for example, in employing option football an offense need not even block certain defenders.

3. The classic dilemma in this regard involves pass defense. Maximal coverage and maximal rush *both* prove productive, yet may not be implemented on the same play; one area of defense always must be subordinated in the interests of the other.

4. Also disconcerting to passing teams (to some degree it appears), occasionally prealigning the safety(s) at twenty-eight yards then shifting to free-safety depth just prior to the snap, or prealigning at twelve to eighteen yards, then shifting into deep-safety.

5. And, the authors are aware, oversimplified; in chapter 9 the complexity and problems which

specific plays present to the defense are discussed in greater detail.

6. See figure 23 for First Level alignments which isolate various personnel with no one immediately to either side of them, e.g., the nose in 11, in 2-link and 2-rip one of the defensive tackles, etc.

7. If the offensive play *is* sweep, pitch, sprintout, etc., stunting *through* that off-tackle/off-end area can prove very effective; however, if it is *not*, removing these key personnel from pursuit endangers the entire defense.

8. There are several grading systems, the simplest at *this* point in the week being +1 for successful execution of responsibility, -1 for failure, or 0 for noninvolvement in a play: the sum must be a *positive value* for a passing grade.

9. Winning does not vindicate indecisions or tactical errors; ineffectiveness in the decision-making process itself must be redressed.

10. Note also that this analysis can be applied to evaluate offensive strategy by reversing each negative sign in table 16 to a positive, and the two positive signs (in right-hand column at top) to negatives.

References

1. LLOYD H. HELGESON, *Total Pass Defense* (West Nyack, N.Y.: Parker Publ. Co., Inc., 1982), pp. 212-213.

2. BOB WILLIAMS, "Complete flexible monster defense," *The Best of Football from Scholastic Coach* (New York: Scholastic Coach Athletic Services, 1970), pp. 24-31.

3. DALE FOSTER, *The Slanting Monster Defense in Football* (West Nyack, N.Y.: Parker Publ. Co., Inc., 1970), pp. 15-19.

4. GAILORD BELLAMY, *Complete Guide to the Split-Pro Defense* (West Nyack, N.Y.: Parker Publ. Co., Inc., 1971), pp. 19-22.

5. CHARLES ROCHE, *Football's Stunting Defenses* (West Nyack, N.Y.: Parker Publ. Co., Inc., 1982), p. 23.

6. RALPH KIRCHENHEITER, *Coaching Footballs Invert Defense* (West Nyack, N.Y.: Parker Publ. Co., Inc., 1974), pp. 18-21.

7. HELGESON, *Total Pass Defense*, pp. 125-129; 182-185.

8. ROCHE, *Football's Stunting Defenses*, pp. 57-58.

9. VINCE LOMBARDI, *Vince Lombardi On Football*, edited by G.L . Flynn (New York: Galahad Books, 1973), pp. 18-36.

10. PETE DYER, *Coaching the Wishbone-T Triple Option Attack* (West Nyack, N.Y.: Parker Publ. Co., Inc., 1973), pp. 17-23.

11. JIM WACKER and DON MORTON, *The Explosive Veer Offense for Winning Football* (West Nyack, N.Y.: Parker Publ. Co., Inc., 1980), pp. 15-18.

12. PEPPER ROGERS and HOMER SMITH, *Installing Football's Wishbone T Attack* (West Nyack, N.Y.: Parker Publ. Co., Inc., 1973), p. 58.

13. PHIL JACK DAWSON, *Defeating Triple-Option Offenses with the Backbone Defense* (West Nyack, N.Y.: Parker Publ. Co., Inc., 1974), pp. 41-50.

14. TOM OLIVADOTTI, "Defensive analysis of pass offense," *Scholastic Coach*, 54(1): 48-49 and 69, 1984.

15. THOMAS FAY and JOSEPH KIMBALL, "Presenting your pass defense concepts," *Athletic Journal*, 65(7): 32-33, 1985.

16. BILL WALSH, "Controlling the ball with the passing game," *Football Coaching*, compiled by the American Football Coaches Association; editor: Dick Herbert (New York: Charles Scribner's Sons, 1981), pp. 85-93.

17. TERRY DONAHUE and HOMER SMITH, "U.C.L.A.'s passing attack: successful patterns and adjustable routes," *Athletic Journal*, 65(2): 8-13, 1985.

18. ROGER THEDER, "Attacking zone coverages," *Football Coaching*, compiled by the American Football Coaches Association; editor: Dick Herbert (New York: Charles Scribner's Sons, 1981), pp. 109-111.

19. DARWIN SEMOTIUK, "Defensive game adjustments" (Paper presented to the Ontario Amateur Football Association, Super Clinic III, at the University of Western Ontario, London, Canada, May, 1979).

20. PETER C. BELL, "Analysis of strategies in the Canadian Football League," *Infor*, 20: 116-125, 1982.

21. V. CARTER and R. E. MACHOL, "The value of field position," *Optimal Strategies in Sports*, edited by S. P. Ladany and R. E. Machol (Amsterdam: North-Holland, 1977), pp. 94-96.

Chapter 9

ANALYSIS OF OFFENSE: SYSTEMS EVALUATION

There appears to be general agreement among coaches (1, 2, 3) on the scope of today's *multiple* offense: running plays include dives and isolations inside, power off-tackle, quick-pitch, sweeps and the option outside, with delayed reverse, counter, and search plays; passing includes specific combinations of dropback-, quick-, sprintout- and play-actions coupled with complementary patterns. While literally hundreds of companion plays as well as entire systems have been discarded through the evolutionary process of offense, these handful of plays have survived successive buttressment by the defense. To better understand the reasons why, this chapter analyzes the major systems of offense,[1] highlighting the few plays from each that eventually were incorporated into the multiple offenses of the eighties. A system of offense features a unique set of mechanisms that manipulates the defense: synchronized action according to the movements of the football. Since 1940, the beginning of the modern era (fig. 122), each successful system has incorporated patterns of blocking and actions by ball carriers or receivers that manipulated the three-level model of defense at a *particular stage* in its evolution, applied leverage that compromised a *particular working model*; each remained successful until it forced the defense into further modification and change.

Throughout this evolutionary cycle offensive football developed along three mechanistic lines, the most popular being a *balanced* attack featuring both running and passing. Run-oriented and passing attacks produced several popular systems of offense as well, although a fine line always existed between predominantly running or passing attacks and the more balanced philosophy of offense. For purposes of this analysis, therefore, two criteria were imposed arbitrarily in order to classify the various systems.

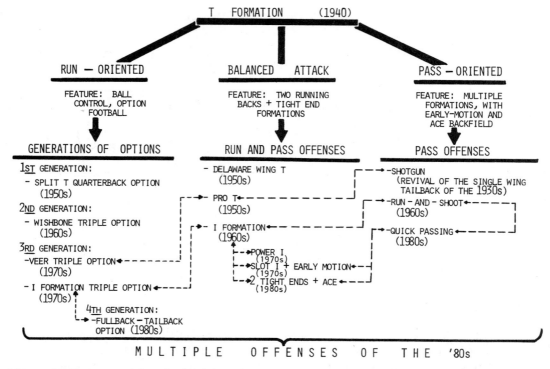

Figure 122 The successful mechanisms (formations+ball movement+plays) from past systems of offense have been incorporated into the multiple offenses of the eighties.

Offenses which featured option mechanism(s) are classified primarily as run-oriented (fig. 122, righthand column). The remainder are classified as either balanced or pass-oriented systems according to the personnel that were positioned in the offensive core (at the snap): respectively, two running backs + one tight end (middle column) *versus* spread formations with ace backfield (fig. 122, righthand column). It can be argued legitimately that considerable overlap exists in these arbitrary divisions (follow dashed arrows in fig. 122); however, the focus of this chapter is on the *multiple* offense employed almost universally at the present time, rather than on these individual systems per se.

ANALYSIS OF RUN-ORIENTED SYSTEMS OF OFFENSE: OPTION FOOTBALL

Contemporary coaches must marvel, as they do at so many of the brilliant concepts in this game, at option football. Now so finely tuned and sophisticated, this offensive mechanism that requires that designated defenders *not* be blocked, yet guarantees that however they react will be wrong. How did such a radical concept ever become operational?

To fully appreciate its evolution one must go back in time, to the years prior to World War II, to the single-wing system (and its variations) which climaxed fifty years of power football (4). On offense, the ball was snapped directly to a fullback or tailback five yards deep, then power blocking attempted to hold open the hole for the ball carrier, preceded by his escort blockers; given this lengthy time and with passing still weaponry of the future, the defense also massed its pursuit at this point of attack. Suddenly, in 1940 the late George Halas, whose Bears popularized the T formation, and Clark Shaughnessy, who carried out its early development first at the University of Chicago then at Stanford (5), transformed football (see fig. 4 and accompanying text); through the forties the split-T, a concept *requiring* gaps of three to four feet between each lineman, modified this offense even further. Coach Don Faurot of the University of Missouri is given full credit for the option concept by its two leading proponents in that era, Bud Wilkinson at Oklahoma (whose split-T teams won an unbelievable string of games, forty-seven straight) and Jim Tatum, equally successful at Maryland, both of whom coached under Faurot while in the Navy in 1943 (6, 7).

Four Generations of Option Football

In comparison with single-wing football, the split-T attacked across a wide front *with speed*; faking was executed on the line of scrimmage, and combined with the passing *threat* of the T-quarterback presented unsolvable problems for the defense in the fifties. An integral part of split-T football was the quarterback-option (fig. 123, upper left diagram) which effectively neutralized the *static* defensive ends of that era. Eventually the Oklahoma 5-2 successfully defensed the split-T^2; in turn, however, other offensive systems were beginning to manipulate this new three-level model of defense. The successes of the wing-T and I-formation (fig. 122) forced the defense to install "the monster" (8), a designated defender who always aligned against the strength side of the offensive formation or to the wideside of the field when the ball was scrimmaged from a hashmark.

Having played quarterback for Wilkinson at Oklahoma in the late forties and coached the split-T in both the U.S. and Canada, Darrell Royal was well schooled in the T-formation and quarterback option when he took over as head coach at the University of Texas in the fifties. To take advantage of the five defenders positioned *away from* the monster yet control rotational pursuit by the deepbacks to the side of the option, in the sixties a *second generation* of option football was perfected at Texas (fig. 123, upper right diagram):

1. the T-backfield was realigned and dubbed a wishbone,
2. one offensive end was split wide, *forcing* the cornerback to move out as well and thereby removing his immediate containment on the option-pitch, and
3. the triple mechanism (review fig. 119) was instituted.

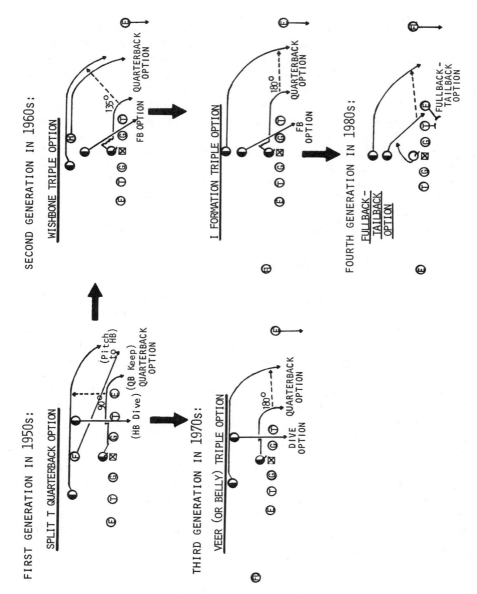

Figure 123 Four generations of option football.

310

From fig. 123 it can be seen how the fullback dive of the wishbone replaced the halfback dive from the split-T and, at the same time, facilitated the quarterback-fullback mesh for the *first* option; the quarterback-halfback option was transferred intact, with only the pitch technique updated (one-handed, more forward, with greater velocity). It is noteworthy that *two decades later* the No. 1 ranked college team in the country (1985: University of Oklahoma) employed this same base formation and option mechanism very successfully.

Obviously the option *mechanism* has never been eradicated by the defense, as the split-T and many other systems were; however, for short periods several defensive adjustments proved effective. Essentially, clever manipulations provided the mechanism for getting a sixth (and even seventh) defender to the side of the option without completely destroying the existing defensive continuity and structure. For the most part, these adjustments positioned additional defenders near the center of the offensive formation in order to provide immediate support to either side; in turn, this precipitated the next generation of option football by exposing the defensive flanks. Even though the veer and I-formation versions (fig. 123, lower half) appeared at the same time as the wishbone, for purposes of this analysis the latter are both labelled as *third generation*, for two reasons. First, operationally, note how the veer- and I-options blended two generations of refinements: the veer triple evolving directly from the first-generation split-T with the halfback dive becoming a dive-option (9), the I triple being identical to the second-generation wishbone, but with the lead tailback removed, and the quarterback's option-pitch becoming a forward lateral in both versions (without any lead blockers to get in the way). More importantly, second, the two wide receivers in the base formations of both the veer-and I-options posed a greater passing threat against the defensive flanks, already weakened by the triple mechanism. These combinations of offensive leverage advanced the multiple concept one stage further: threaten with as many mechanisms as necessary (run and pass) in order to lever and control the defense.

The jury is still out on the most recent option innovation, out of the I-formation a fullback-tailback option (fig. 123, lower right diagram). This variation of the option has recently evolved out of the need to spare quarterbacks further punishment, particularly in pro football, yet retain the option *mechanism* (and its leverage) within the multiple repertoire.

Defensing The Triple-Option Mechanism

Since there now exist many variations of the option mechanism, three *overriding* principles are suggested as guidelines for planning defense.

First Principle: In implementing the 2-level system of defense never alter primary (I) run responsibilities in order to defense any particular variation (fig. 124, upper portion).

On offense, options are always planned in conjunction with several other mechanisms; on defensive, commit too many personnel to stopping a specific variation and most offenses will go immediately to their passing game or to other components of their

PRIMARY ASSIGNMENTS:

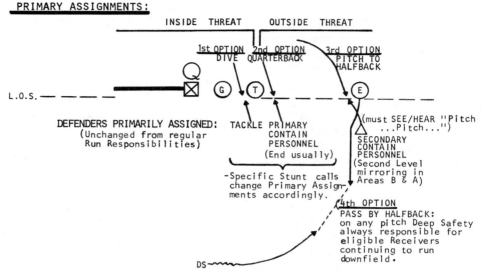

SUPPORT PATTERNS:

—MANY SUPPORT PATTERNS ARE POSSIBLE INVOLVING SECOND LEVEL PERSONNEL; HOWEVER, ONLY SELECT (AND PERFECT) UP TO FOUR FOR A SPECIFIC OPPONENT.

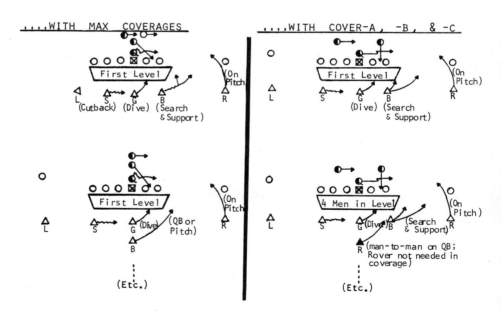

Figure 124 Defensing the triple-option mechanism with the 2-level defense: primary option assignment (to the dive, quarterback, and pitch) is dictated according to each personnel's run responsibility; however, numerous Second Level support patterns are possible.

running game, concentrating its attack wherever the defense has left itself vulnerable. In the eighties it is seldom a point of pride, even with traditional option teams, that they win *with* their option (only that they win).

  Second Principle: In implementing the 2-level system, constantly vary the attack mode.

  While this principle may seem to contradict the first, it does not: secondary (II) run responsibilities can be constantly manipulated, and there are numerous possibilities within the 2-level Defense (fig. 124, lower portion). By its very nature, an option practiced to perfection becomes very mechanical, and thus, for the defense, highly predictable within the limits of that offense's system; in turn, this recognition factor allows specific *support* responsibilities to be assigned on a game-plan basis, according to an offense's personnel and the option employed.

  Third Principle: In implementing the 2-level system convert the option pitch into quick pitch by forcing the quarterback very early.

  This strategy consolidates several advantages and lies at the heart of this system's very effective defense against option football. Foremost, is the fact that many plays during a game are *not* options, and this strategy requires the defense to play with normal aggressiveness *on every play*. In particular, First Level ends can crash aggressively, penetrating to the meshpoint of the first option, contacting the quarterback *forcefully*; as the game wears on this will pay greater dividends than slo-playing the quarterback (10), although this less aggressive technique must be interspersed as well (see below). More critical however, for Second Level personnel outside the core only the quarterback's pitch triggers *the key* for initiating their (II) containment; therefore, the sooner these personnel see or hear "pitch...pitch..." the more immediate becomes their containment.[3] Lastly, forced immediately and pitched *deep* inside the offensive core, the quarterback option essentially becomes a quick-pitch, *not* the dangerous forward lateral made at the line of scrimmage, often well outside the core. With option defense reduced to an extension of quick-pitch, containment and pursuit actually become more effective, for several reasons: the various backfield patterns are so recognizable that defenders' anticipation of the pitch-option is heightened, yet the pitch itself is slower (compared to a quick-pitch) and often there are no blockers ahead of the halfback; also, when the wide receivers find they cannot run off their Second Level mirror (by sprinting down field), they adjust by gradually setting up to stalk-block closer and closer to the line of scrimmage, thereby *neutralizing* this critical leverage mechanism of the triple concept.

  Guided by these principles, coaches have important decisions to make when planning defense against an opponent's specific option package.

  Planning First Level Alignments. The *base* alignment against any option mechanism must be 11 because this alignment positions the First Level tackles and ends *most advantageously*, open and loose respectively, to both sides of the defense (fig. 124, upper diagram). On the other hand, all single digit alignments compromise one of the tackles positioning that defender at a disadvantage (closed) to execute his dive-option assignment. Since the defense cannot play an entire game using only the 11-alignment, appreciate that with single-digit calls it is a Second Level personnel who, effectively, assumes this primary responsibility, in lieu of a *support* assignment usually designated the Second Level (see examples of various support patterns in lower diagrams). That is:

1. in the 11-alignment *two* defenders—one First Level and a supporting Second Level—have each of the option possibilities double-covered;
2. with all single-digit alignments however, to one side of the defense *one* of the options will be only single-covered (the rest remain double-covered on both sides) and,
3. it must be the Second Level defender designated to support who takes over the *primary* assignment for this option.

Planning Support Patterns. While it is not absolutely essential in all instances, against strong option teams it is advisable to incorporate the 11-alignment with cover-A, -B and -C and to plan single-digit alignments only with max coverages; these combinations ensure that every option possibility (to both sides) must have at least one defender assigned to it, and guarantee pass coverage at the same time. By the same reasoning, against the split-backs of the veer a 1-stack can only be planned in combination with a cover (fig. 124, lower righthand diagrams); max coverage would require *two* 2-stacks against the veer. For the most part one deep safety should be employed against strong option teams, but if outside containment by Lou or Rose on the pitch is breaking down "...,Cover/Two-Deep" with a zone roll planned *to the side of the option* allows these personnel to anticipate and gamble more. In planning various support patterns against the option, of lesser concern is the problem of concealment: basically, as long as the First Level remains in its balanced 11-alignment prior to the snap, the offense can only assume that to *both* sides all of the options are well covered. For this reason, it is advisable to shift out of 11-alignment into any single-digit alignment *as late as possible* against option teams; on the other hand, shifting from a single-digit alignment into 11 *after* the quarterback has audibled conceals the defense's intention of double-covering each triple possibility until the snap. While there is always an element of risk in defensing the triple option, one means of double-checking the support patterns planned is through the use of the numerical rating scheme outlined in chapter 8: according to the option mechanism, will a particular support pattern result in the defense being over-matched or outmanned?

Planning Change-Ups. There are two commandments of defense that always hold, independent of the situation: a defense dare not be predictable, yet prior to the snap its mechanisms must be absolutely concealed. Therefore, the basic strategy of always attacking the dive-and quarterback-options cannot be employed constantly despite the variations built in; change-ups must be interspersed. Only two are recommended, however, because each breaks with defensive solidarity, which may be read by the offense. The simplest to incorporate are planned stunts, because these mechanisms are already components of the system; specifically (fig. 125):

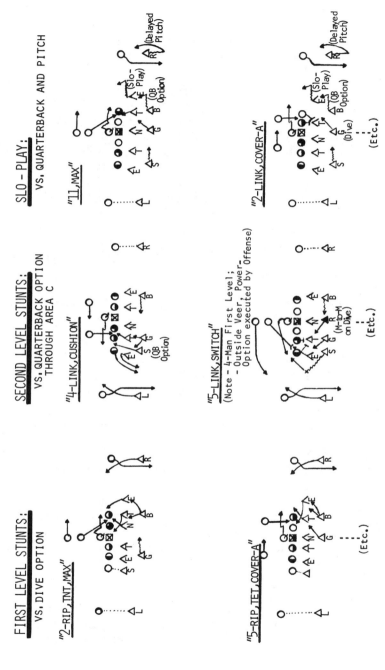

Figure 125 Recommended change-ups against the triple option: these are planned according to the option mechanism(s), and interspersed judiciously during the game.

315

- as change-up against the dive-option, appropriate First Level twists, T.N.T. and/or T.E.T. (see examples, left-hand side);
- as change-up against the quarterback-option, Second Level stunting *through Area C (fig. 125, middle portion)*.

On the other hand, the technique of slo-play, the First Level end to the side of the option playing soft along the line of scrimmage and allowing the football to advance, yet never fully committing to either the quarterback or pitchman, presents several difficulties for the 2-level style of defense (fig. 125, right hand side). Not being an integral part of First Level play, this softer technique, if employed excessively, creates a structural weakness in the core; used sparingly, it proves effective against the quarterback-option for this reason, however. In addition, to execute slo-play both ends must be aligned loose in their two-point stance, which, in turn, restricts the First Level to 11-, 2-, and 3-alignments; further, in the 2- and 3-alignments, without the end aggressively attacking the quarterback, there is a possibility that both the dive-and quarterback-options will have only one defender assigned to each (fig. 125, lower right-hand diagram). Finally, with slo-play, if the quarterback pitches, he does so much later in the play, and by this point secondary (II) contain personnel have been run off by the wide receivers downfield. Therefore, appreciate that slo-play is absolutely necessary to defense the triple option, *but only as a change-up* because it is such a departure from the 2-level style of play. When planning slo-play, therefore, *concealment* must be one of the predominant considerations.

ANALYSIS OF BALANCED SYSTEMS OF OFFENSE: RUN AND PASS

In football vernacular, a *balanced attack* refers to an offense that runs approximately 50-percent of the time and passes the other 50-percent; however, defensive coaches should appreciate that this is primarily an offensive description. In defensive terms, balance always is defined according the the *potential* threats posed by the opponent. How a specific offense chooses to implement its system is (usually) determined by the opposing defense, and the three-level model with its balance has generally dictated running and passing in equal measure. In the present era of multiple offense, a balanced threat is best identified by nine personnel positioned in the offensive core at the snap (with two wide receivers outside), but this has not always been the case. This section analyzes the evolution of the balance football attack and the reasons why specific plays were incorporated into today's multiple systems (fig. 126).

In the years prior to 1940 and during the first decade of the modern era, the offense traditionally positioned all eleven of its personnel in the core in tight power formations (although there were exceptions); therefore, the play variation within a given system established the balance of its attack. In 1940, however, this concept was revolutionized when, from the tight T-formation, running and passing were combined as never before. By the late forties, three additional innovations were begun which have transformed the *system* on offense many times over.

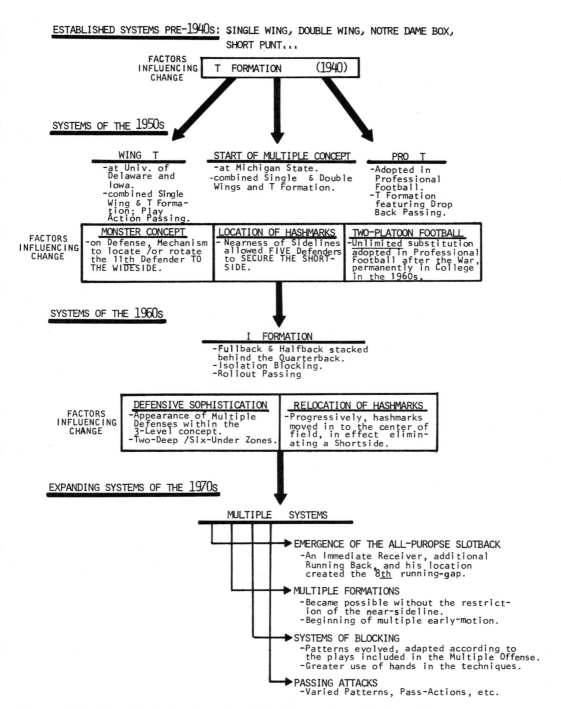

ESTABLISHED SYSTEMS PRE-1940s: SINGLE WING, DOUBLE WING, NOTRE DAME BOX,
SHORT PUNT...

FACTORS
INFLUENCING   T   FORMATION   (1940)
CHANGE

SYSTEMS OF THE 1950s

WING   T
-at Univ. of
Delaware and
Iowa.
-combined Single
Wing & T Forma-
tion; Play
Action Passing.

START OF MULTIPLE CONCEPT
-at Michigan State.
-combined Single & Double
Wings and T Formation.

PRO   T
-Adopted in
Professional
Football.
-T Formation
featuring Drop
Back Passing.

FACTORS
INFLUENCING
CHANGE

MONSTER CONCEPT
-on Defense, Mechanism
to locate /or rotate
the 11th Defender TO
THE WIDESIDE.

LOCATION OF HASHMARKS
-Nearness of Sidelines
allowed FIVE Defenders
to SECURE THE SHORT-
SIDE.

TWO-PLATOON FOOTBALL
-Unlimited substitution
adopted in Professional
Football after the War,
permanently in College
in the 1960s.

SYSTEMS OF THE 1960s

I   FORMATION
-Fullback & Halfback stacked
behind the Quarterback.
-Isolation Blocking.
-Rollout Passing

FACTORS
INFLUENCING
CHANGE

DEFENSIVE SOPHISTICATION
-Appearance of Multiple
Defenses within the
3-Level concept.
-Two-Deep /Six-Under Zones.

RELOCATION OF HASHMARKS
-Progressively, hashmarks
moved in to the center of
field, in effect elimin-
ating a Shortside.

EXPANDING SYSTEMS OF THE 1970s

MULTIPLE   SYSTEMS

EMERGENCE OF THE ALL-PURPOSE SLOTBACK
-An Immediate Receiver, additional
Running Back, and his location
created the 8th running-gap.

MULTIPLE FORMATIONS
-Became possible without the restrict-
ion of the near-sideline.
-Beginning of multiple early-motion.

SYSTEMS OF BLOCKING
-Patterns evolved, adapted according to
the plays included in the Multiple Offense.
-Greater use of hands in the techniques.

PASSING ATTACKS
-Varied Patterns, Pass-Actions, etc.

Figure 126 Evolution of the balanced attack, multiple offense: major contributions of the
systems of offense.

1. Combining of specific mechanisms from different systems into one unified offense: this innovation was best exemplified by the still popular wing T, which combined the principles of single-wing football and the T-formation (11, 12, 13).

2. Integration of *individual* offenses into a multiple system: credit for this concept is generally given to Coach Biggie Munn, who combined both pre- and post-1940 systems into his highly successful multiple attack at Michigan State (14).

3. Success of the pro T, popularizing the strategy of *spreading* the offensive receivers. One event in particular entrenched this innovation: in 1949 the mighty Philadelphia Eagles, champions of the N.F.L., were humbled 35-10 by a team of upstarts from the defunct All-American Conference that employed the pro formation (15, 16).[4]

Through the 1950s, however, three circumstances continued to hamper the offense's development along these lines, particularly in college football. The offense was, in effect, continually pinned against one sideline because the football was being scrimmaged from the hashmarks, located *only thirteen yards* from the sideline, over 75 per cent of the time. (In professional football the hashmarks already had been moved inward, twenty yards from each sideline.) And this situation was further aggravated by the monster concept: in college one defender was anchored in the center portion of the field before the snap. (In the pros, zone rotation *after the snap* achieved this same effect.) Also, until unlimited personnel substitution was legislated, full development of the offensive specialist was retarded, as college players were required to play both on offense *and* defense in so-called one-platoon football (17). As a result, the techniques and development of offense naturally progressed at a slower pace.

In the early sixties another *major* component of the balanced offense appeared: in order to combat the monster and with the hashmarks moving progressively inward (per rule changes), the I-formation with its unique backfield-action, isolation blocking, and rollout passing began attacking *the shortside of the field*. Although Coach John McKay (University of Southern California) was not the originator of the I-formation, his great Trojan teams and succession of Heisman-winning tailbacks popularized this system; by the mid-sixties all of the top-ranked college teams had converted to the I-formation (18), and even the pros were experimenting with this backfield set, which was to revolutionize their game as well. Grudgingly, through the 1960s, the *multiple* concept of defense superseded the monster. From the outset, however, the multiple approach embodied two distinct advantages. First, it accommodated situational defense, enabling personnel to be positioned in the right place at the right time. In turn, this constant variation rendered static blocking systems (for example, the wing-T's post-lead system) obsolete, and new, dynamic principles of both run (19) and pass (20) blocking emerged which have lead, ultimately, to legal use of the hands on offense. Equally important, was the fact that by incorporating multiple defenses within the three-level model wider variety in pass coverage was also accommodated, particularly the two-deep zone that facilitated both combination zone coverages and saturation zoning underneath. In spite of each defensive innovation, the I-formation gained in popularity through the sixties while, at the same time, the final chess piece in the offense's multiple arsenal was being refined and readied for the seventies. Where the idea of the slotback originated is unclear; texts expounding the advantages of this all-purpose player appeared early in the sixties (21, 22), and Spilsbury in his text (23) claimed to be experimenting with a backfielder of this genre as early as 1952. In any case, the slotback was to offense in the seventies what the linebacker had been to defense two decades earlier (see chapter 1). The slotback personified balance: a core blocker with his location creating the eighth running gap in the offensive line (fig. 5), a potential ball carrier, an immediate receiver (but faster than most tight ends), and now, in the seventies, a player providing the perfect mechanism for effecting early-motion. Again, it is unclear where the concept of multiple formations *for purposes of reading the defense* originated. Certainly the 1970 Super Bowl Champion Kansas City Chiefs popularized this strategy (24), but, it was the slotback's versatility more than anything that facilitated this means of leverage with such ease: multiple formations achieved by constantly relocating the slotback, both with and without early-motion.

Components Of The Balanced Multiple-Offense

Essentially, the basic mechanisms of three systems have been amalgamated to achieve offensive balance in the eighties (independent of the option and uniquely pass-oriented systems, that is); figure 127 attempts to synthesize these basic components: from the single-wing and T-formation arose the wing-T system; professional football developed the pro-T, with its potential for passing and multiple formation; then within the existing structure the I-formation superimposed the power of the tailback and versatility of the slotback. Throughout this evolutionary process the techniques and systems have evolved slowly, though much faster than on defense; nearly a half century later, however, only the T-quarterback has been instituted universally in *every* multiple system; in additional, innumerable secondary systems have made important contributions to the whole. Therefore, in the eighties, when planning defense it often becomes difficult "to see the trees for the forest," the basic mechanisms have become so obscured by the multiplicity built into many of the present-day systems.

1. Formation. Examining figure 127, if the offense intends to manipulate the defense by threatening a balanced attack, it is obvious in the first place that a set of common characteristics predetermine formation; that is, over generations of trial and error the balanced attack will not operate, at least not with consistency, unless specific formational prerequisites are met:

- at least nine offensive personnel must be positioned in the core,
- in turn, forcing the defense to defend a minimum of seven offensive line-gaps,
- at least two (potential) ball carriers in the backfield,[5]
- with a *wide receiver* split out near each sideline to force the defense to cover the breadth of the field.

WING T (1950s)

-WINGBACK <u>FORCED</u> DEFENSE TO OVERSHIFT.
-THREATENED OVER A WIDE FRONT: INSIDE FULLBACK DIVE; HALFBACK (OR WINGBACK) POWER SWEEP TO ONE SIDE; QUARTERBACK'S BOOTLEG THREAT TO OTHER SIDE.
-ADAPTED THE SINGLE WING'S POWER BLOCKING SYSTEM.

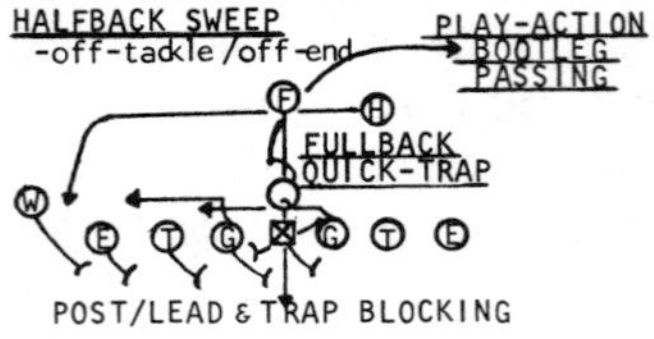

HALFBACK SWEEP
-off-tackle/off-end

PLAY-ACTION
BOOTLEG PASSING

FULLBACK QUICK-TRAP

POST/LEAD & TRAP BLOCKING

PRO T (1960s)

-SPREAD FORMATIONS, SOPHISTICATED PASSING, OFF STRAIGHT DROPBACK-ACTION.
└─FULLBACK DRAW PLAY.
└─SCREEN PASS.
- GREEN BAY SWEEP TO STRENGTH, WING T SWEEP UPDATED (BUT WITHOUT BENEFIT OF THE WINGBACK'S BLOCKING).
-FULLBACK RUN-TO-DAYLIGHT AWAY FROM STRENGTH: ADAPTED T AND SPLIT T OPTION-BLOCKING.

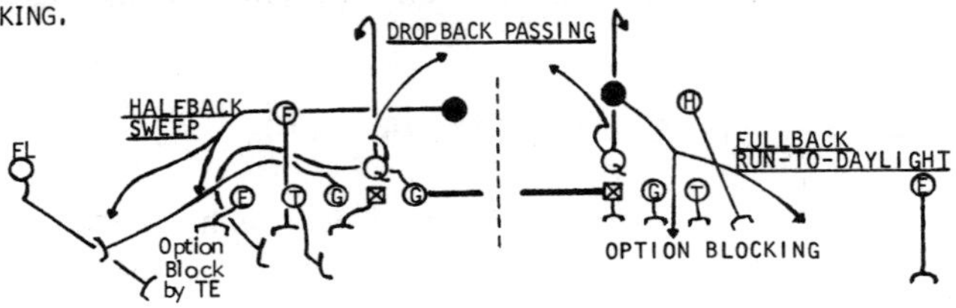

DROPBACK PASSING

HALFBACK SWEEP

FL

FULLBACK RUN-TO-DAYLIGHT

Option Block by TE

OPTION BLOCKING

I FORMATION (1970s)

-FULLBACK ISO BLOCKING FOR THE TAILBACK: INSIDE, OFF-TACKLE, QUICK PITCH.
VERY EFFECTIVE TO THE SHORTSIDE.
-QUARTERBACK ROLLOUT, OFF PLAY-ACTION TO THE TAILBACK DIVING.
-SLOTBACK'S VERSATILITY <u>CREATED</u> MULTIPLE FORMATIONS.

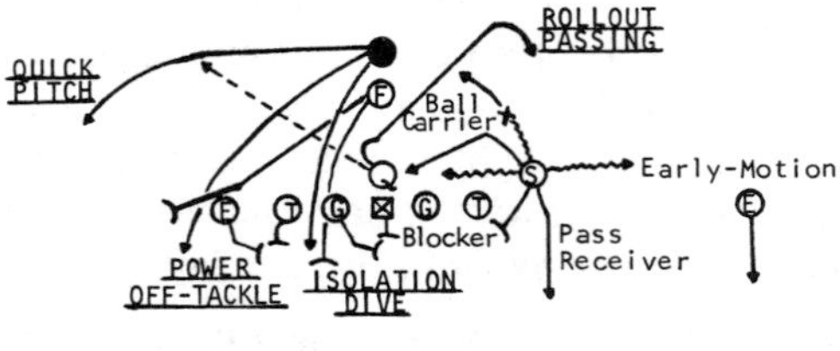

QUICK PITCH

ROLLOUT PASSING

Ball Carrier

Early-Motion

Blocker

Pass Receiver

POWER OFF-TACKLE

ISOLATION DIVE

Figure 127 Balanced offensive attack in the 1980s: amalgamation of these major components, with infinite variation and adaptations.

While variations are always possible, in the long run if these formational dictates are not adhered to, the *basic* run and pass mechanisms from the wing-T, pro-T and I-formation simply cannot operate with their designed effectiveness.

2. Run Offense. Three defensive areas are threatened to varying degrees by the balanced attack, *inside* between the offensive tackles, and *outside* the tackles to both sides (i.e. to strength and away from strength); also, a specific opponent may run power off-tackle so effectively that this gap to strength must be considered separately in planning defense. Otherwise, seldom do these areas need to be subdivided further in game planning. Most multiple offenses possess the capacity to attack each area with the four types of running plays, as defined in chapter 8; however, various play mechanisms operate *most effectively against specific areas.*[6]

INSIDE: SPEED-AND-POWER. Quick-hitting dives still work, but no longer with guaranteed consistency; similarly, against today's pursuit-oriented defenses, power running inside (the protracted counter-trap plays of the wing-T and short reverses) has been all but eliminated. For an offense to run inside with consistency, the speed-and-power mechanism must be employed and three specific plays have proven very successful.

- The fullback dive in the triple option run off the double-team block (fig. 119).

- The fullback *quick* trap from the wing-T (fig. 127, upper diagram): this brilliantly designed play hits precisely over center, and in conjunction with its speed, angle blocking maximizes the offensive line's advantage without requiring the double-team. The guard's quick trap is deadly against he heart of an attacking, penetrating defense, and the quarterback's handoff occurs with his back completely turned to the defense. More recently, this play mechanism has reappeared incorporated with the quarterback-option (25, 26).

- From the I-formation, the tailback dive, hitting off-guard with the lead fullback iso blocking an inside linebacker (fig. 127, lower diagram): another brilliantly designed mechanism, this play takes advantage of the inside linebacker, who must assume *primary* run responsibility for a designated line-gap in the three-level model; run off an effective double-team block *with speed* this momentarily isolates the linebacker, giving the blocking advantage to the hard-charging fullback. Recently, the tight end in jet-action early-motion has been substituted as the lead blocker in this mechanism.

In addition to these three, the tailback-search play has provided consistency running inside because the back only cuts inside when he sees daylight. This play evolved from the fullback draw and run-to-daylight plays[7] of the pro-T (see middle diagram on the right, figure 127); at the present time this mechanism is best operated from the I-formation and run by the tailback.

OFF-TACKLE: POWER. From the I-formation, the tailback running to the tight end's side behind his lead fullback (fig. 127, lower diagram) has provided the consummate off-tackle play for gaining vital yardage (in short yardage situations, on the goal line, etc.). On the other hand, defensive speed and pursuit now is capable of shutting down most of the other off-tackle mechanisms which have proved troublesome in the past: slower sweeps hitting off-tackle, speed plays employing "geo" blocking (short-trapping by the onside guard), cross-blocking the off-tackle hole by the onside tackle and tight end, the quarterback-keeper in the triple option, etc.

OUTSIDE: BOTH POWER AND SPEED. Protecting its flanks will remain the most difficult task for run defense because it is such an expansive area, and now to both the shortside of the field as well as wideside; in addition, as the ball carrier advances outside the core, defensive personnel must progress to containment and pursuit responsibilities, the least structured portion during any play. For these reasons, over the years outside running plays have proven successful employing three basic mechanisms.

- The Power Sweep: featuring the ball carrier following massed blockers, sweeps have been an integral mechanism of offense since the inception of the game. Succession into the modern era evolved from the single-wing through the wing-T (fig. 127, upper diagram); then as the wingback position gradually disappeared from football in the late fifties, the sweep *mechanism* had to be further modified. At the present time, however, even though several variations have been developed in the interim, this modification of the basic mechanism made in the early sixties is still referred to as the Green Bay sweep (29), because it became such a potent weapon in the hands of Coach Lombardi and his Packers (see middle diagram on the left).

- Quick Pitch: there have been many variations of this speed mechanism, which feature *minimal* blockers, with the ball carrier attempting to outrace the defense: the extension play popular at the turn of the century (30), the buck-lateral of the single-wing (31), the halfback pitch from the T-formation, and so on. Almost universally at the present time, out of the I-formation the tailback quick-pitch with or without the fullback leading (i.e., from ace backfield) is the mechanism employed by most offenses (fig. 127, lower diagram).

- Tailback Search Outside: when the tailback is handed the football deep in the backfield this simulates power off-tackle; however, either by design or when the off-tackle area is plugged, the tailback breaks to the outside. The other dominant feature of the search play is option-blocking, which Lombardi popularized as an integral part of the run-to-daylight concept (32); each blocker ties up one defender (in the eighties by excessive grappling), using the defender's own momentum to wrestle him *where he wants to go*. Because of this, keys are difficult to read, particularly any hint that the tailback might make his cut to the outside.

3. Passing. The least predictable feature of the balanced offense, its passing, has more than anything, been responsible for the persistent growth of the multiple attack over the last three decades. Initial impetus toward this outcome, however, arose out of the defense's *universally* adopting zone coverage through the fifties: by its very nature, saturation coverage concentrated the defensive resources downfield against the offensive receivers, rather than exerting pressure to control the *entire* offensive action. As a result, the various systems of offense were given leeway to develop unique concepts of passing which best complemented their running; now, in any number of viable sets, the offense may execute *any one* of these pass mechanisms.

- Passing by the Quarterback: by far, the most dramatic stage in this evolution occurred in 1940 when the T-formation placed the football in the hands of the quarterback; this revolutionized the game itself.

- Play-Action Passing: the wing-T threatened the defense over a much wider front than earlier systems, inside with fullback dives, to strength with halfback sweeps, away from strength with play-action by the quarterback (fig. 127, upper diagram). This led, in turn, to complementary pass patterns that *required* backfield-action in order to gain time for their development downfield, as well as to create that moment of indecision in the underneath coverage.

- Dropback Passing: the Pro-T was developed along an entirely different set of tactical precepts (fig. 127, middle diagram). The offensive formation−flanker set out to the wideside/split end at the shortside sideline−threatened the defense across a broad front; then, the straight dropback-action and obvious blocking by the line, immediately showing pass, forced the zone mechanism to defend the entire field. As complementary plays, but unlike play-action with its ball-faking and subterfuge, off dropback-action screens and draws were executed audaciously *in full view of the defense*.

- Rollout Passing: out of the I-formation, the dive fake to the tailback froze the defense for at least one full second after the snap, while the split end, slotback, and often the fullback released downfield; in the next instant the defensive flank was threatened first by these receivers flooding the zones to that side, and then by the quarterback continuing to run outside, with the option to run with the football should the zone defenders to that side not move up to contain him (fig. 127, lower diagram). In the sixties, rollout shortside (away from the monster) proved so successful that both the mechanism and the concept of a mobile quarterback became entrenched as viable offensive threats.

- Quick Passing: also in the sixties, the run-and-shoot (33) further modified these principles of rollout-action (see final section of this chapter). Experiencing only modest success at the time, the concepts of run-and-shoot passing−ultrashort routes with quick release of the football by the quarterback−have been resurrected in the eighties (34, 35, 36), adding yet another dimension to the offense's pass repertoire.

Defensing The Balanced Multiple System

Three operating principles are again strongly suggested as guidelines for analyzing and planning defense against balanced attacks. And to provide continuity, considerable *overlap* has purposely been incorporated into the three outlined below, and the principles detailed in the last section (for defensing the option). Most multiple systems include at least one option mechanism, and thus, option defense can easily be intergrated within the larger defensive scheme. Additionally, for an option mechanism to operate efficiently, nine or more personnel must be positioned in the offensive core at the snap (examine the formations in fig. 123-125).

First Principle: In implementing the 2-level system, identify the common denominators of defense.

When analyzing a multiple system, group the plays in such a way that only the minimum of defensive mechanisms need to be planned; stated another way, identify *as few mechanisms as possible* that will defense all the multiple features.[8] For example: the 2- and 4-alignments, overshifted to strength, with Second Level stacks placed strategically, may be planned to defense both an inside running game and runs to strength; aggressive funnelling (as opposed to steering) of wide receivers in all covers may best disrupt an offense that throws out routes in the majority of its patterns; and so on. Against multiple offenses these *common denominators* must be determined in order to condense and simplify the defensive game plan as much as possible.

Second Principle: In implementing the 2-level system, constantly vary the attack mode.

Identical to the *second* principle for defensing the option, in this wider context against a balanced offense both the First and Second Levels can be moved and adjusted more freely (i.e., against an option offense, 11 must be planned as the *base* alignment). Planning run defense and pass coverage, the same personnel alignment and mechanisms should not be employed repeatedly: once the defense becomes predictable, for the multiple offense it becomes defeatable.

Third Principle: In implementing the 2-level system, restrict the scope of the balanced offense by attacking.

Defense cannot eliminate all of the play possibilities within the multiple system at the same time; therefore, playing situational defense and *pressuring the football directly* provides the best means for limiting various features. For example, it was suggested earlier that attacking the dive- and quarterback-options aggressively provided the best means for controlling the option *mechanism*; this same principle of attack should be applied to limit other possibilities, particularly the range of pass mechanisms that an offense may choose (see below).

Guided by these principles, coaches must again consider several crucial questions in planning defense against a versatile, balanced attack: how best to juggle and adjust alignment, stacking, stunts, and coverage?

Planning the Outside Defense. In preparing for a well-balanced offense it is suggested that game planning proceed from the outsides of the defense to the inside of the core: statistics indicate that long runs result more frequently penetrating one to four yards outside the tight end (37) than at any other point along the line of scrimmage, and immediately behind this area threatened by the run a majority of the passes are thrown to medium depth; compounding this situation, compared to the defensive core the outsides are sparsely filled with personnel, limiting the adjustment possibilities in this area of the defense. Therefore, unless there are reasons for planning otherwise (i.e., opposing a strong option team or a pass-oriented offense), against the balanced attack planning should *begin outside.* First, group the opponent's outside running plays together (fig. 128, left hand diagram); from the standpoint of defensive execution the differences between these plays require less structural adjustment, as they rely more on recognition (formational tip-offs, blocking patterns, etc.) and appropriate reactions (expecting a particular running back to bounce outside, and so on). Also, on the left-hand side in figure 128 the unique structure for defensing the outside is diagrammed; in combination with cover-A this is the strongest personnel alignment possible.

1. The First Level. The right end (in the diagram), aligned loose and crashing, attacks these outside running plays, adapting his technique accordingly: against pitches he must breakdown sooner, and let the play come to him; against slower sweeps he may crash to the fullback or pulling guards to break up the play earlier. If a large tight end will block him one-one-one on any of these plays, the First Level end should assume his three-point stance. Also, when runs outside are anticipated the adjacent First Level tackle should be aligned open to provide immediate tear support (examine the examples on the right-hand side, fig. 128).

2. The Second Level. Most critically, a 2-stack on the offensive tackle (Gael in this diagram) accomplishes two tactical objectives: first, this Second Level defender is positioned most advantageously to scrape, supporting the end's crash; together with cover-A, this allows the tight end's mirror (Strong in this diagram) to walkaway to a commanding position where he can support both inside and outside on runs as well as providing effective zone coverage in the flat area immediately behind him.

3. Cover-A. Only Rose (in this diagram) would have the deep 1/3 responsibility; thus on sweep-action, when it is still uncertain whether a run or a pass will result, Strong and Gael are permitted more time to read (i.e., neither is forced to drop-off immediately to the deep 1/3 in cover-A).

4. Change-Ups. On the right in figure 128 possible change-ups are diagrammed; however, note that each adjustment *subtracts* from the stability of the basic structure (diagrammed on the left). Also, two stunts may be planned, accord-

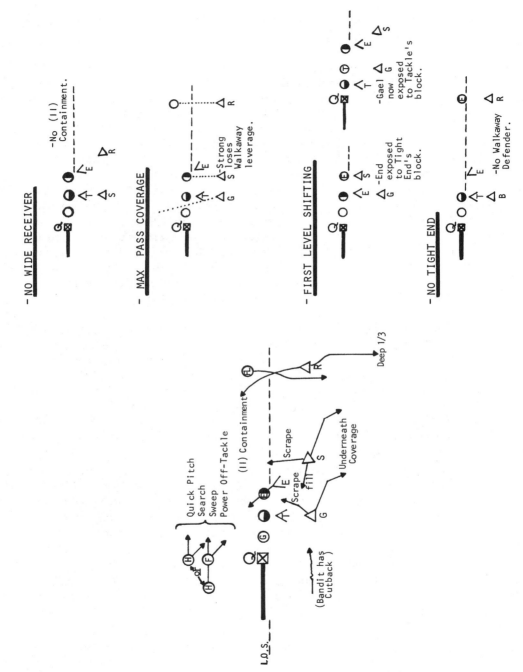

Figure 128 Defending the outsides: in conjunction with Cover-A., the unique structure of the 2-level defense (left-hand side) and variations (right-hand side).

ing to the running plays expected: T.E.T. (tackle-end twist) and switch. The latter is particularly effective against *wide* running plays or quarterback sprint-out with the *double* crash by the end and Strong.

Planning the Core Defense. When shifting by the First Level is planned for inside the core (and single-digit calls create an *overshift*), the defense's strength should in most instances be *counterbalanced* against the balanced offensive attack. This can only be accomplished through adjustments by the Second Level (fig. 129); however, two questions must be carefully considered in planning various attack combinations: will specific stack(s) create a structural weakness against the opponent's inside running game; and will specific combinations result in the defense being outnumbered at another location according to the numerical rating scheme designed for the core (fig. 117)? In Fig. 129 the most reliable stack combinations against both power running and tapping inside are diagrammed.

Rule No. 1: Repeatedly over the years, experience has proven that against inside running the core is strongest when one defender is aligned over the offensive center.

In the *odd* alignments the nose is assigned over-center, and therefore 2-stacks (usually) are planned for the Second Level (fig. 129, upper left hand diagram). As change-ups, several stack adjustments can be planned, including realignment of 2-stacks over-guard, inserting Rover as the sixth Second Level defender in a 1-stack, etc; also, when confronted by major formational changes by the offense it must be the Second Level that counterbalances the defense's personnel strengths through its stack readjustments (fig. 129, right-hand side). In the *even* alignments, the Second Level defender to the side that the nose aligns (usually) counterbalances by moving over-center (fig. 129, lower left-hand diagram); with the nose and one First Level tackle over the offensive guards, even alignments are structurally stable against power running inside with a Second Level defender in 1-stack. On the other hand, even alignments are more vulnerable to quick-trapping and must be planned cautiously: for example, the Split 4-4 Defense (38) all but eliminated the quick-trap two decades ago, and therefore the mechanism, stacking over-guard, may be planned as a change-up (fig. 129, lower right hand diagram). Finally, any major changes in formation again must be counterbalanced by appropriate Second Level adjustments (fig. 129, right-hand side).

Although the second core rule may seem redundant, its relevance will emerge as the intricacies of First Level shifting, Second Level stacking, and core stunting are carefully reexamined during each stage of planning.

Rule No. 2: Double-check that Rule No. 1 is seldom violated.

In other words, for optimal core stability against running plays inside, time and again coaches must recheck to ensure that the *correct* defender has been assigned over-center as more defensive mechanisms and greater complexity are incorporated into a game plan (fig. 130).

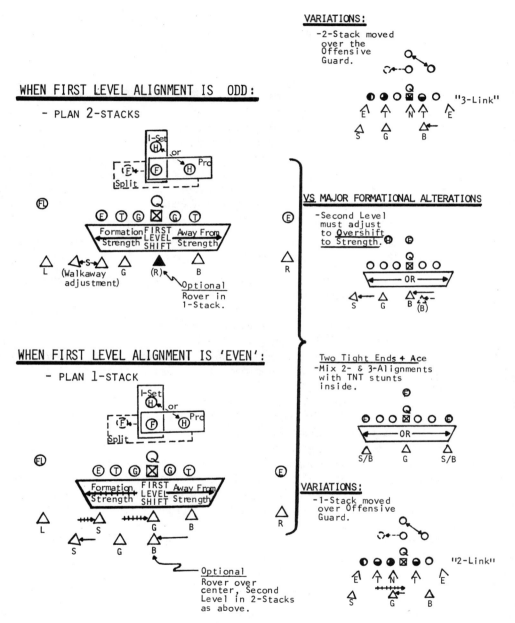

Figure 129 Counterbalancing defensive strength in the core: rules for planning Second Level stacking against the balanced attack.

FIRST LEVEL STUNTING

ODD ALIGNMENTS

"11, Slant,..."
-Stunting to Even after the snap, therefore, prealign the 1-Stack.

"5-Link, TNT,..."
-Right Tackle assigned over-Center, therefore, prealign the two 2-Stacks.

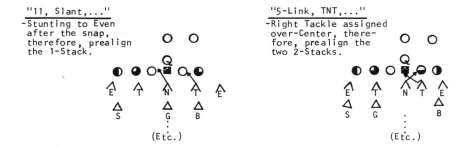

EVEN ALIGNMENTS

"2-Link, Slant,..."
-Actually stunting into Odd after snap, therefore, prealign the two 2-Stacks.

"4-Link, TNT,..."
-If the Offense traps inside effectively, plan the 1-Stack.

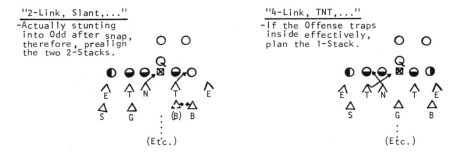

SECOND LEVEL STUNTING

"5-Link, Dog"
-Bandit finds the <u>open</u> gap through center.

"2-Rip, Dog"
-The 2-Stack over Guard may be planned.

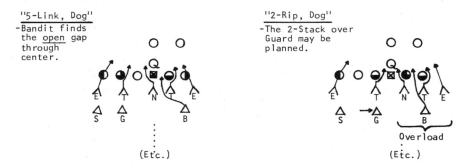

Figure 130 Core Rule #2: with the intricacy of core planning, First Level shifting and Second Level stacking pre-snap then stunting post-snap, always ensure that the correct defender has been assigned over-center (Rule #1).

Finally, faced with nine personnel in the offensive core, against the balanced attack mirroring has the tendency to cluster defenders in the core at the expense of the defensive flanks, a distinct disadvantage against both outside running and play-action passing. Therefore, the following adjustments should be implemented sequentially as the need increases to *counterbalance* defensive strength outside the core yet still defend against running inside.

Rule No. 3: Deepen the stack alignments accordingly. Plan 2-stacks (only). Widen the prealignment of the stacks, particularly in area C. Plan cover-A.

Each of these adjustments includes advantages as well as some disadvantages. For example, by deepening their stack alignment Second Level defenders become more exposed to offensive blocking; beginning five yards off the line of scrimmage Second Level stunting is less effective, yet any pre-snap adjustment may tip the stunt; with the C-stack defender in an *extreme* walkaway, a cover must be called and this can be read by the offense; and so on. In the planning stages a coaching staff must carefully weight the pros and cons of these various decisions.

Planning Pass Defense. Passing has become the least predictable feature of the balanced attack. The overriding mechanism of pass defense in the 2-level system is *pressure*, and only through its deliberate application can this unpredictability be reduced to any extent. In the eighties *the source* of the pass must be controlled–the quarterback and various pass-actions. Planning pass defense, therefore, the following steps should be considered in order to force an offense to modify its passing accordingly. *First,* determine the pass-actions which have similar characteristics, the common denominators of the opponent's passing game. Usually a balanced offense does not employ all of the pass-actions or executes some much better than others because of the quarterback's passing abilities (or lack thereof). Often dropback and play-action, both 2 $1/2$-second passes, can be grouped together, particularly when both involve a five- to seven-step drop by the quarterback; on the other hand, sprintout and quick may be classified together because of the similar patterns and reception areas (primarily the flats). *Second*, control the number of receivers in the patterns by *threatening* pressure prior to the snap (and applying concerted pressures a majority of the time when a pass occurs). In planning, determine if the quarterback is a running threat. If so, the First Level ends should be aligned loose (11-, 2-, and 3-alignments) to better contain him, with stunting from the outsides planned (switch and cushion); if the quarterback is not a runner, then more dog stunts through center can be planned. Establish the personnel mismatches, which pass rusher(s) dominate their blocker; then, plan First Level alignments accordingly to force these matchups in passing situations. Analyze the opponent's pass blocking scheme: against area blocking the overload mechanism is best, while well-executed twists prove more difficult for man-protection schemes to handle. *Third*, constantly vary the pass coverage according to the patterns expected, ensuring that each is well concealed prior to the snap; in employing max coverage, however, several cautions should be observed. Max affords the most efficient use of defensive personnel–one assigned per receiver with the remainder freed to pressure the quarterback; on the other hand, a superior receiver mismatched against a defender can render max coverage a liability in certain situations, particularly when an offense maximally protects its quarterback. In addition, excessive crossing-action by the offensive backs proves more difficult for the mirroring Second Level defenders (stacked in the core) to max; and when an offense may run as often as it passes, employing max excessively can also reduce core stability against complementary running plays.

ANALYSIS OF PASS-ORIENTED OFFENSES: THREE UNIQUE SYSTEMS

Essentially only three offenses have predicated a system almost entirely on their ability to pass the football, utilizing unique combinations of pass-action and patterns: the shotgun, run-and-shoot, and quick passing (fig. 122). The features that these offenses share in common are their base formations, spread receivers with ace backfield, and use of early-motion prior to the snap to manipulate the defensive coverage. In this final section these three systems are analyzed individually. The *principal* mechanisms of each have been incorporated into most multiple offenses, however, the capability of a specific opponent to utilize these specializing passing attacks should be carefully evaluated during pre-game planning: for example, effective use of either the shotgun or quick passing requires a strong-armed quarterback; the sprintout mechanism requires a rugged, running quarterback who can throw accurately on the run; and so on.

The Shotgun

This pass-oriented system is so called because of the prealignment of the quarterback, five yards deep, receiving the longer snap from center then spraying passes both medium and deep across the field. A revival of the single-wing concept, the quarterback specialist has replaced the triple-threat tailback, who was a runner and punter as well as the passer (fig. 131). Receiving the snap from center in the shotgun, the quarterback in effect has already dropped back, and this provides the main advantage of the formation: many coaches feel the quarterback can, without having to set up, scan the defensive coverage immediately to better observe the offensive pattern as it develops. The disadvantage of the shotgun is its reliance upon the pass and a reduced running threat, particularly when the quarterback is not a scrambler. However, more and more the shotgun is being utilized by offenses in long yardage when the opposition employs *situational* defenses: they would rather gain the formational advantage for the quarterback and receivers than pose any run threat, which the majority of defenses all but ignore in passing situations.

Against the shotgun, several unique problems confront the 2-level Defense. A majority of the time medium and deep passes are thrown, and for this reason running plays and shorter passes (screens, delays, etc.) can gain yardage, since this defense is already preoccupied with pressure and pass rush. In addition, the shotgun formation possesses the flexibility to protect the quarterback maximally at any time (fig. 131), and

SINGLE WING FORMATION
(OF THE THIRTIES)

TAILBACK TRIPLE THREAT :
Running, Punting & Passing

SHOTGUN REVIVAL

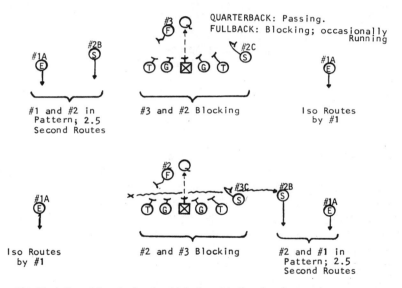

QUARTERBACK: Passing.
FULLBACK: Blocking; occasionally Running

#1 and #2 in Pattern; 2.5 Second Routes

#3 and #2 Blocking

Iso Routes by #1

Iso Routes by #1

#2 and #3 Blocking

#2 and #1 in Pattern; 2.5 Second Routes

Figure 131 Evolution of the single wing triple threat to the singular passing threat of the shotgun: a spread formation with the quarterback aligned 5 yards deep, and 2.5-second pass patterns.

most quarterbacks, already set up, and seeing the rush closing in, are able to get rid of the football before being sacked. For these reasons a very disciplined approach is suggested as the best way to plan for the shotgun.

Planning Run Defense and Pass Rush. Planning the 33-alignment with T.N.T. stunts *over-center* accomplishes two objectives. By varying their stunting pattern the nose and tackles continually attack the most vulnerable offensive lineman,—the center, who must snap the ball. By twisting at the center of the formation, one First Level rusher automatically is staggered in the event of a delayed running play. Planning the even-alignments, shifting *to the side of* the fullback as late as possible concentrates the overload rush against this side while the opposite side of the First Level should throttle down (execute a more cautious rush) in case the fullback is handed the football on a running play (which must come their way, examine fig. 131).

Planning Pass Coverage. More zone and combination coverages should be planned against the shotgun, regularly inserting two deep safeties into the defense or substituting Rover as the sixth Second Level defender. In addition, with a minimal threat of quick passing Second Level defenders should align at medium-to-soft depth, *concealing their shade* as much as possible. Therefore, the constantly varying defensive personnel, techniques, and coverages prove more difficult for the quarterback to read despite the advantages of the formation. Finally, with the reduced running threat of the shotgun a *special* verification of covers-A, -B, and -C may be planned for anytime the No. 3 mobile player aligns on the wideside of the quarterback, i.e., either as a backfielder[9] or—the usual verification of the -A, -B, -C mechanism,—as an immediate receiver to that side.

The Run-And-Shoot

Coach Ellison published his text, *Run-And-Shoot Football....*, in the mid-sixties, after joining Woody Hayes' staff at Ohio State as its freshman coach, and following highly successful years at Middletown High School (in Ohio) where he developed the run-and-shoot. Both its full title, ... : *Offense Of The Future*, and many of the pass mechanisms described in the text (fig. 132) were ahead of their time, for the run-and-shoot made little impression upon football in the sixties. For example, in the text's foreword written by Coach Hayes, complimentary phrases such as "revolutionary ideas" and "fantastic success" embellished Woody's prose (39), yet in his own text, published in late 1969, little in the Ohio State passing attack remotely resembled the run-and-shoot philosophy. Nevertheless, some two decades later the rebirth of run-and-shoot precipitated a minor revolution on offense, as prophesied by Ellison:

> "This *is* the football of the future ... provided ... coaches will open their eyes and stir their imaginations and put the oval-shaped ball on display...." (40)

- Run-and-shoot was the first system to employ early-motion on every play, unbalancing the offensive formation in order to read the defensive readjustment (fig. 132, upper diagram).
- This system was the first to report the use of both hand signals and *automatic* adjustments made in individual routes within a pattern (lower left-hand diagram). Ellison explained how, before the snap, signals were exchanged between the split ends and the quarterback :

> "[the ends] flashed baseball signals to the quarterback ... if the quarterback found one of our ends ... toying with his face bar..." (41)

I)FROM THIS BALANCED SPREAD FORMATION, <u>LONG EARLY-MOTION</u> BY
EITHER ONE OF THE SLOTBACKS <u>UNBALANCING</u> THE OFFENSIVE
STRENGTH SO THE DEFENSE'S READJUSTMENTS COULD BE READ :

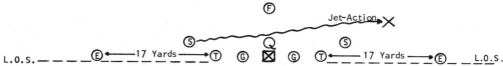

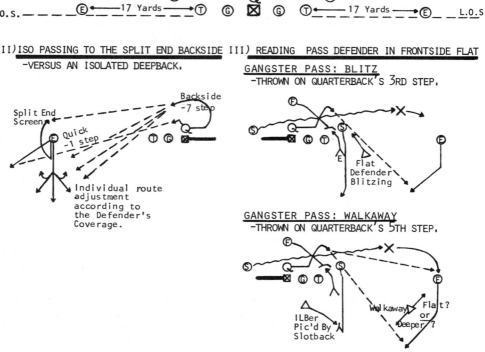

Figure 132 Basic mechanisms of the run-and-shoot: long early motion to read the
defensive coverage; backside iso passing; frontside gangster passing (adapted
from Glenn Ellison, Run-And-Shoot Football: Offense of the Future. West Nyack,
N.Y., Parker Publishing Company, Inc., 1984, 1965; with permission).

- And after the snap, the cut that a receiver would make downfield was
  dictated by the defense and read (ahead of time) by both quarterback
  and receiver:

"if [the deepback] stayed back, there was the hook pass in front of him.... if he
moved right, there came a pass to his left.... if he moved left, there was the ball on
the right...." (42)

- Run-and-shoot emphasized frontout technique by the quarterback in order to get quicker release of the football (lower right-hand diagrams); Ellison described their timing:

"... short passes ... thrown instantaneously with [the receiver's] break ... the blitz pass on his third step ... the walkaway pass on his fifth step...." (43)

- The gangster walkaway pass (fig. 132, lower right) initially developed the pic technique that, while *still* illegal today under the rules, nonetheless has become an integral part of every pass offense. Ellison rationalized its usage in 1965 as offensive coaches still argue today:

"surely a harmless basketball cherry-pick often used in this non-contact sport could not be termed unsportsmanlike in the rough and rugged sport of American football." (44)

- Even Ellison's writing style broke with coaching tradition, eclipsing its prosaic literature to that point with colorful syntax:

"co-ordination of the moving bodies in harmony with the bobbing ball..." (45)

"spring from Hell into the deep Blue ... leave Heaven and go to Boston..." (46)

- And even Nathaniel Hawthorne was quoted,[10]

"'You must begin to hurt if you would become great!'" (47)

With an effective sprintout quarterback , the passing mechanisms of the run-and-shoot present several concerns for the 2-level Defense. A majority of the time 11-, 2-, and 3-alignments must be employed to keep the First Level ends aligned loose for quarterback containment. Also, the number of Second Level personnel in the core—and thus, the adjustment capability of the Second Level in the core—is minimal because of the ace backfield set. For these reasons, the defense against any complementary running attack must be carefully planned; in the original run-and-shoot system, Ellison outlined three series (48): dive plays inside featuring man-blocking, called the Mudcat Series; quick trapping inside, dubbed the Pop Corn Series; and power sweep outside, dubbed The Wagon Train. On the other hand, several features of the run-and-shoot are *highly* predictable and provide a foundation for game planning.

1. With the limited offensive personnel in the core available for blocking, the fullback must *always* race to the frontside against the 2-level Defense to block the crashing First Level end, and this can be instantly read; Ellison stressed that:

"The fullback's block was extremely important....always....at the far knee of Frontside Three....this block was an absolute 'must' in our offense." (49)

2. With the football thrown so quickly, receivers seldom get deep; thus, the ma-

jority of the run-and-shoot patterns employ *horizontal stretching* as their mechanism of attack on the frontside (50).

3. Almost exclusively on the backside (away from early-motion), iso passing is employed, and often the receivers' routes are predictable (fig. 103, upper right hand-diagram).

Planning Pass Rush. With the First Level ends aligned loose, three mechanisms are suggested to both pressure the quarterback *from the outside* and limit his sprint out of the core.

- In the majority of situations, plan aggressive crash for the First Level ends: frontside, to engage the fullback as deep in the backfield as possible while maintaining outside leverage on the quarterback; from the backside, to chase the quarterback, discouraging iso passes or scrambling in that direction.

- While switch may be used *occasionally* against this ace formation, planning tackle-end twists (T.E.T.) *in effect* can accomplish the same objective, a double-crash from the frontside: mirroring the fullback's actions 100 percent, the First Level end completes his twist inside if the fullback dives; however, if the fullback sprints laterally, the end follows his tackle (already slanting to the outside in T.E.T.) by crashing from the outside as usual.

- In addition, *follow-up* can be planned with max coverage (fig. 133, upper diagram): as change up the (front-side-First Level end crashes through the *inside* of the fullback, rather than maintaining his leverage on the quarterback; anticipating that the fullback will block the First Level end, Bandit (in this diagram) scrapes full speed, outside, to follow-up the end's aggressive penetration; and Gael must ensure that Bandit's scrape-action is not pic'd by the slotback by steering his mirror outside.

Planning Pass Coverage. Employing hard-to-medium alignments by the Second Level, max and cover/two-deep should be planned as the basic coverages: implement the former when maximal rush pressure is desired, the latter to maximally saturate the underneath zones against horizontal stretching (review fig. 121). Also, a number of change-ups can be interspersed within these coverages:

- Zone roll (review fig. 112) both *to* and *away from* the early-motion can be planned when a frontside pattern /or iso pass backside (respectively) is expected;

- Rover can be substituted as the sixth defender into the Second Level, *primarily* to increase the saturation coverage underneath, occasionally to double-cover a designated receiver (see example in middle diagram of fig. 133, Rover's double coverage against the isolated split-end).

PASS RUSH: THE FOLLOW-UP PRINCIPLE

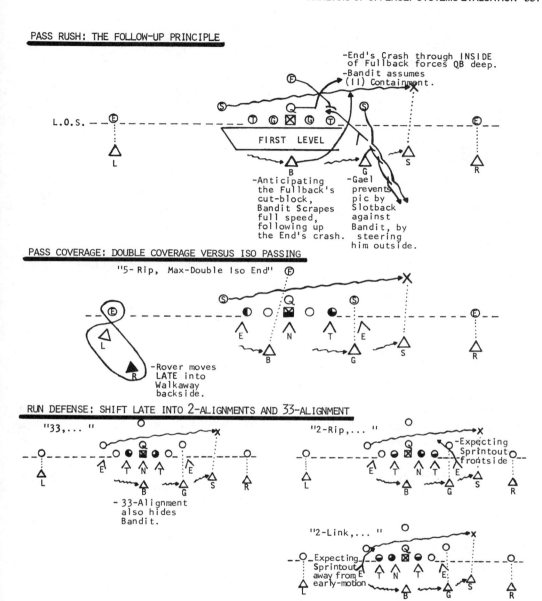

-End's Crash through INSIDE of Fullback forces QB deep.
-Bandit assumes (II) Containment.

L.O.S.

FIRST LEVEL

-Anticipating the Fullback's cut-block, Bandit Scrapes full speed, following up the End's crash.

-Gael prevents pic by Slotback against Bandit, by steering him outside.

PASS COVERAGE: DOUBLE COVERAGE VERSUS ISO PASSING

"5-Rip, Max-Double Iso End"

-Rover moves LATE into Walkaway backside.

RUN DEFENSE: SHIFT LATE INTO 2-ALIGNMENTS AND 33-ALIGNMENT

"33,... "

-33-Alignment also hides Bandit.

"2-Rip,... "

-Expecting Sprintout frontside.

"2-Link,... "

-Expecting Sprintout away from early-motion

Figure 133 Game planning against the run-and-shoot.

Planning Run Defense. Since the adjustment capability of the Second Level is so limited, First Level alignments (with shifting *as late as possible* prior to the snap) must be planned as the primary mechanisms of run defense. On the other hand, twists inside are not particularly advantageous against the sprintout attack, while slanting should be employed cautiously; a defender's getting caught slanting in the wrong direction (away from the sprintout) heightens the quarterback's run-pass options. When a running play inside is expected, the 33-alignment both solidifies the center of the defensive core and hides the Second Level defender in 1-stack (mirroring the ace fullback). Against quarterback sprintout, a 2-Alignment to the side of early-motion frees the First Level end to that side to secure his most advantageous crash angle (fig. 133, lower diagrams). In addition, preparing for a sprintout quarterback tear should be emphasized for nose and defensive tackle personnel.

Quick Passing

A number of the recent developments in offensive football, in particular quick passing and the ace fullback formations, can be traced directly to the run-and-shoot; however, the multiple offenses of today have taken these basic mechanisms several steps further. First and foremost, the philosophy of wide-open football argued so eloquently by Ellison has been universally adopted, even by the most conservative offensive coaches:

> "a revolution ... [has] started...a new order of things on the football field...in the wake of that revolution...an explosion of touchdowns...popping at the rate of one touchdown every ten plays..." (51)

In one form or another multiple formations, with early-motion, are now incorporated into every offensive system; also, passing formations utilizing four immediate receivers, timed pass routes, and automatic route adjustment within patterns are all commonplace (52). What Ellison termed "a harmless basketball cherry-pick" has, with today's high-powered offenses, evolved into a covert, highly sophisticated technique ...because the pic is *just as illegal* as it was a quarter-century ago. The quick mechanism of the run-and-shoot—short passes thrown almost immediately—is revolutionizing the game in the eighties: the sprintout quarterback has been replaced by taller personnel who can throw over huge offensive linemen; the line gaps between these linemen have all but disappeared, and pass rushers are now repulsed by a wall of arms and hands as these linemen stand shoulder-to-shoulder. The defensive flanks are still being threatened, only now by strong-armed quarterbacks throwing quickly out to one side or holding the football slightly longer, then throwing deep. The fullback's cut block frontside against the taller defenders of today remains the most predictable element in the quick passing attack, only now cut blocking serves to force the defenders to lower their hands (so that they cannot interfere with the pass).

Threatening Pass Rush. Its proponents claim the quick passing is impossible to rush effectively, because the football is released so quickly. Therefore, *threatening* maximal pass rush a majority of the time provides the next best alternative, in order to *predict* the type of pass with a degree of certainty: with spread receivers and ace (or empty) backfield, the pass protection afforded by this formation does not permit $2\frac{1}{2}$-second passing against the First Level's 5-man rush. Besides threatening pressure, the only other mechanism recommended against quick involves various twists, again shifting as late as possible into the required First Level alignment: tackle-nose twists

AGAINST PIC PATTERNS

-ZONE MECHANISM:

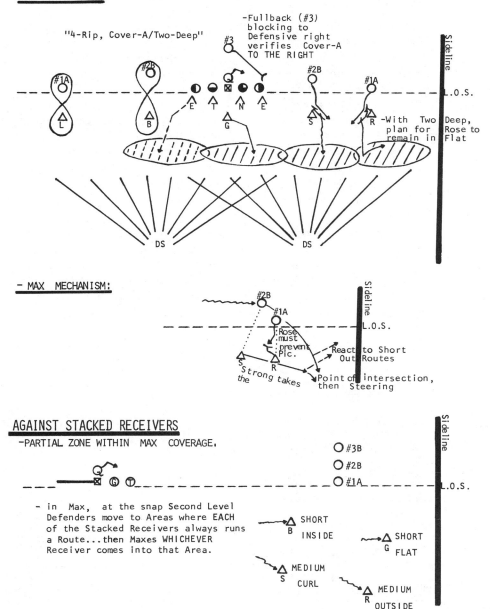

"4-Rip, Cover-A/Two-Deep"

-Fullback (#3)
blocking to
Defensive right
verifies Cover-A
TO THE RIGHT

-With Two Deep,
plan for Rose to
remain in Flat

- MAX MECHANISM:

Rose
must
prevent
Pic.

React to Short
Out Routes

Strong takes
the

Point of intersection,
then Steering

AGAINST STACKED RECEIVERS

-PARTIAL ZONE WITHIN MAX COVERAGE.

- in Max, at the snap Second Level
Defenders move to Areas where EACH
of the Stacked Receivers always runs
a Route...then Maxes WHICHEVER
Receiver comes into that Area.

SHORT
INSIDE

SHORT
FLAT

MEDIUM
CURL

MEDIUM
OUTSIDE

Figure 134 Technical adjustments in pass coverage against quick passing.

(T.N.T.) should be planned as change-ups to add variation into the First Level's short-lived rushes, while the pass-block mechanism is initiated by a tackle-end twist (see final section of chapter 4).

Planning Pass Coverage. Since so much of the defensive responsibility falls to coverage personnel, many elements in the 2-level system are tailor-made to defend against quick passing. Hard-to-medium alignment against *every* immediate receiver is possible with mirroring, and this may be followed up by aggressive directional technique; therefore, until one full second has elapsed most coverages appear (almost) identical. And the system itself is very adaptable: for example, employing Rover for special double-coverages (fig. 133, middle diagram); special verification of the -A/-B/-C mechanism according to the *initial* movement of the No. 3 mobile offense personnel (fig. 134, upper diagram); and so on. In addition, technical adjustments can be implemented against the unique patterns that are an integral part of quick passing: saturating specific underneath zones; playing max but fighting through any pic's; even planning a partial zone mechanism within max coverage (fig. 134, upper through lower diagrams, respectively).

Planning Run Defense. Finally, even though running is not the primary offensive mechanism of the quick-pass offense, run defense must be carefully planned according to the specific mechanisms an offense employs, particularly against the variety of delayed running plays developed in the eighties. Primarily, this becomes the responsibility of the First Level, because often there are few Second Level personnel in the core at the snap to make adjustments, as explained in the last section.

Notes

1. To be included, a system must have been *widely* accepted over a period of years, with several coaching texts published on that system.

2. Ironically, Coach Wilkinson and his staff also were forced to defense the split-T, so many teams began using this offense *against* Oklahoma.

3. Conversely, the longer a pitch is delayed, the further downfield wide receivers are able to run off the Second Level, negating their containment.

4. This upset was at the time comparable to one of the recent Super Bowl champions being humiliated 35-10 by one of the recent U.S.F.L. champions, a seemingly improbable event; in 1949, it was the newly formed Cleveland Browns, upstarts at that time but superbly coached by Paul Brown, who upset the Eagles.

5. At the present time this dictates *two* running backs; however, this appears to be changing rapidly: the combination of two tight ends (creating eight line-gaps) and only an ace backfielder is also proving very successful in the eighties and, as running quarterbacks become more prevalent, with only an ace backfielder this would satisfy the requirements for two running backs.

6. The triple option provides a case in point: a play mechanism specifically designed to operate *against the weakside*; in fact, more effective than running to strength the majority of the time.

7. The draw was perfected initially by the Cleveland Browns in the fifties (27); the run-to-daylight was one of several mechanisms popularized by Vince Lombardi and his great Packer teams of the six-

ties. (Coach Lombardi preached its principles so much that his first book on football was entitled *Run to Daylight* (28)).

8. An opponent's triple-option package would be an example of such a grouping.

9. Mirroring an offensive backfielder, normally if that Second Level defender were to sprint to deep

coverage at the snap, the core defense *against the run* could be seriously weakened.

10. Interestingly, five years later in his own text Woody Hayes' prose was laced with quotes from Sun Tzu (c. 500 B.C.) to Shakespeare to President Harry Truman, with anecdotal reflections from "Billy" Sherman (as Coach Hayes referred to the famous general of the Civil War).

References

1. PEPPER ROGERS and HOMER SMITH, *Installing Football's Wishbone-T Attack* (West Nyack, N.Y.: Parker Publ. Co., Inc., 1973), p. 9.

2. PETE DYER, *Coaching Football's Split 4 - 4 Multiple Defense* (West Nyack, N.Y.: Parker Publ. Co., Inc., 1980), p. 215.

3. ARA PARSEGHIAN and TOM PAGNA, *Parseghian and Notre Dame Football* (Notre Dame, Ind.: Men-In-Motion, 1972), pp. 94-104.

4. H. O. FRITZ CRISLER, *Modern Football* (New York: McGraw-Hill Book Co., Inc., 1949).

5. CLARK SHAUGHNESSY, RALPH JONES, and GEORGE HALAS, *The Modern "T" Formation with Man-In-Motion* (Chicago: copyrighted and published by Shaughnessy, Jones & Halas, 1941).

6. CHARLES BUD WILKINSON, *Oklahoma Split-T Football* (Englewood Cliffs, N.J.: Prentice-Hall, Inc., 1952), pp. vii-x.

7. JIM M. TATUM and WARREN K. GIESE, *Coaching Football and the Split-T Formation* (Dubuque, Iowa: Wm. C. Brown Co. Publ., 1953), pp. 153-154.

8. DALE FOSTER, *The Slanting Monster Defense in Football* (West Nyack, N.Y.: Parker Publ. Co., Inc., 1970).

9. JIM WACKER and DON MORTON, *The Explosive Veer Offense for Winning Football* (West Nyack, N.Y.: Parker Publ. Co., Inc., 1980), pp. 15-18.

10. ESCO SARKKINEN, "Defensive end play," *Football Coaching*, compiled by the American Football Coaches Association; editor: Dick Herbert (New York: Charles Scribner's Sons, 1981), pp. 136-137.

11. DAVID M. NELSON and FOREST EVASHEVSKI, *Scoring Power with the Winged-T* (Dubuque, Iowa: Wm. C. Brown Co. Publ., 1957).

12. DAVID M. NELSON and FOREST EVASHEVSKI, *The Modern Winged-T Playbook* (Dubuque, Iowa: Wm. C. Brown Co. Publ., 1961).

13. JIM BOUMA and JOHN C. CAPLIN, Jr., *The Delaware-Style Wing-T for High School Football* (West Nyack, N.Y.: Parker Publ. Co., Inc., 1975).

14. HARRY CLARKE, *Wing-T Multiple Offense for High School Football.* (Englewood Cliffs, N.J.: Prentice-Hall, Inc., 1962), pp. 20-23.

15. WOODY HAYES, *Hot Line To Victory* (Columbus, Ohio: copyrighted by W. Woodrow Hayes, 1969), pp. 129-131.

16. NORM VANBROCKLIN, *Passing, Punting, Quarterbacking* (New York: Ronald Press Co., 1961), pp. 19-30.

17. DARRELL ROYAL and BLACKIE SHERROD, *Darrell Royal Talks Football* (Englewood Cliffs, N.J.: Prentice-Hall, Inc., 1963), pp.61, 171.

18. HAYES, *Hot Line To Victory*, p. 64.

19. VINCE LOMBARDI, *Vince Lombardi on Football*, edited by G.L. Flynn (New York: Galahad Books, 1973), pp. 92-96.

20. NICK METROKOTSAS, *The Complete Book of Offensive Line Play* (West Nyack, N.Y.: Parker Publ. Co., Inc., 1977), Part III: pp. 130-173.

21. HAMPTON POOL, *Fly-T Football* (Englewood Cliffs, N.J.: Prentice-Hall, Inc., 1960).

22. MAX R. SPILSBURY, *Slot-T Football* (Englewood Cliffs, N.J.: Prentice-Hall, Inc., 1961).

23. Ibid, p. 3.

24. LEN DAWSON and BOB BILLINGS, *Inside Quarterbacking* (Chicago: Henry Regnery Co., 1972), pp. 59-63.

25. LARRY GIOVACCHINI, "The iso-Veer series with a dash of Wing-T". *The Best in Football from Scholastic Coach* (New York: Scholastic Athletic Services, 1970), pp. 125-128.

26. VINCE CAPARO, "Specialty plays from the Delaware Wing-T," *Athletic Journal*, 48: 32-33, 1978.

27. HAYES, *Hot Line To Victory*, pp. 129-130.

28. VINCE LOMBARDI and W. C. HEINZ, *Run To Daylight*, series edited by Red Smith (Englewood Cliffs, N.J.: Prentice-Hall, Inc., 1963).

29. LOMBARDI, *Vince Lombardi on Football*, pp. 19-53.

30. J. F. EDWARDS, *Canadian Football* (Toronto: Copp Clark Co., Ltd., 1947), pp. 87-89.

31. CRISLER, *Modern Football*, pp. 75, 131.

32. LOMBARDI, *Vince Lombardi on Football*, pp. 107-111.

33. GLENN ELLISON, *Run-and-Shoot Football: Offense of the Future* (West Nyack, N.Y.: Parker Publ. Co., Inc., 1965).

34. HOWARD SCHNELLENBERGER and GARY STEVENS, "Miami's 50 series: 3-step dropback pass," *Athletic Journal*, 63: 8-13, 1983.

35. HAL LOCKHART, "A simple one-step, drop-back, short passing game," *Scholastic Coach*, 53:28-30 & 106, 1983.

36. WALT HARRIS, "Tennessee's quick game package," *Scholastic Coach*, 54:28-31 and 77, 1984.

37. ESCO SARKKINEN, "Defensive end play," *Football Coaching*, p. 136.

38. DYER, *Coaching Football's Split 4 - 4 Multiple Defense*, pp. 21-22, & 31.

39. ELLISON, *Run-and-Shoot Football: Offense of the Future*, p. vii.

40. Ibid, pp. ix and xi.

41. Ibid, p. 38.

42. Ibid, p. 43.

43. Ibid, pp. 55 and 64.

44. Ibid, p.62.

45. Ibid, p. x.

46. Ibid, p. 8.

47. Ibid, pp. 1-2.

48. Ibid, chapters 12, 11, and 10, respectively.

49. Ibid, pp. 70 and 72.

50. Ibid, p. 59.

51. Ibid, p. ix.

52. HARRIS, "Tennessee's quick game package," pp. 28-31 and 77

GLOSSARY*

ACE. The offensive backfield formation containing only one running back, usually the fullback, positioned directly behind the quarterback.

ACTION; BACKFIELD-ACTION. The synchronized, directional movement of the backfielders executing the offensive play, including the quarterback's actions.

ALIGNMENT.* The positioning of the First Level along the line of scrimmage in the core.

ALLEY. Assigned lanes for First Level defenders through which they can rush the passer.

AREAS.* The seven locations in the offense's formation — designated Areas A, B, C and the Back Area (fig. 40) — where its mobile personnel may be positioned.

BACK; BACKFIELDER. At the snap, the mobile personnel positioned in the offensive Back Area who carry the football and are eligible to catch passes.

BACKSIDE. The side of the offensive formation away from the direction in which the football moves after the snap.

BALL CARRIER. The back who carries the football on running plays.

BANDIT.* The Second Level defender mirroring the No. 2 mobile offensive personnel to the opposite side of the offensive formation from Strong.

BLITZ. An augmented defensive pass rush, with personnel other than the normal linemen rushing the passer.

BLOCKER. An offensive player who initiates contact with a defender for the express purpose of preventing him from tackling the ball carrier.

BOOTLEG; BOOTLEG-ACTION. On passes, a move made in which, while the backfield action moves to one side of the formation, the quarterback, faking but keeping the football, moves in the other direction.

BUMP-AND-RUN. A very close, aggressive, inside technique of man-to-man pass coverage.

CADENCE. The words and numbers called by the quarterback at the line of scrimmage to initiate the offensive play.

CALL. Verbalization of a set of instructions (words, numbers, etc.) in the defensive huddle which designate First Level alignment, possible stunt(s), and specific pass coverage.

CHECKOFF. The quarterback's *verbal* changing of the offense's play, or portions of it, at the line of scrimmage.

CLOSED; CLOSED ALIGNMENT.* Positional alignment of a First Level tackle on an offensive guard.

CONTAINMENT; CONTAIN RESPONSIBILITY. A defensive responsibility to force the ball carrier (or quarterback, on sprintouts) to turn inside, into pursuit tacklers.

CORE.* An eliptical area along the line of scrimmage encompassing the offensive line and backfield and the defenders directly opposing them.

CORNER; CORNERBACK. Name usually given to the two *widest* deepbacks in the defensive backfield's alignment across the field.

COVERAGE. The action of defending against a pass.

CRACK; CRACKBACK. Term used to alert a defender inside that an outside wide receiver is in early-motion and may block back on him.

CRASH.* Technique whereby a defender immediately pressures the ball carrier

---

* Starred terms throughout the glossary have a meaning or wording unique to the 2-level defense; ones not starred include the more general football terminology or jargon.

from the outside, maintains his outside leverage and forces the ball carrier to turn upfield inside of him.

CROSSING. A pass route commencing from one side of the offensive formation across the defense at plus five to fifteen yards' depth, to a reception area on the other side.

CUE.* A defender's *pre-snap* read.

CUSHION; TIGHT CUSHION.* Max pass coverage of the tight end (usually) by the First Level end; and double coverage by both the First Level end and the mirroring Second Level defender against a tight end or slotback.

CURL. A semicircle run by a receiver at the end of his pass route to the inside back towards the quarterback.

CUTBACK. A secondary run responsibility assigned to backside Second Level personnel in the core: if the ball carrier cuts backside away from the intended hole, by trailing the football this defender remains in a position to move up and make the tackle.

CUT BLOCK. A block made against the lower portion of the defender's body in an effort to topple or trip the defender.

DEEPBACK. The player positioned the deepest off the line of scrimmage in the three-level model of defense.

DEEP 1/3.* Name designating the two outside, deep defensive pass zones beginning at plus fifteen to eighteen yards deep.

DEEP 2/3.* Name designating the Middle 1/3 *plus* one of the adjacent Deep 1/3 pass zones, beginning at plus fifteen to eighteen yards deep.

DEEP SAFETY.* The defender positioned twenty-eight yards deep from the line of scrimmage who enforces the end line across the field at eighteen-plus yards; in the two-level Defense, there may be one or two deep safeties on the field.

DOG.* Term that calls Second Level de-

fenders mirroring offensive backfielders in the core to fire (i.e., to join the First Level in rushing the quarterback).

DOUBLE COVERAGE. Max technique whereby two defenders are assigned to cover one pass receiver man-to-man.

DOWN AND DISTANCE. A means of defining strategical situations during a game; third down and long yardage usually defines a passing situation.

DRAW. A delayed running play which initially looks like a pass.

DRILL. Performance of repetitive football skills; formats include fundamental, small group, and larger team drills.

DROP-BACK. Type of pass-action in which the quarterback drops straight back from center, setting up to throw.

DROP-OFF. Technique by which zone pass defenders move away from the line of scrimmage to their assigned target areas.

EAGLE. An inside-eye alignment by First Level defenders against the offensive linemen across from them on the line of scrimmage.

EARLY-MOTION; IN MOTION. Prior to the snap, lateral movement across the offensive formation by a mobile offensive player (*see:* JET, ROCKET, WAGGLE).

ELIGIBLE RECEIVERS. The offensive ends, backfielder(s), and wide receiver(s) who are eligible to catch forward passes, including the quarterback.

EMPTY.* An offensive formation with no backfielders (other than the quarterback).

ENDS. The defensive ends are two of the five defenders in the First Level, positioned on the outsides; opposite the offensive tight ends, eligible pass receivers possessing size (of a blocking lineman).

END LINE.* An area across the field enforced by the deep safety, beginning at eighteen-plus yards from the line of scrimmage.

ENVELOPE. A combination of two or three

pass routes; with *all* eligible pass receivers executing their assignments, this is referred to as a pattern.

EVEN; EVEN ALIGNMENT.* The nose's alignment head-on one of the offensive Guards.

EXECUTION. The planned action of sequenced movements and techniques: implemented by the offense to advance the football, or by the defense to stop its advancement.

FILL. Forward movement by Second Level defenders in the core to meet offensive movement (and the ball carrier) coming directly at them.

FIRST LEVEL.* The five defenders (nose, two tackles and two ends) positioned along the line of scrimmage and opposing the offensive linemen.

FLAG. A pass route in which the receiver breaks deep and towards the sideline at the goal line.

FLANKER. *See* IMMEDIATE RECEIVER.

FLARE. An offensive backfielder moving outside into the shallow flat area to catch a forward pass.

FLAT. The defensive pass zones immediately adjacent to each sideline and from twelve to fifteen yards deep off the line of scrimmage.

FLEX. Term used to describe when the tight end splits out from his offensive tackle five to seven yards.

FLOOD. A universal pass pattern against one of the flat areas, sending more receivers into that zone than pass defenders assigned to the area.

FOLLOW-UP. In the core the action of the second defensive personnel scraping aggressively off the tail of a teammate, the initial penetration defender, in order to exert pressure, secure secondary (II) containment against a sprintout quarterback or running back moving outside.

FORCE UNIT. In the three-level model of defense, the personnel responsible for defending against the run and rushing the passer.

FOREARM LIFT. Use of the forearm and upper arm to deliver a forceful blow in a lifting motion to the chest of a blocker.

FORMATION. Alignment of the offensive personnel at the snap.

FOUR POINT. A defensive stance in which both hands and both feet, in contact with the ground, form the base of support.

FREE SAFETY. In the three-level model of defense, the defender aligned twelve to fifteen yards off the line of scrimmage and playing *centerfield* in most zone coverages.

FRONTSIDE. The side of the offensive formation to which the football immediately moves post-snap.

FULLBACK. The offensive backfielder positioned directly behind the T-quarterback.

FULL HOUSE. When there are three backfielders in the offense's formation aligned in the shape of a T (*see also* POWER I *and* WISHBONE *for variations*).

FUNDAMENTALS. Coordinated body movements oriented towards football; the basic physical skills of the game—blocking, tackling, passing, catching, etc.

FUNNEL.* From a hard-to-medium depth alignment and outside shade, the aggressive directional technique employed by Second Level personnel to force an immediate receiver to the inside.

GAEL.* The Second Level defender always positioned in the middle of the Second Level, mirroring the No. 3 mobile offensive personnel.

GAME PLAN. A comprehensive summary of three to six pages handed out to defensive personnel detailing the upcoming opponent's offense and the defensive plan of attack (*see text's* Teaching Supplement).

GAPS. The two-foot areas between adjacent offensive linemen; in the 2-level Defense, six gaps are formally defined.

GOAL LINE.* An area defined as high risk for the defense, always inside its own eight-yardline and closer.

HALFBACK; RUNNING BACK. The offensive backfielder positioned beside the fullback.

HANDSHIVER. The use of hands, with arms locked, to prevent a blocker from reaching the defender's body; the point of contact is the blocker's upper arms at the shoulder pads.

HARD.* The alignment depth assumed by Second Level defenders against immediate receivers one to two yards off the line of scrimmage.

HASHMARKS. The small lines bisecting each yard stripe eighteen to twenty-two yards (depending upon the league) from each sideline and running vertically the length of the field.

HEAD-UP. Positioning of a defender, aligned nose to nose and squarely opposite an offensive blocker across the line of scrimmage from him.

HOOK PASS. An inside receiver's pass route turning in and back towards the passer at plus eight to fifteen yards downfield.

HOOK ZONE. The three defensive zones inside the flats, in the middle area of the field, up to twelve to fifteen yards deep: the shortside-, middle-, and wideside-hooks.

HUDDLE. Gathering of players prior to each play to get instructions; the play call.

I FORMATION. An offensive backfield alignment with two (or more) backs positioned in tandem directly behind the quarterback.

IMMEDIATE RECEIVER.* An offensive pass receiver positioned on or within one yard of the line of scrimmage at the snap.

INSIDE. The center of the core between offensive tackles.

INTERCEPTION. The catching of a forward pass by a defender, rather than by the intended offensive receiver: a "bingo."

ISO; ISOLATED.* When only one immediate receiver is positioned in the offensive formation to a particular side (either an Area C tight end, or an Area A or B wide receiver).

ISO-TREE. The pass routes run by a wide receiver aligned near a sideline (usually) by himself, against the Second Level defender who is isolated.

JAM.* The technique of delaying an immediate receiver on the line of scrimmage, preceding tight max pass coverage.

JET; JET ACTION.* Term designating an immediate receiver in long early-motion, towards the center, crossing from one side of the offensive formation, through the back area, coming out the other side.

KEY; KEY READING. After the snap, movement and actions by offensive personnel which give information to the defenders reading them (as the play is in progress).

LAUNCH; LAUNCH POINT. The action of and location where the quarterback releases the football on a pass downfield.

LEVELS; FIRST AND SECOND LEVELS.* A defensive level is composed of defenders executing similar techniques and performing equivalent functions in the overall scheme of the defense.

LEVERAGE; OUTSIDE LEVERAGE. An advantageous angle of approach that a defender gains against the ball carrier, by being aligned further to the outside, then maintaining this positional advantage throughout the play.

LINEBACKERS. The *third* level of defense in the three-level model (see chapter 1); positioned two to five yards off the line of scrimmage, these personnel have primary responsibility for defending both a running gap and a pass zone coverage.

LINEMEN *(offensive).* The *static* personnel positioned on the line of scrimmage: the center, two guards, and two tackles.

LINK.* Directional indicator which shifts the First Level *left* into its final alignment along the line of scrimmage.

LIVE. In drills and scrimmage, full contact between defense and offense, as in the game situation.

LOCK-UP. In drills, only initial contact is made between the defensive and offensive personnel; the defense is designated to win in lock-up, if the defender's technique is correct.

LONG EARLY-MOTION. Rocket - and jet - actions, where a mobile offensive personnel moves a substantial distance across the offense's formation to a new alignment before the snap.

LOOSE; LOOSE ALIGNMENT.* Positional alignment of a First Level end outside-eye on the offensive tight end.

L.O.S. Line of scrimmage.

LOU.* The Second Level defender mirroring the No. 1 mobile offensive personnel to the (defensive) left side of the offensive formation.

MAN BLOCKING. The offensive pattern in which each blocker is assigned to block a specific defender.

MAX; MAX-SOFT.* An aggressive technique of pass defense with an end line in force at eighteen-plus yards' depth, employing man-to-man principles; soft appended means traditional man-to-man coverage, and usually there is no end-line coverage.

MEDIUM.* The alignment depth assumed by Second Level defenders against immediate receivers three to five yards off the line of scrimmage.

MEDIUM DEPTH. The pass reception areas plus eight to fifteen yards downfield over the line of scrimmage.

MIDDLE 1/3.* Term designating the deep defensive pass zone in the center of the field, between the Deep 1/3 zones, beginning at plus fifteen to eighteen yards.

MIRROR; MIRRORING.* A positional adjustment carried out by the Second Level prior to the snap: each defender aligns himself directly across the line of scrimmage from his "mirror" (one of the five mobile offensive personnel — the backfielders and immediate receivers).

MOBILE.* Term describing the offense's five eligible pass receivers (other than the quarterback): the backfielders and immediate receivers.

MOTION. *See* EARLY-MOTION.

NEAR BACK. Usually referring to the halfback in a pro alignment, the near back is the offensive backfielder closest to the defenders aligned at the perimeters of the core.

NON-CONTACT. Drill format in which there is minimal physical contact between players: non-contact precedes LOCK-UP, THUD, and LIVE.

NOSE.* The defender always aligned in the middle of the five First Level personnel (synonyms: middle guard, nose guard).

NUMBERING.* The five mobile personnel are assigned No. 1, 2, 3, 2, and 1 according to their alignment positioning across the field in the offensive formation.

ODD; ODD ALIGNMENT.* Positional alignment of the nose head-on the offensive center.

OFF-TACKLE. The running gaps immediately outside the two offensive tackles (and inside the tight end if present in the offensive formation).

OKIE; OKLAHOMA DEFENSE. Developed in the 1950s, this defense featured a five-man line and two inside linebackers positioned over the offensive guards (2 1/2 yards off the line of scrimmage).

OPEN; OPEN ALIGNMENT.* Positional

alignment of a First Level tackle aligned on an offensive tackle.

OPTION. *See* TRIPLE OPTION.

OPTION PASS (*halfback*). On sweeps and quick pitches when the ball carrier suddenly stops and throws a forward pass.

OUTSIDE. The area towards the perimeter of the core, outside both offensive tackles.

PATTERNS. The highly structured actions and movements by offensive personnel on a given play: the coordinated movements of its blocking, the backfield's action, or the complementary routes run by the receivers on a pass play.

PERSONNEL. Synonym for player; defensive or offensive must be designated.

PLAY-ACTION. On pass plays, a specific backfield action faking a running play before showing pass.

POCKET. The protected backfield area from which the quarterback throws the football that is secured by his blockers.

POINT OF ATTACK. On running plays the gap/hole/area in the offensive line through which the ball carrier penetrates the line of scrimmage.

POSITIONS. On both offense and defense, formal player positions, with designated names, responsibilities, and techniques.

POST-SNAP. After the football has been put into play by the offensive center.

POWER I. Like the I backfield, the fullback and tailback aligned behind the quarterback, but with a fourth backfielder aligned in the halfback position either to the left or right of the I.

PREALIGNMENT. Alignment of a defense or offense before the football is snapped, but not necessarily that team's *final* alignment.

PRE-SNAP. Before the football is put into play, before the play begins.

PRO; PRO BACKFIELD. Two backs in the offense's formation with the halfback aligned beside the fullback.

PURSUIT. The course taken by defensive personnel in order to overtake and gang-tackle the ball carrier or a pass receiver (after the reception).

QUAD.* An offensive formation with four immediate receivers positioned on one side (one in Area A, two in Area B, one in Area C).

QUICK PASS PATTERNS. Passes thrown within less than 2 seconds after the snap to immediate receivers running short slant-in or -out routes, the quarterback executing a three-step dropback.

QUICK PITCH. A running play that hits outside *very quickly* by the football being lateralled (not handed) by the quarterback to the running back.

READING. *See* CUES *and* KEYS.

RECEPTION AREA. The designated location on the field for the receiver to catch a particular pass (hook, curl, etc.).

RESPONSIBILITY. Duties and field areas that personnel must defend after the snap: each defender has a hierarchy of primary and then secondary responsibilities to be carried out in rapid sequence.

RIP.* Directional indicator which shifts the First Level *right* into its final alignment.

ROCKET.* Term designating an offensive back in long early motion before the snap, leaving the backfield area moving to a C, B, or A area.

ROLL.* In "...,Cover/Two-Deep," a game-plan option for moving the two safeties immediately into the frontside Deep $1/3$ and Middle $1/3$ with quarterback sprintout action.

ROSE.* The Second Level defender mirroring the No. 1 mobile offensive personnel to the (defensive) right side of the offensive formation.

ROUTE. The course traversed by an individual receiver within a pass pattern.

ROVER. A *sixth* Second Level defender.

RUNNING BACK. *See* FULLBACK, HALF-

BACK, TAILBACK.

RUSH; PASS RUSHERS. Defenders assigned to pressure the quarterback on passes.

SCRAPE. Technique employed by Second Level player in the core to move outside to meet the football (on running plays) at the point of attack.

SCRIPT; SCRIPTED PRACTICE. The offensive plays and simulated plays to be run against the defense, carefully selected ahead of time and sequenced according to the defensive calls, in effect loading this phase of practice *in favor of* the defense.

SCREEN PASS. The defensive rush is allowed to penetrate; the quarterback, dropping very deep, loops the ball over them to the receiver (usually a running back) still on the offensive side of the line of scrimmage.

SCRIMMAGE; POINT OF SCRIMMAGE. Where the referee places the football on or between the hashmarks, in preparation for the next play.

SEAM. That point which is equidistant between two zone pass defenders; thus, a seam pass pattern attempts to take advantage of the seams in zone coverage.

SECOND LEVEL.* The five defenders (Lou, Strong, Gael, Bandit, and Rose) positioned just off the line of scrim-mage up to five to seven yards deep, who *by rule* mirror the five mobile offensive personnel (according to their numbering).

SERIES; SEQUENCE OF PLAYS. Offensive plays with similar backfield-action and blocking patterns that attack the defense at different points and areas of the core.

SHADE.* The positioning of a Second Level defender against his mirror (immediate receiver) either on his inside or outside.

SHIFTING.* A maneuver to confuse the offense's blocking patterns: rapid change from one defensive alignment to another just before the snap.

SHORTSIDE. The side of the offensive formation to the nearest sideline.

SHORTYARDAGE SITUATION. When the offense has less than two yards to go for a first down.

SHOTGUN. A special pass-oriented formation employed by the offense in long-yardage situations: the quarterback five yards behind the center, immediate receivers spread along the line of scrimmage to both sides of the formation.

SLANT.* A First Level stunt executed by the nose and one tackle: at the snap, both slant in unison in a predetermined direction.

SLOTBACK. An offensive position: the immediate receiver located in Area C, one yard off the line of scrimmage, just outside the offensive tackle.

SNAP. The action which *by rule* initiates every play: the offensive center passing the football between his legs to the quarterback.

SOFT.* The alignment depth assumed by Second Level defenders against immediate receivers seven yards off the line of scrimmage.

SPLIT-BACKS. The offensive backfield set with two running backs in the halfback positions, no personnel in the fullback position.

SPLIT END. An offensive end positioned at least seven to ten yards outside his tackle on the line of scrimmage; a passing threat more than a blocker.

SPLIT; SPLIT RULE. The rule permitting no more than seven feet maximum between adjacent First Level defenders.

SPREAD FORMATION. An offensive formation with at least two immediate receivers to either side; more a passing than a running formation.

SPRINTOUT. A play in which the quarterback, running with the football, moves out of the back area in order to pass or continue running (Synonym: quarterback rollout; however, *roll* has a unique meaning in the 2-level defense)

STACK.* A Second Level defender's positioning himself directly behind a First Level teammate in the core.

STAGGER. The heel-to-toe relationship between the feet.

STALK-BLOCK. A blocking technique employed in the open field by wide receivers against their mirroring Second Level defenders.

STANCE. The body positioning of personnel (both defensive and offensive) preparatory to the snap.

STATIC.* The descriptive term for the five offensive linemen — the center, two guards, and two tackles — whose positioning in their formation almost never varies.

STEER.* From a hard-to-medium-depth alignment and inside shade, the aggressive directional technique employed by Second Level personnel to force an immediate receiver to the outside.

STRENGTH; TO STRENGTH. The side of the offensive formation where the greatest number of potential blockers align; usually to the tight end's side.

STRONG.* The Second Level defender mirroring the No. 2 mobile offensive personnel to the strength side of the offensive formation.

STUNT; STUNTING. Coordinated games executed by First and Second Level defenders in the core to confuse offensive blocking, to strengthen the defensive core against the run, or to augment its pass rush.

SWEEP. A power running play that hits through the off-end area with blocker(s) preceding the running back through the hole.

SWIM TECHNIQUE. Final move in pass rush technique, in which the defender, after turning the blocker's shoulders and moving by him, brings his trailing arm up and over the blocker's helmet.

SWING PASS. A pass to a backfielder still behind the line of scrimmage who is running laterally (toward a sideline rather than upfield).

SWITCH.* A Second Level stunt where two defenders switch pass coverage assignments: the defender in the 2-Stack maxes the tight end immediately to his outside; the defender mirroring the tight end (in Area C) crashes and maxes the near back (if the play is a pass).

TACKLE. The technique of bringing the ball carrier to the ground.

TACKLES.* Designated positions on both offense and First Level defense.

TAILBACK. In the I formation, the deepest running back positioned directly behind the fullback.

TECHNIQUE. The pattern and sequencing of various body parts and movements in performing the fundamental skills of football (see fundamentals).

T-FORMATION. *See* FULL HOUSE.

THREE POINT. A defensive stance in which only one hand and both feet, in contact with the ground, form the base of support.

THUD. In drills, a continuation of lock-up with sustained maximal force and resistance by both defense and offense; not yet full-out live contact. The aim is for no one to fall to the ground (where injuries occur) during each drill sequence.

TIGHT; TIGHT ALIGNMENT.* Positional alignment of a First Level end outside-eye on the offensive tackle to his side.

TIGHT CUSHION.* *See* CUSHION.

TIGHT END. An offensive position: the immediate receiver who is also a blocking threat, located in Area C on the line of scrimmage in a three-point stance, just outside of the offensive tackle.

THROWBACK PASS. A passing play in which the quarterback, sprinting in one direction, stops, sets up, then throws back across the field.

T-QUARTERBACK. A play in which the quarterback is handed the snap directly by the offensive center, being positioned immediately behind the center.

TRAILER.* The backside First Level end who chases the ball carrier from behind is responsible for containing reverses and bootleg passes.

TRAP. On running plays, an inside-out block against a defender at the point of attack by an offensive blocker, travelling parallel to and back of the line of scrimmage.

TREE; PASSING TREE. The repertoire of pass routes that can be run by any individual offensive receiver.

TRIPLE. An offensive formation with three immediate receivers positioned on one side (one receiver in Area A, B, and C, respectively).

TRIPLE OPTION. An offensive running play in which the ball carrier, one of three backs—the fullback, quarterback, or a halfback—is determined by the reactions of defense *during* the play, and not predetermined by offense's huddle call.

TWIN. An offensive formation with two immediate receivers positioned on one side (in Areas A and B, two wide receivers; in A and C, a flanker-tight end; or in B and C, a wingback-tight end formation).

TWIST. A First Level stunt where two defenders initially cross, one behind the other, then assume each other's run and pass responsibilities throughout the remainder of that play.

TWO-POINT. A standing stance in which only the defender's feet form the base of support.

UNCOVERED LINEMAN (*offensive*). A static lineman whom no First Level defender aligns directly in front of across the line of scrimmage.

UNDERNEATH; UNDERNEATH COVERAGE. The five defensive zone targets across the field from sideline to sideline, located (approx.) twelve to fifteen yards deep; their exact locations vary according to the offensive pass pattern on any given play.

WAGGLE.* Term designating an immediate receiver in short early-motion, toward a sideline, moving from one area (C, B, or A) to another on the same side of the offensive formation (*compare with* JET *and* ROCKET).

WALKAWAY. An alignment adjustment for implementation by a Second Level defender mirroring the tight end, against a strong outside running offense: moving to the outside and deepening to secure greater leverage against the threat of this formation (fig. 29).

WEAKSIDE. The side of the offensive formation away from strength, where fewer potential blockers are aligned.

WIDE RECEIVER. *See* IMMEDIATE RECEIVER.

WIDESIDE. The side of the offensive formation to the furthest sideline, across the field.

WINGBACK. An offensive position: the immediate receiver located one yard off the line of scrimmage, just outside of the tight end, in a three-point stance; this player is (usually) positioned on the imaginary boundry separating Area C from B, but is identified as being in Area B.

WISHBONE. An offensive formation in which there are three backfielders, with the two halfbacks aligned 1 1/2 yards deeper than the fullback, forming a Y.

YARDLINES. The lines that mark off the 100-yard field between the two goal lines lengthwise in yards; YARDSTRIPES are painted across the field every five yards.

ZONES. Designated pass defense areas.

INDEX

Ace, 121, 331, 335, 338
Alignment:
    head-on, 137
    inside eye, 137
Alternate pass read, 238
Alternate run keys, 247
Analysis of offense, 274, 282
Arm-over/arm-under, 198

Backfield-action, 283
Backpedal, 235
Balanced attack, 316, 320
Balanced offense, 322
Bandit, 33, 85, 102, 246, 280, 281, 336
Blitzing, 18
Breakdown, 138
Bump-and-run, 228
Byte, 45

Camp, Walter, 3, 5, 8
Chicago Bears, 111, 309
Coaching pyramid, 1
Combination coverage, 333
Common denominators of defense, 324
Concealment, 316
Containment, 79, 153, 313, 335

Contain unit, 16
Core defense, 327
Core receivers, 290
Core structure, 280
Cornerback, 84, 309
Counters, 173, 179, 287
Cover, 49, 96, 101
Coverage adjustments, 281
Crack-back, 173, 238
Crash, 33, 52, 144, 150, 172, 313, 325, 335
Cutback, 144, 156, 164, 168
Cut blocking, 206, 208, 215, 338

Deepbacks, 217
Deep safety, 31, 35, 45, 97, 132, 253, 281
    action-decision, 262, 264
    bounce and glide, 264
    enforcement, 255
    enforcement drills, 262
    outfielder drill, 264
    read drills, 264
    read sequence, 253, 257
    zone technique, 259
Deep zones:
    deep 1/3, 96
    middle 1/3, 96
Defenses:

Defenses *(cont.)*
  3-4 defense, 4, 15, 118, 132
  6-1 defense, 4, 6
  6-5 goal line defense, 24, 26, 124, 128
  goal line defense, 123, 128
  monster defense, 17, 275, 309, 318, 323
  multiple defense, 318
  okie 5-2 defense, 4, 118, 309
  pro 4-3 defense, 4, 6, 15
  shortyardage defense, 123
  situational defense, 324
Defensive:
  concealment, 23, 82
  continuity, 24
  mobility, 21
  simplicity, 24
Defensive game adjustments, 303
Defensive pursuit, 284
Defensive responsibility:
  containment, 79, 143, 313, 335
  primary, 137, 158
  pursuit, 79, 137, 156, 173
  secondary, 137, 158
  trailer, 143, 172
Delayed running, 207, 287, 331
Diagrams (color-coded), 135
Directional techniques, 291
Dive-option, 313
Dives, 321
Double-coverage, 96, 113, 128, 236, 258, 336
Double-team blocking, 275, 321
Draw, 12, 207, 287, 321
Drills:
  1-stack drills, 162, 223
  1-stack + area C drills, 173, 223
  2-stack drills, 164, 223
  alley drill, 200
  area C stack drills, 116, 223
  basic unit drill, 160
  beaten outfielder drill, 248, 268
  cone signal drill, 208
  crash drill, 150, 207, 215
  cross-key drill, 168, 223, 284
  down-out-down drill, 248, 268
  half-line drill, 202, 207, 215
  I-backs drill, 170, 223, 284
  jam technique drill, 173
  lock-up, 139
  lollipop drill, 246
  mirror drills, 227, 250, 268
  one-on-one drill, 150, 200, 207
  slant key drill, 140, 152, 200
  stack drill, 153, 159, 202
  team drills, 193
  three-on-one, 140, 150

Eagle adjustment, 279
Early-motion, 10, 17, 21, 88, 230, 238, 247, 252, 276, 290, 319, 321, 331, 336, 338
Ellison, Glenn, 333
Empty, 338
End, defensive, 6, 32, 83, 97, 102, 143, 279, 309, 324, 327
  fundamentals, 50, 204, 210
  key reading, 205
  leverage angle, 279
  loose alignment, 53, 206, 335
  pass coverage, 210, 212
  tight alignment, 53, 205, 279
  zone drop-off, 213
End line, 37, 233
Enforcement, 96, 113, 248

Faurot, Don, 309
Field organization, 133, 134, 192
Fill, 154, 158, 164, 168, 172
Film analysis, 274, 300
Finesse technique, 199
First-and-ten analysis, 303
First level, 3, 31, 279, 324
  alignments, 48, 54, 111, 313, 330
  call, 58
  personnel, 43
Flat zone, 295
Follow-up, 336
Force unit, 16, 37
Forearm lift, 154
Forearm shiver, 164, 170, 172
Formation:
  strength, 278
  tendencies, 278
Forward pass, 4
Free safety, 260
Fullback quick trap, 321
Funnel, 231, 259
Future models of defense, 21

Gael, 33, 85, 104, 245, 281, 325
Game plan, 37, 54, 57, 95, 109, 150, 158, 164, 168, 175, 296, 303, 324
Geo blocking, 321

Halas, George, 309
Halfback option-pass, 173
Half-time adjustments, 298, 303
Hashmarks, 252, 276, 318

Hayes, Woody, 333
Hook pass, 334
Hook zone, 295

I-formation, 17, 309, 311, 318, 319, 322
Immediate receivers, 90
In-game:
    analysis, 296
    communication, 297
    implementation, 272
Initial contact, 198
Isolated, 102
Isolation blocking, 318

Jam technique, 65, 154, 173
Jet-action, 87, 321

Key reading, 138, 146, 158, 194
    basic keys, 140, 194
    key-man, 138, 146
    key-triangle, 138, 146
    secondary keys, 138, 140, 194

Launch-point, 262
Leverage, 118
Linebackers, 6, 215, 217, 275, 280, 321
    drills, 223
    interchanging, 275
Line play, 4, 11
Link, 54, 59
Long-yardage, 281
Lou, 33, 44, 84, 106, 146

Machinery of offense, 272
Mirroring, 31, 104, 276, 331
Misdirection plays, 72
Mismatching, 294
Mobile offensive personnel, 33, 84, 87, 89, 102
Multiple attack, 322
Multiple formations, 10, 84, 87, 319, 338
Multiple offense, 10, 316

Nose, 32, 338
    even, 52, 279, 327
    fundamentals, 194
    odd, 52, 327

Numerical rating, 275, 314, 327

Offensive areas, 88, 90
Offensive formations:
    quad, 102
    triple, 88, 102
    twin, 87
    visual definition, 89
Offensive keys, 136, 267
Offensive line-gaps, 33, 319
Offensive linemen:
    covered, 156
    uncovered, 158
Offensive mechanisms, 273
Offensive personnel, 319
Off-tackle play, 173, 284
Ohio State, 39
One-platoon football, 318
Option-pitch, 309
Outside linebacker, 6, 12, 144, 173
Outside running, 275
Overshift mechanism, 76

Pass blocking, 138, 195
Pass defense, 192, 278, 281, 300
    combinations, 86, 96, 100, 106
    cover-A, 106, 128, 294, 314, 324, 330, 333
    cover-B, 106, 128, 294, 314, 333
    cover-C, 104, 294, 314, 333
    cover/two deep, 111, 115, 291, 294, 314, 336
    curl zone, 122
    deep zones, 95
    flat zones, 95
    hook zones, 95
    horizontal landmarks, 93
    man-to-man, 5, 18, 235, 286
    max, 49, 83, 96, 219, 221, 233, 291, 295, 300, 336
    max/double, 97, 113, 281
    max-soft, 97, 235
    max/two deep, 111
    saturation, 96
    shortside square, 95, 109, 115
    tight cushion, 97
    traditional zones, 96
    two-deep, 281, 318
    underneath coverage, 95, 109
    vertical landmarks, 93
    zone, 5, 12, 18, 83, 86, 90
Passing game:
    bootleg pass, 144, 146, 173, 208, 267
    curl patterns, 243, 291
    dropback passing, 12, 118, 197, 239, 295, 323, 330

Passing game *(cont.)*
  flood patterns, 243, 291
  hook patterns, 244
  horizontal stretching, 336
  iso passing routes, 336
  play-action, 166, 175, 197, 239, 267, 294, 330
  quick, 12, 239, 323, 330, 338
  rollout, 323
  run-and-shoot, 12, 333
  screen, 4, 12, 197, 207, 331
  seam patterns, 243, 244
  sprintout, 12, 83, 144, 208, 223, 239, 279, 327, 330
  throwbacks, 268
Pass pattern recognition, 238
Pass patterns:
  curl, 291
  exploiting normal movement, 295
  flood, 291
  horizontal stretching, 291
  individual routes, 239
  isolating, 294
  responsibility dilemma, 294
  seam, 291
  vertical stretching, 291
Pass read, 213
Pass rush, 12, 44, 83, 96, 106, 120, 194, 278, 291, 295, 300, 331
Pass scrimmage, 227, 250, 268
Pass skeleton, 227, 250, 268
Personal match-ups, 274
Photo sequences, 176-189
Pic-action, 227, 335, 338
Positional manipulations, 279
Post-game analysis, 272, 274, 299
Power formations, 275, 309
Power off-tackle, 320
Power of stacks, 281
Power running, 284
Power technique, 198
Pre-game preparation, 272
Pre-snap shifting, 136, 143, 194, 279, 314, 327, 338
Principles of leverage, 273
Professional football, 4
Pro-T, 318, 321

Quarterback-option, 309
Quick pitch, 144, 153, 173, 322
Quick trap, 327

Reverses, 144, 146, 170, 173, 287
Rip, 54, 59
Rose, 33, 44, 84, 106, 246

Rotation, 156
Rover, 128, 281, 327, 333, 336, 340
Royal, Darrel, 309
Run defense, 16, 44, 72, 74, 278, 300
Run offense, 282
Run-to-daylight, 321

Scouting, 273
Scrape, 154, 164, 172, 325, 336
Search, 146, 172
Second level, 4, 31, 279, 327
  directional techniques, 231
  hard alignment, 228
  inside shade, 229
  medium alignment, 229
  not-stacked, 227
  outside shade, 229
  pass coverage, 219, 233
  personnel, 44
  soft alignment, 229
  stacked, 46, 62, 219
  stance, 219
  zone technique, 222, 236
Shaughnessy, Clark, 309
Shortside, 93, 102
Shotgun, 331
Shoulder technique, 145, 164
Shuffle technique, 145, 154, 170, 230
Sideline adjustments, 297
Signals, 29, 45, 71
Single-digit alignments, 54, 314
Single-wing, 309, 318, 322, 331
Sixth offensive line-gap, 78
Slo-play, 313, 316
Slotback, 12, 87, 154, 319, 323, 336
Speed running plays, 283
Split end, 17, 333
Spread formation, 8, 331, 338
Stacks, 62, 279
  1-stack, 62, 290, 327, 338
  2-stack, 62, 290, 325, 327, 330
  area C stack, 62, 71
  power of stacks, 74
Stalk-block, 313
Static offensive personnel, 32
Statistical analysis, 301
Steer, 231, 246, 259
Strategy analysis, 302
Strong, 33, 85, 102, 246, 280, 325, 327
Stunts, 48, 66
  cushion, 49, 71, 212, 330
  dog, 49, 69, 284, 330
  slant, 48, 66, 137, 152, 284

switch, 49, 64, 71, 173, 330, 336
twists, 48, 67, 121, 152, 284, 316, 336, 338
Support patterns, 314
Support personnel, 80
Sweeps, 144, 156, 173, 279, 284, 322
Swim technique, 198
Systems of football, 29
    balanced offenses, 316, 324
    pass-oriented offenses, 331
    run-oriented offenses, 308

Tackle, defensive, 32, 325, 338
    closed alignment, 52
    fundamentals, 194
    open alignment, 52, 325
Tackling the quarterback, 199
Tailback, 88, 319, 322, 331
Tailback search, 72, 146, 287, 322
Tatum, Jim, 309
Teaching model, 135
Teaching supplement, 132
Tear, 72, 138, 325, 338
T-formation, 5, 10, 273, 309, 316, 319, 322
Third level of defense, 5
Throttleup, 138
Tight end, 11, 154, 275, 321, 324
Time-outs, 298
Trailer, 72
Trap-blocking 275
Triple option, 17, 286, 311
Two-level defense, 31
    concealment, 40
    continuity, 42

core, 48
multiple alignments, 40
outnumbering, 38
simplicity, 42
tactical principles, 36
Two-platoon football, 6

U.C.L.A., 39, 241
Universal pass patterns, 241, 253, 267
Universal rules, 54-57, 97, 100, 101
University of Oklahoma, 311
University of Texas, 309
Uppercut technique, 199

VanBrocklin, Norm, 6
Veer-option, 311
Visual verification, 84

Walkaway, 64, 281, 285, 290, 330
Wide receivers, 287, 316, 319
Wideside, 93, 102
Wilkinson, Bud, 309
Wingback, 275, 322
Wing-T, 309, 318, 321
Wishbone, 286, 309

Zone coverage, 281, 291, 294, 322, 333
Zone roll, 259, 314, 336
Zone rotation, 318